LIBRARY OF HEBREW BIBLE/
OLD TESTAMENT STUDIES
556

Formerly Journal for the Study of the Old Testament Supplement Series

Editors
Claudia V. Camp, Texas Christian University
Andrew Mein, Westcott House, Cambridge

BROTHERHOOD AND INHERITANCE

A Canonical Reading of the Esau and Edom Traditions

Bradford A. Anderson

t &t clark

Published by T & T Clark International
A Continuum imprint
80 Maiden Lane, New York, NY 10038
The Tower Building, 11 York Road, London SE1 7NX

www.continuumbooks.com

Visit the T & T Clark blog at www.tandtclarkblog.com

Library of Congress Cataloging-in-Publication Data
A catalog record for this book is available from the Library of Congress.

ISBN: HB: 978-0-567-03473-1

Typeset and copy-edited by Forthcoming Publications Ltd. (www.forthpub.com)
Printed and bound in the United States of America

CONTENTS

ACKNOWLEDGMENTS

This book is a revised version of a doctoral thesis submitted to Durham University. I would like to thank the editors of this series, Claudia Camp and Andrew Mein, for accepting it for publication, as well as Duncan Burns, for his meticulous editing and formatting of the manuscript.

The project would not have been possible without the input and encouragement of numerous family members, friends, and instructors. First and foremost, I am grateful to have had the chance to work with Walter Moberly as my supervisor. While Professor Moberly has obviously influenced my approach to reading the Bible, there are numerous other areas where my thinking has been formed while studying under him these many years, and for this I owe him a debt of gratitude. Indeed, his interest and encouragement have made this process not only intellectually rewarding, but personally enriching and enjoyable as well.

Several friends, colleagues, and instructors have read, commented upon, or decisively shaped significant aspects of this project. Iveta Dimitrova introduced me to the Hebrew language as well as the ambiguities of the Jacob narratives during my undergraduate studies, setting me on the path towards this subject. I am grateful to Robert Hayward for his instruction in Hebrew, Aramaic, and the targumim, and for graciously helping me track down several sources throughout my research. I wish to thank my examiners, Terence Fretheim and Stuart Weeks, who provided stimulating conversation and probing questions on the project that sharpened my thinking on several key issues. Joel Kaminsky and Rob Barrett both read sections of this project and offered much needed feedback, while Richard Briggs helpfully talked me through several hermeneutical issues. Special mention needs to be given to Joel Lohr, who has proved an indispensable conversation partner along the way; his friendship and encouragement have been immeasurable.

Much of the research for this project was undertaken as a part-time and long-distance student, a reality that brings its own particular set of challenges. Daniel Caldwell graciously allowed time for me to work on this research while teaching. A very big thank you to Conrad and Lyn White, who have warmly opened their home to me on visits to Durham through the years. Likewise, Janice Macfarlane kindly allowed me to invade her space and set up office in her home. The staff at the Durham University library, particularly those involved with inter-library loans, has been an immense help, as has the administration of the Theology and Religion department, notably Ellen Middleton. All of these have helped alleviate some of the stress of part-time and long-distance research.

Finally, I would like to thank my family, and dedicate this work to them. My parents Dean and Leata Anderson have not only instilled an appreciation of Scripture in me from a young age, but have continued to support me in all my endeavors, including reading large portions of this project along the way. As I complete this study, which touches on the issue of brotherhood, I cannot help but be grateful for my brother Alex, who has provided perceptive feedback on my work and, more importantly, invaluable friendship. My wife Georgie has been patient, encouraging, and supportive during these years of study, and I am certain I could not have done this without her. She has been and continues to be my best friend and biggest fan. And my daughters Molly and Maeve have been a daily reminder that there is life beyond these stacks of books. Their arrival during these years of research has brought unspeakable joy.

ABBREVIATIONS

AASOR	Annual of the American Schools of Oriental Research
AB	Anchor Bible
ABD	*Anchor Bible Dictionary*. Edited by D. N. Freedman. 6 vols. New York, 1992
ABRL	Anchor Bible Reference Library
ABS	Archaeology and Biblical Studies
ACCS	Ancient Christian Commentary on Scripture Old Testament
Alleg. Interp.	Philo, *Allegorical Interpretation*
ANES	*Ancient Near Eastern Studies*
ANET	*Ancient Near Eastern Texts Relating to the Old Testament*. Edited by J. B. Pritchard. 3d ed. Princeton, 1969
Ant.	Josephus, *Jewish Antiquities*
AOAT	Alter Orient und Altes Testament
AOTC	Abingdon Old Testament Commentaries
ApC	Apollos Commentaries
ArBib	The Aramaic Bible
ATANT	Abhandlungen zur Theologie des Alten und Neuen Testaments
ATD	Das Alte Testament Deutsch
BA	*Biblical Archaeologist*
BAGD	Bauer, W., W. F. Arndt, F. W. Gingrich, and F. W. Danker. *Greek–English Lexicon of the New Testament and Other Early Christian Literature*. 2d ed. Chicago, 1979
BASOR	*Bulletin of the American Schools of Oriental Research*
BBB	Bonner biblische Beiträge
BDB	Brown, F., S. R. Driver, and C. A. Briggs. *A Hebrew and English Lexicon of the Old Testament*. Oxford, 1907
BHS	*Biblia Hebraica Stuttgartensia*
Bib	*Biblica*
BibLeb	*Bibel und Leben*
BibOr	Biblica et orientalia
BJS	Brown Judaic Studies
BKAT	Biblischer Kommentar, Altes Testament
BLS	Bible and Literature Series
BN	*Biblische Notizen*
BO	Berit Olam
BTB	*Biblical Theology Bulletin*
BZ	*Biblische Zeitschrift*
BZAW	Beihefte zur Zeitschrift für die alttestamentliche Wissenschaft

CBC	Cambridge Bible Commentary
CBQ	*Catholic Biblical Quarterly*
CC	Continental Commentaries
CJ	*Conservative Judaism*
CLJ	*Cambridge Law Journal*
ConBOT	Coniectanea biblica: Old Testament Series
CTJ	*Calvin Theological Journal*
DBSup	*Dictionnaire de la Bible: Supplément*
Deut. Rab.	*Deuteronomy Rabbah*
DOTP	*Dictionary of the Old Testament: Pentateuch.* Edited by T. Desmond Alexander and David W. Baker. Downers Grove, 2003
DTIB	*Dictionary for Theological Interpretation of the Bible.* Edited by Kevin J. Vanhoozer. Grand Rapids, 2005
EdF	Erträge der Forschung
EncJud	*Encyclopaedia Judaica*
EstBib	*Estudios Biblicos*
ET	English translation
EvT	*Evangelische Theologie*
ExAud	*Ex Auditu*
FAT	Forschungen zum Alten Testament
FB	Forschung zur Bibel
FOTL	Forms of the Old Testament Literature
Gen. Rab.	*Genesis Rabbah*
GKC	*Gesenius' Hebrew Grammar.* Edited by E. Kautzsch. Translated by A. E. Cowley. 2d. ed. Oxford, 1910
HALOT	Koehler, L., W. Baumgartner, and J. J. Stamm, *The Hebrew and Aramaic Lexicon of the Old Testament.* Translated and edited under the supervision of M. E. J. Richardson. 4 vols. Leiden, 1994–99
HAT	Handbuch zum Alten Testament
HB	Hebrew Bible
HCOT	Historical Commentary on the Old Testament
HSM	Harvard Semitic Monographs
HTR	*Harvard Theological Review*
HUCA	*Hebrew Union College Annual*
IBC	Interpretation: A Bible Commentary for Teaching and Preaching
ICC	International Critical Commentary
IEJ	*Israel Exploration Journal*
Int	*Interpretation*
JAAR	*Journal of the American Academy of Religion*
Jastrow	Marcus Jastrow, *A Dictionary of the Targumim, the Talmud Babli and Yerushalmi, and the midrashic literature.* 2 vols. London, 1903
JBL	*Journal of Biblical Literature*
JBQ	*Jewish Biblical Quarterly*

JC	Judaica et Christiana
JES	*Journal of Ecumenical Studies*
JHS	*Journal of Hebrew Scriptures*
JJS	*Journal of Jewish Studies*
JM	Joüon, P. *A Grammar of Biblical Hebrew*. Translated and revised by T. Muraoka. 2 vols. Subsidia biblica 14/1–2. Rome, 1991
JNES	*Journal of Near Eastern Studies*
JPS	Jewish Publication Society
JPSTC	Jewish Publication Society Torah Commentary
JSOT	*Journal for the Study of the Old Testament*
JSOTSup	Journal for the Study of the Old Testament Supplement Series
JQR	*Jewish Quarterly Review*
JSS	*Journal of Semitic Studies*
JTS	*Journal of Theological Studies*
KAT	Kommentar zum Alten Testament
KJV	King James Version
LASBF	*Liber annuus studii biblici franciscani*
LCBI	Literary Currents in Biblical Interpretation
LCC	Library of Christian Classics
Lev. Rab.	*Leviticus Rabbah*
LHBOTS	Library of Hebrew Bible/Old Testament Studies
LSAWS	Linguistic Studies in Ancient West Semitic
MdB	Le Monde de la Bible
MLBS	Mercer Library of Biblical Studies
MT	Masoretic Text
NASB	New American Standard Bible
NCB	New Century Bible
NIB	*The New Interpreter's Bible*
NICNT	New International Commentary on the New Testament
NICOT	New International Commentary on the Old Testament
NIDOTTE	*New International Dictionary of Old Testament Theology and Exegesis*. Edited by W. A. VanGemeren. 5 vols. Grand Rapids, 1997
NIV	New International Version
NKJV	New King James Version
NRSV	New Revised Standard Version
NVBS	New Voices in Biblical Studies
OAN	Oracles Against the nations
OBT	Overtures to Biblical Theology
OTG	Old Testament Guides
OTL	Old Testament Library
OTM	Oxford Theological Monographs
OTR	Old Testament Readings
OTT	Old Testament Theology
PAT	Die Propheten des Alten Testaments
PBM	Paternoster Biblical Monographs

PEQ	*Palestine Exploration Quarterly*
PLO	Porta Linguarum Orientalium
RB	*Revue biblique*
RBL	*Review of Biblical Literature*
RQ	*Revue de Qumran*
RHR	*Revue de l'histoire des religions*
SAM	Sheffield Archaeological Monographs
SamP	Samaritan Pentateuch
SBAB	Stuttgarter biblische Aufsatzbände
SBLDS	Society of Biblical Literature Dissertation Series
SBLSymS	Society of Biblical Literature Symposium Series
SBT	Studies in Biblical Theology
SemeiaSt	Semeia Studies
SFSHJ	South Florida Studies in the History of Judaism
SHBC	Smyth & Helwys Bible Commentary
SNTSMS	Society for New Testament Studies Monograph Series
SOTSMS	Society for Old Testament Studies Monograph Series
SSN	Studia Semitica Neerlandica
STI	Studies in Theological Interpretation
TDNT	*Theological Dictionary of the New Testament.* Edited by G. Kittel and G. Friedrich. Translated by G. W. Bromiley. 10 vols. Grand Rapids, 1964–76
TDOT	*Theological Dictionary of the Old Testament.* Edited by G. J. Botterweck and H. Ringgren. Translated by J. T. Willis, G. W. Bromiley, and D. E. Green. 8 vols. Grand Rapids, 1974–
Tg. Neb.	*Targum of the Prophets.* K.J. Cathcart and R.P. Gordon, *The Targum of the Minor Prophets.* Edinburgh, 1989
Tg. Neof.	*Targum Neofiti.* Martin McNamara, *Targum Neofiti 1: Genesis.* Edinburgh, 1992; and Martin McNamara, *Targum Neofiti 1: Deuteronomy.* Edinburgh, 1997
Tg. Onq.	*Targum Onqelos.* Bernard Grossfeld, *The Targum Onqelos to Genesis.* Edinburgh, 1988; and Bernard Grossfeld, *The Targum Onqelos to Deuteronomy.* Edinburgh, 1988
Tg. Ps.-J.	*Targum Pseudo-Jonathan.* Michael Maher, *Targum Pseudo-Jonathan: Genesis.* Edinburgh, 1992; and Ernest G. Clarke, *Targum Pseudo-Jonathan: Deuteronomy.* Edinburgh, 1998
THAT	*Theologisches Handwörterbuch zum Alten Testament.* Edited by E. Jenni, with assistance from C. Westermann. 2 vols., Stuttgart, 1971–76
TLOT	*Theological Lexicon of the Old Testament.* Edited by E. Jenni, with assistance from C. Westermann. Translated by M. E. Biddle. 3 vols. Peabody, Mass., 1997
TMJ	*Torah U-Madda Journal*
TOTC	Tyndale Old Testament Commentaries
TRE	*Theologische Realenzyklopädie*
TWOT	*Theological Wordbook of the Old Testament.* Edited by R. L. Harris, G. L. Archer Jr. 2 vols. Chicago, 1980

TZ	*Theologische Zeitschrift*
VAB	Vorderasiatische Bibliothek
VT	*Vetus Testamentum*
VTSup	Supplements to Vetus Testamentum
WBC	Word Biblical Commentary
WC	Westminster Commentaries
WeBC	Westminster Bible Companion
WMANT	Wissenschaftliche Monographien zum Alten und Neuen Testament
WW	*Word and World*
YNER	Yale Near Eastern Researches
ZAW	*Zeitschrift für die alttestamentliche Wissenschaft*

Chapter 1

INTRODUCTION

Esau. His name is associated with gluttony, simple-mindedness, and even godlessness. One is hard-pressed to think of a biblical character that has received as much bad press as Jacob's brother. Indeed, the stories concerning Isaac's elder son have sparked countless diatribes in the history of interpretation, whether in the targumim, Philo, and Rashi, or in the New Testament, Augustine, and Luther. But what should the biblical reader make of Jacob's brother? Is he deserving of what happens to him in the biblical narratives? Should he be pitied? Or is something else at work?

Edom. Arguably no other nation in the Hebrew Bible is spoken of in such harsh language, and held in such low esteem, as Israel's neighbor to the southeast. What is the basis of the vitriol which the prophets have for Edom? Is this simply one more example of long-standing hatred of an "other" in Israel's history?

"Esau is Edom." So says the genealogist of Gen 36. And yet, critical biblical scholarship has shown this association to be problematic on a number of levels. How, then, might these traditions be understood in relation to one another in light of critical biblical studies?

Much ink has been spilled in the history of biblical interpretation in attempting to answer exactly these types of questions. There is vast disagreement about how these traditions—those of Esau, Jacob's brother, and Edom, Israel's neighbor—should be understood in their own right. Not surprisingly, there is even less agreement as to what the relationship of these two traditions might be.[1] Three particular issues have dominated

---

1. I am using the term "tradition" in a broad sense here to denote the materials that represent, as a whole, the character Esau and the people/nation of Edom. This usage is not without problems, as the two "traditions" overlap one another at points throughout the Hebrew Bible, and are obviously themselves collections of disparate texts and traditions. Nevertheless, the term seems appropriate as a heuristic tool for the present study, as it offers a point of entry into the broader discussion.

these various discussions concerning Esau and Edom, and are worth reconsidering.

The first issue is an overwhelming tendency to interpret Esau in a negative light. Esau, from a very early stage, has been interpreted as at best a bumbling fool, and at worst godless and unworthy of the birthright and blessing. But does this do justice to the complexity of his character in the Genesis narratives? And what are the literary and theological ramifications if we *do not* interpret him in this negative light? The second issue has to do with the interpretation of Edom in the prophets. The Edom tradition has been explored in a variety of ways, but several literary and theological motifs concerning Edom that recur in the prophetic corpus and in other canonical voices, particularly Deuteronomy, have largely been ignored. What might these voices contribute to the biblical portrayal of Edom when read in light of one another? And thirdly, studies on the relationship of the Esau and Edom traditions have, by and large, focused on either the historical continuity that connects the two traditions (as in most pre-modern exegesis), or their historical discontinuity (as in the preponderance of modern scholarship). What has been left unexplored are literary and theological motifs that span the two traditions, and which may offer us a frame of reference for understanding the relationship of the Esau and Edom traditions.

This study attempts to address these issues, and to shed new light on the depiction of Esau and Edom, by focusing on literary and theological dimensions of these traditions. This is done by offering a canonical reading of the Esau and Edom traditions within the Hebrew Bible, using the theological concept of "election" as a framework for the discussion. As such, a brief word on the issues of both a canonical reading as well as election as a heuristic framework might be in order.

The basic assumption of a canonical reading is that the texts of the Bible, in all their textual and theological diversity, were collected, shaped, and passed down by particular communities of faith.[2] This is not to deny the complex literary and historical development of these texts; rather, it is a conscious decision to read the biblical text in the form in

---

2. This has been highlighted helpfully in R. W. L. Moberly, *The Theology of the Book of Genesis* (OTT; Cambridge: Cambridge University Press, 2009), 1–20; see also Moberly, "The Nature of Christian Biblical Theology," in *From Eden to Golgotha: Essays in Biblical Theology* (SFSHJ 52; Atlanta: Scholars, 1992), 141–57. I am also broadly following the work of Brevard S. Childs, as outlined in his *Introduction to the Old Testament as Scripture* (Philadelphia: Fortress, 1979), and *Biblical Theology of the Old and New Testaments: Theological Reflection on the Christian Bible* (Minneapolis: Fortress, 1992).

which it has been received by the church (and, *mutatis mutandis*, the synagogue).[3] Thus, one question which undergirds this study is: From the perspective of the final form of the Hebrew Bible,[4] how might these traditions concerning Esau and Edom be understood?[5]

A major impetus of this study, meanwhile, is the issue of election. The concept of election or chosenness in the Hebrew Bible is a subject which has been receiving renewed attention in recent years, not least because the issue of particularity is a contentious one in the contemporary Western world.[6] A God who chooses some, whether simply as the object of his[7] affection or for a specific purpose, while rejecting others, is not a fashionable idea today. One of the by-products of this revival of interest in election, however, has been the study of the non-elect and their role in the Hebrew Bible.[8] Indeed, such studies have shown that the non-elect

---

3. Christopher R. Seitz, "Canonical Approach," *DTIB*, 100–101.

4. While Moberly, Seitz, and Childs are all emphatic that a canonical reading in the Christian tradition includes both testaments, the present work will be focusing on the canon of the Hebrew Bible, and I refer to the collection as such. Any reference to the New Testament will be done from the vantage point of the reception history of particular texts.

5. All translations are my own, unless stated otherwise, and are based on the MT, though other traditions and variants are referenced throughout. For more on "received text" and "final form," see Moberly, *Theology of Genesis*, 40–41. Note also the issues highlighted in Erhard Blum, "Gibt es die Endgestalt des Penta-teuch?," in *The Congress Volume: Leuven, 1989* (ed. J. Emerton; VTSup 43; Leiden: Brill, 1991), 46–57.

6. Because of the focus on election, this study builds on the work done in recent years on this subject. Notable works include Horst Dietrich Preuss, *Old Testament Theology* (2 vols.; trans. Leo G. Perdue; Edinburgh: T. & T. Clark, 1995; 1996), which is structured around the idea of election; Jon D. Levenson, *The Death and Resurrection of the Beloved Son: The Transformation of Child Sacrifice in Judaism and Christianity* (New Haven: Yale University Press, 1993); Joel S. Kaminsky, *Yet I Loved Jacob: Reclaiming the Biblical Concept of Election* (Nashville: Abingdon, 2007). Other standard works on the topic include H. H. Rowley, *The Biblical Doctrine of Election* (London: Lutterworth, 1950); T. C. Vriezen, *Die Erwählung Israels nach dem Alten Testament* (ATANT; Zurich: Zwingli-Verlag, 1953), and Seock-Tae Sohn, *The Divine Election of Israel* (Grand Rapids: Eerdmans, 1991).

7. The ideological and theological issues concerning the use of masculine pronouns in relation to the Jewish and Christian deity are many; however, I retain the usage in this study out of convention.

8. Joel N. Lohr, *Chosen and Unchosen: Concepts of Election in the Pentateuch and Jewish-Christian Interpretation* (Siphrut 2; Winona Lake: Eisenbrauns, 2009); R. Christopher Heard, *Dynamics of Diselection: Ambiguity in Genesis 12–36 and Ethnic Boundaries in Post-Exilic Judah* (SBLDS 39; Atlanta: Society of Biblical Literature, 2001); Roger Syrén, *The Forsaken First-Born: A Study of a Recurrent*

have a much more nuanced role within the Hebrew Bible than is often assumed. And yet, as Lohr notes, "There is much regarding the unchosen that has not been explored in scholarship."[9] With this in mind, it would seem that the biblical traditions concerning Esau and Edom may be informative to this discussion, as both are non-elect and yet in close proximity to those who are chosen. Hence, another question I wish to ask is: How might a canonical reading of the Esau and Edom traditions inform our understanding of the theological dimensions of the Hebrew Bible, particularly the issue of (non-)election? In this sense, the issue of election will serve as a heuristic frame of reference from which to examine these texts in their canonical form.

The outline of this study is straightforward. To begin with, I sketch a brief history of the interpretation of both the Esau and Edom traditions. Secondly, I offer close readings of the relevant passages in Genesis concerning Esau. The relative length of the section dealing with Genesis is due to the amount of material in Genesis concerning Esau, the complexity of these texts, and the need to reconceptualize Esau's portrayal in them. Third, the portrayal of Esau's descendants in Deuteronomy is examined. Following on from this, the depiction of Edom in the prophetic corpus is investigated, focusing on Obadiah and Malachi. Finally, I ask how reading the Esau and Edom traditions canonically might inform the broader discussion on election and chosenness in the Hebrew Bible.

My argument is as follows:

The character of Esau, although not the bearer of promise in the line of Abraham, is portrayed, on the whole, in a positive light in Genesis. In terms of election, this would suggest that the non-election of Esau in no way entails that he is cursed, still less excluded from the divine economy (or, to use language that is distinctively Christian, that he is damned). Indeed, I will argue that Esau is blessed in his own right, is seen as a model of gracious brotherly behavior, and, in the world of the text, becomes a nation with a land of his own. Moreover, Esau eventually responds well to his (chosen) brother, and thus the Hebrew Bible may be portraying him as an example of how the non-elect might respond to this reality. In sum, one might say that this section is an attempt to rehabilitate the character Esau in light of the disparagement he has received in the history of interpretation.

Motif in the Patriarchal Narratives (JSOTSup 133; Sheffield: JSOT, 1993); Joel S. Kaminsky, "Did Election Imply the Mistreatment of Non-Israelites?," *HTR* 96 (2003): 397–425.
    9. Lohr, *Chosen*, xii.

Deuteronomy, in turn, offers an important voice in the canonical portrayal of Esau and his descendants as it reinforces the motifs found in Genesis with overtly theological language: not only are the descendants of Esau to be considered kin, but the land of Seir has been given to them by YHWH[10] as a possession or inheritance. Thus, in Genesis and Deuteronomy, Esau and his descendants may not be the chosen line, but they are depicted in a positive light: as brothers of Jacob/Israel they have a special relationship with the elect, and they are blessed in their own right by YHWH, Israel's God.

The portrayal of Edom in the prophetic material, on the other hand, is extremely negative. Nonetheless, I hope to show that the motifs found in the pentateuchal material resurface in the prophets, namely, the subjects of kinship and the land. Indeed, I will suggest that these issues are important elements of the strong prophetic critique of Edom: according to Israel's prophets, Edom respects neither their relationship with Israel, nor the lands apportioned by YHWH. Because of this, they are dispossessed and their inheritance is taken from them.

Finally, I will propose that these two traditions—those of Esau and Edom—can be seen to have resonance in recurring literary and theological motifs, heuristically labeled brotherhood and inheritance.[11] When read canonically, these traditions might helpfully be understood as commenting on the interplay between divine initiative and human response: in both blessing and judgment, the Hebrew Bible portrays YHWH as responsive to those with whom he is involved—even the non-elect.

This study is not exhaustive; indeed, there are substantial elements of the Hebrew Bible which are left untouched, particularly the historical books as well as the poetic and wisdom literature (to borrow the nomenclature of the Christian Old Testament). I do hope, however, that this study will contribute to the textual study of Esau and Edom, as well as theological reflection on the complex issue of election.

---

10. When quoting other authors I have retained their usage of the tetragrammaton. In my own usage, however, I have left it unvocalized.

11. Although in places I do use the term "inheritance" in its technical sense, I employ the term in the title and elsewhere in a broad, heuristic sense, denoting that Esau and his descendants have not been left empty-handed, but have been "blessed" with, among other things, land, nationhood, and prosperity. The same might be said with regard to the term "brotherhood." While I do use the terms "kinship" and "brotherhood" interchangeably throughout the study, I have retained the literal translation in the title to emphasize the fraternal relationship of Isaac's sons.

Chapter 2

ESAU AND EDOM IN THE HISTORY
OF BIBLICAL INTERPRETATION

Before looking in detail at some of the key biblical texts which focus on Esau and Edom, it may be helpful to revisit briefly the various ways in which both Esau and Edom have been interpreted through the years, as well as how they have been understood in light of one another. As the history of interpretation will also be dealt with throughout the study on individual texts, what is offered here are soundings from history that highlight the diversity of the reception of these texts, in order to orient us for the task at hand.

1. *Interpretation of Esau in Genesis*

From an early stage, post-biblical tradition (both Jewish and Christian) would interpret the character of Esau, the son of Isaac and Rebekah and brother of Jacob, in a negative light.

For instance, the ancient Jewish tradition had a tendency to denigrate Esau while simultaneously extolling Jacob's virtues. While this is not exclusively the case, it is a strong recurring theme. Thus, *Jubilees* notes that as the brothers developed, "Jacob learned to write; but Esau did not learn, for he was a man of the field and a hunter, and he learnt war, and all his deeds were fierce."[1] In *Genesis Rabbah* we find the famous re-telling of Jacob and Esau's reunion, where instead of Esau embracing and kissing his brother (Gen 33:4), we are told that Esau fell on Jacob's neck and bit him; only Jacob's neck turned to stone, hurting Esau's teeth,

---

1. *Jub.* 19:14. For more on the portrayal of Esau in *Jubilees*, see Gerhard Langer, "Esau im Buch der Jubiläen," in *Esau – Bruder und Feind* (ed. Gerhard Langer; Göttingen: Vandenhoeck & Ruprecht, 2009), 55–62; Roger Syrén, "Ishmael and Esau in the Book of Jubilees and Targum Pseudo-Jonathan," in *The Aramaic Bible: Targums in Their Historical Context* (ed. D. R. G. Beattie and M. J. McNamara; JSOTSup 166; Sheffield: Sheffield Academic, 1994), 310–15.

thus causing Esau to weep![2] Developments such as these can be seen throughout the later targumim and elsewhere in the rabbinic traditions.[3] During the Roman period, Esau was identified with Rome (as was Edom), an equation which would eventually shift to the Christian (Roman) church as well.[4] This identification of Esau with Israel's worst enemies would solidify Esau's role as a typological enemy of not only the Jewish people, but also of their God.

The early Christian tradition tended to be just as negative about Esau. Hebrews 12:16, for instance, equates Esau's loss of the birthright with his being "godless," an idea of which the tradition would take hold. Several centuries later, Augustine would note that the twins wrestling in Rebekah's womb are symbolic of good and evil people fighting in the church—with Esau representative of evil.[5] At the time of the Reformation, Calvin would label Esau as the epitome of all "reprobate" men, given over to earthly desires and without spiritual concern (unlike Jacob).[6] When discussing Esau's genealogy in Gen 36, Luther mentions that the Jews have regarded Rome and the Christians as Esau and Edom; he retorts that it is actually the Jews who are "that cursed and condemned people" from the lineage of Esau.[7]

Thus, at some point along the way, Esau (and by extension Edom) became an insult that Jews and Christians hurled at one another, or was an image used to depict those at odds with the ways of God.

2. *Gen. Rab.* 78:9.

3. *Targum Neofiti* and *Targum Pseudo-Jonathan* are both overtly negative toward Esau. Examples can be seen in C. T. R. Hayward. "A Portrait of the Wicked Esau in the Targum of Codex Neofiti 1," in Beattie and McNamara, eds., *The Aramaic Bible*, 291–309; and Hayward, "Targum Pseudo-Jonathan to Genesis 27:31," *JQR* 84 (1993–94): 177–88.

4. Harry Freedman, "Jacob and Esau: Their Struggle in the Second Century," *JBQ* 32 (1995): 107–15. Cf. Mireille Hadas-Lebel, "Jacob et Esau ou Israel et Rome dans le Talmud et le Midrash," *RHR* 201 (1984): 369–92; Carol Bakhos, *Ishmael on the Border: Rabbinic Portrayals of the First Arab* (Albany: SUNY Press, 2006), 250–62. For later periods, see Gerson D. Cohen, "Esau as Symbol in Early Medieval Thought," in *Jewish Medieval and Renaissance Studies* (ed. Alexander Altmann; Cambridge: Harvard University Press, 1967), 19–48. For more on the interpretation of Esau in Jewish tradition, stretching from biblical to contemporary usage, see the recent collection of essays in Langer, ed., *Esau – Bruder und Feind.*

5. *Tractate on the Gospel of John* 11.10.2–3, in ACCS 2:146.

6. John Calvin, commenting on Gen 25:29–34 in *Commentaries on the First Book of Moses Called Genesis*, vol. 2 (trans. John King; Edinburgh: Calvin Translation Society, 1850), 47.

7. Martin Luther, *Lectures on Genesis, Chapter 31–37* (Luther's Works 6; ed. Jaroslav Pelikan; Saint Louis: Concordia, 1966), 233.

With the advent of historical criticism, scholarship began to focus less on the characterization of Esau than on what might lie behind it. Hence, as the historicity of the ancestral narratives came to be seen as dubious, scholars such as Gunkel and Maag began to assign socio-historical importance to Esau (and Jacob), with Esau seen as representing the hunter-gatherers, a socio-economic class different from the shepherding Jacob.[8] Source critics also began to notice fissures in the portrayal of Esau. Most notably, it was argued that the Esau of Gen 25 and 27 is an uncouth boor, to be distinguished from the nobler Esau of Gen 33.[9] Finally, as archaeological research developed, the connection of Esau and Edom was seen to be quite a late development, and it was assumed that the two traditions originally would have had very little to do with one another.[10] In all of these readings, the characterization of Esau is only important insofar as it is related to issues which lie behind the text or its development.

In recent decades, however, with the re-emergence of final-form readings in close conjunction with literary and narrative criticism, there have been several studies which have once again paid closer attention to the characterization of Esau and his role in the larger cycle of stories concerning Jacob. Several of these have offered a corrective to both the traditional and the historical-critical readings. Heard, for example, has offered a thorough re-reading of the Genesis texts concerning Esau, focusing on literary aspects, and has convincingly demonstrated their ambiguous nature, in opposition to the rather flat (and negative) way in which the text is often understood to portray Esau.[11] Additionally, Spina has offered a constructive and more theological reading of Esau in Genesis, noting that he is an exemplary model of an outsider becoming "the face of God" to the elect.[12] These and others have recognized that when due attention is given to the text in its received form, Genesis

8. Hermann Gunkel, *Genesis* (trans. Mark E. Biddle; LMBS; Macon: Mercer University Press, 1997), 291–93; Victor Maag, "Jakob–Esau–Edom," *TZ* 13 (1957): 418–29.

9. John Skinner, *A Critical and Exegetical Commentary on Genesis* (ICC; Edinburgh: T. & T. Clark, 1930), 415.

10. This is seen in a good deal of J. R. Bartlett's work, notably *Edom and the Edomites* (JSOTSup 77; Sheffield: JSOT, 1989), and "The Land of Seir and the Brotherhood of Edom," *JTS* 20 (1969): 1–20.

11. Heard, *Dynamics*, 97–137.

12. Frank A. Spina, "The 'Face of God': Esau in Canonical Context," in *The Quest for Context and Meaning: Studies in Biblical Intertextuality in Honor of James A. Sanders* (ed. Craig A. Evans and Shemaryahu Talmon; Leiden: Brill, 1997), 3–25; Spina, *The Faith of the Outsider: Exclusion and Inclusion in the Biblical Story* (Grand Rapids: Eerdmans, 2005), 14–34.

offers a much more nuanced portrayal (contra pre-modern readings) and coherent characterization (contra religio-historical and source-critical readings) of Esau than has often been assumed.[13]

Thus, while the history of interpretation has been quite harsh on Esau, close readings in recent years have begun to shift the general perception of Jacob's brother. While taking on board the gains made from the past several hundred years of historical-critical work, as well as the insights of pre-modern interpretation, it is my contention that these literary developments are important for a canonical reading. Indeed, the present work is indebted to and builds upon these readings that are attuned to the narrative and literary elements of the text.

2. *Depiction of Edom in the Prophets*

Any ambiguity evident in Genesis regarding Esau is not found in the prophets regarding Edom. Indeed, the prophetic corpus is so stringently negative toward their neighboring country that Cresson calls this a "damn Edom" theology.[14] However, even here there is disagreement in the reception history of these texts as to *why* Edom is portrayed in this negative light.

Pre-modern interpreters in both the Jewish and Christian traditions generally offered ahistorical accounts of Edom; however, it was assumed that Edom deserved any punishment it might receive. It was not until the Reformation that commentators began to equate the harsh prophetic critique of the prophets with particular historical circumstances, most notably the events of 587 B.C.E. and the destruction of Jerusalem.[15] This

---

13. See also Gerhard Langer, "Esau in der hebräischen Bibel," in Langer, ed., *Esau – Bruder und Feind*, 17–31; R. J. D. Knauth, "Esau, Edomites," *DOTP*, 219–24. At an advanced stage in my research I encountered Il-Seung Chung's 2008 dissertation from Sheffield entitled, "Liberating Esau: A Corrective Reading of the Esau–Jacob Narrative in Genesis 25–36" (Ph.D. diss., University of Sheffield, 2008). We come to many similar conclusions on how the Esau narratives should be (re)read. However, our overarching concerns are different in that Chung's study focuses on the Esau material in Genesis from a literary-critical perspective, while the present study also incorporates Deuteronomy and the prophetic material as well as theological considerations.

14. Bruce C. Cresson, "The Condemnation of Edom in Post-Exilic Judaism," in *The Use of the Old Testament in the New and Other Essays: Studies in Honour of William Franklin Stinespring* (ed. James M. Efird; Durham, N.C.: Duke University Press, 1972), 125–48.

15. This interpretation dates back at least to Luther, and has been the majority view since. See Martin Luther, "Lectures on Obadiah," in *Lectures on the Minor*

interpretation holds that the relationship between Israel and Edom seems to have been tenuous for a long time, and included periods of Israelite dominance, most notably under David.[16] However, when Jerusalem finally fell to the Babylonians, Edom either did nothing to help their brothers the Israelites, or they actually participated in their downfall.[17] In this reading, Edom's actions toward their neighbor at that fateful event became the proverbial last straw.[18]

This understanding of the prophetic hostility toward Edom was followed by an overwhelming majority in the history of interpretation. One can understand why; it is difficult to read many of these prophetic texts without envisioning some historical action on Edom's part, and the events of 587 B.C.E. seem a reasonable place to start. However, this traditional understanding has been questioned over the past century.[19] To begin with, it has become more and more difficult to pinpoint the dating of particular texts, and thus virtually impossible to note which texts are written before or after the events of 587 B.C.E. Thus, tying the prophets' vitriol toward Edom to a particular historical event is not as sure-footed an interpretive move as it once was. Moreover, as scholarship has rediscovered the rhetorical dimensions of the prophetic voices, there has also been a realization that reconstructing history from these books is a difficult task, and other elements might be at work.

Various interpretations have arisen in light of these difficulties in order to account for the hostility toward Edom. First, it has become commonplace to speak of Edom as a type or symbol representing "the nations." In this view, Edom came to function as a stand-in for the nations in

---

Prophets I: Hosea, Joel, Amos, Obadiah, Micah, Nahum, Zephaniah, Haggai, Malachi (ed. Hilton C. Oswald; trans. Richard J. Dinda; Luther's Works 18; St. Louis: Concordia, 1975), 193–94; cf. Beth Glazier-McDonald, "Edom in the Prophetical Corpus," in *You Shall Not Abhor an Edomite For He is Your Brother: Edom and Seir in History and Tradition* (ed. Diana Vikander Edelman; ABS 3; Atlanta: Scholars Press, 1995), 23–32; J. M. Myers, "Edom and Judah in the Sixth–Fifth Centuries B.C.," in *Near Eastern Studies in Honor of William Foxwell Albright* (ed. Hans Goedicke; Baltimore: The Johns Hopkins University Press, 1971), 377–92.

16. See 2 Sam 8:13–14.

17. This is hinted at or implied in several texts, such as Ps 137:7; Lam 4:21–22, and Obad 11–14.

18. See W. W. Cannon, "Israel and Edom: The Oracle of Obadiah - I," *Theology* 15 (1927): 129–40 (140), who comments that the events of 587 B.C.E. "extinguished finally and for all time any such momentary feelings of friendliness."

19. One of the earlier examples of this is Max Haller, "Edom in Urteil der Propheten," in *Vom Alten Testament. Festschrift K. Marti* (ed. K. Budde; BZAW 41; Giessen: Töpelmann, 1925), 109–17.

opposition to Israel and YHWH based on a host of factors, including their actions toward Israel (usually still associated with 587 B.C.E.)[20] and Edomite settlements in the Negeb, implying that Edom inhabited parts of Israel's promised land. This symbolic function has been applied to individual prophetic voices,[21] and to the prophetic books as a whole.[22] Secondly, this symbolic function has led some to posit that Edom's negative portrayal is based more on literary and liturgical tradition than on historical factors. Kellermann, in the form-critical tradition, argues that the vitriol shown toward Edom developed out of liturgical laments used after 587 B.C.E. Thus, Edom came to have a symbolic and liturgical function for Israel in the dark days of exile and beyond.[23] Dicou offers a more nuanced view incorporating all of these elements: Edom's actions toward Israel in the events of 587 B.C.E. and their settlement of the Negeb may have led to their role in the exilic and post-exilic lamentation cult, solidifying their status as the enemy *par excellence*.[24]

Commentators have also begun to highlight the ideology behind the prophetic critiques of Edom. One such example can be found in the recent contribution of O'Brien, who in her book focusing on the ideological dimensions of the prophets singles out the portrayal of Edom in Obadiah.[25] Bringing together some of the arguments highlighted above, O'Brien argues that the "brotherhood" language used of Esau and Edom

20.   Bartlett (*Edom and the Edomites*, 156–57) has argued that the Edomites have been falsely accused in the events of 587 B.C.E., an idea which has not gained widespread acceptance, though it has been picked up in ideological critiques of the prophetic depiction of Edom (see below).

21.   On Isaiah, see Bernard Gosse, "Isaïe 34–35 Le châtiment d'Edom et des nations, salut pour Sion," *ZAW* 102 (1990): 396–404; and Gosse, "Détournement de la vengeance du Seigneur contre Edom et les nations en Isa 63,1–6," *ZAW* 102 (1990): 105–10; on Ezekiel, see M. H. Woudstra, "Edom and Israel in Ezekiel," *CTJ* 3 (1968): 21–35; and Horacio Simian, *Die theologische Nachgeschichte der Prophetie Ezechiels: Form- und traditionskritische Untersuchung zu Ez 6; 35; 36* (FzB; Würzburg: Echter, 1974).

22.   Cresson, "The Condemnation of Edom," 144.

23.   U. Kellermann, "Israel und Edom. Studien zum Edomhass Israels n 6.–4. Jahrhundert v. Chr." (unpublished Habilitationsschrift. Münster, 1975). See also Kellermann, "Psalm 137," *ZAW* 90 (1978): 43–58.

24.   See Bert Dicou, *Edom, Israel's Brother and Antagonist: The Role of Edom in Biblical Prophecy and Story* (JSOTSup 169; Sheffield: JSOT, 1994), 196–97; Dicou, "Jakob en Esau, Israël en Edom: Israël tegenover de volken in de verhalen over Jakob en Esau in Genesis en in de grote profetieën over Edom" (Ph.D. diss., University of Amsterdam, 1990).

25.   Julia M. O'Brien, *Challenging Prophetic Metaphor: Theology and Ideology in the Prophets* (Louisville: Westminster John Knox, 2008), 153–73.

in Obadiah is metaphorical, rather than historical.[26] She notes that the traditional idea that Obadiah and other prophets were drawing on a well-known kinship relationship between Israel and Edom does not hold up in light of contemporary scholarship which has dated the Pentateuch to the Persian period. Moreover, not all of the prophetic books use "brother-hood" language when speaking of Edom. Hence, "brotherhood" is not necessarily a common or apt description of Edom.[27] With regard to Edom's supposed crimes against Judah, O'Brien again pokes holes in the traditional argument: the biblical evidence concerning Edom's crimes is vague and at times contradictory, the ambiguity of which she believes the archaeological evidence corroborates.[28] All of this leads to O'Brien's conclusions: Obadiah's use of "brother" language is ideological, and is used to underscore Edom's behavior. This, for O'Brien, means that *"Obadiah's use of brother language, as well as its particular recounting of charges against Edom, reflects a self-interest, particularly regarding land."*[29]

As we can see, there are several interpretive approaches which have been taken to explain why Israel's prophets were so negative in their portrayal of Edom: a general assumption that Edom deserved punishment; Edom's behavior toward Judah at the time of the fall of Jerusalem; the symbolic role which Edom came to play representing "the nations"; and the ideological bent of the prophets. All of these are offered as possible reasons for this harsh literary treatment of Israel's neighbor. Indeed, these various understandings of the role of Edom in the prophets are insightful, and I hope to build on their respective strengths. However, I hope to show that exploring some of these particular motifs which occur throughout the prophetic critique of Edom—notably kinship and relationship to the land—may give us yet further insight into the nature of this harsh treatment by the prophets.

3. *Esau and Edom: The Relationship of the Traditions*

Given the close connection between Esau and Edom in the Hebrew Bible, surprisingly few attempts have been made to understand how and why these two traditions might be connected.[30]

26. These are O'Brien's categories (ibid., 154).
27. Ibid., 161–62.
28. Ibid., 164–65.
29. Ibid., 166. Italics in original.
30. Most reference material separates Esau and Edom into separate entries (e.g. *ABD*, *EncJud*). One entry that does deal with the two issues together is Knauth,

One way this issue has been addressed is with a linear reading of the biblical text that takes the biblical history at face value. This was the pre-modern reading which held precedent before the rise of critical biblical studies (and one which, presumably, many readers of the Bible hold today): Jacob and Esau, the sons of Isaac, were the eponymous ancestors of neighboring nations, Israel and Edom. These nations would have a tenuous relationship, with Edom deserving any eventual punishment it might receive. The conflict between the brothers foreshadows the conflict of the nations.[31]

The strength of this approach is that it takes the canonical shape of the Esau and Edom material seriously, and this needs to be recognized. This type of reading is also encouraged by the Bible itself, particularly in texts such as Gen 36, where the connection between Esau and Edom is made explicit. However, there are several shortcomings to this approach. To begin with, modern scholarship has shown that historical claims regarding the patriarchal period are difficult to substantiate.[32] Moreover, the connection of the patriarchs with the nations that bear their names, and how this came to be, has been called into question.[33] Even from the standpoint of sources, a reading which assumes that the prophetic traditions drew from the Genesis material, and not the other way around, can no longer be taken for granted. Taken in sum, these various complexities have problematized a straightforward historical and linear reading of the biblical account of Esau and Edom.

A second approach to the relationship of Esau and Edom, and one which rose out of the difficulties of the traditional reading, is to recognize that the Hebrew Bible has various independent traditions which have been fused together.[34] This approach became commonplace with the rise of critical biblical studies in the modern era. In this view, the Jacob and Esau stories existed independent of their connection to the nation-states, but were made to fit together with national ideas at a later time. (Indeed, it has been observed that there were also disparate Jacob and Esau materials which were joined together as well.[35]) Esau's description

"Esau, Edomites," 219–24. However, because the focus is on the pentateuchal traditions, little connection is made with the prophetic hostility or the possible reasons for it.

31. For an example of this, see Calvin, especially at Gen 36.

32. See, e.g., Thomas L. Thompson, *The Historicity of the Patriarchal Narratives* (BZAW 133; Berlin: de Gruyter, 1974).

33. J. R. Bartlett, "The Brotherhood of Edom," *JSOT* 4 (1977): 2–27.

34. Bartlett, *Edom and the Edomites*, 175–80.

35. Gunkel, *Genesis*, 285–87.

as "red" and "hairy," on top of phonetic similarities, matches the physical description of Edom and Seir. Moreover, the congruences in the stories of Jacob/Esau and Israel/Edom (exile and return, sibling hostility, etc.) suggest that the narratives have been edited together to reflect these similarities.

Several more nuanced approaches to Esau and Edom have surfaced in recent years, reflecting the methodological pluralism of the field of biblical studies. One such example is offered by Dicou, whose work is perhaps the most thorough attempt to answer this question.[36] Providing readings of both the Genesis texts concerning Esau and the prophetic texts about Edom, Dicou concludes that "The Jacob–Esau stories and the oracles against Edom originated mostly in the second half of the sixth century B.C.E., in a mutually influencing development."[37] In both cases, Esau and Edom serve a typological function as representative of the nations. However, Genesis and the prophetic books paint a different picture regarding the outcome: while the prophetic books see no solution other than the destruction of Edom, the Genesis stories can be seen to show that it is indeed possible for Israel and its neighbors to coexist in relative peace.[38] Dicou's research has been an important addition to studies on Esau and Edom, offering both thorough readings and thoughtful reflection. He is sensitive to the texts and traditions, and handles them with a deft touch. Moreover, his use of both synchronic and diachronic methods allows the texts to speak on their own, while being understood in light of historical-critical issues.

Another instructive and important reading of the Esau and Edom traditions has been put forward by Stiebert, who highlights the ideological nature of these traditions.[39] She argues that the portrayal of Esau in Genesis is, for the most part, positive, where Esau is a character who is mistreated. The negative "bad press" which Esau receives in the prophets "belongs to a larger pattern of prophetic inversion and anti-foreign Second Temple ideology. The radical reinterpretation was

36.   Dicou's dissertation ("Jakob en Esau") focuses on the synchronic elements of the relevant texts, while the diachronic elements are dealt with in his subsequent work, *Edom, Israel's Brother*.

37.   Dicou, *Edom, Israel's Brother*, 198.

38.   Ibid., 202–4.

39.   Johanna Stiebert, "The Maligned Patriarch: Prophetic Ideology and the 'Bad Press' of Esau," in *Sense and Sensitivity: Essays on Reading the Bible in Memory of Robert Carroll* (ed. Alastair G. Hunter and Phillip R. Davies; JSOTSup 348; London: Sheffield Academic, 2002), 33–48.

possibly the upshot of making sense of a world where everything appears to have been turned upside down."[40] She concludes:

> Esau, the patriarch who according to the story of Genesis was maligned by his own brother, is wronged yet more in the prophetic literature where he receives very bad press indeed. He epitomizes all that is within the parameters of Second Temple ideology detestable: foreignness, defilement and shamefulness. His fraternal feeling (evident in the Genesis account) is here utterly corrupted; his kinship with Judah/Israel has become so diminished that he is numbered among the abhorred foreigners; even his masculinity is undermined. What has Esau done to deserve this? It could be that his exogamy became the target of ideologues, seeking to find explanations (and scapegoats) for the violent turbulence of the relatively recent past. On the basis of Esau's depiction in the Hexateuch, the reinterpretation of him in Jeremiah, Obadiah and Malachi is not "fair" and consequently draws forceful attention to damaging ideological subtexts.[41]

Again, Stiebert's reading has much to be commended. Her positive reading of Esau in the Hexateuch has much in common with my own, and her ideological critique of the prophets is a helpful reminder that these are difficult texts indeed that need to be read and understood with care.

Finally, two readings which highlight theological dimensions of these traditions need to be mentioned. One of these is offered by Assis, who argues that the hostility Israel feels toward Edom is related to the issue of election. He writes,

> Israel's attitude to Edom in the sixth century B.C.E. is related to the people's feelings of despair, deriving from the view that the destruction meant that God had abandoned His people. Since Edom was seen as an alternative to Israel, being identified with Esau, Jacob's brother, it was thought possible that God had now chosen Edom as his people in place of Israel. Two facts supported these thoughts. The first was the Edomite participation in the destruction of Jerusalem and the temple and the exiling of Judah from their country. Since the exile of Judah and the destruction of the temple were interpreted by the people as severing of the relationship with God, Edom's participation in the act of rejection of Israel by God could have been interpreted easily as an expression of God's wish to choose Edom in their place. Because Israel saw Esau and Edom as being identical, the Edomite participation in the destruction of Judah was not interpreted in a regular political context between two rival neighbouring peoples. Edom's participation received a theological significance in light of the conflict of Jacob and Esau over the election in the Book of Genesis... A

---

40. Ibid., 33.
41. Ibid., 47.

second fact that supported the view that Edom was now chosen instead of Israel is the colonization of the land of Judah by the Edomites... The Edomites invaded Judah's part of God's inheritance and settled there... It was not the fact that Edom participated in the destruction or even the fact that they colonized Judah that led to the exceptional attitude towards Edom in the Biblical sources. Acts of this type were also carried out by other peoples. The ideological and theological significance that Judah assigned to Edom's acts is what led the prophets to focus on Edom.[42]

Assis's study helpfully highlights the theological dimension of the relationship between the Esau and Edom traditions. He notes the particularity of the Esau/Edom story, over against the generalized typological views outlined above. Moreover, the importance of the land, and its relation to the issue of election, is also rightly noted.

Another study that has recognized a further element of this election motif—brotherhood—is that of Spina. After focusing primarily on the Esau texts in Genesis, and finding a remarkably positive portrayal there, Spina notes:

> Quite simply, the nation of Edom, as depicted in the biblical stories, did not follow in the footsteps of Esau the man. The later prophetic condemnations of Edom, therefore, are a function of an appalling (from Israel's point of view) transition from a most gracious brotherhood to a most malignant sibling rivalry expressed at the national level.[43]

Again, Spina's careful readings are instructive, and his focus on theological elements of the texts is helpful. His reading of Esau does not negate the difficulty of election, but instead holds in tension this complex theological idea with the often unrecognized role that the unchosen play in the biblical story. Indeed, my understanding of the Esau story, particularly in Genesis, has much resonance with the work of Spina. Moreover, Spina's understanding of the importance of the brotherhood theme for both the Esau and Edom traditions is vital, though, as we will see, there is a great deal more on this theme to be mined within both these traditions.

In summary, there are several approaches that can be taken with regard to understanding the relationship of the Esau and Edom traditions: (1) traditional, linear readings which see continuity from Esau, down through the people of Edom (Calvin); (2) religio- and source-critical approaches, which argue that the Hebrew Bible has incorporated different

---

42. Elie Assis, "Why Edom? On the Hostility Towards Jacob's Brother in Prophetic Sources," *VT* 56 (2006): 1–20 (14–15).

43. Spina, *Faith*, 32.

traditions, and these traditions have been fused together so as to connect Jacob/Israel and Esau/Edom (Gunkel, Bartlett); (3) the argument that the Esau and Edom traditions both offer typological portrayals of Esau and Edom, that both developed under similar circumstances, but in the end they offer possible alternatives for post-exilic Yehud (Dicou); (4) ideological readings, which note that Esau was mistreated by Jacob, and that Edom is similarly mistreated by Judah as a scapegoat, high-lighting the ideological nature of Israel's Scriptures (Stiebert); and (5) readings which are more theological in nature, focusing on the issue of land and election (Assis) or on the brotherhood motif (Spina). All of these are helpful in their own ways for understanding the relationship of the Esau and Edom traditions in the Hebrew Bible. In this work I hope to utilize elements of all of these approaches, where appropriate, in order to offer a more coherent reading of the complex of materials concerning Esau and Edom in their present canonical shape, one that is particularly attuned to literary and theological resonances.

Having visited (however briefly and selectively) the various ways in which the Esau and Edom traditions have been received, I turn now to the texts themselves, offering readings of the relevant passages, begin-ning with the narratives concerning Esau in Genesis.

Chapter 3

BEGINNINGS: ORACLE, BIRTH,
AND BIRTHRIGHT (GENESIS 25:19–34)

1. *Esau in Genesis: Preliminary Issues*

The cycle of stories focusing on Jacob and Esau is found in Gen 25–36.[1] As Jacob is the primary focus of these narratives, Esau's presence in them is sporadic, occurring primarily at the beginning and the end of the cycle of stories. With this in mind, the following chapters will examine events occurring in Gen 25, 27, 32–33, and 36. While source-critical and redactional issues will be dealt with as necessary when important for the discussion at hand, the following will focus on the received form of these texts. Because the bulk of the relevant texts in Genesis are narrative in form, methods related to literary and narrative criticism will be employed, including a focus on character development, plot development, and the use of key terms and motifs.[2] At the end of each chapter, we will explore how the text in question affects the portrayal of Esau in general, as well as how the conclusions which have been drawn might impact our understanding of the issue of election.

1. A helpful introduction to the Jacob Cycle can be found in Stanley D. Walters, "Jacob Narrative," *ABD* 3:599–608. This cycle of stories has been approached in a variety of ways, a selection of which includes Erhard Blum, *Die Komposition der Vätergeschichte* (WMANT 57; Neukirchen–Vluyn: Neukirchener, 1980); Michael Fishbane, "Composition and Structure in the Jacob Cycle (Gen. 25:19–35:22)," *JJS* 26 (1975): 15–38, reprinted in *Biblical Text and Texture: A Literary Reading of Selected Texts* (Oxford: Oneworld, 1979), 40–62; Terence E. Fretheim, "The Jacob Traditions: Theology and Hermeneutic," *Int* 26 (1972): 419–36; Joseph Blenkinsopp, "Biographical Patterns in Biblical Narrative," *JSOT* 20 (1981): 27–46; Albert de Pury, "Le cycle de Jacob comme légende autonome des origines d'Israël," in Emerton, ed., *Congress Volume: Leuven, 1989*, 78–96.
2. My understanding of biblical narrative has been shaped by many of the standard works in the field, including Robert Alter, *The Art of Biblical Narrative* (New York: Basic, 1981); Adele Berlin, *Poetics and Interpretation of Biblical Narrative* (BLS; Sheffield: Almond, 1983); Shimon Bar-Efrat, *Narrative Art in the Bible* (London: T&T Clark International, 2004).

2. *Introduction to Genesis 25:19–34*

In Gen 25:19–34, the story of Jacob and Esau begins at pace, moving from pre-birth events, to a report of their birth, to their first recorded interaction. Just how these verses hang together (if at all) is unclear.[3] Nevertheless, this passage is important for the present study, not least because it introduces and sets up the remainder of the Jacob Cycle. Here we encounter not only the brothers, but also key themes, words, and theological motifs that will resonate throughout the cycle of stories. Thus, to understand the dynamics of the Jacob–Esau narratives, we need to understand their beginnings.

When one first encounters the events of Gen 25:19–34, particularly in contemporary translations, the verses seem straightforward with regard to the elevation of Jacob over Esau and the nature of their relationship. To begin with, their mother Rebekah receives a word from YHWH declaring that the elder will serve the younger—and Esau happens to be born first. Then, Esau gives up the rights of the firstborn for a mere bowl of lentils, despising this important right of primogeniture. At this point in the story, it seems the odds are stacked against Esau from the beginning, with things getting progressively worse. Because of this, Esau is often written off by readers as irrelevant to the larger story or unworthy of being the bearer of the Abrahamic promise.

However, as is often the case, the story is more complex than it first appears, for a number of reasons. We might first note the presence of grammatical ambiguity, making any reading of these verses somewhat tenuous for the contemporary interpreter. Secondly, the reader is faced with moral complexity, as we are unsure of the characters' motives or how their actions should be understood. And finally, these verses are theologically difficult, as issues of divine and human agency are introduced

---

3. The presence of a *toledot*, divine oracle, birth report, and short narrative has left commentators perplexed as to how these differing forms might all be related. See Jean Louis Ska, "Genése 25,19–34—Ouverture du Cycle de Jacob," in *Jacob: Commentaire à plusieurs voix de Gen 25–36: Mélanges offerts à Albert de Pury* (ed. Jean-Daniel Macchi and Thomas Römer; MdB 44; Geneva: Labor et Fides, 2001), 11–21; Gordon J. Wenham, *Genesis 16–50* (WBC 2; Dallas: Word, 1995), 172–73. This has led to difficulty in isolating sources as well as dating this passage. For instance, Gunkel isolates J and E, while Westermann says it is too hard to distinguish after the hand of a redactor, and Blum sees unity in this passage. See Gunkel, *Genesis*, 288; Claus Westermann, *Genesis 12–36* (trans. John J. Scullion; CC; Minneapolis: Fortress, 1995), 411; Blum, *Die Komposition*, 66–88. On related problems of dating, see David M. Carr, *Reading the Fractures of Genesis: Historical and Literary Approaches* (Louisville: Westminster John Knox, 1996), 224–25.

with little guidance offered to the reader as to how these might be related. All of these issues add to the question of how these verses might inform our reading of the rest of the stories concerning Isaac's sons.

Therefore, this chapter will explore a number of underlying questions regarding Jacob and Esau and their beginnings, including: What do these introductory verses tell us about these characters, and why? In what ways do they shape our reading as the cycle of stories continues? And what might they tell us about the nature of election?

We will attempt to answer these questions by breaking Gen 25:19–34 down into constituent parts, based around pre-birth events, the birth itself, and the birthright scene. I hope to show that while these introductory scenes might set in motion a series of events that will push the subsequent story in a particular direction, the ambiguity and complexity which permeates these verses should give the reader pause before making evaluations as to how this passage might inform our understanding of the character Esau as well as his role as the unchosen son.

3. *Pre-Birth Events (Genesis 25:19–23)*

a. *Conception (vv. 19–21)*

Genesis 25:19 introduces us to a new section of the book of beginnings by means of the *toledot* formula: "This is the account (תולדת) of Isaac, son of Abraham." This follows on immediately from Ishmael's *toledot*, which has preceded these verses in 25:12–18. As is often the case in Genesis, Isaac's *toledot* introduces not so much the story of the man himself, but of his offspring.[4]

We are told that Abraham fathered Isaac, and that Isaac married Rebekah at the age of forty. None of this is new information at this point in the narrative; however, the details given reinforce the fact that Isaac—and not Ishmael—is the one through whom the chosen line will continue. Indeed, the next verse (25:21) introduces a familiar obstacle from the story of Abraham, as the "natural chain of procreation is interrupted, and can proceed only through divine intervention, as was true for Abraham."[5] Consequently, the patriarch prays for his barren wife, and YHWH answers his prayer.[6]

4. George W. Coats, *Genesis, with an Introduction to Narrative Literature* (FOTL 1; Grand Rapids: Eerdmans, 1983), 183–84.

5. Robert Alter, *Genesis: Translation and Commentary* (New York: W. W. Norton, 1996), 126.

6. As several scholars have noted, this is one of the few scenes where Isaac is portrayed as active rather than passive, and perhaps the one area where he out-

And yet, while there is continuity with the barrenness of Abraham and Sarah, there is discontinuity as well, as Isaac and Rebekah face a different set of problems. Humphreys notes,

> In Isaac's story, and in contrast to his father's, the issue is not will there be a son. Rebekah's barrenness is introduced only to be dealt with in one sentence. The real issue, by contrast, is the relationships of the two sons born to Isaac and Rebekah, their relationship to each other, their parents, and especially the promise and blessing established and sustained by God. The disparity in the relationship between narration and narrated time in this opening segment of Isaac's story shows the weight of emphasis. *If God is so slow in granting Abraham and Sarah one son, thus complicating the fulfilling of his promise, in granting Isaac and Rebekah two sons he triggers quite other complications for this family of his choice.*[7]

b. *Rebekah's Word from YHWH (vv. 22–23)*

The story continues in v. 22, where we are told that the children struggled in Rebekah's womb, making life difficult enough that she questions the purpose of it all, and goes to inquire of YHWH.[8] Before moving to the

---

performs his father. See Wenham, *Genesis 16–50*, 174; Victor P. Hamilton, *The Book of Genesis, Chapters 18–50* (NICOT; Grand Rapids: Eerdmans, 1995), 175. Indeed, the Jewish and Christian traditions would both make much of Isaac's powerful prayer. Later Jewish tradition laid stress on the fact that Isaac prayed on the mountain of worship, where his father had bound him, and that this prayer changes the intentions of God. See *Targum Pseudo-Jonathan* to Gen 25:21; cf. Rashi, *Pentateuch with Targum Onkelos, Haphtaroth and Prayers for Sabbath and Rashi's Commentary: Genesis* (ed. M. Rosenbaum and A. M. Silbermann; London: Shapiro, Vallentine & Co., 1929), 114, and Ibn Ezra, *Ibn Ezra's Commentary on the Pentateuch: Genesis (Bereshit)* (trans. H. Norman Strickman and Arthur M. Silver; New York: Menorah, 1988), 248.

7. W. Lee Humphreys, *The Character of God in the Book of Genesis: A Narrative Appraisal* (Louisville: Westminster John Knox, 2001), 156–57 (italics in original). This is not to say that Isaac and Rebekah's wait will be a short one; we find out in 25:26 that Isaac is sixty years old when the boys are born. However, the length of time does not seem to lie at the heart of the story in the way that it does in the Abraham and Sarah narrative.

8. Rebekah's question is somewhat puzzling, the MT reading ותאמר אם־כן למה זה אנכי. Scholars seem to be divided as to whether Rebekah is bemoaning her pregnancy or her life in general. Neither understanding detracts from the general tenor of the passage. *BHS* suggests inserting היה with the Peshitta, conferring with 27:46 where Rebekah makes a similar statement concerning her lack of will to live. Alter (*Genesis*, 127) translates Rebekah's plea as "Then why me?," but notes that it can almost read like a broken-off sentence: "Why am I...?"

oracle which Rebekah receives, it is worth mentioning the issue which brings about the word from YHWH: the fact that the children "struggle" in the womb.

(1) *The Struggle*. The word used for "struggle" (וַיִּתְרֹצְצוּ) is the Hithpalel form of the verb רצץ, the basic meaning of which in the Qal form is "to oppress, wrong, crush."[9] This is the only occurrence of the verb in this form in the Hebrew Bible, denoting reflexive action.[10] Accordingly, Ringgren translates this as the children "struggled together."[11] It is, at this stage, a struggle with no instigator and no victor—just struggle.[12]

Early traditions seem to have transmitted the sense of the MT here regarding a mutual struggle. *Targum Onqelos* uses ודחקין, from דחק, a fairly literal translation indicating struggle.[13] Meanwhile, the LXX has ἐσκίρτων, denoting "stirring," "moving," or "leaping."[14] While this term may not carry the force inherent in the Hebrew, there is no hint of judgment of the lads in this rendering.

However, the history of interpretation shows that this impartiality would not last long. Jewish tradition tended to highlight the close similarity between the root רצץ and the root of the verb "to run," רץ. Thus, as Rashi notes, "whenever [Rebekah] passed by the doors of the Torah (i.e. the schools of Shem and Eber) Jacob moved convulsively in his efforts to come to birth, but whenever she passed by the gate of a pagan temple Esau moved convulsively in his efforts to come to birth."[15] The Christian tradition does not fare much better. Augustine, for instance, takes the wrestling in the womb as metaphoric concerning good and evil people fighting in the church.[16] And Origen understands the struggle as

9.   H. Ringgren, "רצץ," *TDOT* 13:641–43.
10.   See JM §59g; GKC §55d.
11.   Ringgren, *TDOT* 13:642.
12.   Frederick E. Greenspahn, *When Brothers Dwell Together: The Preeminence of Younger Siblings in the Hebrew Bible* (Oxford: Oxford University Press, 1994), 118.
13.   Jastrow suggests "press, squeeze, crowd, or stamp" (Jastrow 1:293). For the Aramaic text, see Moses Aberbach and Bernard Grossfeld, *Targum Onkelos to Genesis: A Critical Analysis Together with an English Translation of the Text (Based on A. Sperber's Edition)* (New York: Ktav, 1982), 150–51.
14.   G. Fitzer, "σκιρτάω," *TDNT* 7:401–2. The same verb is used in Luke 1:41, 44 as Elizabeth's baby leaps in her womb when Mary arrives.
15.   *Rashi's Commentary: Genesis*, 115; Cf. *Gen. Rab.* 63. Ibn Ezra was a voice of reason here, noting the semantic similarity between the roots of these words, but refusing to read any more into it. *Ibn Ezra's Commentary, Genesis*, 249.
16.   Augustine, *Tractate on the Gospel of John* 11.10.2–3, in ACCS 2:146.

the good and evil virtues struggling within each one of us.[17] In each of these cases, it is Esau who embodies evil. Thus, commentators in both the early Jewish and Christian traditions introduce moral evaluations of the characters Jacob and Esau even before they are born.

And yet, while moral evaluation may be inappropriate at this stage, the fact that there is a struggle cannot be denied. From the perspective of the narrative, this strife does indeed set the tone for the rest of the brothers' relationship, and is the reason Rebekah goes to inquire of YHWH.[18]

(2) *The Oracle from YHWH*. Rebekah's inquiry proves fruitful,[19] as YHWH answers her in v. 23: "Two nations (גוים)[20] are in your womb, and two peoples (לאמים) from within you will be separated (יפרדו). And a people will be stronger (יאמץ) than a people, and the greater the younger will serve (ורב עבד צעיר)." And yet, the oracle is far from clear; indeed, it seems to raise more questions than it answers. In light of this, we will explore several areas which need further investigation: grammatical ambiguity, individual and national identity, and hermeneutical implications.

The first half of v. 23 is, grammatically speaking, relatively clear. The reason for Rebekah's discomfort is that there are two peoples within her. The terms גוים and לאמים are often used in poetic parallelism to refer to nations or peoples, and either term seems appropriate in both instances here.[21]

The term found at the end of 25:23a, יפרדו, also seems straightforward. From the root פרד, the basic meaning of this term is "to separate."[22] However, one might ask if this separation refers to the twins themselves, their descendants, or both. And if the lads are in view, does this separation denote enmity or simply physical separation? The term is found

17. Origen, *Homilies on Genesis* 12.3, in ACCS 2:147.

18. Terence E. Fretheim, "The Book of Genesis," *NIB* 1:319–674 (521).

19. Interestingly, Josephus is the only ancient commentator I came across who takes issue with the fact that it is Rebekah, and not the patriarch Isaac, who seeks YHWH and receives an answer. In Josephus's retelling, it is Isaac who inquires of YHWH. See *Ant.* 1.18.1.

20. *BHS* reads גוים for גיים. Further text-critical issues in the oracle are dealt with in Robert A. Kraft, "A Note on the Oracle of Rebecca (Gen. xxv.23)," *JTS* 13 (1962): 318–20.

21. See R. E. Clements and G. J. Botterweck, "גוי," *TDOT* 2:426–33 (428); H. D. Preuss, "לאם," *TDOT* 7:397–98; B. Jacob, *Das erste Buch der Tora: Genesis, Übersetzt und Erklärt* (Berlin: Schocken, 1934), 543.

22. M. Hausmann, "פרד," *TDOT* 12:76–79. Here it is found in the Niphal, which is the most common form.

elsewhere in Genesis, most notably when it is used to describe the
separation of Abram and Lot in Gen 13:9, 11 and 14, where strife might
be implied, but is not necessary.[23] It may be that the ensuing narratives
speak to this, as the brothers separate in their lifestyles and temperaments,
ultimately leading to conflict. However, while conflict does follow the
brothers throughout the cycle of stories, the final scene (Gen 33) has the
brothers separating in relative peace.

The next clause, 25:23bα, states that "a people will be stronger than a
people (ולאם מלאם יאמץ)."[24] The ambiguity here relates to who is being
referred to as אמץ, "stronger," and how this relates to the subsequent line
about serving.[25] Steinberg offers a common interpretation:

> The construction of the poetic piece leads the reader to believe that the
> stronger one is actually the older twin—the one whom Yahweh informs
> Rebekah will be a servant to the younger, weaker twin. The poem sug-
> gests that, if indeed there was a customary priority given to the firstborn,
> as many assume, this right will be overturned in the case of Jacob and
> Esau.[26]

And yet several issues remain: Does the use of לאם imply that the
descendants of the twins are being referred to here, rather than the
ancestors as Steinberg suggests? Even if one chooses to understand the
reference here as the twins, questions remain: Which one is "stronger"?
Will Esau be weaker, and serve the younger, stronger brother? Or will
Esau be stronger, and yet serve the weaker?[27]

The ambiguity is compounded in 25:23bβ, where we read, ורב יעבד
צעיר. The first point of contention here is the terminology used. Who (or
what) is being referred to with the terms רב and צעיר? Are we still being
told about the "peoples" from the previous clause, or are we now dealing
with individuals? Speiser has noted that there is an exact parallel in
Akkadian family law using the terminology of רב and צעיר regarding

23.   Laurence A. Turner, *Announcements of Plot in Genesis* (JSOTSup 96; Sheffield: JSOT, 1990), 128; cf. J. P. Fokkelman, *Narrative Art in Genesis: Specimens
of Stylistic and Structural Analysis* (SSN 17; Assen: Van Gorcum, 1975), 89.

24.   On the singular usage of לאם, see Preuss, *TDOT* 7:397.

25.   On this term, see J. Schreiner, "אמץ," *TDOT* 1:323–27.

26.   Naomi Steinberg, *Kinship and Marriage in Genesis: A Household Economics
Perspective* (Minneapolis: Fortress, 1993), 89–90.

27.   In light of the ambiguity here, Rashi offers an interesting reading. He understands "one stronger than the other" as "they will never be equally great at the same
time: when one rises, the other will fall" (*Rashi's Commentary: Genesis*, 115). This
reading makes sense not only of the national level of Israel and Edom, but also of the
individual characters of Jacob and Esau.

inheritance.[28] And Sæbø has highlighted that צעיר is often used in poetic parallelism, indeed, at times in juxtaposition with terms such as בכור and related terminology, including רב.[29] Thus, reference to the individual children and birth order is not out of the question. Others, however, argue that this clause has nothing to do with the birth order of the children, as the entire oracle has the national context in view.[30]

Moreover, the terms רב and צעיר can also be rendered as "greater" and "lesser," removing any sense of birth order from the equation. All of this is compounded by a possible wordplay on the names of the boys in this clause. The word which is usually translated as "younger," צעיר, is a homonym of שער, "hairy," the term used in the description of Esau in the birth report of 25:25, and which will recur in the events of Gen 27. Meanwhile, the verb used here for "serve," יעבד, has similarities with Jacob's name, יעקב.[31] It could be argued that this casts doubt as to who should be considered the "greater" and the "lesser."

This leads us to one last area of ambiguity in 25:23bβ, namely, who will be serving whom. Translations unanimously render this phrase as "the older will serve the younger," and this seems to be the way the early translations understood this as well.[32] However, the syntax is not straightforward; the ambiguity can be seen to some extent in rendering this as, "the older the younger will serve." Heard elucidates the issues:

> In typical poetic style, neither "older" nor "younger" is marked for case…
> The lack of explicit case markers requires recourse to other factors to deter-
> mine the subject and object of the verb *'ābad*. Both *rab* and *ṣā'îr* agree in

28. E. A. Speiser, *Genesis: A New Translation with Introduction and Commentary* (AB 1; Garden City: Doubleday, 1983), 194–95.

29. M. Sæbø, "צעיר," *TDOT* 12:424–28. For more on רב, see H.-J. Fabry, "רב," *TDOT* 13:272–98.

30. Jacob, *Das erste Buch der Tora*, 343; Greenspahn, *When Brothers*, 118; cf. Burke O. Long, *The Problem of Etiological Narrative in the Old Testament* (BZAW 108; Berlin: Töpelmann, 1968), 49, who notes that the oracle to Rebekah appears to be more concerned with tribal issues, while the birth narrative takes pains to describe the individuals. While this distinction is somewhat helpful, it is also a simplification, as there are definite "national" overtones in the birth narrative as well, particularly in the wordplays relating to Esau, Seir and Edom.

31. These are noted by Wenham, *Genesis 16–50*, 176; Hamilton, *Genesis 18–50*, 177.

32. For contemporary translations which follow this, see NRSV, NASB, NIV, and NKJV. The LXX clarifies the syntax of the clause by noting the subject: καὶ ὁ μείζων δουλεύσει τῷ ἐλάσσονι. *Targum Onqelos*, meanwhile, concludes the verse with ורבא ישתעבד לזעירא. The addition of the preposition *lamed* here indicates that the greater will be subject *to* the lesser.

number and gender with *ya'ăbōd*, so the syntax of the verb alone is of no help in resolving the ambiguity... In Hebrew, verbal clauses are most frequently structured *verb–subject–object*, with *object–verb–subject*, *verb–object–subject*, *subject–object–verb*, and *object–subject–verb* as well-attested alternatives... Reading 23bβ "the older will serve the younger," however, produces the pattern *subject–verb–object*, which though normal in English is rather peculiar in Hebrew. Of course, the line could be parsed as if it began with a nominative absolute (*casus pendens*), but it lacks the normal syntactical markers of a nominative absolute, such as the shift to an independent clause with its own explicit subject... The lack of such markers does not mean that *wĕrab* in v. 23bβ *cannot* be read as a nominative absolute, but it does mean that such a reading, while possible, is not necessary. Readers are thus faced with the uncomfortable choice of reading "the older will serve the younger," against the most frequent constructions of Hebrew grammar (or construing *wĕrab* as an unmarked nominative absolute, with no supporting syntactical features of the clause), or "the younger will serve the older," against Israelite ethnic pride *vis-à-vis* Edom.[33]

Heard continues by pointing out that the parallelism with v. 23bα might help clarify the meaning of this clause. However, the question then becomes how the *waw* which connects the two lines should be interpreted: Is this a comparative (and thus heightening) or antithetical (and thus distinguishing) parallelism? This goes back to the question which was posed above, namely, which "people" is the stronger: "Will the one serve the other (v. 23bβ) *because* the other will be stronger than the one (v. 23bα), or will the one serve the other *in spite of the fact that* the one is stronger than the other?"[34]

The ambiguity of who will be serving whom has been noted on occasion by commentators, with various responses. Ibn Ezra implicitly referenced this issue by commenting that רב must be the subject here, citing a similar case in Mal 1:6 (בן יכבד אב).[35] B. Jacob and Alter both note the ambiguity of the clause, but opt to render it in traditional fashion, as this in their view makes the most sense in context.[36] Others, however, feel that the ambiguity in v. 23bβ is important in that it forces the reader to rethink other aspects of the story, such as the subsequent

---

33. Heard, *Dynamics*, 99; cf. Richard Elliot Friedman, *Commentary on the Torah* (San Francisco: HarperSanFrancisco, 2001), 88. On agreement in parts of sentence with gender and number, see GKC §145; on word order in sentences, see GKC §142; JM §155ng.

34. Heard, *Dynamics*, 100.

35. *Ibn Ezra's Commentary, Genesis*, 250.

36. Jacob, *Das erste Buch der Tora*, 543; Alter (*Genesis*, 127) translates it as "the elder, the younger's slave."

actions of the mother and her younger son, and whether or not these are in line with or in opposition to the oracle which was given.[37]

In sum, the reader is left with several levels of ambiguity in this oracle: Who will be stronger, and is this referring to the brothers or their descendants? Who will be serving whom? And should these terms be understood as "elder" and "younger," or "greater" and "lesser"? These ambiguities necessarily affect how one interprets the oracle to Rebekah, and in turn how the larger cycle of stories concerning her sons are understood.

The ambiguities in the oracle given to Rebekah obviously have implications beyond the immediate context. What should be made of YHWH's words to Rebekah in terms of how they inform the larger narrative concerning Jacob, Esau, and their descendants? The most pressing issue relates to the question of identity. The use of גוים and לאמים in the oracle brings to the fore an issue which affects not only our understanding of the Genesis narratives, but indeed all references to the brothers throughout the Hebrew Bible. Are Jacob and Esau to be understood as individual characters in their own right, or as ciphers for the nations that will bear their names?

This tension of individual and national concerns is evident in both ancient and contemporary interpretation. For instance, while early Jewish tradition certainly saw Jacob as the chosen son, this oracle came to be understood as dealing primarily with future national concerns. In *Genesis Rabbah* and the targumim, this is not so much about Israel and Edom as Israel and *Rome*: one day the small, less powerful people will break free and rule the other.[38]

The Christian tradition, on the other hand, understood the oracle as dealing with the theological issue of election, with the individual characters in the story serving as an example of the ways of God. The most famous example of this is found in Rom 9:10–13:

> Rebekah's children had one and the same father, our father Isaac. Yet, before the twins were born or had done anything good or bad—in order that God's purpose in election might stand: not by works but by him who calls—she was told, "The older will serve the younger." Just as it is written: "Jacob I loved, but Esau I hated." (NIV)

---

37. David W. Cotter, *Genesis* (BO; Collegeville: Liturgical, 2003), 189; Heard, *Dynamics*, 100.

38. *Gen. Rab.* 63:7. Cf. *Targum Onqelos* and other targumic traditions, which use the word "kingdom" in place of "people."

As Dunn notes, Paul is underlining the fact that Jacob and Esau do not just come from the same father (as Isaac and Ishmael did), but from the same act of intercourse. Indeed, Paul goes on to say that God's choice is made before good or evil has been done, and the use of ἵνα in v. 11, "in order that," points to intended purpose. For Paul, the election of Israel is not the point here, but rather "how God's purpose of election comes into effect."[39]

The use of Gen 25:23 in Romans would go on to provide fertile ground for the history of Christian interpretation. In his *City of God*, Augustine quotes Paul, noting that God's choice was an obvious work of grace, as neither son deserved to be God's chosen.[40] Similarly, Calvin would argue that this oracle informs Rebekah that the younger will be the elect of God, meaning that one was chosen and the other rejected. Moreover, God inverts the birth order to show that "the heir of the promised benediction was gratuitously elected."[41]

Interestingly, contemporary commentators tend to be divided along precisely these same lines, understanding the oracle as referring primarily to national events, or as concerned with the idea of election.

The reading strategy employed by historical-critical scholars in response to Gen 25:23 has been to understand the oracle as a retrospective nationalistic statement, referring most likely to Israel's later subjugation of Edom under David. As Westermann remarks, we see in the oracle "the pride of the victor speaking who has overcome a larger people (2 Sam 8:13f.)... The generation of the early period of the monarchy sees in a simple family event of the remote patriarchal period the beginning of what it now experiences."[42] Some have argued that David's reign should be seen as the earliest possible date for this understanding, but that a later date, related to other national conflicts, is also possible.[43] Regardless, this historical approach makes sense of the oracle by relating it to later, national circumstances.

A second contemporary approach to the oracle in Gen 25:23 follows Paul's understanding of this as concerned with election. Here the focus tends to remain on the individuals in the narrative itself, even if the tension of individual and national concerns is noted. This can be seen in

39. James D. G. Dunn, *Romans 9–16* (WBC 38B; Dallas: Word, 1988), 542–43.
40. Augustine, *City of God* 16.35, in ACCS 2:148.
41. Calvin, *Genesis*, 44–45.
42. Claus Westermann, *Genesis 12–36*, 413; Cf. S. R. Driver, *The Book of Genesis* (WC; London: Methuen, 1909), 245–47.
43. J. Alberto Soggin, *Das Buch Genesis, Kommentar* (Darmstadt: Wissenschaftliche Buchgesellschaft, 1997), 341.

the work of Brueggemann, who highlights the scandalous nature of the oracle and the surrounding narrative:

> The text credits the shattering career of Jacob to the speech of God. God does not explain or justify. God simply announces... Like its main character, this narrative is indiscreet and at times scandalous. It shows God and his chosen younger one aligned against the older brother, against the father, and against the cultural presumptions of natural privilege. Jacob is announced as a visible expression of God's remarkable graciousness in the face of conventional definitions of reality and prosperity. Jacob is a scandal from the beginning.[44]

Levenson, meanwhile, describes the situation using stark language, stating that "the oracle to the pregnant matriarch was not only a prediction but a statement of YHWH's own preference," an idea which he says finds validity in Mal 1:2–3.[45] Drawing in the events of Gen 27, he concludes,

> we are faced with a much larger problem than that of a mother and a brother who refuse to adhere to the principle of primogeniture, employing loathsome trickery to accomplish their ends. We are faced as well with a Deity who disregards the principle of order no less than they, even preferring the unscrupulous trickster over the uncouth first-born.[46]

In summary, the hermeneutical tension of individual and national concerns has led to two broad interpretive approaches to the oracle of Gen 25:23. The oracle has been understood (1) as a forward-looking or retrospective statement regarding nationalistic domination in Israel's history; or (2) as dealing with the theological issue of election. What are we to make of these interpretive approaches?

It would seem that both vantage points are important for a holistic understanding of the oracle. Indeed, many interpreters understand that a careful reading will need to incorporate both individual and national aspects. This requires care, however, as the two cannot be collapsed into one. As Clifford comments,

---

44. Walter Brueggemann, *Genesis* (IBC; Atlanta: John Knox, 1982), 215, 217.

45. Levenson, *Death*, 63.

46. Ibid. As Barth states, "There was much to praise in the later nation Israel (and in Jacob too), and much to blame in Ishmael (and in Esau too). But whatever we may find to praise or blame, the election of the one and the rejection of the other certainly bears no relation to it." See Karl Barth, "The Election of the Community," in *Church Dogmatics* 2.2 (trans. G. W. Bromiley; Edinburgh: T. & T. Clark, 1968), §34, p. 216.

> The national meaning of the Genesis stories of the ancestors becomes
> clear only when the drama of the individual actors is taken seriously on
> its own terms. The stories are not allegories with a one-to-one correspon-
> dence of individual and nation. The human actors, however, are ancestors
> who somehow include and prefigure their descendants.[47]

If the oracle is concerned with both individual and nationalistic issues,
then the "nationalistic" reading is a helpful reminder that there is more
going on in these stories than a small family feud. Nevertheless, it is
clear as the story progresses that issues of family succession and the
chosen son are also at stake, and this needs to be kept in mind. As such,
the idea of "election" may be a helpful framework here, as the election of
Jacob and non-election of Esau have obvious ramifications for their
descendants as well. Any later Israelite dominance would be understood
as a byproduct of YHWH's favor, and a continued reflection of this
chosenness. Thus, the two horizons of individual and national concerns
are not easily separated in a canonical frame of reference.

If election is indeed an important motif at work in Gen 25:23, as I
believe it is, one might ask whether this forecloses any meaningful
developments as subsequent narratives unfold. An assumption that often
accompanies the view of election is that this idea entails pre-determi-
nation. While this is understandable, it can also be argued that, in the
broader context, this oracle does not pre-determine future events, but
simply sets things in motion in a particular direction. The fullest example
of this can be seen in Fretheim's commentary. Fretheim begins by noting
that "God is not described as an agent in these [subsequent] developments, which underscores the importance of human activity." Thus, "the
move from present oracle to future reality was not necessary or inevitable."[48] For Fretheim, the oracle pushes things in a particular *direction* for
the future:

> One might claim that the future of the two boys has been predetermined
> by this divine word. Yet, it shortly becomes clear that Rebekah does not
> understand that the oracle absolutely determines her sons' futures... The
> future about which God speaks is not set in concrete. This is true of divine
> announcements about the future generally, particularly in prophetic mate-
> rial... These utterances express the future as God sees it (or would like to

47.   Richard J. Clifford, "Genesis 25:19–34," *Int* 45 (1991): 397–401 (397–98).
Similar sentiments can be found in R. W. L. Moberly, *Genesis 12–50* (OTG; Sheffield: Sheffield Academic, 1992), 29; Fretheim, "Genesis," 520; Blum, *Die Komposition*, 79; Kevin Walton, *Thou Traveller Unknown: The Presence and Absence of
God in the Jacob Narrative* (PBM; Milton Keynes: Paternoster, 2003), 16–17.
48.   Fretheim, "Genesis," 521.

see it). God's knowledge of future human behaviors is not absolute…
Moreover, the divine will can be frustrated by human behaviors (e.g., sin);
though God's way into the future cannot, finally, be stymied.[49]

Fretheim's reading may be corroborated by an analysis of the oracle as a
speech act. White's investigation is an example of this, highlighting the
ambiguity that is caused by the oracle. With regard to 25:23, White
notes,

> as a speech act with the form of a declaration rather than a promise, no
> "uptake" is required by its addressee. Instead the oracle functions to make
> Rebekah the central figure of this narrative by disclosing to her the divine
> foreknowledge (and the narrator's foreknowledge) of the end toward
> which the narrative is moving. The eventual subordination of the elder to
> the younger is not promised here, but declared… The tension is not gen-
> erated by the conflict between faith and doubt, but by the question of how
> this predetermination of the future will be actualized. It thus is not a ques-
> tion of Rebekah's faith in this oracle, but of how the events will transpire,
> and what role, if any, she will play in its fulfillment since this fore-
> knowledge has been given to her.[50]

White continues:

> This narrative strategy thus provides a divine utterance in a micro-dia-
> logue which sets in motion the events, while leaving its actualization up to
> what appear to be independent forces operating in the dynamics of the
> family related in the third-person narrative framework and the dialogue
> between the personages. Along the divine/human axis is the performative
> announcement to Rebekah that injects discontinuity into the natural order
> of succession. At the level of human communication the subsequent
> discourse is redolent with marital discord and the emotions of parental
> favoritism as motivating factors. Thus the story appears to have two
> motivating systems which have little to do with each other. If one takes the
> oracle as dominant then a case can be made for Rebekah's sainthood due
> to the sacrifices she makes in order to implement it. If one takes her favor-
> itism for Jacob and manipulation of her husband as the fundamental forces
> in this plot, then the harsh charges of betrayal and deceit which have been
> leveled at her in many commentaries become justified. But it is in the
> friction between the performative speech of the divine oracle and the
> representation of the characters made in the narrative framework and its
> related direct discourse, that the narrative will retain a degree of semantic
> openness, and it is in this openness that the narrative preserves its sym-
> bolic character. Though the action at the level of the human characters

49. Ibid., 522–23.
50. Hugh C. White, *Narration and Discourse in the Book of Genesis* (Cambridge:
Cambridge University Press, 1991), 207.

> achieves the closure of the representative narrative, the subjective source
> of the action is blurred by incorporating two explanations for the events,
> leaving the characters and their actions shrouded in ambiguity, and seman-
> tically undecidable, as the vacillation of the commentaries illustrate.[51]

Thus, while the oracle pushes the story in a particular direction, this by
no means renders meaningless the remainder of the narratives concerning Jacob, Esau and their descendants. On the contrary, it would seem
that the subsequent narratives are prime examples of the fact that everything is not set in stone. Instead, what we see is the open-ended nature of
YHWH's word, and, theologically speaking, the working out of the
tension of divine and human agency.

c. *Pre-Birth Events: Preliminary Conclusions*

This section explored the pre-birth events of Gen 25:19–23, including the
conception and the oracle which Rebekah receives from YHWH. The
issue most relevant for the present study is the oracle, which, as von Rad
once wrote, speaks of "great and enigmatic things."[52] Can any conclusions be drawn with regard to Gen 25:23? To begin with, some of the
difficulties noted above will remain unresolved. With regard to the identity of the "greater/elder" and "lesser/younger," the grammatical ambiguity entails that there is no definite answer. Moreover, the question
of who will be "stronger" and who will be serving whom is complex,
especially in light of what we know from other stories regarding the
twins and their descendants. That being said, I am inclined to agree with
Kaminsky, who, highlighting the ambiguity of the oracle, notes that a
non-traditional reading does not fit with the overall picture we find in the
Bible: "The oracle makes much more sense if it is announcing that the
normal societal expectation that favored the elder child was being chal-
lenged... It would be strange to find an oracle announcing the preeminence of an elder child."[53]

There are, however, other elements of the oracle that are less ambiguous. For instance, it seems safe to say that there are individual *and* future
nationalistic concerns at stake. The oracle is given as a response to
Rebekah's concern regarding her difficult pregnancy, the result of which
will be two sons (Jacob and Esau), who go on to be two nations (Israel
and Edom). Thus, to draw too hard a line of distinction may be unhelp-
ful. Furthermore, it is intimated that the subsequent relationship(s) will

---

51. Ibid., 208.
52. Gerhard von Rad, *Genesis: A Commentary* (trans. John H. Marks; rev. ed.;
OTL; London: SCM, 1972), 265.
53. Kaminsky, *Yet I Loved Jacob*, 44.

have strife, as there is strife in the womb: there will be separation, one will be stronger, and one will serve the other, and all of this signaled by the pre-birth struggle. Finally, the reading strategy offered by Fretheim (and White) seems a fruitful one: while the oracle pushes the story in a particular direction, this by no means entails that the subsequent narratives are of no consequence.[54] Rather, these stories are the (sometimes complex) working out of YHWH's word. Indeed, it may be that an ambiguous and complex oracle is a fitting introduction for a cycle of such ambiguous and complex stories, as the reader is forced to take stock of the ensuing narratives in light of this tension.

4. *The Birth (Genesis 25:24–26)*

Following the oracle to Rebekah, the story jumps to the birth scene. In Gen 25:24 we are told explicitly what up until now has only been implied: there are two children, twins (תומם), in Rebekah's womb.[55] In vv. 25–26, the boys emerge, and we are told aspects of their appearance, their actions, and the etymologies of their respective names.

a. *Esau*
In Gen 25:25 we are told that "The first came out red (אדמוני), all of him as a hairy garment (כאדרת שער); and they called his name Esau (עשו)."[56] Two issues need to be examined from this verse: the physical description of Esau, and the giving of his name.

The initial description concerning the first born is that he came out אדמוני. From the root אדם, this occurrence traditionally has been rendered as "red." This "redness" is often understood as an ominous sign. *Genesis Rabbah* states that Esau was red because he was a shedder of

---

54. Fretheim, "Genesis," 521–23.

55. It may be that the use of הנה at the beginning of the clause implies that Rebekah is comprehending the oracle for the first time. While the MT has תומם in Gen 25:24, the Samaritan Pentateuch has תאמים, a form closer to that found in Gen 38:27, the next occurrence of the word. For more on the forms in which this word occurs, see *HALOT* 4:1694. The rabbis made much of this "defective" spelling of twins in 25:24. As both *Gen. Rab.* 63:8 and Rashi point out, the term is written defectively here, but correctly in the case of Tamar in 38:27. Why? Because both of Tamar's sons were righteous, while in Rebekah's case, only one was righteous, while the other was defective.

56. The main textual difficulty in this section is that in v. 25 the plural ויקראו is used in the naming of Esau, while the naming of Jacob uses the singular ויקרא in v. 26. The Samaritan Pentateuch and Cairo Geniza render both as plural, while the LXX, Peshitta and Vulgate opt for singular in both instances.

blood.[57] Similarly, Vawter contends that "red" is used in a disparaging manner because "red" has derogatory connotations in much of literature.[58]

And yet there is more to it than this, for two reasons. First of all, this same term, אדמוני, is used to describe David in 1 Sam 16:12 and 17:42. However, in these cases it is usually understood as referring to David as a "ruddy" or even "handsome" youth, and few would consider these texts as disparaging David.[59] Secondly, אדם in the Hebrew language denotes a broad range of colors, and is much less restricted than our modern understanding of the term red. In the Hebrew this color term can range from brown, to yellowish brown, to the color of blood, to crimson and wine, depending on the context.[60] Moreover, there is no substantial reason for understanding this term as having negative connotations in the Hebrew Bible, much less in the wider world of literature.[61]

The main purpose in using this term is most likely to equate Esau with Edom (אדום), the future home of Esau and his descendants, a play on words that will be reinforced in the narrative of 25:29–34.[62] As Brenner points out, the wordplay used here between אדום/אדם/אדמוני is more concerned with phonetics than with colors, as it is the paronomasia which is important. The connection of these terms requires a loose framework for interpreting the "color."[63]

The second thing we are told is that Esau came out "all of him as a hairy garment." There is again a double play on words here, as not only will Esau grow up to be a hairy man (שער, 27:11), but he will be associated with the region of Seir (שעיר, 32:3). What should be made of this reference to a "hairy garment"? Hairiness plays a notable role in other

57. *Gen. Rab.* 63:8; *Rashi's Commentary: Genesis*, 115.

58. Bruce Vawter, *On Genesis: A New Reading* (London: Chapman, 1977), 288.

59. Susan Niditch, *"My Brother Esau is a Hairy Man": Hair and Identity in Ancient Israel* (Oxford: Oxford University Press, 2008), 114. The rabbis noticed this as well, but explained the similarity with the following: Esau killed "out of his own will and consent, but this one [David] puts people to death only upon the decision of the Sanhedrin" (*Gen. Rab.* 63.8).

60. Cf. Athalya Brenner, *Colour Terms in the Old Testament* (JSOTSup 21; Sheffield: JSOT, 1982), 58–80.

61. Stiebert, "Maligned Patriarch," 34.

62. Cf. Gammie, who notes how proper names of people and places are played upon throughout the Jacob Cycle. John G. Gammie, "Theological Interpretation by Way of Literary and Tradition Analysis: Genesis 25–36," in *Encounter with the Text: Form and History in the Hebrew Bible* (ed. Martin J. Buss; Philadelphia: Fortress, 1979), 117–34 (124–25).

63. Brenner, *Colour Terms*, 62.

biblical stories, most memorably in the narratives of Samson and Absa-lom. Kunin argues that both of these men are portrayed as impure and lacking sexual control, and thus we may be invited to see Esau in the same light.[64] Meanwhile, Bakhos notes that both Esau and Ishmael are presented as "wild" in how the Bible depicts them, and this "wildness" may have some connection to another wild, hairy man from the literature of the ancient Near East, Enkidu from the *Epic of Gilgamesh*.[65]

And yet, it can be asked how helpful these negative comparisons truly are. As has been pointed out, in the stories of Samson and Absalom the abundance of hair points to strength and vigor more than wild ferocious-ness (Judg 16:17; 2 Sam 14:26). Indeed, Niditch argues that the connec-tion of hair with manly vigor and heroism in Hebrew narrative is so strong that "at the outset, Esau looks like a promising patriarch."[66] In this sense, the fact that the "smooth" Jacob is the patriarch of Israel, and not the hairy Esau, may point yet again toward the counterintuitive nature of Israel's origins.

Therefore, it may be that, like the use of אדמוני, the term שער is not used in a derogatory fashion, but rather because of its verbal resonance with the future home of Esau's descendants (Seir). Taken together, it is not clear that the reader is to make a negative value judgment about Esau based on his physical description as is so often done.

The final piece of information we are given concerning the birth of the firstborn is his name, "Esau" (עשו). The connection between עשו and the previous two terms, אדמוני and שער, is not obvious. Various possibilities have been given, the most plausible being some relation to the root עשה, "to make." Later Jewish tradition understood Esau's name this way, as can be seen in *Targum Pseudo-Jonathan*'s addition: "because he was born fully completed, with hair of the head, beard, teeth, and molars."[67] However, as has been pointed out numerous times, "Neither of these folk etymologies is linguistically correct, but, of course, such is not their intention."[68] Indeed, they serve another purpose: "What the etymology

64. Seth D. Kunin, *The Logic of Incest: A Structuralist Analysis of Hebrew Mythology* (JSOTSup 185; Sheffield: Sheffield Academic, 1995), 200–201.

65. Bakhos, *Ishmael on the Border*, 23–24; Ronald S. Hendel, *The Epic of the Patriarch: The Jacob Cycle and the Narrative Traditions of Canaan and Israel* (HSM 42; Atlanta: Scholars Press, 1987), 116–21, 128–29.

66. Niditch, *"My Brother Esau"*, 114.

67. Also found in others, such as *Rashi's Commentary: Genesis*, 115. The rabbis (e.g. *Gen. Rab.* 63.8) also made a connection between Esau's name and a word which has some phonetic similarities, שוא, meaning "worthless." Cf. BDB, 996.

68. Hendel, *Epic*, 111.

explains is not the proper name itself, but the nature of Esau's connection
with his land. He is, so to speak, the embodiment of Seir-Edom."[69]

b. *Jacob*

The text continues in Gen 25:26: "And after this, his brother came out,
and his hand was grasping the heel (וידו אחזת בעקב) of Esau; and he
called his name Jacob (יעקב)." We are given less information about
Jacob than his brother, and yet what we are told is revealing.

First of all, the initial word used to describe Jacob here is אחיו, "his
brother." While this may seem a banal observation, it is in fact quite
important, as kinship terminology permeates the surrounding narrative,
and indeed, the entire Jacob Cycle. This is heightened by the next clause,
where we are told that Jacob is "grasping the heel" of his brother. Here
we see the juxtaposition of kinship and strife, which again is a theme that
will drive the narrative.

The grasping of Esau's heel serves as the basis for the etymology of
Jacob's name in the next part of the verse (יעקב/עקב). There is a general
consensus that the "original" name of Jacob comes from יעקב־אל, "may
God protect," a designation widely attested in the ancient Near East.[70]
And yet, it is interesting that if this is the case, Israel chooses to remem-
ber its eponymous ancestor not as related to God's protection, but as
grasping his brother's heel. Thus, according to the text, Jacob's name
should be equated with "heel grabber." While this designation can be
understood as related to the act of supplanting, one can reasonably
assume the text is commenting on Jacob's character as well, as other
texts seem to imply.[71]

---

69. Syrén, *Forsaken*, 85.

70. See D. N. Freedman, "The Original Name of Jacob," *IEJ* 13 (1963): 125–26.

71. The root עקב occurs elsewhere in relation to the Jacob story: in Gen 27:36,
Hos 12:3, and Jer 9:4, the verbal form is used with negative connotations regarding
Jacob's actions, and seems best understood as "supplanted" or "deceived." It is
unclear whether there is simply one root word or two, or if one original root developed into several more nuanced meanings. For more on this, see Eugene Carpenter
and Michael A. Grisanti, "עקב," *NIDOTTE* 3:504–6; William D. Whitt, "The Jacob
Traditions in Hosea and Their Relation to Genesis," *ZAW* 103 (1991): 18–43 (28–
31). Smith has argued that Jacob's grasping of Esau's heel is a euphemism for
genitals, as "in ancient Hebrew thought the sexual organs were regarded as the seat
of a man's procreative power" (S. H. Smith, "'Heel' and 'Thigh': The Concept of
Sexuality in the Jacob–Esau Narratives," *VT* 40 [1990]: 464–73 [465]). Consequently, Jacob is attempting to replace Esau as the firstborn. Malul has offered a
rebuttal, stating that there is no need to see sexual connotations here. However, he
ends up agreeing with Smith that issues of succession are at stake. Thus, to "grasp

c. *Purpose of the Birth Narrative.* What is the overall purpose of 25:24–26? We might first note that, although we are told that the boys are twins, it is their differences which are highlighted even from birth. Moreover, the lads are portrayed in terms of their subsequent relationship: Esau's description focuses on his physical appearance, while Jacob's focuses on his actions.[72]

Additionally, the birth narrative offers several pieces of information that are necessary for understanding the subsequent stories. Esau being described as אדומני and שער are not only themes which will recur in the birthright and blessing scenes, but they serve as literary allusions to Esau's connection with Edom and Seir. Jacob's attempts to supplant his brother, meanwhile, will carry through the rest of their relationship as well.[73] These elements come together in Gen 27, where Jacob's deceptive actions require him to assume the physical characteristics of his brother.

While some commentators argue that Esau is portrayed here as wild even from birth, it could just as persuasively be argued that Esau's description is primarily etiological, while it is Jacob's description as a "heel grabber" that is the more negatively critical of the two. Thus, it might be best at this stage in the story to reserve judgment, and to take these descriptions as important for the unfolding narrative.

5. *The Birthright (Genesis 25:27–34)*

The remaining verses of Gen 25 deal succinctly with the lads' development, followed by an episode which recounts, for the first time, their interaction.

a. *The Development of the Brothers (vv. 27–28)*
In Gen 25:27 we are told that, "As the lads grew up, Esau became a man knowledgeable in hunting (ידע ציד), a man of the field (איש שדה). But Jacob was a simple man (איש תם), staying among the tents (ישב אהלים)." The juxtaposition of the brothers continues in this verse, although here we are given information in parallel: an action element (knowledgeable in hunting/simple) and a spatial element (man of the field/staying among the tents).[74] What is meant by these descriptions?

the heel" became synonymous with "supplanting" and "deceiving." See M. Malul, " 'āqēb 'Heel' and 'āqab 'to Supplant' and the Concept of Succession in the Jacob–Esau Narratives," *VT* 46 (1996): 190–212.
72. Fretheim, "Genesis," 521; Fokkelman, *Narrative Art*, 90.
73. Blum, *Die Komposition*, 72–73.
74. White, *Narration and Discourse*, 210; Fokkelman, *Narrative Art*, 91.

The information supplied here has fuelled much commentary, often furthering the denigration of Esau and the exaltation of Jacob. *Targum Onqelos*, while retaining the literal understanding of Esau's description, "a man who would go out into the field," goes on to describe Jacob as "a perfect (שלים) man who attended the house of study."[75] Two issues are introduced here, namely, what one is to make of the Hebrew תם, and what is meant by the fact that Jacob stayed among the tents.

The word תם comes from the root תמם, meaning "completeness, totality without diminution."[76] The adjectival תם can denote a range of things, from "perfect," "innocent," and "faultless," to "healthy," or "simple." Kedar-Kopfstein points out that positive uses of the term are almost always assessments of moral or ethical conduct, and the root is used elsewhere to describe Noah, Abraham, and Job.[77] Yet, there are negative connotations to the word as well, and "Every attempt to use the immediate or situational context to distinguish among neutral, negative, and positive nuances shows clearly that it is not rare for these nuances to overlap."[78]

Most early Jewish tradition followed *Targum Onqelos* by stating that Jacob was "perfect."[79] However, if this description of Jacob is taken as parallel to the description of Esau (a man knowledgeable in hunting), is this a proper understanding? Many contemporary commentators opt to stay with the traditional rendering; B. Jacob, for example, comments that Jacob is depicted here as "friedlichen, arglosen, sanften."[80] However, from as early as Calvin there have been those who see this description of Jacob as the antithesis of Esau's robust pursuits.[81] In this vein, von Rad proffers "orderly," or "respectable," in comparison to the (uncivilized) hunter, and Heard translates this as "responsible," related to Jacob's duties nearer to home.[82]

---

75. The LXX uses the term ἄπλαστος, a fairly literal rendering which means "simple," "innocent," or "upright," and which is a common translation of תם; see Otto Bauernfeind, "ἀπλοῦς, ἀπλότης," *TDNT* 1:386–87.

76. B. Kedar-Kopfstein, "תמם," *TDOT* 15:699–711 (702).

77. Ibid., 15:705–7. See Gen 6:9; 17:1; Job 12:4.

78. Ibid., 15:704. Thus, Alter renders תם as "simple" in his translations, but notes that the implication of Jacob being "innocent" may be ironic in light of Jacob's subsequent actions. Alter, *Genesis*, 128.

79. Cf. *Targum Pseudo-Jonathan* and *Targum Neofiti*. See also *Gen. Rab.* 63:10.

80. Jacob, *Das erste Buch der Tora*, 545. Blum (*Die Komposition*, 74–75) offers a similar construal with "fair" or "good."

81. Calvin, *Genesis*, 49.

82. Von Rad, *Genesis*, 266; Heard, *Dynamics*, 102–3. Hamilton (*Genesis 18–50*, 181) offers a different understanding and origin for תם, noting that there is a similar

What, then, should be made of Jacob "staying among the tents"? The biblical depiction of Israel's ancestors is one of nomads, having lived in tents.[83] Thus, a literal understanding might be that Jacob was more of a homebody than his brother. However, as was shown in *Targum Onqelos*'s translation, this came to be understood early on as Jacob attending the "tents of study."[84] *Targum Neofiti* would say that Jacob "dwelt in the schoolhouses," while *Targum Pseudo-Jonathan* noted that Jacob "ministered in the schoolhouse of Eber, seeking instruction from the Lord."

It is not hard to imagine how these various interpretations of Jacob led to some less flattering depictions of Esau. *Genesis Rabbah* played on the fact that Esau was a skillful hunter by claiming that he was a "trapper" of people, stealing from them and killing them.[85] *Targum Pseudo-Jonathan* carries this even further: "Esau became a skilled hunter (able) to hunt birds and wild beasts, a man who would go out into the field to kill people. It was he who killed Nimrod and his son Henoch." Another line of thought, seen in the work of Rashi, interpreted Esau's cunning ability in hunting to mean that he knew how to trap his father with his words (hence Isaac's affection). Jacob, however, was described as תם because he was a person of integrity, whose thoughts and words matched up.[86]

Of all the ancient commentators, it is Philo who gives the most space to the descriptions of Esau and Jacob, mostly in relation to Jacob being settled, or "dwelling in a house," as opposed to Esau, who is without a house. This, for Philo, is a sign of wickedness, as "the wicked man is destitute of a city and destitute of a home... For it is not natural for vice which is inclined to be subservient to the passions to inhabit the city of virtue, inasmuch as it is devoted to the pursuit of rudeness and ignorance, with great folly."[87]

Again, however, it appears that "staying among the tents" might be more helpfully understood in relationship with the previous spatial statement of Esau being a "man of the field," something which the ancient commentators tended to miss (or ignore). Hence, modern scholarship has understood this as referring to Jacob's shepherding or pastoral

---

Arabic root (*tîm*) which means "be kept in subjection." Thus, the idea here in 25:27 would be "homebody," which he feels fits nicely with Jacob's dwelling in tents, and in comparison with the roaming Esau.

83. K. Koch, "אהל," *TDOT* 1:118–30 (120).

84. Cf. *Jub.* 19:13–14, which states that Jacob learned to read because of the tents of learning.

85. *Gen. Rab.* 63:10. Ibn Ezra also noted this was a possibility, as hunting required deception and trickery (*Ibn Ezra's Commentary, Genesis*, 251).

86. *Rashi's Commentary: Genesis*, 116.

87. *Alleg. Interp.* 3.1.2.

vocation, which would have required that he stay closer to the camp than did the hunting Esau. We are thus presented with two vocations, life-styles, or cultures—hunter/gatherer and shepherd/farmer—that further distinguish the brothers.[88]

In 25:28 we are given one further piece of information that will inform subsequent narratives, particularly Gen 27: "And Isaac loved (ויאהב) Esau because of the hunting he put in his mouth (כי־ציד בפיו), but Rebekah loved (אהבת) Jacob." The syntax of the first clause is somewhat unclear, but the sense is evident: Isaac has affinity for Esau, the hunter, and he has a taste for the game he brings home, a theme which will recur in Gen 27.[89] As Cohen notes, the fact that Esau seems to be more like Ishmael than Isaac, and that Isaac himself was the younger son, makes the father's love of his elder son somewhat ironic.[90] Meanwhile, we are given no reason for Rebekah's love of Jacob. We are left to wonder (suppose?) if Rebekah's affection is in any way related to the oracle.[91]

Another dimension of this verse is that the verb אהב, "love," has connotations related to the idea of "election," particularly in Deuteron-omy and the prophetic tradition.[92] This will be expressed in explicit language in Mal 1:2–5, where YHWH says, "I have loved Jacob, but Esau I have hated." For now, though, it is the mother who favors the one who will turn out to be the beloved of God. As Kunin remarks, "The text begins with an interesting inversion. The father loves the rejected son while the mother, who is from the outside, loves the chosen son."[93]

88. Driver, *Genesis*, 247; Jacob, *Das erste Buch der Tora*, 545. Ibn Ezra did note this as well, while eschewing the "tents of learning" idea as baseless (*Ibn Ezra's Commentary, Genesis*, 251).

89. As Alter notes (*Genesis*, 128), we are not quite sure whose mouth the game is in: is Esau bringing the game home in his mouth, like a lion, or is it being put into Isaac's mouth? *BHS* notes that ציד is rendered as צידו in the Samaritan Pentateuch and LXX, and that the בפיו of the MT is probably better read as לפיו. These emenda-tions would give a reading of "because of his [Esau's] game for his [Isaac's] mouth."

90. Norman J. Cohen, "Two that are One: Sibling Rivalry in Genesis," *Judaism* 32 (1983): 331–42 (336).

91. *Jub.* 21.15–31 offers an interesting rewriting here, noting that Isaac loves Esau, but Abraham and Rebekah love Jacob. Abraham tells Rebekah that Jacob is more worthy of the blessing than Esau, and Abraham then blesses Jacob in the presence of Rebekah. The marginalization of Isaac in this account is noteworthy.

92. Deut 4:37; 10:15; 21:15–16; Hos 11:1. Cf. William L. Moran, "The Ancient Near East Background of the Love of God in Deuteronomy," *CBQ* 25 (1963): 77–87.

93. Kunin, *Logic of Incest*, 113. Few ancient commentators mention any moral dimension of this parental preference, one exception being Ambrose, who notes that this favoritism is not something to be emulated, but actually compounds the familial strife. See Ambrose, *Jacob and the Happy Life* 2.2.5, in ACCS 2:151.

Thus, the differences between the lads are once again at the forefront of the text, and the divide between them (and throughout the family) is widening.

b. *The Bartering of the Birthright (vv. 29–34)*

The story once again takes us to another undefined moment in time where we encounter the famous scene of Esau selling his birthright to his brother for the proverbial "mess of pottage." The story finds Esau returning home famished from the hunt one day, only to encounter his brother cooking. When Esau asks for some of the food, Jacob refuses unless Esau is willing to give up his birthright.[94] Esau eventually agrees and, after an oath is sworn, Jacob gives Esau his food, which he promptly consumes, and goes on his way. There are numerous interesting aspects of this story, and the commentary on it is voluminous. However, for the purpose of this study we will focus on two issues: the depiction of the brothers, and the hermeneutical significance of the narrative.

(1) *The Depiction of Esau.* Much of this short narrative actually focuses on Esau. Thus, it is not surprising that a good portion of commentary on these verses has focused on the characterization of him. The question is, how should we understand the depiction of Esau here? While the

---

94. The term בכרה, "birthright," only occurs twelve times in the entire Hebrew Bible. Of these occurrences, all but two occur in Genesis (25:31–34 [×4]; 27:36; 43:33), Deuteronomy (21:15–17), and 1 Chronicles (5:1–3 [×3]). All of these, with the exception of Deut 21, are dealing with or commenting on the patriarchal families, specifically Isaac's and Jacob's sons. Indeed, many argue that this is precisely the reason that Deut 21 was written, to counteract the tendencies of the patriarchs. As such, the biblical portrayal of the birthright is limited, and primarily concerns the patriarchs. See my "The Inversion of the Birth Order and the Title of the Firstborn," *VT* 60 (2010): 655–58. Much work has been done on the biblical concept of the firstborn and the laws of primogeniture, including comparisons with similar terminology and concepts in the ancient Near East. While at times this research has looked promising, it has produced divided results. What scholars seem to have some agreement on is the fact that the rights of the firstborn entail a larger portion of the inheritance, and possibly familial succession. See M. Tsevat, "בכור," *TDOT* 2:121–27; Greenspahn, *When Brothers*, 30–48; I. Mendelsohn, "On the Preferential Status of the Eldest Son," *BASOR* 156 (1959): 38–40; Eryl W. Davies, "The Inheritance of the First-Born in Israel and the Ancient Near East," *JSS* 38 (1993): 175–91. With regard to the inheritance of the birthright, it would seem that this entitles one to a double portion of what is received by the other male siblings. See especially Eryl W. Davies, "The Meaning of *pî šenayim* in Deuteronomy XXI 17," *VT* 36 (1986): 341–47.

majority of the history of interpretation has judged this portrayal as negative, there are reasons for approaching the issue with caution.

The first thing we are told about Esau occurs in 25:29, where we learn that "he came in from the field (ויבא עשו מן־השדה), and he was famished (והוא עיף)." Even at this point in the story, ancient interpreters found elements of Esau worth critiquing. The rabbis noted that Esau coming in from the field implies that he slept with a betrothed girl (Deut 22:25) and being famished tells us that he had murdered someone (Jer 4:31).[95] *Targum Pseudo-Jonathan* takes this further: while Jacob is preparing lentils to comfort his father on the day of Abraham's death, Esau has been out committing five transgressions: he practised idolatry, shed innocent blood, had gone in to a betrothed maiden, denied the life of the world to come, and despised his birthright.

Meanwhile, contemporary commentators have noted negative connotations as well. Coats observes that the description of Esau as coming back empty handed from the hunt can be seen as a sly comment on the previous description of Esau as a skilled hunter: the man knowledgeable in hunting comes home with nothing.[96] Furthermore, Levenson has pointed out that Esau's profession as a hunter (and his wild, hairy physical nature) would "suggest uncouthness and even a certain degree of danger" to an ancient Israelite, thus already influencing the audience at this point in the story.[97] Hence, from the very first verse of this short scene, we have early interpreters inferring that Esau has been up to no good while out in the field, and modern commentators pointing out that Esau is being depicted as dangerous or inept.

The next thing we are told about Esau (v. 30) is that he sees what his brother has been cooking, and, as he is famished, desires some. One of the critical aspects of this verse is the word Esau uses when requesting the food, הלעיטני. From the root לעט, this is a *hapax legomenon* in the Hebrew Bible. However, the term would be more widely used in the rabbinic period as referring to how one would feed an animal, particularly pouring food down a camel's throat.[98] The rabbis thus understood this as referring to Esau's animal-like behavior.[99]

Contemporary scholarship has tended to follow this rabbinic reading. The most influential translation may be that of Alter, who renders this

---

95. *Gen. Rab.* 63:12. Cf. *Rashi's Commentary: Genesis*, 116.

96. Coats, *Genesis*, 187.

97. Jon D. Levenson, "Genesis," in *The Jewish Study Bible* (ed. Adele Berlin and Marc Zvi Brettler; Oxford: Oxford University Press, 2004), 53.

98. Nahum M. Sarna, *Genesis* (JPSTC; Philadelphia: The Jewish Publication Society, 1989), 182.

99. *Gen. Rab.* 63:12.

word as "let me cram my maw," which he cites as an example of "inarticulate appetite."[100] Some have noted that an appropriate correspondence in German might be "fressen" as opposed to "essen."[101] For B. Jacob, this indeed implies Esau is a crude animal, and this one word seems to sum up Esau's character in this scene.[102] Speiser thinks Esau is portrayed as an "uncouth glutton," and Westermann notes that we have here a very crude characterization of Jacob's brother.[103]

The verse continues by telling us what it is that Esau wants to "gulp down," and this raises the second issue in this verse, namely, how Esau describes the food: מן־האדם האדם הזה. This generally has been understood as a continuation of Esau's inarticulate speech, and is often rendered along the lines of "this red red stuff."[104] Thus, Esau is being portrayed in a derogatory fashion and his limited intelligence is on exhibit.[105]

The next few verses (25:31–34) describe the transaction between Jacob and Esau whereby the birthright switches hands. In v. 31, Jacob tells Esau he will not give him any of the food unless Esau will forfeit his birthright. Esau responds in v. 32 by saying, "Behold, I am going to die (הנה אנכי הולך למות); so what is this birthright to me (ולמה־זה לי בכרה)?" But Jacob persists, and demands that Esau swear to him. Esau relents, and the birthright is transferred to Jacob. Esau is given the food, which he promptly eats, and this is followed by his exit. One final note that we are given in 25:34 is that Esau despised (ויבז) the birthright.

The combination of Esau's description of his current state and the narrator's comment that Esau "despised" the birthright have led to a general agreement that Esau is depicted here in a negative manner. In the Jewish tradition this was seen as an example of Esau's unworthiness of possessing the birthright. Some targumic traditions note that Esau's despising the birthright on account of his being near to death is actually a "denial concerning the vivification of the dead and [a denial of] the life of the world to come."[106] Rashi, meanwhile, following another tradition, justifies the transfer of the birthright based on sacrificial duty. The

---

100.   Alter, *Art of Biblical Narrative*, 44. Numerous scholars note Alter's rendering of this word, e.g. Cotter, *Genesis*, 191. In his subsequent translation of Genesis Alter translates this as "Let me gulp down" (Alter, *Genesis*, 129).

101.   Soggin, *Das Buch Genesis*, 344.

102.   Jacob, *Das erste Buch der Tora*, 545.

103.   Speiser, *Genesis*, 195; Westermann, *Genesis 12–36*, 418; cf. W. Gunther Plaut, ed., *The Torah: A Modern Commentary* (New York: Union of American Hebrew Congregations, 1981), 174.

104.   Cotter, *Genesis*, 191; Alter, *Genesis*, 129; Fokkelman, *Narrative Art*, 96.

105.   Vawter, *On Genesis*, 289; Kunin, *Logic of Incest*, 114.

106.   Quote from *Targum Neofiti*; cf. *Gen. Rab.* 63:14.

firstborn was responsible for all sacrificial service, and Jacob recognized Esau was unfit for this role. When Jacob explains to Esau all that is required, along with the prohibitions and punishments, Esau wants nothing to do with it, as it will inevitably lead to his death. Thus, Esau's despising the birthright shows signs of Esau's wickedness in that he despised the service of the Holy One.[107]

Early Christian tradition also used these verses to depict Esau as unworthy, and as an example not to be followed, though in a more vaguely didactic sense. This is seen in the epistle to the Hebrews, where we read in 12:15–17:

> See to it that no one misses the grace of God and that no bitter root grows up to cause trouble and defile many. See that no one is sexually immoral, or is godless like Esau, who for a single meal sold his inheritance rights as the oldest son. Afterward, as you know, when he wanted to inherit this blessing, he was rejected. He could bring about no change of mind, though he sought the blessing with tears.[108]

Accordingly, Esau, a man of the moment, is rejected because of his inability to control himself over "a single meal." Augustine would make a similar claim, noting that Esau is a slave to temporary pleasures, a sentiment later echoed by Calvin, who labels Esau as a profane person, interested only in the flesh.[109]

Modern interpreters have come to similar conclusions. As Sarna notes, Esau's statement that he is "about to die" is either a reference to his (dangerous) life as a hunter, or else "is an exaggerated description of his present condition."[110] As for those that might take Esau at face value, this does not make things any better: "because of his weariness [Esau] loses sight of proportion and of his self-respect."[111]

Meanwhile, much comment is made on the narrator's use of the word בזה at the end of the narrative.[112] According to Wenham, who translates the word as "contempt," this is "important, because explicit moral commentary is rare in the Bible."[113] As Görg notes, "In the linguistic usage of

---

107.   *Rashi's Commentary: Genesis*, 117.

108.   NIV. For comment on these verses, see Harold W. Attridge, *Hebrews* (Hermeneia; Philadelphia: Fortress, 1989), 368–69. The correlation of Esau with sexual immorality and godlessness seems to imply that the writer to the Hebrews was influenced by early Jewish tradition, which, as noted above, also depicted Esau in this way.

109.   Augustine, *Sermon* 4.12, in ACCS 2:151; Calvin, *Genesis*, 54–55.

110.   Sarna, *Genesis*, 182.

111.   Fokkelman, *Narrative Art*, 96.

112.   For more on this term, see M. Görg, "בזה," *TDOT* 2:60–65.

113.   Wenham, *Genesis 16–50*, 178; cf. Fretheim, "Genesis," 522.

the OT, the behavior suggested by the root *bazah* touches mainly on Yahweh's sphere of activity."[114] Thus, Esau's "despising" the birthright can be seen as a parallel to the usages found in the description of those who refuse to give Saul a present (1 Sam 10:27), Goliath "disdaining" the young David (1 Sam 17:42), and Michal's childlessness because of her "despising" David (2 Sam 6:16).[115]

One final element of 25:34 is often noted with regard to the depiction of Esau, and that is the collection of "rapid-fire verbs" that describe Esau's actions.[116] The quick succession of verbs—"and he ate and he drank and he rose and he departed and he despised" (ויאכל וישת ויקם וילך ויבז)—was noted as far back as Calvin as an indication of Esau's blatant disregard for the ramifications of this encounter.[117] This, as Bar-Efrat comments, depicts Esau "as a man of action who does not spend time in contemplation."[118]

In summary, throughout this short story, commentators have found reason to see Esau as portrayed in a negative light. From his inarticulate language and bestial appetite, to his thoughtless actions and "disdaining" of his birthright, Esau is seen as unworthy of being the chosen son. Indeed, Kunin sees this portrayal as "consistently ideologically negative," putting Esau in the unenviable company of characters like Nimrod and Ishmael.[119]

There are, however, various issues which might imply that Esau has been commonly misinterpreted in this narrative, if not entirely, then at least in part. The first issue is the nature of Esau's language. As noted above, many commentators take Esau's language as an indication of uncouthness, particularly the use of the term הלעיטני and the reference to the food as האדם האדם הזה. But are these as overtly boorish as is often assumed?

To begin with, the translation of הלעיטני requires some interpretive modesty. The fact that there are no other uses in the Hebrew Bible with which to compare this occurrence might imply that we are reading our "bestial" preconceptions of Esau into this text.[120] In fact, both *Targum Onqelos* and *Targum Pseudo-Jonathan* tone down the passage by using the word אטעימני, which means "to taste," a word that does not even

114.   Görg, *TDOT* 2:63.
115.   So ibid.
116.   The phrase is Alter's (*Genesis*, 130).
117.   Calvin, *Genesis*, 54.
118.   Bar-Efrat, *Narrative Art*, 217.
119.   Kunin, *Logic of Incest*, 113.
120.   Heard, *Dynamics*, 103–4.

evoke the image of normal eating.[121] This might imply that the animal-like insinuation in the term לעט was not as widely held as is often noted.[122] Furthermore, as Prouser points out, at the beginning of Esau's description of the food stands the preposition מן, "from" or "of." This entails that Esau is asking for a taste *from*, not demanding the entire dish, which would call for the accusative את.[123]

Another element which is often overlooked is the fact that Esau uses the particle of entreaty ("please") in his request for food (הלעיטני נא), a pleasantry which Jacob does not return when he demands the birthright in v. 31. As Prouser notes, the fact that translators omit Esau's "please" (נא) here is not unusual, as in many translations there is more than a little disparity in the depictions of Jacob and Esau throughout the entire Jacob Cycle. For instance, translators rarely omit the term when translating Jacob's words to Esau in Gen 33:11, "please accept my gift." However, a few verses later, Esau's plea to leave some of his men in 33:15 also has the particle, but once more this is often omitted in translations.[124]

The next issue of contention with regard to Esau's coarse language is the phrase מן־האדם האדם הזה. Again, this is often understood as Esau being too tired or too crude to bother calling the food by its proper name. There are, however, alternative understandings. First of all, as Heard comments, historical and cultural distance should give us some pause over issues such as this:

> Interpreters also point to Esau's use of "the red, that red" to identify Jacob's stew as another element in the narrator's portrayal of Esau as a boor. More recent interpreters seem content simply to identify Esau as "stupid" for his inability to call the stew by name. None of these commentators, however, detail the basis for their own implicit claim that "red" is *not* the name of the dish.[125]

Furthermore, Prouser offers an alternative reading based on syntax, as words are often repeated in Hebrew to depict a sense of heightening or intensity. The same may be the case here, as in Sarna's suggestion of

121.   See Aberbach and Grossfeld, *Targum Onkelos*, 152. Ibn Ezra follows this understanding.

122.   See Joseph H. Prouser, "Seeing Red: On Translating Esau's Request for Soup," *CJ* 56, no. 2 (2004): 13–20 (14).

123.   Ibid., 15–16. For more on the partitive aspect of מן, see GKC §119w, particularly n. 2.

124.   Prouser, "Seeing Red," 15. The NIV is guilty of all of these inconsistencies, as is the NRSV. The NASB offers the most balanced use of the particle.

125.   Heard, *Dynamics*, 104. Along these lines, it is interesting that the LXX and Vulgate replace the first האדם with translations of נזיד, the stew or food that is being cooked. Cf. Brenner, *Colour Terms*, 60.

"deep red" to describe the stew.[126] Thus, interpretations which focus on Esau's impatience, vulgarity, or lack of competence are not necessarily warranted. Contrary, this would possibly point to a "thoughtful description" from Esau: "Interpreting repetition as signifying emphasis or intensity, rather than haste, is consistent with, for example, the translation of טובה הארץ מאד מאד as 'The land is an exceedingly good land.' Nothing unseemly or inarticulate is evident in Isaiah's שלום שלום or in Zechariah's חן חן."[127] To be sure, for those who are not convinced by this purposeful, heightening repetition, one might expect that text-critical proposals would include deleting one occurrence of האדם as an example of dittography. However, the lack of such proposals is again suggestive that interpreters bring assumptions to the text that color the portrayal of characters and events.[128]

One might also note that it is at this juncture the story explicitly links Esau with Edom (על־כן קרא־שמו אדום). As with the birth scene, the text here seems to be interested in connecting Esau with Edom by use of the wordplay between אדם and אדום, and as such the etiological dimensions need to be kept in view. And finally, it should be remembered that Esau's description of his own state as עיף, "famished," "tired," or "faint," echoes the words of the narrator in 25:29.[129] This needs to be kept in mind when considering the sincerity of Esau's words.

For Prouser, all of these elements add up not to an uncouth boor, but to a son similar to his father: "Esau is not impatient for food, he is (not unlike his father, Isaac) enamored of food, a personal trait that may pervert his priorities, but has not adversely impacted the quality his [*sic*] verbal communication."[130] Accordingly, Prouser thinks a plausible case can be made to translate Esau's words here as, "Please may I have just a taste of that lovely red soup, weary as I am."[131] This is not to say that Esau is without blame in this episode. Prouser concludes that although Esau's "actions in Genesis 25 may show Esau to be a morally short-sighted spiritual diminutive, his words are eminently polite and—perhaps uncharacteristically—elegant."[132]

126.   Sarna, *Genesis*, 182.

127.   Prouser, "Seeing Red," 16–17, quoting Num 14:7; Isa 57:19, and Zech 4:7.

128.   *BHS* offers no amendments; neither do Gunkel (*Genesis*, 291) and Westermann (*Genesis 12–36*, 417–18), the latter noting, "Gk and Vg appear to differentiate…however, the repetition is deliberate" (418).

129.   Alter, *Art of Biblical Narrative*, 44. For more on the range of meaning of this term, see *HALOT* 2:820.

130.   Prouser, "Seeing Red," 17.

131.   Ibid., 18.

132.   Ibid., 14.

A second area where we may need to rethink the negative portrayal of Esau is the understanding of why he sold his birthright. The traditional understanding of this has been to portray Esau as a man more interested in immediate fleshly desires than in spiritual or eternal matters. There are, however, other possibilities. One option that has been set forth is that Esau was deceived by Jacob, something which Esau himself declares in Gen 27:36. The fullest example of this is Daube's "blood soup" theory.[133] Daube begins by asking, why does Esau not refer to the soup by name? Instead of seeing "this red, red" as crude speech, Daube thinks it is a reference to blood soup, for a variety of reasons. First of all, why are we not told until the end of the story that the food is merely lentil soup?[134] Secondly, why does Esau repeat the word "red"? And finally, why does Esau claim that he was deceived in Gen 27:36? Daube then makes the observation that red is not only the color of blood, but in Hebrew the two words are verbally similar (אֹדֶם, דָּם). For Daube, this makes sense of Esau's desire to "gulp" the soup. "Evidently, he thought that Jacob was preparing a blood-broth (the fare, it may be recalled, of the Spartan warriors)."[135] This, Daube concludes, is a further example of trickery by Jacob; once more he is preying on someone's desires and needs to get what he wants, something he will continue to do throughout his life.[136]

Daube's thesis is not without its critics. One isue is that this understanding rests too heavily on a "blood red" understanding of אֹדֶם, a color which is unlikely with lentils, as they tend to lose their color when cooked. Furthermore, Daube's reference to blood broth being the fare of the Spartan warriors is interesting, but not overly helpful, as we have no other examples in the Hebrew Bible of people imbibing blood for vigor or power. Nevertheless, Daube's reading does highlight the fact that Esau's subsequent claim of deception in Gen 27 needs to be taken into account, and that the historical and cultural distance that stands between the reader and the text should also be kept in mind when judging Esau's actions.

A second interpretation, and one that has been around for some time, is the notion that Esau was willing to part with the birthright because of

---

133. David Daube, "How Esau Sold His Birthright," *CLJ* 8 (1942–44): 70–75. This is also found in Daube, *Studies in Biblical Law* (Cambridge: Cambridge University Press, 1947), 190–305.

134. On "lentils," עֲדָשִׁים, see *HALOT* 2:794. While the MT of 25:29 has only נָזִיד, LXX MSS add φακοῦ, "lentils," as in v. 34. Whether or not one agrees with Daube's theory, this addition does seem to break the narrative tension of the story.

135. Daube, "How Esau," 73.

136. Ibid., 74–75.

the dangerous nature of his profession as a hunter. The logic is that Esau may die before his father does; as such, what good is a birthright to him? Ibn Ezra espoused this view, and also noted the rabbinic tradition that says Isaac had no wealth, so that the double share of the inheritance would be of no import to Esau.[137] Hence, in Ibn Ezra's understanding, Esau's statement has two parts: I am about to die (because of my profession), and what good is it to me anyway (as father has no wealth)? While this reaction may not be laudatory, it does not necessarily mean that Esau is spiritually bankrupt.

This leads us to another issue, the meaning of the term בזה. As noted above, the term is usually translated here as "despise," and is seen as an explicit judgment from the narrator on Esau's inner disposition. However, this term can mean more than "despised"; it can also be construed as "disregard" or "ignore."[138] One might also inquire as to the verb's relation to the other "rapid fire" verbs in Gen 25:34 (ויאכל וישת ויקם וילך ויבז). Could this term be one last verb of action, describing what Esau does, and not a commentary on his actions? Heard notes that as this is a sequence of *waw*-consecutive verbs, this can be read as a temporal verb, similar to Gunkel's translation of, "and he did not think about the birthright again."[139] Consequently, "Recognizing the breadth of the semantic range of *bāzâ* creates a broader range of readerly assessments of Esau here. Readers' evaluations of Esau's attitude may hinge precisely on their decision as to Esau's attitude, and 'despising' the birthright is a far cry from simply 'underestimating' it."[140]

Thus, while Esau is usually thought to be portrayed in an extremely negative light in this episode, there is cause to rethink this, or at least to reconsider the severity of the depiction.

(2) *The Depiction of Jacob.* It is not surprising that with the denigration of Esau came justification of his brother. An element which was stressed as early as *Targum Onqelos* was the legal, and thus binding, result of the transaction. Not only does Jacob demand that Esau swear (שבע) to him,

---

137. *Ibn Ezra's Commentary, Genesis*, 253. This is also discussed by Reuben Ahroni, "Why Did Esau Spurn the Birthright? A Study in Biblical Interpretation," *Judaism* 29 (1980): 323–31 (327–30).

138. For example, Ps 102:18 (102:17 ET), which reads, "He will respond to the prayer of the destitute, and will not despise/ignore (ולא־בזה) their prayer."

139. Gunkel, *Genesis*, 292. Malul argues that בזה conveys a legal meaning in Gen 25:34, which he renders as "to relinquish." Again, this would make this a verb of action that stands in correspondence with those before it. See Malul, "'aqab, 'Heel'," 205–6.

140. Heard, *Dynamics*, 107.

but the legal language of "selling" (מכר) and "giving" (נתן) is used as well.[141] Thus, Jacob is one who is meticulous in following laws and customs, and this is to be respected.

Commentators on Gen 25:27–34 have not left Jacob untouched, however, as several indicting elements of the younger brother's words and actions have been highlighted as well. To begin with, the reader is left wondering why Jacob happens to be cooking just when and where Esau returns from the hunt. White builds on this, noting that the verb יזד, because it is in the unusual Hiphil, can be understood as "to act presumptuously," or "with wilful forethought."[142] For White, the implications are clear: "These associations could scarcely have been absent from the mind of the ancient writer or reader. The meaning seems to be similar to the colloquial expression in English 'to cook up' in the sense of to scheme, though is perhaps much stronger in its negative implications."[143] He continues,

> The strategy that Jacob has used here upon Esau is a mirror image of the technique by which Esau himself related to his father. Just as Esau gets what he wants from Isaac through the preparation of a desired dish of venison, so now Jacob will use a pot of lentils to gain what he wants from Esau. Unlike Esau, however, for whom such action is a natural part of his character, for Jacob it is a conscious, premeditated plot. The same strategy will then be used by Rebekah against Isaac in the next scene.[144]

Jacob's words can also be seen as less than flattering. For example, as noted above, Esau uses the particle of entreaty (נא) in his request for food, while Jacob's reply to Esau in vv. 33–34 ("swear to me at once") lacks this courtesy, and instead can be read as a "curt three-word reply," one that is "cold and calculating."[145]

Taken together, interpreters have noted that neither brother comes across as ideal. Calvin—no admirer of Esau—states that Jacob was "inhuman" in not serving his brother, and that in this scene we see "brought to light what lay hid in both."[146] As Walton remarks, even if the

---

141. On שבע, see I. Kottsieper, "שבע," *TDOT* 14:311–36. With regard to מכר, see E. Lipiński, "מכר," *TDOT* 8:291–96, who argues, quite convincingly, that "sell" is not a good translation here, as the meaning is closer to "barter" or "trade."

142. White, *Narration and Discourse*, 211. This sense occurs in Deut 1:43b, which reads, "You rebelled against the command of the LORD and presumptuously (ותזדו) went up into the hill country" (NRSV). Cf. Deut 18:20 and Exod 21:14.

143. Ibid.

144. Ibid., 213.

145. Wenham, *Genesis 16–50*, 178.

146. Calvin, *Genesis*, 51. Note, however, that Calvin goes on to justify Jacob's actions and condemn Esau (53–54).

narrator does judge Esau, the "passage remains open-ended and refuses any black and white judgements in favour of one or the other of the brothers."[147]

c. *Reading Strategies for the Birthright Narrative*

One final aspect which needs to be explored is the significance of the birthright story, and various reading strategies which have been employed in order to make sense of the narrative. Three such interpretive approaches will be highlighted here: first, that in order to understand the story one needs to look to the pre-history of the text, which is most likely the depiction of opposing cultures or lifestyles; second, that Esau is shown to be unworthy of the birthright, thus legitimating Jacob and Israel; and third, that what is at stake here is the question of the outworking of the theme of election, or the human response to the divine initiative.[148]

One way of understanding this story is to see the key as lying in the pre-history of the narrative. Maag argued that this is a civilization myth, as the shepherd gains the upper hand over the hunter. This story, according to Maag, was later co-opted into the story of the patriarchs to explain why Esau as a hunter lives "away from the fat of the earth," as do his descendants the Edomites at the time of David, when the "younger" had subdued the "older"; thus, the Edomite connection to the Esau tradition was added around the Davidic period to add validity to the current political climate.[149] Westermann, following Maag, sees this in a similar light. "The older civilization of the hunter and gatherer, which once dominated the whole region, must withdraw into the wilds and lose its significance. When the narrative about the lentil soup is understood in this way, it provides a valuable attestation to the history of civilization, the only one among the patriarchal stories."[150]

---

147. Walton, *Thou Traveller Unknown*, 21. Cf. Spina, who says, "If Esau is crass and stupid, Jacob is coldly extortionary" (Spina, *Faith*, 16–17).

148. There are other understandings which do not fit into these categories, but which are beyond the scope of this study. One such reading is offered by Niditch, who sees Gen 25:29–34 as "an initial and incomplete working out of the trickster pattern fully articulated in chapter 27." See Susan Niditch, *Underdogs and Tricksters: A Prelude to Biblical Folklore* (NVBS; San Francisco: Harper & Row, 1987), 101.

149. See Maag, "Jakob–Esau–Edom," 418–29. Cf. Friedemann W. Golka, "BECHORAH und BERACHAH: Erstgeburtsrecht und Segen," in *Recht und Ethos im Alten Testament - Gestalt und Wirkung: Festschrift für Horst Seebass zum 65. Geburtstag* (ed. Stefan Beyerle, Günter Mayer, and Hans Strauss; Neukirchen–Vluyn: Neukirchener, 1999), 133–44 (134); Gunkel, *Genesis*, 291.

150. Westermann, *Genesis 12–36*, 417; cf. Golka, "BECHORAH," 135. For a critique of Maag and Westermann, see Blum, *Die Komposition*, 88, 190–202, who

A second interpretive option, popular in both Jewish and Christian tradition (as seen above), is to read this story as proof of Esau's unworthiness of the birthright and, subsequently, the blessing. By virtue of extension (and the direct mention of אֱדוֹם), this includes the Edomites. Contemporary scholars are not opposed to this understanding. Alter, for instance, thinks the story is clear in depicting Esau as unfit to be the vehicle of divine election. Jacob, on the other hand, is concerned about the future and "this qualifies him as a suitable bearer of the birthright: historical destiny does not just happen; you have to know how to make it happen."[151] White offers a similar understanding in suggesting that this narrative is about what happens before the promise is given and realized, and thus how one set of traits is more worthy of bearing the promise. Unlike Abraham, where faith was needed in the promise, here action is required before the promise is given. Thus, one brother's traits are more "consistent with the deeper values implicit in the earlier narratives," and that is the use of the mind to take advantage of another.[152] Ultimately, then, this scene is an apologetic Israelite comment, as the undeserving Esau is appropriately relieved of his birthright.[153]

These are both reasonable approaches, especially if one sees the depiction of Esau as inherently negative. However, when one takes into account that Esau's portrayal might not be as overtly negative as is often assumed, these readings seem less persuasive.[154] That leads to one further reading strategy: understanding the story as depicting the outworking of the election motif, most notably the tension between divine and human agency as introduced in the oracle to Rebekah.[155] In this reading, the present pericope continues to set the stage for the subsequent stories concerning the brothers and, once again, we are left with more questions than answers. How does this story relate to the oracle which was given before the lads' birth? And if the oracle is about God's elective purposes,

---

argues that these are not "kulturmythen" but are constitutive for the substance of the story itself and, if anything, are etiological.

151. Alter, *Art of Biblical Narrative*, 45.

152. White, *Narration and Discourse*, 213–14.

153. Golka, "BECHORAH," 135.

154. Moreover, Walton (*Thou Traveller Unknown*, 26) has rightly observed the following paradox: many who interpret the oracle of Gen 25:23 as demonstrating YHWH's election irrespective of the worth of those chosen subsequently go on to argue for Esau's unworthiness in the birthright narrative, without any explanation of how these two issues might be related. Walton directs these comments at Calvin and Augustine, but many others could be added.

155. Ahroni, "Why Did Esau Spurn?," 324–26; Walton, *Thou Traveller Unknown*, 26.

what should be made of the actions of these brothers? Fretheim helpfully comments on this:

> The story of Jacob and Esau begins with a struggle, which sets the stage for a complex and difficult journey for everyone within this conflicted family. At the same time, the texts witness to a God at work in and through this situation. The problems and possibilities created by the inter-action between God and this family constitute the essence of the story of Jacob and Esau. … At the same time, we may have difficulty in discerning when and how [conflict] stands in service of God's purposes.[156]

From a literary and theological perspective, this seems the most promising framework for understanding this text, even if many questions remain unanswered.

d. *The Birthright Scene: Summary*

As we have seen, Gen 25:27–34 carries forward the ambiguity and complexity which began in the oracle given to Rebekah. The preponderance of interpretation sees an extremely negative portrayal of Esau in these verses. And yet, when given due attention, the text is much more subtle than this, causing us to reconsider how Esau is to be understood. With regard to the significance of this short narrative, it was noted that there are various stances taken, including looking to the pre-history of the text for a civilization myth, or understanding this as a story which denigrates Esau and thus legitimizes Jacob and Israel. A further way of reading this story is to see here the outworking of the theme of election. What we are left with is an ambiguous narrative which leaves the rights of the firstborn in the hands of Jacob. This act will continue to push the larger cycle of narratives in a particular direction, one filled with strife and tension.

6. *Beginnings: Preliminary Conclusions*

This chapter has explored Gen 25:19–34, looking in turn at sections concerning pre-birth events, the birth of the twins, and the subsequent birthright scene. It was my intention to show that while the beginnings of the Jacob Cycle might set in motion a series of events that will push the subsequent story in a particular direction, the ambiguity and complexity which permeates these verses should give the reader pause before making evaluations of either the characters in the text or what the passage as a whole might be saying.

---

156. Fretheim, "Genesis," 522.

In the first scene, it was noted that the oracle given to Rebekah is ambiguous both grammatically and in terms of its hermeneutical implications. Moreover, the fact that election is an important motif does not entail that all events are pre-determined from this point onward. Thus, Rebekah is given an oracle by YHWH which, though ambiguous, sets the story on a particular trajectory. In the second scene we explored the birth narrative. Here the differences between the lads are highlighted from birth, continuing the theme of separation and strife. Although commentators have attempted to show that Esau is being ridiculed or disparaged in the birth narrative, one could just as persuasively argue that it is the heel-grabbing Jacob who is commented upon. Finally, in the third scene we saw the transaction regarding the birthright. This episode, like the oracle, is full of ambiguity and complexity. While the majority of commentators view Esau as negative in this story, a close reading of the text shows that there are alternative understandings. In the end we have Jacob obtaining the birthright, and the story of the brothers continues to move toward a climactic conflict as the tension of divine and human agency becomes palpable.

In conclusion, a few points can be made concerning how Gen 25:19–34 relates to the rest of the stories of Jacob and Esau. It might first be noted that while these verses are foundational for the Jacob Cycle, they need to be understood as part of the larger whole. Consequently, any opinions we may be formulating about Jacob or Esau need to be provisional at this stage in the story. Second, the tendency of commentators to see the portrayal of Esau as negative may be importing preconceptions into the text. In turn, judgments made at this juncture may color our understandings of subsequent narratives, creating a self-perpetuating cycle.[157] Finally, the tension of divine and human agency is introduced into the story of Jacob and Esau, with little explicit guidance for the reader. Thus, major literary and theological questions are raised with few answers given.

What about the issue of election? To be sure, the discerning reader is faced with difficult questions regarding a God who would appear to choose some and not others. Indeed, one can understand the temptation

---

157.   For example, Van Seters and Westermann argue that a distinction needs to be made between the "Esaus" of Gen 25 and Gen 33, as they appear to be completely different characters, and thus must come from another hand. See John Van Seters, *Prologue to History: The Yahwist as Historian in Genesis* (Zurich: Theologischer Verlag, 1992), 284–86; Westermann, *Genesis 12–36*, 417. However, one wonders if a more positive interpretation of Esau in Gen 25 might cohere more closely to the Esau they envisage in Gen 33.

for those who might consider themselves part of the elect to justify the choice of Jacob over Esau. However, attempts at justification are not only theologically misguided, but they also do not do justice to the complexity of these texts. As was highlighted throughout this chapter, interpreters often find reasons to malign Esau, even when the texts themselves are ambiguous. If anything, these texts would seem to reinforce the idea that election is both a mystery and a scandal. Moreover, as Fretheim makes clear, if the oracle poses difficulty for the "unchosen," it also calls forth questions for those who may be "chosen":

> The narrator probably "sets up" the reader with this text. The temptation for later Israel (and all who consider themselves to be God's elect) would certainly be to side with Jacob against Esau, to somehow justify his behaviors or even to suggest that whatever he did to obtain the birthright was appropriate to or congruent with God's choice. At one level, such thinking is ethically dangerous, for it suggests that the elect are free to act as they please, without regard for the consequences. At another level, such thinking is theologically wrongheaded, for personal behaviors did not ground God's choice to have the elder serve the younger... The reader must also use care in discussing primogeniture and the reversal of the rights of the firstborn. To be sure, the oracle overturns traditional customs and understandings and opens the future to possibilities not inherent in existing structures and institutions. But it is just as true that one can idolize the reversal of the traditional for its own sake. Even more, one can be tempted to understand election in terms comparable to primogeniture! Election, too, can be used as a vehicle to exclude others and exalt one's rights and privileges.[158]

Fretheim's caution here is an important one, and it leads us to our next question regarding Esau: If Esau has indeed been passed over, does his status as the unchosen son entail that he is cursed? It is to Gen 27 and this question that we now turn.

---

158.   Fretheim, "Genesis," 523–24.

Chapter 4

GENESIS 27: THE BLESSING OF JACOB AND ESAU

1. *Introduction*

The well-known narrative of Gen 27 is both lengthy and complex.[1] Sensing his impending death, Isaac calls his eldest son, Esau, in order to bless him, instructing him to make a savory dish that will accompany the blessing. As Esau leaves, we are told that Rebekah has overheard this conversation, and that she reports it back to Jacob. Rebekah hastily puts a plan into action whereby Jacob will be the recipient of Isaac's deathbed blessing. This plan includes Rebekah preparing a meal as Isaac likes, putting Esau's clothes on Jacob, and adding animal skins to Jacob's hands and neck to make him appear hairy like his brother. Jacob carries out the deception and, despite what seem to be hesitations on the part of Isaac, the father blesses his younger son. As soon as Jacob is off stage, Esau comes to his father, meal in hand, ready for his blessing. Isaac's reaction is (on the surface at least) one of surprise and consternation; yet he affirms that the first blessing must stand. Esau loses his composure and begins to weep, imploring his father to bless him as well. Isaac finally concedes and gives a second pronouncement to Esau. Esau vows to kill Jacob because of this event, and Rebekah learns of her elder son's intent. Rebekah again intervenes, this time convincing Isaac to send Jacob away to find a wife from her people. Isaac blesses Jacob again as he heads off to the land of his uncle Laban. Esau, meanwhile, takes a wife from the daughters of Ishmael in an effort to appease his father.

---

1. I use Gen 27 here as shorthand for the events of Gen 26:34–28:9. On the relation of Gen 27 to its broader literary context, see Fishbane, *Biblical Text*, 40–62; and Golka, "BECHORAH," 133–44. Various source-critical and redaction issues are dealt with by Jacques Vermeylen, "Le vol de la bénédiction paternelle: Une lecture de Gen 27," in *Pentateuchal and Deuteronomistic Studies: Papers Read at the XIIIth IOSOT Congress, Leuven 1989* (ed. C. Brekelmans and J. Lust; Leuven: Leuven University Press, 1990), 23–40.

What does this episode contribute to the biblical portrayal of Esau? Jacob, without doubt, comes away with the upper hand: he now has both the birthright and the blessing. It seems clear at this point in the story that the chosen line will indeed follow Jacob, and not Esau. But where does this leave Esau, both in relation to his family as well as the larger story-line of the Hebrew Bible?

It would seem that much hinges on the interpretation of the two poetic passages tucked away in the narrative of ch. 27, particularly whether or not Esau is given a blessing or a curse by his father. Isaac's pronouncements over his sons can easily be overlooked because of other note-worthy occurrences in the chapter, namely, Jacob's deception of Isaac with the help of his mother, and his acquisition of Esau's blessing by apparently morally ambiguous means.[2] Nevertheless, Isaac's pronouncements over his sons are key components in understanding the broader biblical portrayal of Jacob and Esau. As such, this chapter will focus on how these pronouncements might be understood, particularly whether we might consider Isaac's words to Esau a "blessing."[3]

In order to gain a better understanding of Isaac's declarations concerning his sons (Gen 27:27–29, 39–40), we will look at several areas, including the history of their interpretation, the literary and syntactical difficulties, the narrative context of the pronouncements, and the sibling blessing narratives found in the other ancestral narratives. I hope to show that one can indeed understand Isaac's pronouncement to Esau as a blessing, even if it is a lesser blessing than that which Jacob receives. This understanding may be a starting point in helping us make sense of the portrayal of Esau and his descendants and their relationship to Israel throughout the Hebrew Bible.

2. *History of Interpretation*

In what follows I will examine how a selection of pre-modern Jewish and Christian interpreters understood these difficult verses, followed by an investigation of how contemporary scholarship has addressed the issues.

---

2. On the issue of moral ambiguity in Gen 27, see David Marcus, "Traditional Jewish Responses to the Question of Deceit in Genesis 27," in *Jews, Christians, and the Theology of the Hebrew Scriptures* (ed. Alice Ogden Bellis and Joel S. Kaminsky; SBLSymS 8; Atlanta: Society of Biblical Literature, 2000), 293–306.

3. For more on the nature of biblical blessings, and how this might relate to the issue of the birthright, see the excursus at the end of this chapter.

a. *Early Translations and Interpretations*

The LXX and MT handle these passages in a very similar fashion. For instance, where the MT uses the preposition מִן in both Gen 27:28 and 27:39, the LXX uses the preposition ἀπὸ in both places. This word has roughly the same range of meanings in the Greek as its Hebrew counterpart.[4]

Targum Onqelos makes a few clarifying adjustments to Esau's blessing, but again uses similar language to the MT—particularly the preposition מִן—in both vv. 28 and 39 in depicting the two blessings. The clarifications that *Targum Onqelos* does make include expanding the Hebrew "become restless" (תָּרִיד) in v. 40 with "when [Jacob's] *descendant*s will transgress the words of the Law." The sense here is that Israel's superior status in the relationship with Esau and his descendants is predicated upon their fidelity to the law. This understanding would become quite common in Jewish tradition, and would serve to give meaning to Israel's later lack of dominion over Edom.[5]

Thus, the ancient translations, and those which we would expect to be closest to the MT, maintain the ambiguity of the text by using prepositions with a similar function as the Hebrew מִן, with little other evidence being given that would push the reader in one direction or the other regarding Esau's blessing/curse. Nonetheless, Jacob's superior status over his brother is upheld.

As we move toward rabbinic Judaism, interpreters become more interested in explaining other aspects of these verses, such as where exactly the "fat places" of the earth might be, and what it means to

---

4. See the references in BAGD, 86–88.

5. For the Aramaic of *Targum Onqelos*, consult Alexander Sperber, *The Bible in Aramaic, Based on Old Manuscripts and Printed Texts*. Volume 1, *The Pentateuch According to Targum Onkelos* (Leiden: Brill, 1973), 42–43. On מִן in the Aramaic, see Franz Rosenthal, *A Grammar of Biblical Aramaic* (PLO 5; Wiesbaden: Harrassowitz, 1995), 39. As is often the case, *Targum Pseudo-Jonathan*'s translation is furthest from the original. In fact, *Targum Pseudo-Jonathan*'s depiction of Isaac's blessing appears self-contradictory as v. 39 reads, "Behold, in the goodness of the fruits of the earth shall your dwelling be, and far from the dew of heaven above." This depends again on one's understanding of the prepositions being used. The confusion in this case is that *Targum Pseudo-Jonathan* uses the preposition *bet* (בְּ) in the first case (בְּטוּב) and מִן in the second (מִטּוּבַךְ). Moreover, *Targum Pseudo-Jonathan* goes on to change v. 40 so that the condition of the future freedom is placed on Esau, not on Jacob/Israel: "But you shall be subjected to your brother; but if you go astray and cause his children to abandon the observance of the commandments of the law, you shall break the yoke of his slavery from your neck." For the Aramaic of *Targum Pseudo-Jonathan*, see M. Ginsburger, *Pseudo-Jonathan (Thargum-Jonathan ben Usiël zum Pentateuch)* (Berlin: Calvary, 1903), 48–49.

"remove the yoke from your neck." However, the issue of Esau's blessing does continue to come up. Ginzberg highlights some of the major
interpretations, including those found in *Genesis Rabbah* and Rashi:

> Esau began to weep. He shed three tears—one ran from his right eye, the
> second from his left eye, and the third remained hanging from his
> eyelash. God said, "This villain cries for his very life, and should I let
> him depart empty-handed?" and then he bade Isaac bless his older son.
> The blessing of Isaac ran thus: "Behold, of the fat of the earth shall be thy
> dwelling," by which he meant Greater Greece, in Italy; "and of the dew
> of heaven from above," referring to Bet-Gubrin; "and by thy sword shalt
> thou live, and thou shalt serve thy brother," but when he casts off the
> yoke of the Lord, then shalt thou "shake his yoke from off thy neck," and
> thou wilt be his master. The blessing which Isaac gave to his older son
> was bound to no condition whatsoever. Whether he deserved them or not,
> Esau was to enjoy the goods of this world. Jacob's blessing, however,
> depended upon his pious deeds; through them he would have a just claim
> upon earthy prosperity. Isaac thought: "Jacob is a righteous man, he will
> not murmur against God, though it should come to pass that suffering be
> inflicted upon him in spite of his upright life. But that reprobate Esau, if
> he should do a good deed, or pray to God and not be heard, he would say,
> 'As I pray to the idols for naught, so it is in vain to pray to God.'" For
> this reason did Isaac bestow an unconditional blessing upon Esau.[6]

Thus, not only was Esau blessed (at God's behest), but he was given an
unconditional blessing ("Your dwelling will be…"), unlike Jacob, whose
blessing invokes God ("May God give to you…").[7]

One other Jewish writer gives us an interesting insight into early
interpretation of this episode. In his *Antiquities*, Josephus writes the
following: "His father being grieved at [Esau's] weeping said, that 'he
should excel in hunting and strength of body, in arms, and all such sorts
of work; and should obtain glory forever on those accounts, he and his
posterity after him; but still should serve his brother.'"[8] Here again we
are presented with the idea that Esau was blessed in some way, but that it
was a limited blessing, in that subservience to Jacob was still involved.

Another interesting interpretation comes from the anonymous New
Testament epistle to the Hebrews. There are two references to Esau in
Hebrews, and taken together they reflect the complexity of the issue.
Hebrews 11:20 states that, "By faith Isaac blessed (εὐλόγησεν) Jacob and
Esau with regard to their future." Scholars seem to be in agreement that

---

6. Louis Ginzberg, *The Legends of the Jews* (trans. Henrietta Szold; Philadelphia: The Jewish Publication Society, 1954), 1:339–40. Cf. *Gen. Rab.* 67; and
Rashi's Commentary: Genesis, 128.

7. *Rashi's Commentary: Genesis*, 126, commenting on Gen 27:28.

8. *Ant.* 1.18.6.

this indicates two blessings.[9] Interestingly, however, a few verses later in Heb 12:16–17, we read the following: "See that no one is sexually immoral, or is godless like Esau, who for a single meal sold his inheritance rights (τὰ πρωτοτόκια ἑαυτοῦ). Afterward, as you know, when he wanted to inherit this blessing (τὴν εὐλογίαν), he was rejected. He could bring about no change of mind, though he sought the blessing with tears." Here the writer of the Hebrews seems to follow other Jewish tradition that associates Esau with immorality, and implies that a blessing was not available to him.[10]

Of the various New Testament commentaries consulted, none notes the tension between these two passages. In fact, many comment that Esau was cursed in Gen 27, without so much as a mention of Heb 11:20.[11] We should be aware, as Attridge points out, that "as is frequently the case in Hebrews' handling of biblical stories, the paranetic point, not the original plot, is determinative."[12] Yet it is strange that within the space of two chapters we have references both to Esau being blessed and to missing out on a blessing. As Heb 12 connects the rights of the birthright which Esau sold to the blessing which he seeks in Gen 27, it may be that the writer of Hebrews understood that Esau received some sort of blessing, but the patriarchal blessing of YHWH was forfeited. Nevertheless, Hebrews seems to highlight the complexity of Isaac's blessing or curse of Esau.

Centuries later, Calvin and Wesley seem to give fairly similar interpretations as that found in Hebrews. Commenting on Heb 12, Calvin wonders how this episode is reconciled with Ezek 18:21 on repentance: "Thus it is that they who are given up to a reprobate mind are never touched with genuine penitence. Hypocrites truly break out into tears, like Esau, but their heart within them will remain closed as with iron bars. Therefore, since Esau rushes forward, destitute of faith and repentance, to ask a blessing, there is no wonder that he should be rejected."[13] This does not mean, however, that Esau was not blessed. Calvin notes with regard to Gen 27:39 that Esau did indeed receive a blessing. This blessing, however, was merely a worldly, material blessing.

9. See Attridge, *Hebrews*, 353; F. F. Bruce, *The Epistle to the Hebrews: The English Text with Introduction, Exposition and Notes* (NICNT; Grand Rapids: Eerdmans, 1990), 313.

10. See ibid., 368.

11. This fact was noted in the recent study by Rainer Kampling, "Wieder kein Segen – Esau im Neuen Testament," in Langer, ed., *Esau – Bruder und Feind*, 231–41 (231–33).

12. Attridge, *Hebrews*, 370.

13. Calvin, *Genesis*, 97–99.

A similar understanding can be seen in the work of Wesley:

> Esau likewise obtained a blessing: yet it was far short of Jacob's. 1. In Jacob's blessing the dew of heaven is put first, as that which he most valued and desired: in Esau's the fatness of the earth is put first, for that was it which he had the principal regard to. 2. Esau hath these, but Jacob hath them from God's hand. God give thee the dew of heaven, ver. 28. It was enough to have the possession, but Jacob desired it by promise... But the great difference is, that there is nothing in Esau's blessing that points at Christ, nothing that brings either him or his into the church, and without that the fatness of the earth, and the plunder of the field, will stand him in little stead. Thus Isaac by faith blessed them both, according as their lot should be.[14]

Thus, both Calvin and Wesley can be understood as following the lead of Hebrews: conceding that Esau was indeed blessed, but with a lesser blessing than that of Jacob. Esau's blessing is entirely material, as opposed to the "spiritual" blessing, the blessing of Abraham and YHWH, which Esau forfeited and which Jacob inherited.

Finally, it is worth mentioning two interpretations of the church fathers. Augustine and Ambrose both understand Isaac's pronouncement to Esau as a blessing, but they qualify this blessing in different ways. Augustine feels that Isaac is "roughly handled," and gives Esau a blessing for the sake of peace. This, for Augustine, is comparable to those in the church who are offered the sacraments for the sake of peace even though they "live by the sword" and constantly stir up dissension. When Isaac speaks to Esau about removing the yoke from his neck, it is an invitation to change his ways. "Yes, you may have this communion in the dew of heaven and the fruitfulness of the earth but all the same you are living by your sword and either rejoicing in the quarrels and dissension, or being scared out of your wits by them. So change yourself, and take the yoke from your neck."[15]

Ambrose agrees that Esau is blessed, but in Ambrose's understanding, Isaac makes the elder subject to Jacob because he is unwise. "But since he had two sons, one without moderation and the other moderate and wise, in order to take care of both of them like a good father, he placed the moderate son over the immediate [*sic*] one, and he ordered the foolish one to obey the one who was wise."[16] Then, borrowing from the Apostle Paul, Ambrose compares Jacob and Esau to the son of the free

---

14. *Wesley's Notes on the Bible*, 672–73. Online: http://www.ccel.org/ccel/wesley/notes.pdf.

15. Augustine, *Sermon* 4.35, in ACCS 2:181.

16. Ambrose, *Jacob and the Happy Life* 2.3.11, in ACCS 2:181.

woman and son of the slave girl, representing the law and grace. Thus, when Esau decides to live by grace and not "the letter," he will break the yoke from his neck.[17]

In summary, pre-modern interpretations in both the Jewish and Christian tradition assume that Esau was blessed, but that this blessing was inferior to Jacob's, and was qualified for various reasons.

b. *Contemporary Interpretations*

There is no shortage of contemporary scholars who see Isaac's speech to Esau as a curse. Many commentators follow Gunkel, who wrote, "Moved by love and compassion, Isaac would like to bless. But the world has been given away. Nothing remains for Esau other than—curse."[18] For those that follow this line of thinking, there are several explanations that are frequently presented: literary and syntactical issues, including the differing uses of the preposition מן and the reversal of some of the language in the two speeches, namely, "dew" and "fat"; the contextual issue regarding the tenor of the entirety of Isaac's statement to Esau; the infertility of the land of Seir/Edom; and the question of how many blessings Isaac was able to give.

A major argument made in defense of Isaac's speech to Esau as a curse is the use of the preposition מן. This term has a broad range of meanings, and in this context, it can be understood as partitive ("from" or "on"), or privative ("away from"). Scholars are agreed that Jacob's blessing in Gen 27:28 uses the partitive sense: Jacob will live from the good land and the dew of heaven. The question is more difficult in the case of Esau in 27:39. Proponents of the privative sense ("away from") in v. 39 include Blum, von Rad, Dicou, Syrén, Turner, Westermann and Zobel.[19] As von Rad writes, "[Isaac's] second 'blessing' is, to be sure, the opposite of what Jacob received. Its effect is especially bitter because it begins with almost the same words. The contrasting meaning is

17. Ambrose, *Jacob and the Happy Life* 2.3.13, in ACCS 2:182. This interpretation is interesting in light of the fact that, as noted above, early Jewish writings such as *Targum Onqelos* understood this passage as the opposite of Ambrose's interpretation: that Jacob/Israel's fidelity to the law would be the condition of Esau/Edom's subservience.

18. Gunkel, *Genesis*, 306.

19. Blum, *Die Komposition*, 82; Gerhard von Rad, *Genesis: A Commentary* (trans. John H. Marks; rev. ed.; OTL; London: SCM, 1972), 279; Dicou, *Edom, Israel's Brother*, 119; Syrén, *Forsaken*, 99; Turner, *Announcements*, 125; Westermann, *Genesis 12–36*, 443; Hans-Jürgen Zobel, "Der bildliche Gebrauch von *smn* im Ugaritischen und Hebräischen," *ZAW* 82 (1970): 209–16 (214–15).

expressed only by the different syntactic use of one and the same preposition, which cannot be duplicated in English."[20]

For those that understand 27:39 as using a privative מִן, contextual issues are often given as the basis of this decision. Kaminsky offers one such reading:

> Esau pleads for a blessing, and he receives one that reads more like a curse. Some commentators attempt to downplay the negative aspects of Esau's blessing by pointing out how similar the first line of Esau's blessing is to one part of Jacob's blessing in the original Hebrew… But Gen 27:40 makes clear that Esau and his *descendants* will experience a difficult life and will be ruled by Jacob and his descendants at least for a while. The Hebrew Bible often employs only slightly variant phrases to describe vastly different outcomes (Gen. 40:13, 19).[21]

One further linguistic issue that has been raised is the reversal of key terms in the speeches to Jacob and Esau, particularly the terms "dew" and "fat." Waltke, for instance, claims that this is a rhetorical device used to highlight difference.[22]

Additionally, an argument for Esau being cursed is often made on agricultural grounds: Seir was considered a barren desert, with little possibility of fertility. Von Rad states that, "The stony Edomite mountain region can scarcely be cultivated."[23] Gunkel writes, "Esau's land was considered, then, to be very infertile, a view which is, however, seen objectively, not absolutely correct for the land of Edom."[24]

And finally, many of these interpretations rely on the idea of scarcity with relation to blessing. As von Rad remarks, "Isaac could not indemnify his favorite son by any blessing anywhere near the equivalent of Jacob's; he had spent himself in blessing Jacob. In these things there is only an either-or."[25] Even when this idea of scarcity with regard to the blessing is not stated explicitly, it often seems to be an underlying assumption of many readers of the Hebrew Bible.

There are several commentators who, laying out the issues involved, refrain from making a decision one way or another with regard to Esau's "blessing." This group includes Sarna, Speiser, Wenham, and Heard.[26]

20. Von Rad, *Genesis*, 279.
21. Kaminsky, *Yet I Loved Jacob*, 46.
22. Bruce K. Waltke, with Cathi J. Fredricks, *Genesis: A Commentary* (Grand Rapids: Zondervan, 2001), 381.
23. Von Rad, *Genesis*, 279.
24. Gunkel, *Genesis*, 306.
25. Von Rad, *Genesis*, 279.
26. Sarna, *Genesis*, 194; Speiser, *Genesis*, 210; Wenham, *Genesis 16–50*, 212; Heard, *Dynamics*, 114–16.

Yet these scholars continue to point out the complexities of these texts. Indeed, most of these commentators make note of the above-mentioned issues, but are not convinced in one direction or another by the evidence. Sarna notes, "Ostensibly, the wording of the pronouncement is identical with that uttered to Jacob, yet it is strangely enigmatic and ambiguous."[27] Speiser concurs: "To treat both passages on a par, implying that Esau too was promised agricultural wealth, would undermine the whole tenor of the context. But to understand the particle as 'without…,' with many older translators and most moderns, is not sanctioned by established Heb. usage."[28]

The most balanced "undecided" account may come from Heard.[29] Noting both blessing and anti-blessing streams in scholarship, he goes on to explore the various issues. He begins by noting the scarcity issue: Should Esau's question to his father in 27:38 as to whether or not there is only one blessing force the readers to ask themselves the same question? There are, after all, other contexts where more than one blessing is given (Ishmael, Jacob's sons). As for the semantic ambiguity of מִן, Heard points out that grammatical rules seem incapable of solving the issue, and so syntactical arguments on this passage often boil down to "interpretive judgment calls," with scholars following their gut feeling on the context. Finally, Heard notes that the historical comments on Seir's fertility were contentious in the past and continue to be so today. In the end, Heard remains neutral on the subject.

The list of those who understand Isaac's words to Esau as a blessing is also notable, including Alter, Levenson, Spina, Brueggemann, Fretheim, and B. Jacob, to name a few.[30] Alter comments on some of the main issues: "The notion put forth by some commentators that these words mean something quite different from what they mean in the blessing to Jacob is forced… [T]he bounty of heaven and earth, after all, can be enjoyed by more than one son, though overlordship, as he has just made clear to Esau, cannot be shared."[31]

27.　Sarna, *Genesis*, 194.

28.　Speiser, *Genesis*, 210.

29.　Heard, *Dynamics*, 114–16.

30.　Alter, *Genesis*, 143; Levenson, *Death*, 62; Spina, *Faith*, 20–21; Brueggemann, *Genesis*, 234; Fretheim, "Genesis," 536–37; Jacob, *Erste Buch*, 570. Cf. I. Willi-Plein, "Genesis 27 als Rebekkageschichte. Zu einem historiographischen Kunstgriff der biblischen Vätergeschichten," *TZ* 45 (1988): 315–34 (320–22); Driver, *Genesis*, 260.

31.　Alter, *Genesis*, 143.

Levenson reiterates this idea of a lesser blessing: "Like Ishmael, also supplanted, Esau does finally receive a blessing but one inferior to that of which Jacob robbed him... For whereas Isaac wishes both brothers natural abundance, he blesses Jacob alone with mastery over his brothers and with the key Patriarchal provision, 'Cursed be they who curse you/Blessed they who bless you' (v. 29; cf. 12:3, to Abraham)."[32]

Perhaps the fullest accounting for a positive blessing in Esau's case, even if a lesser one than his brother, comes from Knauth:

> In view of God's blessings on both Isaac and Ishmael, as well as Jacob's blessings of all his sons together in Genesis 49, the implication of the exchange between Isaac and Esau in Genesis 27:33–38, that Isaac had only one blessing to give, seems odd. Esau had pleaded for his father to bless both of them (Gen 27:34, 36, 38), which Isaac implied was impossible (Gen 27:37). But this is, in fact, exactly what God then proceeded to do: he blessed them both, just as he had also blessed Isaac and Ishmael, though the covenant itself was not extended.[33]

She goes on to note several issues. First, the debatable aspects of מן and the other syntactical issues in these verses are discussed. Secondly, she notes that even if 27:40 predicts a hostile life, such a life is not mutually exclusive from divine favor and blessing, as a similar exchange take place with Ishmael in Gen 16:12. Finally, Knauth highlights the fact that Esau is, in both Genesis and Deuteronomy, a more sympathetic character than is often realized. Future blessing and inheritance seem to be some sort of reality in Esau's future.

c. *Review: Esau's Blessing in the History of Interpretation*
To review, we have seen that pre-modern translations and interpretations are in general open to the idea that Esau was blessed by Isaac. There are, however, caveats in both the Jewish and Christian traditions: in one stream of Jewish tradition, for instance, Esau's blessing does not preclude subservience to Jacob, but Esau is blessed unconditionally because he would not be able to live up to the conditions that are given to Jacob. In the Christian tradition, Esau's blessing is inferior to Jacob's for a variety of reasons: because it is a worldly, material blessing, not the covenantal "spiritual" blessing of YHWH; because it was given for the

32. Levenson, *Death*, 62.
33. Knauth, "Esau, Edomites," 221. Knauth's attribution of God as the source of the blessing in the quote above in place of Isaac is puzzling given that no explanation is proffered. This issue takes on greater significance in light of Terence E. Fretheim, "Which Blessing Does Isaac Give Jacob?," in Bellis and Kaminksy, eds., *Jews, Christians*, 279–92. This issue will be discussed below.

sake of peace; or because Esau was immoderate and unwise and needed to live under the direction of his brother.

In contemporary scholarship, commentators are divided between those who see the pronouncement to Esau as a curse, those who are undecided on the issue, and those who read the text as a positive blessing. There are four disputed factors that seem to affect these interpretations: the literary and syntactical issues, including the semantic ambiguity of the preposition מִן; the contextual issue of whether Isaac's prediction of Esau's future is positive or negative; the perception of Seir/Edom's suitability for habitation; and the question of whether or not there was indeed only one blessing for Isaac to give. In order to get a better understanding of these issues, we will investigate them individually.[34]

3. *Grammatical and Syntactical Issues*

As highlighted above, there are two main literary and syntactical issues that affect our interpretation of these poetic passages and which deserve attention: the use of the preposition מִן, and the word order of the speeches.

a. *The Preposition* מִן

The preposition מִן has a broad semantic range, with the basic meanings of "separation," "distance," or "provenance." However, there do not seem to be any clear grammatical rules that stipulate when and how מִן is used to designate these various meanings.[35]

The main issue with the usage of מִן in Gen 27 has to do with the parallel occurrences in 27:28 and 27:39 and the relationship of Jacob and Esau to the "dew of heaven" and the "fatness of the earth." Are these both partitive uses ("from" or "on"), or is the first partitive and the second privative ("away from")? As noted earlier, scholars are divided on the issue.

---

34. The issue of Seir/Edom's suitability to be a productive land will for the moment not be taken up. For more on the geographical issues from an archaeological perspective, see the essays in Piotr Bienkowski, ed., *Early Edom and Moab: The Beginning of the Iron Age in Southern Jordan* (SAM 7; Sheffield: J. R. Collis, 1992), and Øystein S. LaBianca and Randall W. Younker, "The Kingdoms of Ammon, Moab and Edom: The Archaeology of Society in Late Bronze/Iron Age Transjordan (ca. 1400–500 BCE)," in *Archaeology of Society in the Holy Land* (ed. Thomas E. Levy; London: Leicester University Press, 1995), 399–415.

35. See *HALOT* 2:597–98; JM §133e; GKC §119v-z.

There are a few additional instances in the Hebrew Bible where מן is placed before either שמן or טל, as seen in Gen 27:28 and 39. The most relevant of these, as it occurs in a blessing context, is Deut 33:13. Moses, blessing the tribes of Israel, says of Joseph: "May YHWH bless his land from the choice things of heaven (ממגד שמים), from the dew (מטל), and from the deep waters (ומתהום) which lie below." These are clearly partitive usages meant to convey a positive blessing. In Dan 4:22, the Aramaic portion of the book, we find the text speaking of Nebuchadnezzar's future and saying that he "will be given grass to eat like cattle of the field, and from the dew of heaven (ומטל שמיא) you will be drenched." Though this pronouncement is far from a blessing, this phrase again seems to denote the partitive "from" as opposed to the privative "away from."[36]

The connection of מן and שמן happens most frequently in Leviticus, in relation to the priests pouring "from the oil" (משמן, Lev 8:12; or מן־השמן, Lev 14:26). These two words are also found together in the wisdom literature, often using the comparative sense of מן ("his words are more smoothing than oil [משמן]," Ps 55:22; cf. Ps 104:15; Prov 5:3; Eccl 7:1). The one occurrence which seems most likely to be privative is found in Ps 109:24, where we read, "My knees are weak from fasting, and my flesh is lean, without fat (משמן)."

Taken together, there does not seem to be any clear indication as to when מן is to be understood as partitive or privative in relation to טל and שמן, though the one other occurrence in a blessing appears to be partitive (Deut 33:13). The context of Gen 27:27–29 and 39–40 thus remains vitally important.

(1) *Genesis 40:13 and 4:19.* It was noted above that when discussing these occurrences of מן in Gen 27:28 and 39, several commentators point to the story of Joseph interpreting the cupbearer's and baker's dreams in Gen 40. The argument is that Joseph uses identical language at the beginning of each interpretation, but the meanings are vastly different. Each verse begins, "Within three days Pharaoh will lift your head..." But while 40:13 goes on to say, "and restore you to your office," 40:19 continues with, "from you and will hang you on a tree."

Admittedly, there are similarities between the Gen 27 and Gen 40 accounts, as we have one person predicting the futures of two others and doing so by using similar language. However, the comparison seems to break down because the immediate context of Gen 40:13 and 19 makes

---

36. This terminology recurs in Dan 4:30 and 5:21.

their interpretation abundantly clear, while the Gen 27 texts are not self-evident. Scholars are right to note how similar wording can be used to convey different meanings. However, the overall ambiguity of the speech in Gen 27:39–40 compared with that in Gen 40:13 and 19 makes this comparison less useful than is often realized.

b. *Word Order*

A second grammatical issue which is raised in the discussion of the blessings in Gen 27 is the word order of the speeches. In the blessing of Jacob in Gen 27:28, the order of elements within the verse is (1) the dew of heaven, (2) the richness/fat of the earth, and (3) an abundance of grain and new wine. In the pronouncement to Esau in 27:39, however, the order is (1) the richness/fat of the earth, and (2) the dew of heaven above. Waltke and Grisanti both claim that the reversal of word order in these two verses intensifies the reversal of meaning.[37] However, neither gives reasons for why this is the case, or examples that would support this claim. Instead, the intensity of the reversal noted in these interpretations seems to be predicated on the already established fact of different meanings of מן in the two verses. As Alter notes, this is a forced reading. "The reversal of order of heaven and earth is a formal variation, a kind of chiasm, and it would be imprudent to read into it any symbolic significance."[38]

c. *Review: Literary and Syntactical Issues*

In review, the literary and syntactical issues in the two pronouncements from Isaac are complex and far from self-explanatory. The interpretation of the preposition מן can be understood in various ways, with no clear-cut grammatical rules to settle the issue. Moreover, any meaning behind the change in word order in Gen 27:28 and 39 again is not apparent. In sum, based on syntactical issues alone, the question as to whether or not Isaac's speech to Esau in 27:39 is positive or negative remains unanswerable. We turn next to issues that arise in the context of these pronouncements.

4. *Contextual Issues*

There are, undoubtedly, differences in the speeches Isaac makes to his two sons in Gen 27. This section will focus on the contextual issues surrounding these pronouncements, including what instigates each

---

37. Waltke, *Genesis*, 381; Michael A. Grisanti, "שׁמן," *NIDOTTE* 4:173–74.
38. Alter, *Genesis*, 143.

speech, what is said, and what the reaction of each son is to their father's words.

a. *Instigation*

What instigates the two pronouncements by Isaac? The first is brought about by Isaac's desire to bless Esau before his death. Even with Isaac's doubts and questioning of his son's true identity, there is a sense in which this first pronouncement happens quite spontaneously. Isaac's statement in 27:27 after he smells his son's garments, "Ah, the smell of my son is as the smell of a field which YHWH has blessed," seems to lead directly into his proclamation of blessing.

The second speech, however, comes with some reluctance, and only after much pleading on Esau's part. Esau notes that Jacob stole both his birthright and his blessing; yet he seems to think there should be some sort of blessing for him anyway. In 27:36 he asks, "Have you not reserved a blessing for me?" When Isaac responds with a question of his own, Esau again asks in 27:38, "Do you have only one blessing, my father? Bless me, also me, my father." The reader might then wonder, as B. Jacob comments, why would Isaac respond at all if he was not going to bless Esau? If Esau asked for a blessing, why would Isaac curse him?[39]

b. *Pronouncement*

The difference in these two speeches from Isaac, and particularly the ambiguity of the second, is most clear at the beginning of each pronouncement. We are told explicitly in 27:27 that Isaac's statement is a blessing (ויברכהו). However, in 27:39, after Esau pleads for a blessing, we are simply told that "His father Isaac answered him (ויען)..." Moreover, as the rabbis were keen to point out, Jacob's blessing invokes God's granting these things (ויתן־לך האלהים). Esau's, however, is simply stated: "Your dwelling will be..." (... יהיה מושבך).

The content of the first half of each pronouncement is similar, as noted above. Both contain references to the dew of heaven and the richness or fat of the earth. Zobel has made the case that both טל and שמן connote rain, and others support this view.[40] Whatever the case, the idea here seems to be one of fertility and abundance. The first blessing also contains an additional comment which the second pronouncement does not include: an abundance of grain and new wine. This element is also found in the contexts of blessings in Deut 7:13 and Deut 33:28, both in reference to the land of Canaan.

---

39. Jacob, *Erste Buch*, 570.
40. Zobel, "Der bildliche Gebrauch," 209–16. Cf. Grisanti, *NIDOTTE* 4:174.

The second halves of these pronouncements also deal with similar themes. In 27:29, Jacob is told, "May peoples serve you and nations bow down to you. Be master to your brothers, and may the sons of your mother bow down to you. Those cursing you will be cursed; those blessing you will be blessed." Isaac's statement to Esau also deals with subservience and familial themes. We read in 27:40, "And by your sword you will live. And your brother you will serve. But it will happen when you grow restless that you will break his yoke from your neck."

This latter verse is not without difficulties. First of all, what does it mean to "live by your sword?" Heard notes that while this phrase is often understood as predicting a violent life of warfare for Esau, this is not the only plausible reading:

> But *hereb*, while most commonly used in military contexts, can none-theless denote other bladed implements including flint knives used for circumcision (Josh 5:2, 3) or chisels for stonework (Exod 20:25). Even if this wider sense of *hereb* as "knife" is not recognized, or rejected as being too rare, readers need not automatically suppose that the sword by which Esau lives will be directed against human beings. Animals are candidates too (Deut 13:15), and thus the line comports very well with the overall depiction of Esau as an outdoorsman and hunter. Thus v. 40aα may simply assert that Esau will continue to be successful in his already-chosen lifestyle. On the other hand, Isaac's words do not compel this construal, and readers may choose instead, without doing violence to the text, to read the line as predicting a life of "rapine and raids" (Westermann's phrase) for Esau and his descendants.[41]

Indeed, as Dicou points out, Esau living by his sword could be taken as a counterpart to Jacob's having an abundance of grain and wine, juxtaposing the agricultural and hunting lifestyles.[42]

The next phrase is fairly straightforward: "You will serve your brother." However, this is qualified by the enigmatic final line of the pronouncement: "But it will happen when you grow restless (תריד) that you will break his yoke from your neck." There are two issues here. The first concerns the relatively rare term, תריד, and what precisely it entails. The second is what is meant by the term "yoke," and what it might mean to remove it.

The verb תריד is a second person Hiphil imperfect from רוד, the basic meaning of which in the Qal is "to wander restlessly or roam." The

---

41. Heard, *Dynamics*, 116.

42. See Dicou, *Edom, Israel's Brother*, 119–20, who argues that this can be taken positively even if the מן of Esau's discourse is privative, as the dew and richness of the land would be less important for Esau than for Jacob.

Hiphil, however, has the sense of "showing restlessness" or "freeing oneself."[43] There are textual variations to the MT: the Samaritan Pentateuch has תאדר, whose meaning is unknown, but could possibly come from a root meaning "to make majestic." The LXX, meanwhile, has καθέλῃς, from καθαιρέω, "to take down, destroy, or overthrow."[44] *BHS* proposes תאריך, from the root ארך meaning, "to prolong" or "tarry a long time," or possibly תמרוד, from מרד, "to rebel." Thus, we have variations and proposals of "overthrow/destroy," "tarry a long time," or "rebel." While the MT can be understood in its own right, these emendations are also compatible with the tenor of the text.

The idea that Esau will "break the yoke from his neck" is often understood as referring to later Israelite and Edomite history. David would subjugate Edom during his reign, but Edom would eventually free itself during the reign of Jehoram (2 Kgs 8:20–22).[45] Yet, as Fretheim notes, "It would be too simple to suggest that the known histories of Israel and Edom are here retrojected into early times and thought to have been determined by these early oracles... Certainly the text recognizes that words and deeds do shape history, but not in some detailed, inevitable way."[46] Moreover, as Spina points out, this statement finds resonance in the unfolding story of Jacob and Esau. One could say that Isaac's pronouncement finds its fulfillment in Esau's warm welcome of his brother in Gen 33:4, where he falls on Jacob's "neck" and kisses him. "That is how Esau frees himself. Forgiveness, not the sword, is his preferred 'weapon.'"[47] Heard offers a similar reading:

> If the first few lines of Isaac's pronouncements are ambiguous, the last few hardly seem to qualify as a curse. To be sure, Isaac proclaims that Esau will serve his brother, but this only reconfirms the early blessing to Jacob, which Isaac believes to be irrevocable. Nevertheless, Isaac here mitigates the earlier blessing by placing upon it an "expiration date" that depends completely upon Esau's own attitude toward the subservience: Esau's servitude will end when Esau is ready for it to end.[48]

43. BDB, 923; Elmer A. Martens, "רוד," *NIDOTTE* 3:1067–68.

44. Carl Schneider, "καθαιρέω, καθαίρεσις," *TDNT* 3:411–13.

45. Westermann, *Genesis 12–36*, 443; Gunkel, *Genesis*, 306. Early Jewish translations and interpretations noted above which changed "become restless" to "when Jacob's descendants transgress the law" (see *Targum Onqelos*, for example) may be a variation on this historical reading, as this may have been done to explain why Edom was no longer a part of Israel/Judah's territory in later times.

46. Fretheim, "Genesis," 539.

47. Spina, *Faith*, 27.

48. Heard, *Dynamics*, 116–17.

As such, the pronouncement to Esau remains ambiguous. Jacob is indeed promised fertility and abundance, and is granted lordship over his family and brother. However, Esau too can be understood as being promised fertility, and Jacob's lordship seems to be qualified in Isaac's pronouncement to Esau.[49]

c. *Reactions to the Pronouncements*
The story gives us very little in relation to Jacob's reaction to his father's blessing (27:30). Esau's reaction, however, is given to us in greater detail: "And Esau bore a grudge against Jacob on account of the blessing which his father blessed him…" Contextually, Esau's reaction sets the scene for Jacob needing to leave the land, the younger son's own exile.[50] And it is often argued that Esau's angry and resentful reaction must be a sign that his father had cursed him. Yet, we have already seen in 27:36 that Esau was upset at Jacob's actions, feeling twice deceived and robbed. A more pertinent issue may be which blessing the narrator is referring to in v. 41: is Esau's reaction concerning the blessing which his father had blessed Jacob, or concerning the blessing that he was given? Syntactically, the blessing referred to could belong to either brother. The mention of Jacob in the verse may point to the reference being to him, but the fact that Esau asks for a blessing in v. 38 may indicate that Esau is the referent.[51] The latter reading would reinforce the idea that Esau is indeed blessed, albeit with a lesser blessing than his younger brother received.

d. *Review: Contextual Issues*
In review, the instigation, pronouncement, and reaction to Isaac's declarations to his sons about their futures are informative. While the first speech occurs quite spontaneously, the second one comes after pleading and shedding of tears. Even though "his" birthright and "his" blessing are both gone, Esau asks his father if there is not another blessing for him (27:36, 38). And the reader is left asking the same question as Esau: is there only one blessing?[52]

49. Fretheim, "Genesis," 536–37.
50. Levenson, *Death*, 65.
51. See Fretheim, "Which Blessing?," 289, who takes this to refer to Esau's blessing.
52. Keukens feels that Esau's question does indeed function in this way, probing the reader as well to ask whether Esau is in fact blessed or cursed. See Karlheinz H. Keukens, "Der irreguläre Sterbesegen Isaaks Bemerkungen zur Interpretation von Genesis 27,1–45," *BN* 19 (1982): 43–56 (51).

The pronouncements themselves deal with parallel themes, from issues of fertility to familial relations and subservience. Yet, despite the tendency to read Esau's pronouncement as negative, one can read the text as generally positive. The most obviously "negative" aspect is Esau's subservience to his brother; but even this statement is mitigated. Isaac's response to Esau's request in 27:37 seems to imply he can do nothing for his elder son; yet, interestingly, his pronouncement to Esau in 27:39–40 leaves out the *two very things* which Isaac mentions as having been given away to Jacob: the lordship of the family and the sustenance with grain and new wine (v. 37). Might this imply that Isaac is doing what he can for the son that he loves?[53]

As the syntactical and contextual issues have not been conclusive regarding the intent of Isaac's pronouncements over Esau, we will explore one final area: the idea of blessing in the Hebrew Bible, specifically within the family.

5. *Sibling Blessings in the Ancestral Narratives*

The main question here is that which is asked by Esau in the text itself: Does his father have only one blessing to give? One of the intriguing aspects of the commentaries on Gen 27, and specifically the sections on Esau, is that they rarely mention the relationship of other blessing scenes, particularly those within the ancestral narratives. When commentators do mention other sibling narratives, the one that is commonly raised is Cain and Abel.[54] The connection between Esau and Cain is one of murderous rage: Cain's anger in Gen 4:5 manifests itself in the murder of his brother

---

53. This points to yet another ambiguous aspect of Gen 27, the character of Isaac. If Isaac's character is consistent throughout the chapter, one could even understand Isaac's words to Esau in Gen 27:37 as further comic evidence that Isaac does not know what was going on: first he was fooled by a less than convincing masquerade, and now he does not even know how the familial blessings work. On Isaac as a humorous figure, see Joel S. Kaminsky, "Humor and the Theology of Hope: Isaac as a Humorous Figure," *Int* 54 (2000) 363–75. Other questions of Isaac's understanding of the blessing scenario also come to mind: Is he aware of the earlier oracle or the transfer of the birthright? Does he know that he is blessing Jacob, and simply acting shocked as the narrative progresses? As with so many other issues, the text is for the most part silent on the issue of Isaac's role. On the place of Isaac in this chapter, see Craig A. Smith, "Reinstating Isaac: The Centrality of Abraham's Son in the 'Jacob–Esau' Narrative of Genesis 27," *BTB* 31 (2001): 130–34.

54. See, e.g., Westermann, *Genesis 12–36*, 443.

in 4:8. Meanwhile, we are told in Gen 27:41 of Esau's intent to kill his brother Jacob, only to be cut off (again) by the intervening actions of his mother. While there is a connection here of sorts, it seems to me that the sibling narratives directly preceding and following the Jacob and Esau story—Isaac and Ishmael as well as Joseph and his sons—offer the most compelling comparisons.

a. *Ishmael*

The points of contact between Esau and Ishmael are quite striking: both are counterparts to the promised heirs and end up leaving Canaan (Gen 21:21 and Gen 36:7); both are given their own *toledot* in Genesis (25:12–18 and Gen 36); both have fathers that love them and are distressed by their displacement as heirs (Gen 17:18 and Gen 27:1–4, 30–34); both bury their fathers with their brothers (Gen 25:9 and Gen 35:29); and both are forefathers of nations. As if this were not enough, Esau marries one of Ishmael's daughters as an attempt to appease his father (Gen 28:6–9).

The narratives concerning Ishmael are quite developed, and he is involved in three scenes in which blessing or foretelling is at stake: Gen 16:10–12; 17:20–22, and 21:11–13, 17–18. In Gen 16:10–12 we have an angel of YHWH addressing Hagar after she has fled from an abusive Sarai. In this pre-birth oracle, Hagar is told to return to Sarai, and in v. 10 it is pronounced that her descendants will be increased and be too numerous to count. This seems to be a reference back to Abram's blessing in Gen 13:16. However, 16:11–12 continues the angel's speech, and it is more ambiguous:

> Behold, you are with child,
> and you will bear a son
> And you shall call his name Ishmael,
> because YHWH has heard of your affliction;
> And he will be a wild ass of a man (פרא אדם)
> His hand to all and the hand of all to him (ידו בכל ויד כל בו)
> And he will live against/to the east of (ועל־פני) all his brothers.

The language here is difficult, and raises serious interpretive questions: is "wild ass of a man" inherently negative? Does "his hand to all and the hand of all to him" imply hostility? And should על־פני be understood as "against" or "to the east" of all his brothers? Though the answer to these may seem obvious, Heard has shown how our readerly preconceptions often taint our understanding of what are in reality ambiguous statements. For instance, concerning "wild ass," Heard notes that many understand this as an image for rebellion; however, this can also be taken as pointing to freedom, and other usages in the Hebrew Bible of this terminology are not prescriptively negative or positive.[55] Again, the use of the preposition ב with יד ("hand") tends to imply conflict, but syntactically it can be understood as "adversarial or cooperative."[56] The same can be said regarding the final clause: Ishmael may be "against" his brothers, or he may be "to the east" of them. Heard concludes:

> On the one hand, then, readers may perceive Yahweh's messenger to paint a bleak picture of Ishmael's future, one characterized by violence and mutual enmity with everyone, including kin. On the other hand, the precise wording of the messenger's speech is such that readers may find it easy, even compelling, to perceive in this message things Hagar might well desire for her child: freedom, a relationship of mutual assistance with everyone, and proximity to kin. Of course, these alternatives are not mutually exclusive in all their particulars, so some readers may opt for elements of both.[57]

Thus, in 16:11–12 we have an unequivocally positive statement ("I will increase your descendants") followed by a more ambiguous one. This has similar elements to Esau's blessing in Gen 27, the first half of which can be understood positively, and the latter half of which seems more ambiguous because of the subservience to Jacob.

When we move to Gen 17, the status of Ishmael becomes clearer. Here the covenant with Abraham is reiterated, introducing circumcision and foretelling a son for Sarah, who will be blessed. Abraham's response to this is, "If only Ishmael would live before you" (17:18) God responds by reiterating that Isaac will be the covenant bearer, but then adds the following in 17:20: "And as for Ishmael, I have heard you; behold, I will bless him (ברכתי אתו) and will make him fruitful and I will greatly increase him. Twelve rulers he will beget, and I will make him into a great nation." Thus, Isaac is to be the promised heir, the carrier of the covenant blessing; nevertheless, Ishmael will be blessed and be a great nation.

Finally, in Gen 21 we have the expulsion of Hagar and Ishmael from proximity with Abraham's family. Sarah has decided to get rid of the slave and her son, which again distresses Abraham. In 21:12–13 God reassures Abraham of the fact that Isaac will be the son of promise, but that Ishmael will be made into a great nation. This statement is reiterated

---

55. Heard, *Dynamics*, 69. Cf. Isa 32:14; Jer 2:24; Hos 8:9; Ps 104:11; Job 6:5. Similar language seems to be used of Joseph in Gen 49:22, though the text is not without difficulties. See Levenson, *Death*, 96; Sarna, *Genesis*, 343.
56. Heard, *Dynamics*, 69–70.
57. Ibid., 73. Cf. Syrén, *Forsaken*, 22–24.

a few verses later (21:17–19) when Hagar fears she and her son will die
in the desert. She is told that the boy will become a great nation (21:18).[58]

Levenson ties together nicely the stories of Ishmael and Esau, noting
the way their stories mirror one another as well as how the narrative
connects them:

> In both cases, that of Ishmael and that of Esau, the dispossessed elder
> brother is still awarded an enviable destiny, fatherhood of a great nation
> for Ishmael (17:20; 21:18) and a luxurious abode and occasional inde-
> pendence from servitude for Esau (27:39–40). A Priestly genealogical
> note ties the homology of Ishmael together beautifully. Esau's becoming
> Ishmael's son-in-law doubtless reflects ethnic and political relationships
> in the lands to the south of Canaan. These same relationships have almost
> certainly played a role in the construction of a narrative in which Ishmael
> and Esau resemble each other so much. Apart from the ethnographic
> dimension, however, the image of Esau's fleeing to Ishmael just after his
> relative disinheritance at the hands of Jacob makes a powerful literary
> statement. Now, just outside the land promised to Abraham, these two
> descendants of his make common cause, ruling their mighty nations yet
> utterly powerless to deflect the providential course that has decreed that
> the status of the beloved son shall attach not to themselves, but to their
> younger brothers.[59]

b. *Joseph and His Sons*

Another illuminating instance of sibling blessings comes at the hands of
Esau's brother Jacob. With the family reunited in Egypt and nearing the
end of his life, Jacob blesses his offspring. However, the scene unfolds in
an unusual way, as Jacob first blesses Joseph's sons, his grandsons
Ephraim and Manasseh, and then blesses his twelve sons proper.

Genesis 48 highlights the blessing of Ephraim and Manasseh.[60] The
scene has several similarities with Gen 27: an elderly father, near death,
with failing eyes, summons his strength for a final blessing which
includes a kiss and benediction. Here Jacob reckons Joseph's two sons as
his own (48:5–6), stating that they will both inherit territory as with
Jacob's other sons. When the time comes for the blessing, Joseph brings
the boys forward, Manasseh on Jacob's right, and the younger Ephraim
on his left. In 48:14 we read, "But Israel stretched out his right hand and
set it upon the head of Ephraim, who was the younger (הצעיר), and the
left upon the head of Manasseh, crossing his hands, because Manasseh

58. On source-critical elements and the relationship of the two "Hagar legends"
in Gen 16 and 21, see Gunkel, *Genesis*, 229–30.

59. Levenson, *Death*, 102.

60. Various critical issues are set out by Edwin C. Kingsbury, "He Set Ephraim
Before Manasseh," *HUCA* 38 (1967): 129–36.

was the firstborn (הבכור).” Joseph is displeased with the arrangement, and tries to switch Jacob's hands, informing his father which one is the firstborn (48:17–18).[61] Jacob responds in language reminiscent of both Ishmael and Esau: “I know, my son, I know; he also will become a people (יהיה־לעם) and he too will become great (יגדל). Nevertheless, his younger brother (אחיו הקטן) will be greater than he, and his descendants will be great nations” (48:19). The scene with the boys ends with the terse statement in v. 20, “And he placed (וישם) Ephraim before Manasseh.”

Here again we have the subversion of the tradition regarding the elder brother, with the younger Ephraim promised the privileged position. However, both Ephraim and Manasseh received a shared blessing, and both will become great peoples.[62]

c. *Review: Sibling Blessings in the Ancestral Narratives*
The younger son in the ancestral narratives often seems to obtain the “better” blessing, which includes some sort of familial superiority, if not outright succession. It also seems to invoke fertility and prosperity, elements common to the Abrahamic blessing. Furthermore, and perhaps most importantly from the vantage point of the text itself, it serves to establish the family line through which the storyline will continue. In this respect, Levenson is right to state that this status is “inextricably associated with the theology of *chosenness*.”[63]

But to say that Isaac, Jacob and Joseph (and the latter's sons) are chosen does not mean that others are not blessed. As we have seen, Ishmael is specifically promised blessing, and Joseph's blessing is divided between his two sons, even though one again is given superior status. Thus, the election of some does not imply the cursing or ultimate loss of all others.[64] The same holds true for the narrative of Jacob and

61.   Interestingly, Joseph here joins Abraham and Isaac as a father whose blessed son is not the one he would have chosen. True to form, Jacob is the only patriarch who blesses the son (or grandson) of his choice.

62.   This linkage of these two brothers is evident throughout the various biblical traditions (cf. Deut 33:17). Following on from this narrative, Gen 49 goes on to detail the blessing of Jacob's other sons. On the continuity and discontinuity of both Gen 49 and Deut 33 in relation to Gen 27 and other testamental benedictions, see Christopher Wright Mitchell, *The Meaning of BRK "To Bless" in the Old Testament* (SBLDS 95; Atlanta: Scholars, 1987), 80.

63.   Levenson, *Death*, 59.

64.   This is not to deny that the unchosen suffer pain and loss on account of their status; the story of Ishmael seems especially poignant on this issue. However, one could just as easily point to the pain and loss suffered by the elect on account of their being chosen; Abraham's life is full of such examples.

Esau. As Greenspahn notes, "There is nothing in Jacob and Rebecca's words or deeds to suggest that they thought Esau's blessing was Isaac's only one. Their urgency resulted from their belief that Isaac was about to die. It was not his only blessing that they wanted for Jacob, but the *best* one."[65] In general, a framework which places the scarcity of blessing at the center of these episodes is not warranted.[66]

6. *The Nature and Source of the Blessings*

Before concluding, a brief word on the nature and source of Isaac's pronouncements over his sons may be in order.

a. *Blessing: Magic Words and Speech Act Theory*
Blessing is obviously one of the main themes of the Hebrew Bible, and as such is beyond the scope of the present study.[67] It is worth noting, however, that much work has been done in the past century on the nature of blessings and the source of their power or authority. A previous generation of scholarship saw a magical element to blessing. This developed alongside an understanding of the spoken word as having immense, indeed magical, powers.[68] Yet this idea has been roundly criticized over the past few decades.[69] The main objection has been that blessings (and curses) in the Bible are illocutionary speech acts, based on societal and cultural conventions, not magic. As Mitchell states, "The words *must* be spoken in the socially accepted situation, by the proper person, and in the proper form, or else the utterance is invalid; *the words in themselves*

65. Frederick E. Greenspahn, *When Brothers Dwell Together: The Preeminence of Younger Siblings in the Hebrew Bible* (Oxford: Oxford University Press, 1994), 56.

66. This scarcity theme can be found in the comments of von Rad and Gunkel on Gen 27 noted above, and has more recently been revived in the work of Regina M. Schwartz, *The Curse of Cain: The Violent Legacy of Monotheism* (Chicago: University of Chicago Press, 1997).

67. Broad studies on blessing in the Hebrew Bible can be found in Mitchell, *The Meaning of BRK*; and Claus Westermann, *Blessing in the Bible and the Life of the Church* (trans. Keith Crim; OBT; Minneapolis: Fortress, 1978). Both Mitchell and Westermann offer comprehensive and helpful histories of interpretation on the subject of blessing. Cf. J. Scharbert, "ברך," *TDOT* 2:279–308; Kent Harold Richards, "Bless/Blessing," *ABD* 1:753–55.

68. In relation to Gen 27, this is often seen in Isaac's desire to bless his son with his נפש. This was understood as the transfer of soul power. Proponents included Pedersen, Mowinckel, Hempel, and Scharbert.

69. See Anthony Thiselton, "The Supposed Power of Words in the Biblical Writings," *JTS* 25 (1974): 283–99.

have no power... When the speech act is performed properly and in the appropriate context, society accepts the illocutionary utterance as an accomplished act."[70]

Mitchell notes that testamental benedictions, usually before the father's death, are the most common setting for familial blessing. This informs his understanding of Gen 27:

> Isaac's testamental blessing in Gen 27 is a prime example of...an illo-
> cutionary speech act. When the patriarch refers to his death, and issues an
> oral disposition of his estate in the form of a blessing, then the testament
> is considered legally binding, and it cannot be rescinded. The effective
> power of the benediction has nothing whatsoever to do with magic words
> or the transfer of soul power any more than modern legal oaths or a
> notarized will. As in many modern oaths, Isaac also called upon God to
> enforce the will.[71]

If the words themselves are not magical, why does Isaac not simply undo what he has done in blessing Jacob? Cultural convention may again be the reason: "Isaac's response to Esau's request (v. 37) indicates that Isaac felt that it was impossible for him to rescind the blessing. Since the testamental blessings were normally pronounced shortly before the father's death, it is likely that there was no socially accepted legal proce-dure for rescinding them."[72]

Thus, there is a legal, binding dimension to Isaac's pronouncement over Jacob. While this blessing cannot be undone, Isaac mitigates the first blessing with the conditions in his pronouncement over Esau.[73]

b. *Whose Blessing Does Isaac Give?*

Finally, we have the following question: Which blessing is Isaac intend-ing (or authorized) to give? This subject—which blessing is at stake, and the validity of that blessing—receives its fullest attention from Fretheim.[74] Fretheim distinguishes between two realities of blessing in Genesis: first, God's specific promises to the elect family (blessing of Abraham, son, land, descendants, nationhood); and second, "general, creational realities such as fertility, various forms of prosperity, and

---

70. Mitchell, *The Meaning of BRK*, 174 (italics in original). Cf. William J. Urbrock, "Blessings and Curses," *ABD* 1:755–61 (755).

71. Mitchell, *The Meaning of BRK*, 174.

72. Ibid., 83. Cf. Richard S. Briggs, "Speech-Act Theory," in *Words and the Word: Explorations in Biblical Interpretation and Literary Theory* (ed. David J. Firth and Jamie A. Grant; Leicester: Apollos, 2008), 75–108 (83–84).

73. Fretheim, "Genesis," 538–39.

74. Fretheim, "Which Blessing?," 279–91.

success in the sociopolitical sphere, which all of God's creatures can mediate and experience independent of their knowledge of God."[75] This is important for Fretheim because he feels that the blessing of Jacob by Isaac in Gen 27:27–29 contains only the second of these; the first is commended by Abraham to God in 28:3–4, and then eventually given by God in 28:13–15.[76] In this sense, the blessings of Gen 27 represent a father blessing his children—no less and no more.

What about the latter phrases of 27:29, which seem to allude to the Abrahamic blessing being passed to Jacob? Fretheim notes that it may be possible to distinguish between communal promises and personal promises. "The last two phrases of 27:29 do refer to 12:3, but this is the only time they are recalled in Genesis and hence not integral to the 'blessing of Abraham.' It may be a more personal reference."[77]

Fretheim gives several more points to bolster his argument. First, Jacob later tries to give back this blessing (often translated as "gift") in ch. 33, which leads Fretheim to believe it was never the blessing of Abraham which he stole. And second, he notes that some understand Isaac's language of wanting to give Esau a "personal" blessing (27:4) as proof that it was never going to be the promise of Abraham.[78]

> Even if the deception had not been attempted and Isaac had actually blessed Esau, that act would not have foreclosed what God did in chapter 28. Isaac's blessing of Esau would not have constituted a continuation of God's promises to Abraham and himself. That happens only later after Isaac commends him to God. If Isaac were reserving the constitutive blessing for Jacob all along, that would help explain why he commends Jacob to God without any reference to the deception. Isaac's experience was that God rather than his father or grandfather had transmitted the blessing. Nothing indicates that Isaac now thought that this was to be a human rather than a divine task.[79]

What does Fretheim say regarding the fulfillment of the oracles and blessings concerning the sons of Isaac?

> It is often noted that God's oracle to Rebecca and Isaac's blessing seem to contradict Jacob's later serving Esau and bowing down to him... Moreover, in no instance does Esau "bow down" or "serve" Jacob. But these texts should occasion no such difficulty, for neither God's oracle nor Jacob's blessing is understood to have set the future in concrete or in

75. Ibid., 281.
76. Ibid., 281–82.
77. Ibid., 282.
78. Ibid., 289.
79. Ibid., 290.

detail in the first place. The texts from chapters 32–33 are one more indication that God's oracle and Isaac's blessing do not do what some have claimed for them. Indeed, such a lack of 'fulfillment" is what readers should be prepared to find following a divine oracle or a human blessing! Even if the blessing cannot be revoked, this does not mean its content will inevitably be realized.[80]

Fretheim's reading is important, in that it deals with Gen 27 in light of the other blessings which Jacob receives, something which many commentators simply ignore.[81] One issue with this reading, however, has to do with the complex and ambiguous relationship between divine and human action in the ancestral narratives. Take, for instance, the other sibling blessing narratives discussed above. In the case of Abraham's sons, we have both pre-birth divine oracles to Hagar and Abraham (Gen 16 for Ishmael, Gen 17 for Isaac), and what appear to be post-birth divine blessings (Gen 17 and 21 for Ishmael, given indirectly to his parents, and Gen 26 for Isaac); however, we have no paternal blessing of the sons. Then, when an elderly Jacob blesses his sons in Gen 48–49, there is no divine blessing passed directly to any son, only the blessing of the father. As such, it seems that Jacob's blessing in Gen 48 is the final word on the matter.

Consequently, while Fretheim's reading here is thought-provoking, his attempt to differentiate between the blessings seems perhaps too prescriptive based on the surrounding sibling narratives. Moreover, his argument seems to minimize the complex and symbiotic relationship between divine and human action that is often present (and unexplained) in the ancestral narratives.

Where does this leave us? While these blessings are obviously from Isaac to his sons, they also appear to establish the continued promised line of Abraham.[82] As is so often the case, it is the ambiguous relationship between human and divine action and the lack of clear distinctions that makes these texts so complex. One could say that God's subsequent blessing of Jacob in Gen 28 is a reaffirmation of the outcome of Gen 27, in spite of the treachery. As von Rad writes, "The narrator is convinced that ultimately in the human struggle for the blessing of the dying man divine plans are being worked out, and he intends to show it… The story reckons with an act of God that sovereignly takes the most ambiguous human act and incorporates it into its plans."[83]

80. Ibid., 287–88.
81. For example, Westermann, Gunkel, and Sarna are all silent on the matter, or presume the patriarchal blessing is at stake in Gen 27.
82. Levenson, *Death*, 59–60.
83. Von Rad, *Genesis*, 280.

7. Genesis 27: Preliminary Conclusions

This chapter highlighted Isaac's pronouncements to his sons in Gen 27. A survey of the history of its interpretation showed the broad range of ways in which Gen 27 has been read, and served to highlight the complexity of these texts. We then explored three further areas: the literary and syntactical issues, the contextual elements, and the nature of familial blessing in the ancestral narratives. Finally, we looked at the nature and source of Isaac's blessings.

What does this scene add to our understanding of Esau in terms of his broader canonical portrayal? When read in light of Gen 25, the larger storyline is clearly moving in a direction whereby Jacob has displaced Esau, both within the family, and in the larger context of the succession of the Abrahamic blessing. That being said, I have argued that Isaac's pronouncements to both his sons in Gen 27 should be understood as blessings. Jacob's is superior, without doubt. But Esau's need not be read as a curse or "anti-blessing."

That brings us back to the issue of election. When we understand Isaac's pronouncements as blessings for both Jacob and Esau, we can see that election need not entail a scarcity of blessing. As Fretheim writes, "Divine election does not include a corner on participation in the goodness of God's creation. God's creative activity is ongoing and, through acts of blessing, provides a life-giving, life-enhancing context for all creatures."[84] Though Esau is the unchosen son, he is blessed nonetheless. And while he may be rightfully displeased, this does not negate that there is blessing and a future for the son who is passed over.

EXCURSUS: BIRTHRIGHT AND BLESSING

This chapter has focused on Isaac's pronouncements to his sons in Gen 27. In the previous chapter we touched on Jacob's acquisition of Esau's birthright. Before moving on, it may be helpful to unpack the relationship of these two issues in the Jacob/Esau narratives.

Some commentators simply forgo commenting on the interrelationship of the birthright and blessing, deciding either that there is not enough information provided or that it is not relevant to the reader. Sarna, for example, notes the following concerning Gen 27: "The birthright is not an issue here, and its relationship to the blessing is unclear. Apparently, they were separate institutions. Nothing is said about the disposition of property, and it is striking that Esau expected to receive the

84. Fretheim, "Which Blessing?," 281.

blessing even though he admitted to having lost the birthright."[85] Others, however, have made a concerted effort to understand the relationship of these various issues and what is at stake in Gen 27. I have isolated three examples which seem worthy of mention.

a. *Variant Traditions*

The first approach, exemplified in source-critical scholarship, sees the birthright and the blessing as two originally distinct traditions that told of Jacob usurping Esau's place as the firstborn, and which were later brought together. Gunkel states this explicitly, with little explanation: "Originally the two accounts [Gen 25 and 27] were variants. 'Blessing' and 'birthright' are actually identical."[86] Greenspahn gives textual evidence for originally separate settings of the birthright and blessing scenes:

> Several similarities between them suggest that they may be variants of a common, earlier tradition about how Jacob had come to take Esau's place: Food plays a central role in both, as does Esau's hunting in the fields. Death is also a presence, with Isaac's imminent fate...rhetorically balanced by Esau's observation, "I am about to die..." (25:32)... Rather than progressing from Esau's sale of the birthright under duress to Jacob's exploitation of that status to gain his brother's blessing as well, the narrative seems to have joined two quite separate stories without harmonizing them entirely.[87]

There is an appealing element to this interpretation, particularly because the birthright is a relatively underdeveloped idea in the Hebrew Bible. However, as Fishbane and others have shown, there is a great deal of narrative symmetry and thematic coherence in the Jacob Cycle, and the received form of the text thus deserves greater attention.[88]

b. *Character-based Interpretations*

A second interpretive approach can be seen in readings that are concerned with the issue of the characterization of Jacob and Esau. This approach is not overly concerned with differentiating between the birthright and blessing because what is at stake is the suitability of the characters for these designations.

An example of this is an argument of causation, which states that Esau lost out on the blessing in Gen 27 because of his actions in forfeiting the birthright in Gen 25. This can be seen in how Heb 12:16–17 understands these stories: "See that no one is sexually immoral, or is godless like Esau, who for a single meal sold his inheritance rights (τὰ πρωτοτόκια ἑαυτοῦ). Afterward, as you know, when he wanted to inherit this blessing (τὴν εὐλογίαν), he was rejected. He could bring about no change of mind, though he sought the blessing with tears." A similar understanding is found in the work of Steinmetz, who holds that Esau does not understand the nature of the birthright and blessing, nor the fact that they go together. Without further

85. Sarna, *Genesis*, 189.
86. Gunkel, *Genesis*, 306.
87. Greenspahn, *When Brothers*, 125.
88. Fishbane, *Biblical Text*, 40–62.

explanation she writes, "Esau lacks a sense of destiny, and so the birthright is not significant to him, and the blessing is not appropriate for him."[89]

One might well assume on an initial reading of Gen 25 and 27 that causation is at work here. Yet the text of the Hebrew Bible never makes this connection. Moreover, Esau claims that he was deceived twice by his brother (27:36), and Daube and others have shown that the encounter in Gen 25 can indeed be read this way.[90] The point here is that if the issue of character is at stake, surely Jacob is just as unfit for both the birthright and blessing as his brother.

Another character-based interpretation sees Jacob as a trickster. This follows on from the previous idea, because in this view Jacob's deceitful actions are not seen as wrong, but would have been applauded by the ancient audience, who appreciated these types of characters. Indeed, God's sympathies are with those the story portrays as wise and not those who are foolishly duped.[91]

Again, this seems like a reasonable understanding of these texts because the Bible so often withholds statements of judgment concerning the ethical actions of its characters. And yet, studies highlighting inner-biblical exegesis make it clear that in general the biblical traditions look unfavorably on Jacob's actions in Gen 27. Fishbane has noted that the Laban narratives within the Jacob Cycle give "Jacob his comeuppance and circumspectly redresses the injustice of his original act of deceit."[92] Levenson, meanwhile, has shown that the prophets were no strangers to Jacob's acts of deceit and were not afraid to comment on the issue (e.g. Jer 9:3–5; Mal 3:6–9).[93] Indeed, for Levenson, Greenspahn and others, this is one of the keys to understanding the entire Hebrew Bible: God's election of Israel and its ancestors was prior to and *in spite of* their multitudinous shortcomings.[94]

c. *Differentiating Between Birthright and Blessing*
Greenspahn presents a third option by differentiating between the birthright and the blessing. According to Greenspahn, Jacob was due the double portion of the inheritance after purchasing the birthright from Esau in Gen 25; but even so, both brothers would have had an inheritance of some sort, as the double share implies that there is something for everyone. Instead, what is at stake in Gen 27 is the destiny of the brothers; it revolves around the bigger idea of blessing. Thus, according to Greenspahn, "Esau was not disinherited, nor Jacob granted *patria potestas*."[95] He explains:

89. Devora Steinmetz, *From Father to Son: Kinship, Conflict and Continuity in Genesis* (LCBI; Louisville: Westminster John Knox, 1991), 97–98.

90. Daube, "How Esau," 70–75.

91. See especially Niditch, *Underdogs*, 99–101; and Nahum M. Sarna, *Understanding Genesis: The Heritage of Biblical Israel* (New York: Schocken, 1970), 188. The targumim make similar claims, often replacing any mention of Jacob's deceit in Gen 27 with "wisdom." See Marcus, "Traditional Jewish," 293–306.

92. Fishbane, *Biblical Text*, 55.

93. Levenson, *Death*, 62–64; cf. Greenspahn, *When Brothers*, 129.

94. This seems also to be the thrust of Paul's argument when he invokes Jacob and Esau in Rom 9:10–13: God's election was and is not earned.

95. Greenspahn, *When Brothers*, 56.

[A]ctual leadership and inheritance are not the real focus of these stories at all. As they repeatedly make clear, what is at stake in the patriarchal tales is neither property nor office, but the transmission of a blessing… It is this which resolves the nettlesome legal problem of how the Bible could tolerate Jacob's keeping a blessing he had fraudulently obtained… However, fraud need not be a concern, since it is not a legal proceeding that these stories describe nor, for the most part, the transfer of property. As is clearly stated, their focus is a blessing, a theme that dominates the book of Genesis.[96]

These blessings, according to Greenspahn, do not necessarily offer the patriarchs any obvious benefit. This implies that Isaac's words to Jacob in 27:29, "be lord over your brothers," were not dealing with the issue of succession at all; in fact, Greenspahn notes that Jacob, "despite all that the story has led us to expect, is never placed above Esau at all, but only given a vague and generic kind of superiority… Significantly, neither this nor anything else foretold by the story was actually fulfilled during Jacob and Esau's lifetimes."[97] Greenspahn argues that the only real assurance in these blessings has to do with *descendant*s who will be numerous and perhaps powerful:

Being favored with a blessing—a theological category rather than a legal one—means being an ancestor of Israel, marking the line through which the people traced their descent and justifying the thread of the biblical account… Essentially retrospective, they explain for later generations how God had determined those through whom the line would continue. Whether primogeniture prevailed in ancient Israel or not has little to do with the thrust of these stories, whose focus is religious rather than legal.[98]

Greenspahn's interpretation has much to commend itself. His research on the firstborn is intriguing; he helpfully distinguishes between the birthright and the blessing, and also highlights the fact that the blessing of Gen 27 was not an "all or nothing" scenario, for either brother. And Greenspahn seems like he is heading in the right direction by noting the blessings are theological and that election is an important motif in this.

Yet there are less persuasive elements in Greenspahn's reading as well. For instance, his distinction between the legal and the theological seems forced, and, as a result of this, he appears to short-change the binding dimensions of Gen 27. For instance, what about the dying father, the importance of the ritual meal, and the irrevocability of the blessing? Do these not hint at the fact that there was some binding element to the pronouncements? There is, no doubt, a bigger picture in view of Jacob and Esau's descendants; yet to speak of these blessings as statements of destiny with no legal ramifications seems insufficient. As such, we would do well to keep in mind the fact that, as noted above, these pronouncements are illocutionary utterances with societal implications, and they need to be understood as such.[99]

---

96. Ibid., 55–56.
97. Ibid., 118–19.
98. Ibid., 56.
99. See Briggs, "Speech-Act Theory," 83–84.

d. *Birthright and Blessing: Preliminary Conclusions*
In light of the above discussion, I would suggest the following as a helpful way
forward in understanding the relationship of the birthright and blessing. To begin
with, while inversion of the birth order and the theme of the election of the younger
sibling is without doubt a major thread in the Hebrew Bible, the birthright as such is
not necessarily so. Thus, this cycle of stories is in a sense anomalous, and the interrelationship of blessing and birthright is on the whole underdeveloped in the Hebrew
Bible, something which should be kept in mind.

Nevertheless, taking on board the discussions noted above (primarily Greenspahn), a synchronic reading could run along these lines: Esau sells his rights of the
firstborn (בכרה) to Jacob, swearing an oath to confirm the transaction (Gen 25:29–
34). In light of Deut 21:15–17, it seems best to understand this as solely the double
portion of the inheritance. In the words of Tsevat, "Esau sold this special portion and
nothing else... Esau's rank and position are not affected by this transaction, as chap.
27 shows quite clearly."[100] When Isaac wishes to bless his elder son with his "deathbed" blessing, even though the birthright had been sold, both brothers (and their
mother) think this blessing of Isaac is valuable and worth obtaining (Gen 27:5–10).
Esau, in fact, seems to expect this blessing, and is outraged when it is stolen out
from underneath him. Here Esau also makes it explicitly clear that he has now been
deceived twice by his brother, again distinguishing between the birthright and
blessing (Gen 27:36): "He has deceived me these two times: he took my birthright
(בכרתי), and behold, now he has taken my blessing (ברכתי)!" Thus, reading the
stories as a whole, it seems the two elements of birthright and blessing can be
distinguished.[101]

Consequently, the transfer of the birthright seems to have given Jacob the larger
portion of the inheritance; the rights of the firstborn had been transferred. And yet,
the father still had a blessing for his sons, which Esau expected and which all
involved thought was worth pursuing. This is not to say that the father had one
blessing; as argued above, there was not a scarcity of blessing. What was at stake
was the *better* blessing. However, the blessings which are given are binding, and
cannot simply be undone. Though Esau is not left empty-handed, he can reclaim
neither "his" birthright nor "his" blessing.

There is, then, in the world of the text, some sort of symbiotic relationship
between the birthright and the blessing: both are aspects of Esau's displacement,
even if the text is not completely clear on the details. However, one can begin to
understand Esau's angry reaction in Gen 27:41, even if Isaac's pronouncement to
him in 27:39–40 is understood as a "lesser" blessing: Jacob not only has the double
share of the family inheritance and the honors of family succession, but he also has
the blessing of his father, and appears to be the vessel to carry on the chosen line. It
is now clear that Esau is indeed the unchosen son. Levenson draws out the theological implications of this symbiotic and yet enigmatic relationship:

100.   Tsevat, *TDOT* 2:126.
101.   A similar understanding is put forward by Baruch Levine, "Firstborn,"
EncJud 6:1306–8.

In the case of the Patriarchal narratives of Genesis, the urgent and constantly repeating issue of which son is chosen cannot be disengaged from
the painful question of which shall inherit the status of the first-born, or,
to put it differently, which is the beloved son? For in the narratives of
Israel's origins, chosenness means having the status of the one upon
whose very life God has acquired an absolute claim.[102]

Jacob is the beloved son, the one chosen by God. And, in spite of Esau's rage, Jacob
escapes with his life intact. The question remains for the reader, however, as to what
Esau's response will be should the brothers ever meet again.

102. Levenson. *Death*, 60.

Chapter 5

GENESIS 32–33: THE REUNION OF JACOB AND ESAU

1. *Introduction*

After the tumultuous events of Gen 27, Jacob leaves his homeland and is gone for twenty years. The text tells us much about Jacob's life in these years: his encounter with God at Bethel; his two marriages and tenuous relationship with his uncle Laban; the birth of his children; and his business acumen leading to considerable possessions. However, the text tells us nothing about Esau during this time period. We are left with the depiction of his anger and a desire to kill his brother (27:41), as well as his marriage to a daughter of Ishmael (28:6–9).[1] It is not until YHWH tells Jacob that it is time for him to return to the land of his fathers that the reader is reminded again, somewhat implicitly, of Esau (31:3).

Genesis 32–33 outlines Jacob's reunion with Esau and his return to the land of promise in a narrative that is complex on a number of levels. To begin with, it is a lengthy episode by Hebrew Bible standards, and this should clue us in to the importance it plays in the larger Jacob Cycle. Secondly, this story is complex because it is permeated with ambiguity and tension. The uncertainty of the motives of the characters, coupled with the anxiety related to the relationship in need of resolution, leads to a suspenseful two chapters. Finally, the story is complex because of the literary sophistication and wordplays which it employs, requiring a sustained sensitivity to the text.

In order to deal adequately with these complexities and how they relate to the present study, I will break this account into three sections, and explore the various themes therein: the preparation (Gen 32:1–33); the reunion (Gen 33:1–11); and the subsequent separation of the brothers (Gen 33:12–20).

---

1. Esau's marriages are dealt with in the next chapter.

2. *The Preparation (Genesis 32)*

Genesis 32 is a prelude to the reunion which will take place in ch. 33. This chapter can be broken down into several sub-sections:[2] Jacob's encounter with the angels of God at Mahanaim (32:1–3); Jacob's acts of preparation (32:4–22); and finally, Jacob's night struggle with the stranger at Peniel (32:23–33).

a. *Mahanaim (32:1–3)*

Genesis 32 begins with the final separation of Jacob and his family from Laban, following on from the escape of Jacob and his family in ch. 30, and the subsequent encounter with Laban in ch. 31. What has been a tense and suspense-filled episode ends with Laban making a peace treaty with Jacob (31:51–54), followed by Laban blessing his daughters and grandchildren, and returning home (32:1). This encounter with Laban functions on several levels in the larger narrative. First, the suspenseful encounter that ends with a relatively positive outcome, but still has the parties going their separate ways, may foreshadow the Esau encounter which resolves in a similar fashion. Second, Jacob's encounters with Laban and Esau envelope his encounter with the stranger at Peniel, and so together may reinforce the fact that Jacob (and now Israel) is one who does indeed struggle with both God and man (32:28).[3] And finally, as several commentators have pointed out, these reconciliatory encounters with both Laban and Esau are important for Jacob's story because they are the two relational conflicts that most need repairing. There are several important loose ends which need to be tied up before Jacob's narrative can move on.[4]

In 32:2 we are told that Jacob went on his way, after which the text understatedly comments that, "angels of God (מלאכי אלהים) met him."[5]

---

2.   The verse ordering in the Hebrew and English editions of Gen 32 are slightly different, with ET (following the LXX and Vulgate, among others) one verse behind the Hebrew. The present work will use the Hebrew ordering.

3.   On the similarities of the separations from Laban and Esau, see I. L. Seeligmann, "Hebräische Erzählung und biblische Geschichtsschreibung," *TZ* 18 (1962): 305–25 (309).

4.   Johannes Kühlewein, "Gottesfahrung und Re fungsgeschichte in der Jakob-Esau-Erzählung," in *Werden und Wirken des Alten Testaments: Festschrift für Claus Westermann zum 70. Geburtstag* (ed. Rainer Albertz et al.; Göttingen: Vandenhoeck & Ruprecht, 1980), 116–30 (118).

5.   Several targumim use this as a way to bridge the Laban and Esau encounters. When Jacob sees the angels, *Targum Neofiti* adds, "Perhaps they are messengers

When Jacob sees them, he exclaims, "This is the camp of God (מחנה אלהים)," and he names the place Mahanaim (מחנים).

There are several issues in these verses worth highlighting. First of all, while the proximity of this encounter with the struggle at Peniel might lead us to look for a connection between the two, the fact that Jacob here encounters מלאכי אלהים may in fact remind the reader of Jacob's encounter with angels of God at Bethel in Gen 28. Indeed, the only other place where מלאכי אלהים occurs is in 28:12, where it describes the angelic beings Jacob sees ascending and descending the ladder to heaven.[6] Moreover, while the verb פגע, "to meet," can denote either friendly or hostile intent, this encounter in 32:1–3, as in ch. 28, is a friendly one.[7] Thus, positive encounters with מלאכי אלהים, and with this the idea of God's presence, seem to bookend Jacob's travels away from and back to the land of promise.[8] As Fokkelman notes, "from beginning to end the Mahanaim-scene refers to and builds on the Bethel-scene… Therefore we wonder, just as Jacob has, whether his 'return to the land of his forefathers' will take place *bᵉšālōm*, as 28:21 has it, will be safe and sound."[9] This is one of the important questions that Gen 32–33 addresses.

A second issue here concerns how to best translate מלאכי אלהים. As Westermann notes, when taken in conjunction with 28:12, these are best understood as heavenly beings, and thus should be translated as "angels."[10] However, the theme of "messengers" will play a central role as ch. 32 develops, as will the idea of "camps." Hence, we do well to keep in mind the semantic range of the term מלאך, as it may point back to the angelic beings at Bethel in Gen 28, as well as hint at the messengers that Jacob himself will deploy to meet his brother.

Finally, Jacob's naming of the place as מחנים, "two camps," again foreshadows developments that will unfold in the coming chapters. As with מלאכי אלהים, מחנים here has an element of ambiguity: while it highlights Jacob's encounter with God, it also points forward to when

---

from Laban, my mother's brother, who has returned to pursue after me; or the hosts of Esau, my brother, who comes to meet me, or hosts of angels from before the Lord come to deliver me from the hands of both of them." For a similar idea, see *Targum Pseudo-Jonathan*.

6. See C. Houtman, "Jacob at Mahanaim: Some Remarks on Genesis xxxii 2–3," *VT* 28 (1978): 37–44.

7. Ibid., 37.

8. See Walton, *Thou Traveller Unknown*, 182.

9. Fokkelman, *Narrative Art*, 198.

10. Westermann, *Genesis 12–36*, 505.

Jacob will end up dividing his own camp for strategic purposes (32:8–9).[11] And again in ch. 33, Esau will use this term when questioning Jacob about the gifts which were sent ahead (33:8). Moreover, following on from this reference, the next few chapters will provide several layers of wordplay related to מחנים: מחנה, מנחה, חן, and הנה.[12] These motifs of camp(s), gift, and favor are ultimately all interrelated in this scene.

Thus, the beginning of ch. 32 does more than merely transition from the Laban narrative to the Esau encounter. It also provides, along with Gen 28, a frame for Jacob's exit from and return to the land of promise, as well as introducing several themes which will recur throughout Gen 32–33, many of which highlight the intersection of divine and human in the Jacob story.

b. *Initial Preparations (32:4–22)*
The bulk of ch. 32 outlines several steps Jacob takes in preparation for his encounter with Esau: the sending of messengers with a message for his brother, the division of his camp on hearing the response of his messengers, his prayer to the God of his fathers, and the sending of gifts to Esau. However, the first item worth noting is the reference to Esau himself.

(1) *Esau, Seir, Edom (32:4)*. After the naming of Mahanaim, Jacob sends a message ahead to Esau. This reference to Esau is the first time that Jacob's brother has been mentioned since 28:6–9, which recounts Esau taking one of Ishmael's daughters as a wife. Here in 32:4 we learn that Esau is "in the land of Seir (ארצה שעיר), the field of Edom (שדה אדום)." What are we to make of this geographical note?

The text implies that Esau has moved on to the land which his ancestors would later inhabit. Interpreters throughout history have filled in this gap in various ways. Driver comments that because we are not told of Esau's migration to Edom until 36:6–8 by P, J must picture that migration having happened earlier.[13] Calvin had already pursued this line of thought:

---

11. See Mark G. Brett, *Genesis: Procreation and the Politics of Identity* (OTR; London: Routledge, 2000), 98.

12. Blum, *Die Komposition*, 142.

13. Driver, *Genesis*, 291. Source critics have highlighted other issues. Bartlett, following Gunkel and Skinner, notes that the use of Seir in 33:14 and 16 means that the use of Edom in 32:4 is most likely a gloss. See Bartlett, "Land of Seir," 10.

> It now happened, by the providence of God, that Esau, having left his
> father, had gone to Mount Seir of his own accord; and had thus departed
> from the land of promise, by which means the possession of it would
> remain void for the posterity of Jacob... For it was not to be believed that
> he had changed his habitation, either because he was compelled by his
> father's command, or because he was willing to be accounted inferior to
> his brother. I rather conjecture that he had become greatly enriched, and
> that this induced him to leave his father's house.[14]

However, these references to Seir and Edom work on a literary level as
well. Sarna points out some of the resonances:

> The three Hebrew words *se'ir*, *sadeh*, and *'edom* are deliberately used to evoke
> memories of the hostile relations with Esau, the one covered with
> hair (*se'ar*), a man of the outdoors (*sadeh*) of ruddy complexion (*'admoni*),
> who came in from the field (*sadeh*) and begged for the red stuff (*'adom*),
> and whose hairiness (*sa'ir*) played a crucial role in the deception that
> precipitated Jacob's flight to Laban.[15]

Along with these, another important element, often ignored by commentators, is the narrator's reference to Esau as Jacob's brother (אחיו) in
32:4. Not only does the reference to brotherhood remind the reader of the
earlier familial strife of Gen 25 and 27, but the brotherhood motif will be
an important one as the story in ch. 32–33 unfolds.

Finally, in 32:4 we encounter the first use of the root פנים, which plays
an important role in these chapters.[16] Here we find the root with the
prepositional *lamed*, as לפניו, explaining that Jacob sent his messengers
"ahead of him." This idea of Jacob's position in relation to his "camps"—
behind and before them—will play an important role as the story
develops. But, as we will see, פנים will be used in a variety of ways as a
leitwort throughout these two chapters.

(2) *Messengers and Message (32:4–6)*. Sending messengers was not
uncommon in a predominantly illiterate era, and messengers are prevalent throughout the Hebrew Bible.[17] Thus, after his encounter with the
מלאכי אלהים, the first thing Jacob does is send messengers of his own
(מלאכים) to his brother Esau. However, as noted above, this double use

---

14. Calvin, *Genesis*, 186–87. While this may seem to paint Esau in a relatively
positive light, Calvin goes on to note that this move was done impetuously, to get
away from his parents and have his own life.

15. Sarna, *Genesis*, 224.

16. There are 15 usages between 32:1–33:14. On פנים and its various derivatives,
see H. Simian-Yofre, "פנים," *TDOT* 11:589–615.

17. See Westermann, *Genesis 12–36*, 506, and the literature there cited.

of "messenger" might remind the reader that the human and divine are intimately linked in this narrative, a theme which will continue throughout ch. 32–33.

What is immediately striking about Jacob's message are the titles which he applies to Esau and himself. He refers to Esau, not as his brother, but as לאדני, "my lord." And conversely, Jacob refers to himself as Esau's servant, עבדך. Again, this is conspicuous because in the previous verse (32:4) the narrator has referred to Esau as Jacob's brother, and when the servants of Jacob return having delivered his message, they refer to Esau as Jacob's brother as well (32:7). At this point it is worth noting that the narrator puts the word "brother" on the lips of everyone except Jacob.

The message goes on to give an extremely abbreviated description of Jacob's life since he last saw his brother. He has been staying all these years with their uncle Laban, and has accumulated various belongings: cattle, donkeys, sheep, goats, and servants. The message ends in 32:6 declaring Jacob's purpose: "I am sending to declare to my lord (לאדני), that I might find favor (למצא־חן) in your eyes." There are two salient issues here. First of all, what is meant by "finding favor"? And secondly, why does Jacob catalogue his possessions? What are his intentions, and how does he think this will lead to the favor he so desires?[18]

The term חן carries the idea of "acceptance." In several ancient languages, this term is connected to the face and eyes, as favor was thought to be shown on the face. "To show one's face...means to be favorably disposed toward a person. In anger one's face is hidden."[19] In the realm of human relationships, favor can be sought as a gift, and when sought, often includes the elements of giving gifts, deferential language, and prostration.[20] The scene in Gen 32–33 fits many of these descriptions:

> The account of Jacob and Esau in Gen. 32f. takes us to the pinnacle of the OT teaching on *ḥēn*... The story contains four quotations from Jacob in which he seeks *ḥēn* from Esau... This *ḥēn* is the goal of his activity (32:6,8[5,7]), namely a permanent change of disposition or attitude on Esau's part... He has no request to make; instead he comes with gifts to

18. Another issue on which the text is silent is why Jacob omits reference to his wives and children.

19. D. N. Freedman and J. Lundbom, "חנן," *TDOT* 5:22–36 (24); Terence E. Fretheim, "חנן," *NIDOTTE* 2:203–6; William L. Reed, "Some Implications of HEN for Old Testament Religion," *JBL* 73 (1954): 36–41

20. Freedman and Lundbom, *TDOT* 5:26–27. See Gen 34:11; 42:21; 2 Sam 14:22; Ruth 2:10; Ps 31:10; Esth 4:8.

give, and he compliments Esau with this phrase by urging him to accept these (33:10). Jacob knows that if Esau accepts the gifts it will demonstrate that Esau has accepted him as well, i.e. that Jacob has indeed found favor in his brother's eyes.[21]

However, this does not answer the question regarding Jacob's disposition. How are we to understand Jacob's words and intentions in 32:5–6? There are various ways of interpreting these verses; for the sake of convenience, we will divide them into those who see Jacob as showing (1) humility, or (2) strength and wealth.

Those who identify humility in Jacob's words focus on the use of titles ("lord" and "servant") and Jacob's explicit statement that he is seeking Esau's favor. Driver observes that here we see a Jacob who is "very humble and conciliatory."[22] Indeed, several scholars have noted that Jacob's deferential language goes well beyond ancient oriental courtesy between siblings.[23] Spero has offered the fullest explanation along these lines:

> Jacob reasoned that Esau believed that his (Jacob's) actions in both the *bechora* and *bracha* events were driven by an unbridled ambition to rule over him, to become the head of the family after Isaac, with its material and social benefits. Therefore, in this conciliatory message Jacob: (1) Describes himself as *servant to my lord Esau*—indicating that he does not consider himself superior and has no desire to rule; (2) states that he has become independently wealthy and has no need for the family inheritance; and (3) points out that by being banished from their parents' home for so long, he has been amply "punished" for his alleged misdeeds.[24]

21. Freedman and Lundbom, *TDOT* 5:29. As Zimmerli notes, Jacob's use of this language shows at some level his intention to reconcile with his brother. H. Conzelmann and W. Zimmerli, "χάρις," *TDNT* 9:376–87 (380).

22. Driver, *Genesis*, 291.

23. Wenham, *Genesis 16–50*, 290; Jacob, *Das erste Buch der Tora*, 630.

24. Shubert Spero, "Jacob and Esau: The Relationship Reconsidered," *JBQ* 32 (2004): 245–50 (248). Not all commentators who subscribe to Jacob's humility here agree on the sincerity of this humility. Steinberg, for instance, comments that, "Through the servile attitude he feigns toward Esau, Jacob appears secure in the knowledge that he is presently safe from the vengeance of Esau" (Steinberg, *Kinship and Marriage*, 109). While one can indeed maintain that Jacob's humility might not be totally sincere, the idea that he feels secure and is free from fear does not make sense in the larger narrative. In reality, much of Jacob's reaction to the response he receives from his messengers seems to be predicated on fear, as will be outlined below.

Conversely, those who understand Jacob in 32:5–6 as presenting a show of strength tend to focus on the list of possessions he catalogues. Spina, for instance, understands that Jacob's servants are to inform Esau that their master has become, "fabulously wealthy and would be interested in an accommodation."[25] This is, then, a thinly disguised bribe.

Cohen offers a modifying position, seeing elements of both humility and arrogance in Jacob's message:

> Anyone in Jacob's position, pleading for his life from one whom he feared as a militant pursuer clearly intent on vengeance, would assuredly prepare every word of his plea for clemency with the greatest care and the finest attention to detail. He would couch it in the most conciliatory of terms, present himself in the most self-effacing manner possible... While all this sounds obvious, it would seem, however, that Jacob was ignorant of all those required proprieties. For his submission to Esau was couched in a manner calculated to achieve the very opposite effect: to convince Esau that his antipathy toward his brother over the matter of the birthright was fully justifiable, because clearly Jacob had no feeling of remorse in his heart, but rather the same old dogmatic self-assurance and self-justi-fication for having seized the birthright.[26]

Cohen goes on to maintain that Jacob's speech seems to be "calculated to do no more than show Esau that the birthright and its blessings were truly fulfilled to the letter, leaving Jacob a man of great substance and self-sufficiency quite able to bestow substantial alms upon his less fortunate brother."[27] Yet, even in the midst of all this posturing, Jacob uses the language of lord and servant. Why? This, according to Cohen, is another example of Jacob's ambivalence coming through. Cohen's atti-tude and actions throughout these two chapters reveal the same mixed signals.[28]

Thus, Jacob's message in 32:5–6 has been understood as both a posture of humility, as a show of strength and a possible bribe, or as a confused combination of the two. Whatever the case, the text does not

---

25. Spina, *Faith*, 22. It is interesting that *Targum Pseudo-Jonathan* offers an antithetical understanding to this one regarding Jacob's possessions. *Targum Pseudo-Jonathan* amends 32:6 to read: "*And of all those things with which my father blessed me I have nothing*; I have *but a few* oxen and asses, sheep and menservants and maidservants, and I have sent to tell my master *that that blessing has not profited me*, and so that I might find mercy in your eyes, *that you might not bear a grudge against me because of it*."

26. Jeffrey M. Cohen, "The Jacob–Esau Reunion," *JBQ* 21 (1993): 159–63 (159–60).

27. Ibid., 160.

28. Ibid., 161.

inform us of Jacob's motives. The reader is left with perhaps the same ambivalence that Jacob himself feels about the ensuing encounter.

(3) *Esau's Response and Jacob's Division of the Camp (32:7–9)*. The story jumps directly to the response Jacob's messengers bring to him. Again, reference to Esau as Jacob's brother comes from the lips of someone other than Jacob himself. The response is short, and has two elements. First, Esau is coming to meet Jacob (הלך לקראתך). And second, Esau has four hundred men with him.

As Fokkelman notes, Esau is acting indirectly at this juncture in the narrative and, along with Jacob, the reader is unsure of Esau's motives. The fact that Esau is "coming to meet" his brother is not especially illuminating, as the root קרא can be construed as friendly or hostile.[29] The four hundred men, however, does seem to have ominous overtones. Heard notes in passing that if Esau is semi-nomadic, in the same vein as Abraham and Isaac, this may simply be the size of his traveling group, in which case he is bringing his family to greet Jacob.[30] However, elsewhere in the Hebrew Bible, this is the approximate size of a militia (see 1 Sam 22:2; 25:13).[31] Westermann goes so far as to describe Esau as the leader of a "mercenary army."[32]

The text never does inform the reader regarding Esau's intentions with this large group. If anything, this mention of the four hundred men and Esau's approach is intentionally ambiguous, and is used as a rhetorical device to heighten the sense of tension in the scene in light of the brothers' history.[33] And in this sense, it works. Just as Jacob's message to his brother contained an element of ambiguity, so Esau's approach is ambiguous. Jacob, however, assumes the worst. Afraid and exceedingly distressed, Jacob divides into two camps (לשני מחנות) all of the people and possessions with him (32:8). The reader is informed of Jacob's reasoning: "He said, 'If Esau comes to the one camp and attacks it, then the remaining camp will escape'" (32:9).

Jacob's division of his group into two "camps" reminds the reader of his encounter at Mahanaim. Yet while his encounter with the messengers of God was a peaceful one, the response from his own messengers leads to Jacob essentially cutting his losses in case of emergency. If the encounter with God's messengers was meant to be reassuring on Jacob's

29. See BDB, 896–97.
30. See Heard, *Dynamics*, 128–30.
31. Sarna, *Genesis*, 224.
32. Westermann, *Genesis 12–36*, 507.
33. Spina, *Faith*, 22–23.

return to his homeland, it is not working. And this leads back to our earlier discussion on Jacob's motives. The text makes clear in 32:9 that the overriding motivation for Jacob's actions is fear.

Yet, if Esau has ill intentions, why does he spare the messengers?[34] Why does he not respond with a message of his own? Again, Esau's actions are "off stage," which may serve to remind us that this narrative is ultimately about Jacob, and to focus the reader on his actions. And what the reader sees is familiar: Jacob is a man with a plan. First he sends a message to his brother. Then he divides his camp. The next step will be to seek divine assistance.

(4) *Jacob's Prayer (32:10–13)*. In 32:10–13, the text abruptly shows Jacob breaking into prayer. The prayer consists of (1) invoking the God of his fathers; (2) reminding God that it was the deity himself who told him to return to his homeland; (3) a statement of his own unworthiness and God's faithfulness; (4) a plea to save him from Esau's attacks on himself and his family; (5) another reminder to God, this time of his promise of blessing.

The ambiguity which has been traced throughout the narrative so far continues in Jacob's prayer. On the one hand, this is the first recorded prayer of Jacob, and as such may point to a development in his character.[35] Jacob is deferential to God, acknowledging God's faithfulness and provision, and stating his own unworthiness in relation to God's kindness (חסד) and faithfulness (אמת).[36] He even refers to Esau as "my brother," the first such sign of kinship from Jacob thus far. Moreover, Jacob seems to show a genuine concern for the well-being of his family in the upcoming encounter with Esau. On the other hand, Jacob obviously wants something out of this, which may make his deference suspect.[37] We find here no penitence or remorse, no admission of guilt. Indeed, Jacob is very clear with God: he is afraid (ירא) and wants protection. Jacob is thus not above requesting protection by reminding God of his promises of blessing, and that it was God himself who told Jacob to return home.[38]

---

34. Fokkelman, *Narrative Art*, 201.

35. Moberly, *Genesis 12–50*, 31.

36. Sarna calls this prayer, "an expression of absolute faith in a living God" (*Genesis*, 225).

37. Brueggemann, *Genesis*, 264.

38. See Spina, *Faith*, 23.

(5) *Sending of Gifts (32:14–22)*. Following on from his prayer, the text tells us that Jacob spent the night there. Yet Jacob's preparations for his encounter with Esau continue: we are told that he prepared a gift to send ahead to his brother.[39]

The gift consists of a substantial number of animals, separated into their respective herds. Jacob instructs the servants to "go ahead of me" (לְפָנַי), and to keep some distance between the various herds (32:17). The animals are to arrive in succession, each herd led by a servant of Jacob with a similar message for Esau: these are a gift (מִנְחָה) from Jacob, and he is coming behind us. In these instructions Jacob gives to his servants, the ambivalence of Jacob's actions and thought processes are on full display. When addressing the servants, he refers to Esau as "my brother" (32:18), using the language of kinship. Yet in the message they are to relay to Esau, the language once again has Jacob referring to himself as "your servant" and Esau as "my lord" (32:19).

The narrative once again gives us direct insight into Jacob's intentions. In 32:21 we are told, "He said, 'I will cover his face (אֲכַפְּרָה פָנָיו) with these gifts (בַּמִּנְחָה) I am sending ahead of me (לְפָנַי). After this, I will see his face (אֶרְאֶה פָנָיו), and perhaps he will lift up my face (יִשָּׂא פָנָי).'" This verse raises several important issues: What does it mean to "cover the face" and "lift up the face"? And how might the giving of gifts accomplish this?

As several commentators have noted, it is at this stage that we start to encounter the *leitwort* פָּנִים with greater frequency.[40] In fact, this root occurs five times in 32:21 alone. Jacob states that his desire is to אֲכַפְּרָה פָנָיו, literally "cover/wipe the face" of Esau, a phrase which is usually translated as "appease" or "pacify."[41] This is the Piel form of

---

39. Without forcing the issue too far, the fact that this gift-giving comes directly after his prayer might give us pause if tempted to see Jacob's prayer as a model of "absolute faith" (Sarna, *Genesis*, 225).

40. See Levenson, "Genesis," 67; Fokkelman, *Narrative Art*, 206; Blum, *Die Komposition*, 143.

41. The NASB opts for "appease" while the NIV uses "pacify." There is some debate as to how כפר is best understood conceptually, and this can be seen in various interpreters of Gen 32:21. Westermann notes that when כפר is used alongside פָּנִים, it implies guilt. Hence, with this choice of language, Jacob is implicitly taking some responsibility for the impaired state of the relationship. He thus understands this phrase as "cover the face," as Jacob will cover Esau's face so that he no longer sees guilt. Westermann, *Genesis 12–36*, 510. Averbeck insists this is better understood as Jacob wiping the anger off of Esau's face, a similar sentiment being found in Prov 16:14 and in other ancient Near Eastern writings. Richard A. Averbeck, "כפר," *NIDOTTE* 2:689–710 (698). Regardless, the idea in 32:21 is fairly

כפר, usually meaning "cover over, pacify, propitiate."[42] The term כפר has sacrificial overtones, and is normally used in a cultic context, particularly in ritual passages.[43] Indeed, it is the term most often associated with the idea of atonement in the Hebrew Bible.

Jacob's hope is that once appeasement has taken place, he will then be able to see Esau's face (אראה פניו), and then perhaps Esau will lift up Jacob's face (ישא פני). To "see the face" in the Hebrew Bible can refer to a general meeting with someone, or to having access to an elevated individual.[44] It is also a common phrase used to denote a cultic encounter with a deity. Meanwhile, to "lift the face" is a figurative expression with the idea of showing consideration for, forgiving, accepting, and showing partiality. Usually the person receiving the favor is the one whose face is lifted.[45] Taken as a whole, in 32:21 the root פנים is used in several ways: we have Jacob wishing to appease (אכפרה פניו) his brother (with cultic overtones), so that when he meets him (אראה פניו), his brother will forgive him (ישא פני).

The question remains as to what role the gift giving (מנחה) plays in this pacification. There are three ways that commentators make sense of Jacob's giving gifts in order to appease his brother.[46] The first approach sees Jacob behaving according to the social customs of his day. As Gunkel notes, gift giving was common when meeting a superior (1 Sam 17:18; 2 Kgs 5:18), or if there was reason to fear (1 Sam 25:27). In Gunkel's view, Gen 43:11 and 32:17–22 encapsulate both of these traits.[47] Von Rad picks up on this, but with a sense of the inherent humor in the passage:

clear: Jacob wishes to appease or pacify Esau, in the same way that God might be appeased in a cultic context.

42. BDB, 497–98.

43. The word is used extensively in Exodus and Leviticus, as well as parts of Chronicles and Ezekiel. For an extensive overview, see Averbeck, *NIDOTTE* 2:689–710.

44. Simian-Yofre, *TDOT* 11:604. See Gen 44:23, 26; 46:30; 48:11; Exod 34:35; 2 Sam 3:13; Dan 1:10.

45. Ibid., 11:600. See Gen 19:21; Lev 19:15; Num 6:26; 1 Sam 25:35.

46. This overlooks the rabbinic tendency, as seen in *Jub.* 29:16–20, to rewrite the story as to depict Jacob sending gifts to his parents, and not Esau. As Hayward notes with regard to this tradition, "This piety toward parents contrasts with Esau's wilful behaviour in marrying a foreign wife and leaving his parents." C. T. R. Hayward, *Interpretations of the Name Israel in Ancient Judaism and Some Early Christian Writings: From Victorious Athlete to Heavenly Champion* (Oxford: Oxford University Press, 2005), 119.

47. Gunkel, *Genesis*, 347.

> To give an official gift of honor is a polite custom throughout the
> Orient... The way, however, in which Jacob staggers his gifts, letting the
> bearer announce that he, Jacob, is himself coming behind, his sending of
> another gift and still another—this way in which Jacob hopes to appease
> Esau's anger by stages must cause every reader to smile, in spite of the
> seriousness of the situation.[48]

A second understanding of Jacob's gift looks at the exchange from an
anthropological perspective. Petersen has recently proffered such an
interpretation, drawing on the work of Mauss.[49] Mauss's extensive
research on gifts showed that giving a gift often puts the recipient in debt
to the giver. In this respect, giving a gift is a power play for social
advantage. Petersen argues that Jacob's gifts were not given as a decoy
or flattery, but to "overpower Esau economically."[50]

A third approach to this passage investigates the cultic nature of the
term מנחה. As has been pointed out, cultic and sacrificial language is
already present with the term כפר. While מנחה does generally mean
"gift" or "present," it is also a term used for sacrifices, and the word may
have its roots in that context.[51] Weinfeld teases out how the secular and
sacred might be intermingled in Gen 32–33:

> This *minḥâ* and Esau's acceptance of it function representatively by
> signalling "favor" (*ḥēn*) and "favorable acceptance" (*rāṣâ*) between the
> two hostile brothers. J pointedly draws out the meaning of this *minḥâ* for
> the sphere of human relationships by using it like a sacrificial term...
> Thus even in the case of the profane *minḥâ* the term's cultic-sacral
> connotation can adroitly be brought into play; this presupposes that the
> *minḥâ* offering was accorded an extremely wide sphere of efficacy in
> mollifying the deity...and similarly presupposed such efficacy being
> operative in the secular sphere.[52]

All of these interpretations have some validity. Indeed, it may be that
what we have in these verses is a combination of all three of these ideas:
Jacob sends gifts ahead to a superior of whom he is afraid, as is the
custom of his day. He does this knowing that it might give him the upper
hand upon their meeting. And he trusts that in some way this (sacrificial?) gift will appease his brother.

---

48. Von Rad, *Genesis*, 319.
49. See Marcel Mauss, *The Gift: The Form and Reason for Exchange in Archaic
Societies* (trans. W. D. Halls; New York: W. W. Norton, 1990).
50. David L. Petersen, "Genesis and Family Values," *JBL* 124 (2005): 5–24 (20).
51. See M. Weinfeld and H.-J. Fabry, "מנחה," *TDOT* 8:407–20 (410).
52. Ibid., 8:416. Cf. Wenham, *Genesis 16–50*, 292.

The section comes to a close in 32:22 with the statement that while Jacob's gift (מנחה) went on ahead of him, he himself stayed the night in the camp (מחנה). As Gunkel and others have highlighted, we have here a wordplay on "gift" and "camp," and the two encounters—with God and Esau—of which these terms remind the reader.[53] With these preparations complete, Jacob settles in for what will turn out to be a very long night.

c. *The Struggle at Peniel (32:23–33)*

The next few verses are among the most famous in all of biblical literature. Jacob sends his family and possessions ahead of him, across the Jabbok (32:23–24), leaving him alone.[54] In 32:25 we are abruptly informed, "And a man wrestled with him until the breaking of the dawn."[55] The man cannot overpower Jacob, but then dislocates Jacob's hip. When the man asks to be released because it is daybreak, Jacob insists he will not let go until he is blessed. The man changes Jacob's name to "Israel," and eventually blesses him. However, the stranger refuses to reveal his own name to Jacob. Jacob names the site "Peniel," stating that he saw God face-to-face and lived. As the sun rises, Jacob limps away, and the scene ends with an explanation as to why Israelites do not eat the tendon attached to the socket at the hip: because this is where Jacob was touched during his struggle.

These verses understandably have captured the imagination of interpreters for millennia, and are some of the most commented on in the entire Bible.[56] The present study will limit its focus to how this scene

---

53. Gunkel, *Genesis*, 344.

54. Interestingly, the rabbis already have Esau on the mind here as well. Commenting on 32:22 and Jacob's eleven sons, Rashi writes: "But where was Dinah? He placed her in a chest and locked her in so that Esau should not set his fancy upon her (desire to marry her). On this account Jacob was punished—because he had kept her away from his brother for she might have led him back to the right *path*; she therefore fell into the power of Shechem." See *Rashi's Commentary: Genesis*, 159; cf. William T. Miller, *Mysterious Encounters at Mamre and Jabbok* (BJS 50; Chico: Scholars Press, 1984), 113.

55. There is almost certainly a play on words here. Jacob (יעקב) is wrestling (יאבק) at the Jabbok (יבק). As Sarna and others have noted, the use of this stem for "wrestle" is unique to this story (32:25, 29; see Sarna, *Genesis*, 227), and thus is almost forced in for literary purposes. For more on the various wordplays at work in this encounter, see Stanley Gevirtz, "Of Patriarchs and Puns: Joseph at the Fountain, Jacob at the Ford," *HUCA* 46 (1975): 33–54.

56. Ancient Jewish comments on this scene can be found in Miller, *Mysterious Encounters*, 97–111. See the early Christian interpretations in ibid., 119–38, and ACCS 2:218–24. Contemporary literature on this passage, particularly in light of

contributes to the narrative of Gen 32–33, with specific reference to the identity of Jacob's opponent, and the resultant effects on Jacob's character.

(1) *The Identity of Jacob's Opponent.* Because the text states quite ambiguously that "a man (אִישׁ) wrestled with him," the identity of Jacob's opponent has been the source of much speculation. We will outline four common arguments.

One of the earliest interpretations, offered in the rabbinic tradition, was that this opponent was Esau's guardian angel.[57] Jewish tradition has an aversion to anthropomorphized theophanies; this, combined with the fact that Jacob seems to hold his own in the struggle, makes the idea of the opponent being God unbearable to some. This understanding of Jacob's opponent has its merits. The fact that this "man" might be associated with Esau or his angel is not unreasonable given the preparation made by Jacob in light of an encounter with his brother earlier in the chapter. The tension in the narrative thus far might actually incline the reader to expect this to be Esau-related. Moreover, the rabbis noted the connection between Jacob's statement, "I have seen God/a god face-to-face and have lived" (32:31), and Jacob's response upon meeting Esau and being graciously received in 33:10: "To see your face is like seeing the face of God/a god."

However, this explanation is problematic on two fronts. First, the use of אלהים almost always refers to Jacob's God in the Jacob Cycle. The term occurs over fifty times between Gen 27–35, and with the exception of references to Laban's and his daughters' gods in Gen 31:30 and Gen 35:2, 4, every reference appears to be related to the God of Jacob's fathers. It would seem that Jacob's naming the place Peniel would substantiate this.[58] In the various other places which Jacob names with

<hr/>

ancient Near Eastern literature, is discussed in Esther J. Hamori, *"When Gods Were Men": The Embodied God in Biblical and Near Eastern Literature* (BZAW 384; Berlin: de Gruyter, 2008), 13–25 and 96–103.

57. See *Gen. Rab.* 72:3 and *Rashi's Commentary: Genesis*, 159. In contemporary scholarship, Sarna also espouses this view (Sarna, *Genesis*, 404). This may trace back to the text of Hos 12:4–5, which references this episode and mentions both an angel and God. In Hosea, the two seem to be used in parallel.

58. There is some textual uncertainty regarding "Peniel" here. While *BHS* uses the traditional Hebrew פְּנִיאֵל, in 32:31, a variant פְּנוּאֵל occurs in 32:32. The Vulgate, the Samaritan Pentateuch, and Peshitta versions all use the latter in v. 31 as well, and this form is also used elsewhere, in Judg 8:8 and 1 Kgs 12:25. For some reasons as to why פְּנִיאֵל is used in 32:31, see Westermann, *Genesis 12–36*, 519.

reference to his encounters (Bethel at 28:19; Mahanaim at 32:2–3; the altar at Shechem at 33:20), there is no indication that any being other than the God of his fathers is in view. A second issue which arises when we understand Jacob's opponent as an angel of Esau is what to make of the re-naming and the blessing which occurs. Sarna sees this as Esau's acquiescence of the blessing and acknowledgment that the land belongs to Jacob.[59] However, one is hard pressed to locate other instances where a blessing and re-naming occur at the hands of another god or angel. Moreover, the reiteration of Jacob's blessing and re-naming which occurs in Gen 35:9–10 seems to make clear that it is indeed the God of Jacob's fathers who has blessed and re-named Jacob, and that this is a positive change.

A second interpretive option is a religio-historical one which sees the struggle at the Jabbok as an attack by a river-spirit or demonic being who does not want Jacob to cross the river. This line of thinking is supported by Gunkel and Westermann, both of whom note that ancient sagas often connect geographical places with spirits who guard those places, or with demons who act only at night.[60] Westermann comments, "All the profound theological consequences drawn from Jacob's supposed encounter with God…have no basis in the text."[61]

While there may be some truth to this interpretation in the text's prehistory, there are difficulties in a canonical reading. To begin with, the monotheistic nature of Israelite religion invariably puts Israel's God at the center of any divine action. If Israel and their forbearers are interacting with any divine being, it is the God of their fathers. Moreover, Gunkel's reasoning that this cannot be YHWH because, "Yahweh is the god who loves and helps Jacob," is overly simplistic.[62] After all, this text has been used fruitfully by spiritually minded readers for millennia to highlight the idea of spiritual struggle with God.[63]

This leads us to the most common understanding of Jacob's opponent: that it is Jacob's God, or one of his angels, who is encountered in the struggle. Hosea 12:4–5 seems to confirm this idea, and mentions both of these (God and angel), implying that the distinction might not matter: "In his maturity he contended with God (אֶת־אֱלֹהִים), he struggled with the

59. Sarna, *Genesis*, 404.
60. Westermann, *Genesis 12–36*, 519, 521; Gunkel, *Genesis*, 350–53.
61. Westermann, *Genesis 12–36*, 519, 521.
62. Gunkel, *Genesis*, 352.
63. Calvin, for instance, comments at length here regarding Jacob's God as an antagonist, who tests and tries his people for their betterment. See Calvin, *Genesis*, 195–98.

angel (מלאך) and prevailed."[64] Most commentators who understand the opponent as the God of Jacob stress the fact that although we are not given an explicit name (YHWH), the context and associations are very clear. The fact that Jacob later refers to this being in Gen 32:31 as אלהים is, for many, the clincher.[65] The purpose of such a struggle is compared to a sort of "divine testing," from which Jacob emerges as a new man, ready to face his brother and his new life in the land of promise.

This understanding, like the other interpretive options, is not without difficulties. Most notable are the abounding problems of theophany and anthropomorphism.[66] Reconciling a divine encounter where the deity seems unable to prevail, but yet is able to strike an injurious blow, is difficult.[67] Moreover, the deity's desire to flee before daybreak has also caused consternation for some. In this reading, the former is often explained as showing Jacob's tenacity, while the latter is taken as the man looking out for Jacob's well-being: truly to see God would lead to Jacob's death.[68]

One final interpretive understanding of this struggle is that Jacob is fighting his God as well as his inner demons. B. Jacob stresses that however we understand Jacob's opponent, it is with his past and his guilt that he is now wrestling.[69] Spina makes a similar argument, noting that

64. On the connection of Gen 32–33 and Hos 12, see Francis I. Andersen and David Noel Freedman, *Hosea: A New Translation with Introduction and Commentary* (AB 24; Garden City: Doubleday, 1980), 610; Hans Walter Wolff, *Hosea* (trans. Gary Stansell; Hermeneia; Philadelphia: Fortress, 1974), 205–13; W. L. Holladay, "Chiasmus, the Key to Hosea XII 3–6," *VT* 16 (1966): 53–64 (56–58); L. M. Eslinger, "Hosea 12.5a and Genesis 32:29: A Study in Inner Biblical Exegesis," *JSOT* 18 (1980): 91–99 (92); Steven L. McKenzie, "The Jacob Tradition in Hosea XII 4–5," *VT* 36 (1986): 311–22 (315–16).

65. Hamori, *"When Gods,"* 23; Rolf Rendtorff, *The Canonical Hebrew Bible: A Theology of the Old Testament* (trans. David E. Orton; Leiden: Deo, 2004), 600.

66. For more on these issues, see James Barr, "Theophany and Anthropomorphism in the Old Testament," in *Congress Volume: Oxford, 1959* (Leiden: Brill, 1960), 31–38.

67. How best to render the term ויגע is difficult, with interpreters disagreeing as to whether the term is a violent "strike" or a soft "touch." See the discussion in Hamori, *"When Gods,"* 97.

68. Several of these issues have been explored at length in Hamori, *"When Gods."* On the tension of seeing God face-to-face and the injunction that no one can see God's face and live, see R. W. L. Moberly, *At the Mountain of God: Story and Theology in Exodus 32–34* (JSOTSup 22; Sheffield: JSOT, 1983), 65–66, 80–83.

69. Jacob, *Das erste Buch der Tora*, 643; cf. Konrad Schmid, "Die Versöhnung zwischen Jakob und Esau (Gen. 33,1–11)," in Macchi and Römer, eds., *Jacob,*

the "unnamed man" can be understood as a kind of "everyman" with whom Jacob has struggled throughout his life: Esau, Isaac, and Laban.[70] In this sense the struggle with the divine visitor foreshadows the encounter with the brother which is imminent. Part of the argument for this understanding is the shift in language in this scene. The text initially tells us that Jacob wrestles with a "man" (איש). Jacob later understands that this was more than a man, when in naming the site Peniel, he notes that he saw God (אלהים) face-to-face, and his life was spared. As Spina argues, the struggle with the unnamed "everyman" morphs into a struggle with God himself by the end of the episode.[71] Finally, when the man eventually changes Jacob's name to Israel, he notes that this is because Jacob has "contended with God and with men and has overcome." Again, the text seems to point toward the fact that Jacob's interactions with both his God and his fellow humanity are in view.

What is the reader to make of these options? It may be that elements of all of the above interpretations have something to offer. Moberly helpfully brings these interpretive streams together:

> Of all Old Testament stories, this is perhaps the hardest to comment on, largely because the deliberately allusive and mysterious nature of the text makes the story appeal powerfully to the imagination but leaves it not very amenable to rational, discursive explanation. Is Jacob's adversary a spirit of the night, a river spirit, Esau, a projection of his subconscious, or God? As the text stands, it is clearly none other than YHWH in human form (32:30). But the fact that the story is suggestive of these other interpretations—perhaps because in earlier versions they were an actual part of the story—makes it likely that in a sense they are all true, as they all belong to the immediate or wider context of the story. God confronts Jacob not only in human form, but as Esau, whom he fears, as a night spirit, as a river spirit because he is crossing a perilous boundary into the territory of Israel, and as the embodiment of the deepest hopes and fears of his own mind. The writer boldly incorporates these folkloristic motifs in order to try and convey something of the mysterious depth of the occasion.[72]

211–26 (215). As Visotzky puts it, "Jacob is bound by a web of guilt, covenant, commitment, and responsibilities. He remains wracked by guilt, two decades later, for his treatment of Esau. This much to Jacob's credit—he has a deeply refined sense of guilt" (Burton L. Visotzky, *The Genesis of Ethics: How the Tormented Family of Genesis Leads Us to Moral Development* [New York: Crown, 1996], 182).

70. Spina, *Faith*, 24.
71. Ibid.
72. Moberly, *Genesis 12–50*, 31.

Most important for the present study is the fact that, although Jacob recognizes that this is the God of his fathers that he has encountered, the issue of his brother Esau is not far from the surface. Indeed, it is the impending reunion that serves as the broader literary context for the episode at the Jabbok. This, then, leads us to another important question: does Jacob's name change signal that he is himself a changed man?

(2) *Changed Name; Changed Man?* The name which is bestowed on Jacob by his assailant is Israel (ישראל).[73] Of all the name changes in the Bible, Jacob's change to Israel may be the one with most significance, as it later becomes the name his descendants will assume. However, it is also often noted that name changes can be significant occurrences that signal a change in the life of individuals.[74] Is this the case in the story of Jacob?

Fokkelman argues that this is the definitive change in Jacob's life, noting that after this encounter we see a changed man who is no longer afraid, is leading the way for his family, and is ready to meet his brother. He writes, "The old Adam has been shaken off, 'Jakob' stays behind on one bank of the river. A new man, steeled and marked, Israel, has developed and he continues the journey on the other bank. The completely renewed, purified relationship with God makes a renewed, authentic relationship with his 'brother' possible."[75]

At the other end of the spectrum are those who think Jacob's name may have changed, but little else. Hendel comments that however much we want to talk about this encounter changing Jacob, after the encounter he still seems to be afraid of his brother, using subtle tactics right up until the moment they meet.[76] As Niditch points out, elements of Jacob the trickster seem just as evident here as elsewhere in his story.[77]

The majority of commentators fall somewhere in the middle on this issue. As von Rad notes, "it is exceedingly doubtful that the narrator intends to interest us in Jacob's inner experience. Perhaps the nocturnal

---

73. For an extended treatment on the changing of Jacob's name, and the various interpretations of the name Israel in biblical and extra-biblical traditions, see Hayward, *Interpretations of the Name Israel*.

74. Examples often cited are Abram to Abraham in Gen 17, and, in the New Testament, Simon to Peter in Mark 3.

75. Fokkelman, *Narrative Art*, 222.

76. Hendel, *Epic*, 130. Gunkel sees this legend as originally separate from the larger narrative because "the courageous god-vanquisher and the Jacob who trembles before Esau are actually quite different figures" (Gunkel, *Genesis*, 353).

77. Niditch, *Underdogs*, 116.

event ought really to designate an inner purification in Jacob. But whether, after it, he was 'as God wanted him' is doubtful."[78] Wenham agrees: Jacob is changed; he is a new man with a new name, and is perhaps more ready than before for his encounter with Esau. Nonetheless, elements of the old Jacob remain, and it does not take long for these to resurface.[79] Once again the text leaves us with much ambiguity, and little clarification. Jacob's name has been changed, but as to what extent the man himself is different, we have to infer on our own.

Genesis 32 ends with the following in v. 31: "The sun rose upon him just as he passed Peniel, and he was limping on account of his thigh." Sarna notes how this brings further closure to Jacob's exile from his homeland: "Jacob's ignominious flight from home was appropriately marked by the setting of the sun [28:11]; fittingly, the radiance of the sunrise greets the patriarch as he crosses back to his native land."[80] And yet, this is not a triumphal entry; Jacob carries with him not only the emotional baggage of the past two decades, but also a noticeable, physical limp, signifying the "magnificent defeat" of the previous night's struggle.[81]

Looking at Gen 32:23–33, we are again confronted with the dense ambiguity of the larger narrative. Who is Jacob's opponent, and what does the struggle represent? What does Jacob's change of name signal, and how affective is this change in Jacob's behavior? What does this mean for the relationship of Jacob and Esau and the larger narrative of their reunion? While the text has given us some clues, many of these questions remain unanswered as Jacob moves on to the encounter with his estranged brother.

3. *The Reunion (Genesis 33:1–11)*

The meeting to which the previous chapter has been building is now at hand. As Butterweck-Bensberg notes, "In Gen 33,1–18 finden wir eine der eindrucksvollsten Versöhnungsgeschichten der hebräischen Bibel."[82] And yet, the ambiguities which have punctuated the previous chapter can

---

78. Von Rad, *Genesis*, 324, interacting here with August Dillmann, *Die Genesis* (Leipzig: Hirzel, 1892).
79. Wenham, *Genesis 16–50*, 304; cf. Moberly, *Genesis 12–50*, 31–32.
80. Sarna, *Genesis*, 228.
81. This phrase comes from Frederick Buechner, *The Magnificent Defeat* (San Francisco: HarperOne, 1985).
82. Annelise Butterweck-Bensberg, "Die Begegnung zwischen Esau und Jakob (Gen. 33,1–18) im Spiegel rabbinischer Ausdeutungen," *BN* 116 (2003): 15–27 (15).

be seen in these verses as well. We will explore the following issues in this section: Jacob's approach to Esau; the moment of reuniting; and the interaction of Jacob and Esau subsequent to the reunion.[83]

a. *Jacob's Approach (33:1–3)*
Jacob's initial fears concerning his brother are again brought to the fore, as we are informed in 33:1 that Jacob looks up and sees Esau coming with his four hundred men. Jacob then begins dividing and staggering his wives and children, possibly signaling further maneuvering on his part.[84] However, the beginning of v. 3 signals an unexpected change: "But he himself passed before them (והוא עבר לפניהם)." Moreover, the verse goes on to note that Jacob, "bowed down to the ground seven times (וישתחו ארצה שבע פעמים) as he drew near to his brother (אחיו)."

Jacob's actions in 33:3 are striking, and have provoked much comment from interpreters. To begin with, the fact that Jacob goes before his family signals to some that he is indeed a new man after his Peniel encounter. As noted earlier, Jacob has continually sent servants, gifts, and camps ahead of himself. Now, however, Jacob goes before his family, as seen in the use of לפניהם, once again playing off of the *leitwort* פנים. Moreover, Walton points out that והוא at the beginning of v. 3 disrupts the syntax, taking the reader by surprise, as Jacob acts counter to expectations.[85] Some argue that by putting himself before his family, Jacob is allaying our fears that he might be up to his old tricks.[86]

Yet, not everyone is convinced. Others make the case that the only reason we are impressed with Jacob's actions here is that we already have such low expectations of him. Visotzky and Hendel, among others, have argued that Jacob's actions here can just as reasonably be understood as cowardly and fear-driven, based on the reference to him seeing the four hundred men approaching. To go before his wives and children is hardly chivalrous.[87]

What, then, do we make of the bowing down to the ground? There have been several approaches to understanding Jacob's act of bowing in the history of interpretation. The first approach is to see Jacob as being

---

83. For a thorough treatment of rabbinic interpretations of the encounter in Gen 33, see ibid., 15–27.

84. There is a slight textual question regarding אחרנים in 33:2. Both *BHS* and Gunkel (*Genesis*, 354) suggest an emendation, possibly אחריהם, following the Peshitta and LXX.

85. See Walton, *Thou Traveller Unknown*, 187.

86. Fokkelman, *Narrative Art*, 223.

87. Visotzky, *The Genesis of Ethics*, 189–91; Hendel, *Epic*, 130.

portrayed in a positive light. For instance, one rabbinic tradition held that
Jacob was in fact bowing down to God, not to Esau, and was fervently in
prayer.[88] Another rabbinic view held that Jacob was demonstrating right-
eousness, based on Prov 24:16, which states that, "a righteous man falls
seven times, and he rises up again."[89] A more common contemporary
move, as seen in the work of Fokkelman, understands Jacob's actions in
33:3 as showing his sincerity and humility, further proof that Jacob has
changed after his Peniel encounter.[90]

Another interpretive option has been put forth in light of discoveries
made concerning customs in the ancient Near East. Parallels to this
seven-fold bowing have been found in the Amarna letters. These parallels seem to reflect proper behavior for a court ritual, as if a subject was
approaching a monarch. This reading has Jacob acknowledging his
almost vassal-like status to his brother, and showing him, "the profound-
est marks of deference and respect."[91]

Finally, others have noted that something more than an acknowledgment of Esau's lordship is at work here. Instead, what we have is Jacob's
guilty conscience coming to the surface, and, as Wenham notes, he may
be "trying to undo the great act of deception whereby he cheated Esau of
his blessing."[92] This line of thinking connects the bowing seen here with
that mentioned in Isaac's blessing of Jacob in 27:29: "May peoples serve
you and nations bow down to you (וישתחו). Be lord over your brothers,
and may the sons of your mother bow down to you (וישתחוו)." This verb
does not occur in the Jacob Cycle outside of Gen 27 and 33. Thus, while
Esau is supposed to bow down to Jacob, it is Jacob who is bowing down
to his brother. Some would even say that the blessing of Jacob in Gen 27
has not only gone unfulfilled, it has actually been reversed.[93]

Thus, Jacob's actions at the beginning of Gen 33 continue to reflect
the ambivalence which characterized Gen 32. On the one hand, Jacob

---

88. See *Gen. Rab.* 78:8. Calvin (*Genesis*, 206) subsequently revived this idea.

89. *Gen. Rab.* 78:8.

90. Fokkelman, *Narrative Art*, 223.

91. Driver, *Genesis*, 298. On the correlation of these with Gen 33, see Claus
Westermann, *The Promises to the Fathers: Studies on the Patriarchal Narratives*
(trans. David E. Green; Philadelphia: Fortress, 1980), 81–82; Schmid, "Die Versöhnung," 221. On possible parallels in Ugaritic literature, see Samuel E. Loewenstamm, "Prostration from Afar in Ugaritic, Accadian and Hebrew," *BASOR* 188
(1967): 41–43.

92. Wenham, *Genesis 16–50*, 298; cf. Gunkel, *Genesis*, 346, 354.

93. This idea is highlighted by Turner, *Announcements*, 123; and David J. A.
Clines, *What Does Eve Do To Help?, and Other Readerly Questions to the Old
Testament* (JSOTSup 94; Sheffield: JSOT, 1990), 60–61.

goes before his family, seemingly willing to face his fate head on. More-over, he bows down before his brother, which can be understood as a sign of respect, humility, or even an implicit recognition of the stolen blessing. On the other hand, Jacob still seems to be motivated by the fear of his brother and the four hundred approaching men. And as he pros-trates himself before his brother, we are still not quite sure of his motives. Is this true humility or more posturing on the part of Jacob?

b. *The Meeting (33:4)*

Whether or not Jacob's motives are clear to the reader, the moment of the reunion has arrived. While Esau has been moving "behind the scenes" in the previous chapter, we now encounter Jacob's brother in the flesh for the first time since Gen 28. We are told in the first clause of 33:4 that, "Esau ran to meet him (וירץ עשו לקראתו)." At this juncture the tension has not yet been resolved. Both verbs used here, to "run" (רוץ) and to "meet" (קרא), can be construed positively or negatively.[94] All the reader (and presumably Jacob) knows is that Esau is coming toward his brother, with a sense of urgency.

It is the rest of 33:4 which makes clear Esau's intentions, alleviating the anxiety of the previous chapter: "and he embraced him (ויחבקהו), and fell on his neck (על־צוארו), and kissed him (וישקהו), and they wept (ויבכו)." We now see that Esau's running was not with hostile intent, but may be seen in juxtaposition with Jacob's slow and steady approach, punctuated with his bowing to the ground. A brief comment on each of the subsequent verbs may be in order, as they all have resonance with the broader Jacob–Esau narrative.

First, Esau embraces Jacob. From the root חבק, the meaning of this term is relatively clear: to "clasp" or "embrace."[95] However, there is a phonetic similarity between this verb and the term which was used to describe Jacob's struggle with the man at Peniel the night before, אבק. While Jacob may have been expecting another physical encounter similar to אבק, he instead receives חבק, an unexpected embrace. Both are physical, but with different intentions and outcomes.[96]

Following on from this we are told that Esau falls on Jacob's neck and kisses him. This phrase has evoked an extraordinary amount of interpre-tive ingenuity, as well as a good deal of suspicion, in Jewish tradition.

---

94. P. Maiberger, "רוץ," *TDOT* 13:416–22; on קרא, see BDB 896–97; and Schmid, "Die Versöhnung," 222.

95. See BDB, 287.

96. Cf. Hamilton, *Genesis 18–50*, 343.

Much of the mistrust regarding Esau's kiss stems from the Masoretic "extraordinary punctuation" connected to this word. Each consonant of this word in the Hebrew text has a dot imposed above it, signaling the Masoretes wanted it to be noted for some reason.[97] Some have taken this to mean that this word should be understood as the phonetically similar נשׁך, "to bite." This is, while not unanimous, a common rabbinic interpretive move. An example of this can be seen in *Targum Pseudo-Jonathan*, where Esau falls on Jacob's neck in order to bite him. The fact that both brothers wept is then explained with the following: "Esau wept because of the pain of his teeth that were loosened; and Jacob wept because of the pain of his neck."[98] While there may be reason to distrust Esau in light of his comments in Gen 27:41, the context does not lend any credence to the idea that his kiss was insincere. Indeed, when reuniting with a family member, this sign of affection may have been the appropriate response.[99]

Yet again, the verbs used here have resonance with the larger narrative. Spina points out the significance of Esau falling on Jacob's neck:

> Thinking back to what Isaac said to Esau that fateful day when his brother manoeuvred to acquire the primary blessing for himself, we remember the father's statement that Esau would live by his sword and one day break Jacob's yoke from his neck. This vocabulary certainly evokes thoughts of physical violence. At the same time, while the repetition of the word "neck" in the reunion scene seems to allude to Isaac's prophecy and the potential for its being fulfilled, the manner of fulfilment is not quite what the language leads us to expect. Esau does not use a sword to remove Jacob's yoke, even though Jacob fears that his brother

---

97. On this extra punctuation over "kiss," see *BHS* at 33:4, and the explanation in Page H. Kelley, Daniel S. Mynatt, and Timothy G. Crawford, *The Masorah of Biblia Hebraica Stuttgartensia: Introduction and Annotated Glossary* (Grand Rapids: Eerdmans, 1998), 32–34.

98. Other traditions elaborate on this further, noting that Jacob's neck turned to stone and thus hurt Esau's teeth (*Gen. Rab.* 78:9). Not all Jewish tradition bought into this vilification. Rashi noted that there were several possibilities, including that Esau did not kiss Jacob "with his whole heart," or that God intervened so that it was a meaningful kiss (*Rashi's Commentary: Genesis*, 161). Ibn Ezra, meanwhile, concludes that the kiss was not meant to be harmful, but was indeed genuine, as both brothers end up weeping together, as Joseph and his brothers did in Gen 45:14. See *Ibn Ezra's Commentary, Genesis*, 319. On the various rabbinic interpretations of Esau's kiss, see Mois A. Navon, "The Kiss of Esau," *JBQ* 35 (2007): 127–31; and Butterweck-Bensberg, "Die Begegnung," 18–19.

99. E.g. Gen 45:14. On kissing in a familial context in the Hebrew Bible, see K. M. Beyse, "נשׁק," *TDOT* 10:72–76.

and his four hundred men are undoubtedly armed to the teeth. Instead, with a gesture that is the very antithesis of violence and can only be described as an act of blithe acceptance and reconciliation, Esau falls compassionately on his brother's neck, embracing and kissing him (Gen. 33:4).[100]

Another echo from a previous section of the Jacob–Esau story is the verb "kiss." When Jacob tricked his father into giving him the blessing intended for Esau, the deal was sealed when Jacob kissed his father, allowing Isaac to smell the scent of his son Esau (Gen 27:27). Now, after all these years, Esau's kissing of Jacob "appropriately signals the final resolution of the chain of tragic events precipitated by that other kiss, Jacob's deceitful kiss, that played a crucial role in the original blessing scene."[101] Hence, both the reference to "neck" and "kiss" have resonance with the previous blessing scene and the strife which it brought to the family.

Finally, 33:4 concludes by noting that "they wept" (ויבכו).[102] The reader is reminded again of the original blessing scene when, in Gen 27:38, Esau previously wept at the loss of his blessing: "Bless me, even me, my father. And Esau lifted his voice and he wept (ויבך)." Esau initially wept bitter tears because of the blessing and the familial strife which ensued. He now weeps what we assume are tears of joy, with his brother, at their reunion.

Thus, all four of these actions—embracing, falling on the neck, kissing, and weeping—have reverberations with the larger story of these brothers, and point to the undoing of some of the wrongs which have been previously committed.[103] Moreover, all of these terms are found elsewhere as normal instances of familial greeting.[104] Consequently, aside from certain streams of rabbinic thought, commentators tend to agree

---

100.　Spina, *Faith*, 27.

101.　Sarna, *Genesis*, 229.

102.　The plural verb here seems a bit odd after the succession of singular verbs which have preceded it. *BHS* suggests an amended singular form (ויבך), and Gunkel concurs: "The plural 'they cried' does not suit the situation in which Jacob has entirely different ideas" (Gunkel, *Genesis*, 354); cf. Soggin, *Genesis*, 402. Yet several of the ancient traditions, including LXX and *Targum Onqelos*, retain the plural usage.

103.　This is not necessarily a statement concerning the composition of these texts; rather, it is a recognition that there are resonances with the broader narrative, points of contact which have been commented on by many interpreters.

104.　Wenham (*Genesis 16–50*, 298) notes the following occurrences in Genesis: running (24:17; 29:12), embracing (29:13; 48:10), falling on the neck (45:14), weeping (29:11; 45:14; 46:29).

that Esau is portrayed in a positive light in 33:4. Stiebert claims that Esau's "behavior is nothing short of magnanimous and exemplary."[105]

This, however, leads us to another question: Why does Esau respond the way he does? As is a recurring theme in these chapters, there is disagreement in the history of interpretation as to the motivation behind Esau's actions.

A common refrain in Christian tradition is that while Jacob fretted over Esau's response to him, God had already softened Esau's heart, making him gracious. John Chrysostom understands the passage in this way, and would be followed by the likes of Calvin.[106] As Calvin notes, "It is no wonder, that for the sake of his servant Jacob, he should have composed the fierce mind of Esau to gentleness."[107]

A second approach, more common in Jewish tradition, sees Esau's gracious response as a result of Jacob's preparatory actions in the previous chapter. Rashi, for instance, stresses that Esau's pity was aroused by Jacob's gifts and prostration.[108] Cohen concurs:

> The only explanation we can offer is that Jacob's message, with its subtle yet profound interplay of both strength and fear, power and uncertainty, faith and doubt, submission and aggression pierced the emotional armor of Esau. Jacob's measured words created a shaft of self-discovery and illumination within Esau... Esau realized, for the first time in his life, that the material advantages inherent in the birthright did not in fact secure or guarantee happiness.[109]

These interpretations tend to simultaneously exalt Jacob and denigrate Esau; Esau is not a changed man, he has simply been overcome (or outwitted) once again by his brother Jacob, whose actions in the previous chapter are thus to be commended.

A third way of understanding this change in Esau is to think of it as a development of his character that has happened during the ensuing years following the blessing scene (even off stage, as it were).[110] One idea that

---

105. Stiebert, "Maligned Patriarch," 37. Further examples of this type of language can be found in Jacob, *Das erste Buch der Tora*, 642, 645, and Levenson, "Genesis," 68. It is not uncommon to see 33:4 referenced as a possible model for Jesus' depiction of the father when the prodigal son returns home in Luke 15:20, further highlighting the positive construal of these actions. See, e.g., Moberly, *Genesis 12–50*, 29.

106. Chrysostom, *Homilies on Genesis* 58.3, in ACCS 2:214.

107. Calvin, *Genesis*, 208.

108. *Rashi's Commentary: Genesis*, 161.

109. Cohen, "The Jacob–Esau Reunion," 162. Cf. Spero, "Jacob and Esau," 249; Sarna, *Genesis*, 229.

110. Bakhos, *Ishmael on the Border*, 25; cf. von Rad, *Genesis*, 327.

might lend itself to this "character development" interpretation has to do with the portrayal of Esau in Gen 25 and here in Gen 33. The scene in Gen 25, where Esau sells Jacob the birthright, ends with a succession of five verbs that seem to characterize Esau: he ate, drank, rose, went off, and spurned the birthright (25:34). In Gen 33:4 we encounter another grouping of five verbs given in quick succession: he ran, embraced, fell upon, kissed, and wept. As Sarna notes, the "initial breach," which was characterized by these five verbs, is now paralleled by a corresponding reconciliation, with five verbs of its own.[111] Along these lines, Soggin sees a development in the character of Esau from a bearish and brute man to an able and big-hearted one.[112]

A final way of understanding Esau's actions, and one that can be held in conjunction with the previous idea, is that what we see here are the actions of true brotherhood. Westermann writes the following:

> The narrator of Gen. 27–33 arranges the conclusion of his narrative so that he gives the meeting its individuality by contrasting the two greetings. Esau greets Jacob as one brother greets the other after a long separation (v. 4); Jacob greets Esau as a vassal greets his patron with a ceremonial which has its origin in the royal court… These two types of greeting are so skillfully worked together that the contrast speaks for itself…so as to dominate the whole episode.[113]

Spina makes a similar observation and asks rhetorically, "Is there any more brotherly behavior in the whole Bible?"[114]

In summary, Esau's welcome of Jacob has been explained in a variety of ways: God had already softened his heart; Jacob's ploys from ch. 32 worked; or Esau's character shows development, and this is on display in his brotherly actions. Once again, it is difficult to isolate the motives of the characters involved. While I am sympathetic to the reading which highlights Esau's development and commendable behavior, the other options cannot be dismissed. Indeed, there is no reason why these various readings cannot be held in tension or as complementing one another. Regardless, the brotherly behavior which Esau exhibits is striking in light of the larger cycle of stories, and this needs to be recognized.

c. *The Interaction of Jacob and Esau (33:5–11)*
With Esau's warm welcome, the tension of the narrative has been relieved. But there is more to come, as not a word has yet been spoken

111. See Sarna, *Genesis*, 229; cf. Schmid, "Die Versöhnung," 222.
112. Soggin, *Das Buch Genesis*, 402.
113. Westermann, *Genesis 12–36*, 524.
114. Spina, *Faith*, 31.

between the two brothers. Several themes are continued and find their conclusion in these verses.

Esau begins by asking about Jacob's wives and children. Jacob's response is deferential to both God and Esau (33:5): "The children whom God has graciously given (חנן) to your servant (אֶת־עַבְדֶּךָ)." There are two themes picked up again in this verse. First of all, Jacob tells Esau that his children are graciously given by God. As Westermann and others have noted, the word ברך ("bless") would have probably been more appropriate here, and it is possible that Jacob may be avoiding the word intentionally.[115] However, the use of the verb חנן also reminds the reader that it is Esau's חן that Jacob is seeking, a point Jacob will reiterate shortly.[116] This is a theologically charged word in its own right, as it can denote acceptance and forgiveness alongside favor. The second issue to be aware of in this verse is that even after Esau's warm welcome, Jacob continues to refer to himself as Esau's servant, and, as the text continues, to Esau as his lord.

The next few verses (33:6–7) depict the women and children in Jacob's family parading before Esau, in the order of their importance to Jacob. The reader now sees that Jacob's final division of his family in 33:1–2 may not have been tactical, but instead was arranging them in the order for their presentation to Esau. And just as Jacob prostrated himself before Esau, so too does his family. In fact, the verb denoting their obeisance (שׁחה) is used three times in 33:6–7.

Esau continues with another question for Jacob (33:8): "What do you mean by all this camp (כל־המחנה הזה) which I have met"?[117] Esau seems to be referring to the gifts which were sent ahead. However, there is a touch of irony here as Esau refers to the droves as "camp," a *leitwort* in the narrative, and a reminder that Jacob was dividing his camp just a few verses earlier. Jacob responds by telling Esau the droves were meant, "To find favor (חן) in the eyes of my lord (אֲדֹנִי)." The themes which were picked up in the response of Jacob to Esau's first question in 33:5 resurface in his answer here: he is seeking the favor (חן) of Esau, to whom he continues to show deference (אֲדֹנִי).[118]

---

115.   Westermann, *Genesis 12–36*, 525.

116.   On the verbal use of חנן, see Freedman and Lundbom, *TDOT* 5:23–25; cf. R. Ap-Thomas, "Some Aspects of the Root HNN in the Old Testament," *JSS* 2 (1957): 128–48.

117.   The Hebrew in the first clause is a bit awkward (מי לך), and is literally "Who to you…?" However, the sense seems to be "What do you mean by…?" See Alter, *Genesis*, 185.

118.   There is also a phonetic wordplay at work in these words. Jacob refers to his children as God's graciousness, חן. Esau then asks about the meaning of Jacob's

The next few verses offer a back and forth dialogue between the brothers regarding the acceptance of Jacob's gift. Esau begins in 33:9 by refusing the gift: "I have plenty (רב), my brother (אחי); let what is yours be yours." There is speculation as to Esau's motives in rejecting Jacob's gift. Some have posited that ancient Near East etiquette required the declining and eventual acceptance of gifts.[119] Others have noted a similar rejection made by Abram in response to the king of Sodom in Gen 14:23, where Esau's grandfather states that he does not want his riches in any way to be associated with the king's charity.[120] Finally, others argue that Esau simply does not need anything from his brother, as he has been blessed in his own right, despite not receiving the blessing of the first born.[121]

Three issues lend credence to this last reading. First, if our interpretation of Esau's blessing in Gen 27 is correct, then there is no reason to be surprised by subsequent narratives depicting Esau's prosperity outside the land of promise. Second, it is worth noting that while Jacob continues to refer to Esau as his "lord," Esau here addresses Jacob as "my brother." This intentional juxtaposition of language seems to indicate a lack of malice in Esau's response.[122] Finally, the use of the word רב may again remind the reader of the larger Jacob–Esau narrative, particularly Isaac's blessing of Jacob in 27:28, where Isaac says, "May God give you from the dew of heaven and from the fat of the earth, and an abundance (ורב) of grain and new wine." In spite of the fact that Jacob received the promise of abundance (רב), Esau has plenty (רב).[123] Indeed, the final clause in Esau's statement ("let what is yours be yours") can be seen as Esau's implicit acknowledgment that he has let go of the past.

Jacob responds with a lengthy retort to his brother (33:10–11):

> No, please, if I have now found favor (חן) in your eyes, then accept my gift (מנחתי) from my hand. For I have seen your face (פניך) as one sees the face of God (פני אלהים) because you have accepted me favorably (ותרצני). Take, please, my blessing (את־ברכתי) which was brought to you, because God has been gracious to me (חנני), and because I have all I need.

---

camp, מחנה. Jacob replies by speaking of Esau's favor, חן. And in the subsequent verses Jacob urges Esau to accept his gift, מנחה, as a sign of his favor, חן. On this, see Schmid, "Die Versöhnung," 220.

119.   Sarna, *Genesis*, 230.
120.   Hamilton, *Genesis 18–50*, 345.
121.   Alter, *Genesis*, 185.
122.   Fretheim, "Genesis," 572.
123.   Levenson, "Genesis," 68.

The verse concludes, "And because he pressed it on him, he took it."

There are several interrelated themes from this narrative which culminate in Jacob's response to Esau: the theme of favor (חן), the key word "face" (פנים), and the larger issue of blessing.

(1) *Favor and Gift.* As noted above, the favor which Jacob seeks is related to pacifying Esau (כפר, 32:21), and the terminology which is used is closely related to cultic themes. The fact that gifts (מנחה) are being given and that Esau has received Jacob favorably reiterates the fact that there are juridical and sacrificial overtones at work in the text.[124] Regardless of whether or not Jacob is admitting guilt, the theme of favor, and the cultic overtones of the passage as a whole, seem to be coming to a head in these verses.

However, during this scene there is a change in the dynamic between favor and gift. Earlier in the narrative, the gift was sent ahead in order to gain Esau's favor. Yet at this point in the narrative, Jacob realizes that he has already gained his brother's favor; in this sense, his prayer has been answered. Thus, "The gift is now offered by Jacob, not to obtain favor, but in gratitude for God's favor...made visible in the face of Esau."[125]

(2) *The "Face" Motif.* The second issue revolves around the *leitwort* "face," פנים. As was noted earlier, this term occurs in various forms throughout these two chapters: Jacob had sent messengers and gifts ahead of him (לפניו, 32:4, 17), and then expressed a desire to "cover the face" (אכפרה פניו) of Esau, so that when he saw Esau's face (פניו), Esau might "lift the face" of Jacob (ישא פני, 32:21). Then, following the struggle with his assailant, Jacob names the place Peniel (פניאל), noting that he had seen God "face-to-face" (פנים־אל־פנים, 32:31). Now in 33:10 this language seems to come to a climax as Jacob tells Esau that seeing his face is like seeing the face of God.

This statement has provoked a variety of interpretations. One rabbinic approach was to change the wording so as to avoid anthropomorphism. For example, *Targum Onqelos* amends Jacob's comparison to "seeing your face is as the sight of the face of the great ones," and *Targum Pseudo-Jonathan* has "the face of your angel." Another tradition builds on this, stating that Jacob's intent in mentioning this was to instill fear in Esau, by noting that Jacob had seen his brother's guardian angel and

---

124. See, e.g., Rashi, who notes that the language here, especially רצה, evokes the idea of propitiation (*Rashi's Commentary: Genesis*, 162). For more on this term, see Terence E. Fretheim, "רצה," *NIDOTTE* 3:1185–86.

125. Fretheim, *NIDOTTE* 2:204.

survived. Thus, Esau could never hope to overcome him.[126] A second interpretive option is to see Jacob's words as persuasive rhetoric. Gunkel feels this is mere flattery on Jacob's part,[127] and Petersen argues that Jacob's statement here is a "psychologically compelling speech" which is meant simply to persuade Esau.[128]

A third understanding of Jacob's words draws out the comparison of 33:10 and 32:21. Brueggemann, for instance, concludes that the reconciliation with the brother has to be held in tension with the encounter with God—the face motif makes this clear: "In the *holy God*, there is something of the *estranged brother*. And in the *forgiving brother*, there is something of the *blessing God*. Jacob has seen the face of God. Now he knows that seeing the face of Esau is like that."[129]

Yet in what way are the two encounters similar? Brueggemann admits that "we are not told in what ways it is like the face of God. Perhaps in both it is the experience of relief that one does not die."[130] Indeed, it is the final word of 33:10, ותרצני, which may provide the necessary context. As Alter and others have noted, it is the "you accepted me graciously" of 33:10 which stands in parallel with the "my life was spared" in 32:21.[131] As Wenham writes, "such warmth after so many years of hatred makes this scene one of the most beautiful in Scripture. The full and free forgiveness that Esau displays toward his deceitful brother is, as Jacob himself recognizes, a model of divine love."[132]

While not eschewing any of these readings, this last understanding seems to make the most sense when taken in the context of the two chapters as a whole. Jacob was shown God's mercy in that his life was spared in the encounter with the stranger. Now, after the tension which has been mounting for so long, the reunion with his brother reminds him of that grace which spared his life the night before. As Fokkelman notes, "Esau's behavior is definitively coupled with God's behavior. The meeting with Esau lies in a single perspective with the meeting with God."[133]

---

126.   *Rashi's Commentary: Genesis*, 162.
127.   Gunkel, *Genesis*, 344, 355.
128.   Petersen, "Genesis and Family Values," 20, again drawing on sociological and anthropological perspectives.
129.   Brueggemann, *Genesis*, 272–73.
130.   Ibid., 273. *Gen. Rab.* 78:12 offers another take on this: "Just as the face of God is judgment, so your face is judgment."
131.   Alter, *Genesis*, 186; cf. Heard, *Dynamics*, 132.
132.   Wenham, *Genesis 16–50*, 304. Cf. Fretheim, "Genesis," 573.
133.   Fokkelman, *Narrative Art*, 226.

(3) *Gift and Blessing.* A third and final theme which these verses high-light is the connection of this scene with Gen 27, and the recurrence of the blessing motif. As von Rad points out, Gen 33 needs to be seen as part of the larger whole, "for its relation to the story of deception is unmistakeable."[134] Fishbane and others have elucidated this, arguing that on a structural level the Jacob Cycle can be seen as a series of chiasms, in which case chs. 27 and 33 are paired off.[135] Thus, there are obvious thematic and structural connections between these two scenes. There are also linguistic associations in these two chapters, some of which were mentioned above: key terms such as bowing down, neck, kissing, and weeping all remind the reader of the blessing narratives in Gen 27.[136] The most obvious verbal link, however, is Jacob's use of the word ברכה in place of מנחה in 33:11. While Jacob has throughout the narrative been referring to his gift for Esau with the expected noun מנחה, he abruptly switches his terminology in v. 11 and refers to the gift as ברכה, the word usually used for "blessing."

While a good deal of pre-modern commentary seems to have remarked solely on the fact that ברכה can be understood as a gift or greeting,[137] the majority of contemporary scholarship thinks this choice of terminology is in some way related to the blessing motif. Whether unconsciously, metaphorically, or literally, Jacob appears to be attempting to undo the wrongs which resulted from his receiving the blessing via deception in Gen 27.[138]

After offering Esau his ברכה, Jacob adds another reason as to why Esau should take his gift. Initially it was to show fully his favor toward Jacob. Now, Jacob notes that Esau should take the gift because God has been gracious with Jacob, and he has all he needs. Here Jacob returns to the theme of God's favor; not only has God graciously given him a large

---

134.   Von Rad, *Genesis*, 325. Cf. Schmid, "Die Versöhnung," 214.

135.   Fishbane, *Biblical Text*, 51; Dicou, *Edom, Israel's Brother*, 123; Gammie, "Theological Interpretation," 121–22.

136.   As Fishbane (*Biblical Text*, 51) comments, Gen 33 "bristles with ironic overtones."

137.   See, e.g., *Rashi's Commentary: Genesis*, 152. These secular uses are laid out in Mitchell, *The Meaning of BRK*, 126–27.

138.   Fishbane calls this "an unconscious double-entendre," as Jacob's guilt seeps to the surface (*Biblical Text*, 52). Westermann thinks Jacob is actually trying to return the blessing, as he has enough without it (*Genesis 12–36*, 526). The preponderance of scholarship, however, understands this as a symbolic restitution for past wrongs. Examples include Alter, *Genesis*, 186; Sarna, *Genesis*, 230; Hendel, *Epic*, 130; Spina, *Faith*, 26; Levenson, *Death*, 67; Brett, *Genesis*, 98.

family, but he has shown favor in the abundance of Jacob's possessions. Indeed, the final clause of Jacob's statement here can be seen as a response to Esau's statement regarding his own possessions. Esau has said in 33:9 that he has "plenty" (רב). Jacob, meanwhile, responds in 33:11 that he has "all" (כל). Yet again, Jacob's motives are unclear to the reader. While acknowledging God's graciousness, is he implying that he is indeed the blessed son? And is his statement that he has "all" a further example of one-upmanship on Jacob's part? Or is this instead an act of benevolence, or even of trying to make amends?

d. *Summary of Genesis 33:1–11 and the Reunion*

As we have seen, Gen 33 picks up where Gen 32 left off, building on the tension of the impending meeting between the estranged brothers. Jacob's actions in 33:1–3 are again ambiguous, as he prepares his family to meet Esau and begins his approach to his brother. Esau's reaction upon meeting his brother in 33:4, however, alleviates the fear which had consumed Jacob. Esau responds graciously in welcoming his brother, and the text describes Esau's actions in language reminiscent of the blessing scene of Gen 27. The subsequent interaction between the brothers (33:5–11) brings to a climax several of the themes which have been driving the story, including Esau granting favor to Jacob, and Jacob's comparison of seeing Esau with seeing the face of God.

Nevertheless, this joyful and seemingly productive reunion is not yet the conclusion of the story. Indeed, true to form, the narrative concludes with more ambiguity, and one final unexpected turn after the heart-warming reconciliation.

4. *The Separation (Genesis 33:12–20)*

The reunion having taken place, it is now time for the brothers to move on. Esau expresses a desire to accompany Jacob (33:12), but Jacob offers a variety of reasons why this is not feasible, and urges Esau to go on ahead of him to Seir, where he will meet up with his brother (33:13–14). Esau then volunteers to leave some of his men with Jacob, and Jacob again declines the offer (33:15). So Esau starts back to Seir, but Jacob, we are told, goes on to Succoth (33:16–17). The chapter ends by detailing several more travel notices as Jacob makes his way back to Canaan (33:18–20).

After the reunion and reconciliation we have just experienced, this segment of the story seems puzzling. Once again the reader is left wondering about the motives of the brothers, as well as what their separation means in light of their reconciliation.[139] We will start by looking at some of the ambiguity seen in the key words and themes in 33:12–17, followed by a short analysis of the travel notices and etiologies that mark Jacob's travels into the land of Canaan. Finally, we will explore a few of the explanations which have been given for the separation of the brothers, and how this relates to the narrative as a whole.

a. *Ambiguity in 33:12–17*

The ambiguity which has highlighted much of ch. 32–33 once again plays a prominent role in these verses. To begin with, one would expect that Esau's warm reception of his brother, as well as the eventual acceptance of Jacob's gift, would have cleared the air. In these verses, however, we still find Jacob referring to Esau as "lord" and himself as Esau's "servant." Indeed, Jacob's last recorded word to his brother in the Hebrew Bible is "lord."[140] Secondly, Esau expresses a desire to accompany Jacob in 33:12. Jacob, however, urges Esau to go on ahead (לפניו) in 33:14–15. While Jacob had gone ahead of his family in 33:3, he now desires to shift back behind them, a position he was in throughout Gen 32.[141] Third, while the text tells us that Esau offers to accompany Jacob, it does not tell us where Esau thinks they might be going. It is Jacob who mentions Seir, and that he will catch up with his brother there. And yet when the brothers eventually leave in 33:17, the syntax seems to highlight the fact they depart in separate directions.[142] Finally, it is worth mentioning that while Jacob pressed his gift on Esau until he finally relented and accepted it (33:11), both of Esau's offers to Jacob (33:12, 15) are steadfastly rejected.[143] Indeed, Jacob once again brings up the theme of favor in 33:15, where he seems to imply that now that he has received what he desired from Esau, he would prefer the visit come to a close.

All of these elements are surprising in light of the reconciliation which has just occurred. And yet, they may be a reminder that although these encounters with God and Esau have changed him, "Israel" is still in many ways "Jacob."

---

139.   Coats refers to this as an "anti-climax" after the moving reunion. See George W. Coats, "Strife without Reconciliation: A Narrative Theme in the Jacob Traditions," in Albertz et al., eds., *Werden und Wirken*, 82–106 (103).

140.   Jacob, *Das erste Buch der Tora*, 647.

141.   See Hamilton, *Genesis 18–50*, 347; Fokkelman, *Narrative Art*, 228.

142.   Heard, *Dynamics*, 131.

143.   Hamilton, *Genesis 18–50*, 346–47.

b. *Jacob Returns to Canaan (33:18–20)*

The final verses of Gen 33 finalize Jacob's return to the land of promise, an idea which is stated explicitly and implicitly.[144] First of all, Jacob's actions here are reminiscent of his grandfather Abraham, and Abraham's movements in the land of promise. Like Jacob, Abraham traveled through Shechem (12:6; 33:18), acquired land from strangers (Gen 23; 33:19), and built an altar to his God (12:7, 8; 13:18; 22:9; 33:20). These similarities remind the reader of what has previously taken place when a patriarch was in the land of promise.[145]

Secondly, there are several points of connection with Gen 28, when Jacob originally left Canaan. After his dream at Bethel, Jacob makes a vow which sees him essentially bargain with God (28:20–22): if God will take care of him so that one day he can safely (בשלום) return to his father's house, then YHWH will be his God. In 33:18, we are told that Jacob arrived שלם עיר שכם אשר בארץ כנען. This is generally understood in one of two ways. On the one side are those that take שלם as a proper name, and understand the text to say, "Shalem, the city of Shechem."[146] On the other side are those who translate שלם adverbially, so that it reads, "Jacob arrived safely in the city of Shechem."[147] Wenham opts for the former, translating שלם as the proper noun Shalem. Nevertheless, as he notes, place names often contain other meanings and ironic overtones. Thus, there could be a double entendre in use here, as Jacob goes to the city named "peaceful" after this strife-filled encounter.[148] In this sense, the question of Jacob's peaceful and safe return to the land of promise, as first set out in Gen 28, has been answered, though not without tension and trials. Finally, in 33:20 the text states that Jacob set up an altar

---

144.   These verses also form an introduction to Gen 34 while closing out the Esau narrative. Seeligmann ("Hebräische Erzählung," 309) has shown a connection between the separations Jacob has with Laban and Esau, in that they both have departures followed by etiological explanations. He sees this as part of a departure pattern or formula; cf. Erhard Blum, "Genesis 33,12–20: Die Wege trennen sich," in Macchi and Römer, eds., *Jacob*, 227–38 (232–33).

145.   Moberly, *Genesis 12–50*, 32.

146.   The LXX has a proper noun in its translation. Cf. Westermann, *Genesis 12–36*, 528.

147.   The Samaritan Pentateuch uses שלום here, and this idea is followed by Rashi (*Rashi's Commentary: Genesis*, 164), who translates it as "wholeness." This interpretation is also seen in Alter, *Genesis*, 187; Fokkelman, *Narrative Art*, 198; so too in Hamilton, *Genesis 18–50*, 350, who offers a rebuttal to Westermann's argumentation.

148.   Wenham, *Genesis 16–50*, 300.

and named it אל אלהי ישראל, which can be translated, "El is the God of Israel," and once again can be seen as the fulfillment of his prayer in Gen 28.

c. *Explanations for the Separation of the Brothers*

Given the moving reunion of 33:4, the subsequent separation of the brothers has led to much speculation. Several explanations have been offered.[149]

One approach to understanding Jacob's actions here is to see this as further proof of Jacob's distrust of his brother. This line of thinking attributes continued suspicion to Jacob: has Esau really let bygones be bygones? Why does he want to travel together, and why would he leave some of his men as an escort? Is it a trap of some sort?[150] Some argue that in light of this, we see Jacob acting with wisdom in this situation. This line of thought tends to argue that Jacob was being polite to his brother, but was ultimately trying to avoid damaging the newly restored relationship by providing occasion for further hostility.[151] Since Jacob had received what he came for (favor), there was no use in testing the relationship any further. Indeed, some even justify Jacob's actions by noting that, although the Bible never tells us that Jacob did visit Seir, it also does not tell us that he did not go to his brother at some later time.[152] Others are more suspicious of Jacob's motives, and tend to see this as

---

149.   The interpretations outlined here will focus on explanations which attempt to make sense of the separation in the literary context of the narrative itself. There are, however, other ways of looking at this, including the idea that we see here the anthropological separation of shepherding and hunting lifestyles, or a retrospective explanation for the locations of the people of Edom and Israel, as commented upon earlier with reference to Gen 25. For more on these interpretive options, see Schmid, "Die Versöhnung," 223–24.

150.   See Gunkel, *Genesis*, 355; Alter, *Genesis*, 187; Kaminsky, *Yet I Loved Jacob*, 55–56.

151.   See Driver, *Genesis*, 299; Fredrick C. Holmgren, "Holding Your Own Against God! Genesis 32:22–32 (In the Context of Genesis 31–33)," *Int* 44 (1990): 5–17 (12); Cf. Calvin (*Genesis*, 211), who comments at 33:12 that Jacob "cautiously avoids new occasions of offense: for a proud and ferocious man might easily be exasperated again by light causes."

152.   A popular rabbinic interpretation makes a similar argument by interpreting Jacob's words eschatologically: "But when will he come to him in point of fact? It will be in the age to come: 'And saviors shall come up on Mount Zion to judge the mount of Esau' (Obad 1:21)." See *Gen. Rab.* 78:14; cf. *Rashi's Commentary: Genesis*, 163. This and other rabbinic interpretations are discussed in Butterweck-Bensberg, "Die Begegnung," 25.

further evidence of Jacob's deception of his brother. Von Rad, for instance, thinks that Jacob shows a "stubborn refusal" to accompany Esau, and thus exhibits "the mistrust of one who himself has often deceived."[153] Hamilton comments that the post-Peniel Jacob is "not above making false promises and offering misleading expectations."[154]

Petersen makes the claim that Esau is being duped by his brother and, like his uncle Laban, has to go home on his own, the victim of Jacob's quick wit. However, for Petersen, this does not reflect poorly on Jacob, but on Esau:

> Genesis 33 presented a dire situation, a fraternal encounter that might have eventuated in fratricide. That potential calamity was averted by Jacob's use of the strategy of gift giving and his ability to conduct verbal warfare. Moreover, Esau played by those same rules. By accepting the gift, he agreed not to attack Jacob. And by engaging Jacob in dialogue, he opened the door to a resolution through a war of wits rather than a war of weapons. Esau lost that war, but honoured the game by leaving the playing field after he had lost a second time.[155]

A final understanding of the separation is to interpret it is as the best possible outcome, and a realistic depiction of human interaction. Turner describes the parting as "separation within reconciliation,"[156] an idea that Westermann elaborates on:

> Vividly and cleverly Jacob makes his brother see that the two of them now lead different lives, are involved in different forms of community, and should therefore better not go on together, but remain apart. Jacob's final remark, "until I come to my lord in Seir," is but a polite way of saying in the circumstances that he would not want to contradict his brother. Esau knows quite well that it is not meant to be taken seriously. The decision to separate, veiled though it is, is significant for the narrative as a whole. The narrator wants to say that a reconciliation between brothers need not require that they live side by side; it can also achieve its effect when they separate and each lives his own life in his own way.[157]

This does not entail that Esau's offers are any less sincere than his previous welcome and embrace of his brother; however, the two simply cannot coexist.[158] But this does not mean, either, that there is "strife

---

153.   Von Rad, *Genesis*, 328.
154.   Hamilton, *Genesis 18–50*, 347.
155.   Petersen, "Genesis and Family Values," 21.
156.   Turner, *Announcements*, 133. This is in response to Coats ("Strife," 103), who describes this as "strife without reconciliation."
157.   Westermann, *Genesis 12–36*, 527. Cf. Fretheim, "Genesis," 573.
158.   Blum, "Genesis 33,12–20," 229.

without reconciliation," in the words of Coats. [59] Reconciliation in the Bible is realistic, and allows room for a certain amount of residual complexity. As Kaminsky writes, "Reconciliation neither signals a return to the *status quo ante*, nor does it magically erase the character flaws that people have exhibited all along. Rather, when reconciliation occurs in the Bible, usually the characters have matured, but they remain partially flawed."[160]

Thus, as has been the case for much of Gen 32–33 (not to mention the Jacob Cycle as a whole), we are left with a certain amount of ambiguity. However, the narrative plot has been resolved: Jacob has returned safely to the land of his ancestors. And even if his relationships have not returned to an idyllic state (though they were never ideal, even before birth), there has been reconciliation. Indeed, from this point on, the text gives us no indication that there is any strife between the brothers. In fact, the only other time the two brothers are mentioned together is at the burial of their father Isaac in 35:29, where we read, "And they buried him, Esau and Jacob, his sons."

5. *Genesis 32–33: Preliminary Conclusions*

In light of the foregoing discussion concerning the various complex features of Gen 32–33, I conclude by asking what this episode adds to our understanding of the relationship of Jacob and Esau, particularly in light of their status as elect and non-elect.

First of all, it is obvious that this narrative is primarily concerned with Jacob. The questions these chapters are concerned with are: Will Jacob return safely to the land of his fathers? and, Will the impaired relationship with his brother impede this return? And yet, Esau is more than an ancillary figure here. Indeed, it is Esau's tension-breaking and heart-felt welcome of his brother that makes a peaceful return for Jacob possible. Furthermore, the positive portrayal of Esau in these chapters—his warm welcome and embrace of Jacob and the subsequent likening of Esau to Jacob's God—is unexpected and should cause us to take notice. One could argue that this is highlighted by the ambiguous nature of Jacob's character in these chapters, which stands in contrast to the magnanimous behavior exhibited by Esau. Indeed, many of the various key words and themes which recur throughout the two chapters ("face," "brother," "favor") seem to find their fulfillment in Esau's grand gestures

159.   Coats, "Strife," 103.
160.   Kaminsky, *Yet I Loved Jacob*, 56.

of hospitality. In spite of their past struggles, Esau welcomes Jacob as a brother and shows favor to him, an encounter which leads Jacob to compare seeing Esau's face with seeing the face of his God.

Thus, we are reminded once again that God's choosing of a particular person or people does not correlate to exemplary character on the part of those chosen, nor does it eliminate others from having a significant place in the divine economy. Indeed, these "others" continue to play an important role in Israel's story and development (as seen here in Gen 32–33), and in many ways continue to have stories of their own with Israel's God (as will be seen in Gen 36 and Deut 2). Barth comments on this very theme:

> In Gen. 33 the dispute between Jacob and his elder brother Esau, who in many ways resembles Ishmael, ends in a reconciliation, so that in Gen. 36 the race of Edom, later to be another unpleasant neighbour of Israel, is given a place in the account of the patriarchs. In this prelude to the true history of Israel…it is thus plain that those who are without, the men who surround Abraham, Isaac and Jacob, are certainly men of different and strange peoples which are not elected and called, that they do not belong to the people of God with which we are concerned in the patriarchs, yet that they are not completely cut off from this people, but that they are conjoined with it, so that in their own manner and place they, too, are in the sphere and hand of its God as the one God.[161]

A second and related point is that Gen 32–33 highlights the importance and interrelatedness of Jacob's relationships with both God and humanity. As Walton notes, "Jacob's return to his homeland and to his estranged brother is a masterpiece of tension but also of balance of the human and the divine."[162] Throughout the story, Jacob is interacting and struggling with both his God and his brother (and before that, his uncle). This is seen in several ways: the dual usage of "angels/messengers" and "camps" following the Mahanaim scene; the sacrificial language of appeasement used by Jacob in reference to pacifying Esau; the language used by Jacob's assailant when changing Jacob's name ("one who struggles with both God and man"); Jacob's use of "favor" to refer both to God's provision and Esau's acceptance; and Jacob's explicit comparison of seeing the face of Esau as seeing the face of God. Jacob's status as God's chosen one does not absolve him of responsibility in his relationship to others, and, in some way, Jacob's relationships with

---

161.   Karl Barth, "The Doctrine of Reconciliation," in *Church Dogmatics* 4.3.2, 689.

162.   Walton, *Thou Traveller Unknown*, 223.

humanity and divinity are intertwined.[163] Indeed, as this story makes clear, it is sometimes these "others" that make plain the reality of God's favor. As Spina notes, "In an amazing turnabout, Jacob, the recipient of God's elective grace and thus the one destined to bear the ancestral promise into the future, begins to understand the very essence of that divine grace by experiencing the munificent forgiveness and generosity of Esau, the very one whom God has bypassed."[164]

Esau, meanwhile, has been blessed in his own right outside the land of Canaan, acquiring substantial possessions. Moreover, Esau breaks free from the yoke of Jacob in this scene not with violence, but with forgiveness, another unexpected turn in the story.[165] Levenson elucidates how this informs the larger narrative:

> Without ever giving up the birthright he assumed by deception, Jacob forgoes the hegemony it entails. Without reinstatement as the first-born, Esau forgoes the vengeance that nearly destroyed the family. The act of choosing, God and Rebekah's special preference for Jacob over Esau, has not proven fatal after all; at long last all involved seem able to accept it... God's exaltation of Jacob over Esau nearly destroys the chosen family; it condemns Jacob, Rebekah, and probably Isaac as well to untold misery. Yet the family survives, and when we last see Isaac, he is once more with his two sons, who are not fighting now but cooperating—in the burial of their father. The day when Esau dreamt of killing his brother during the mourning period for their father (27:41) is long forgotten. The twins who struggled with each other even in their mother's womb are now, like their father, at peace.[166]

Thus, one way of understanding Gen 32–33 and its relation to the larger cycle of stories is to see it as the outworking of the dynamics of election. As Kaminsky notes,

> The notion that the tension generated by divine favoritism can be mitigated or eventually overcome is a component of the election tradition that is deepened in each subsequent story... The question of how the narrative portrays the relationship between Jacob and Esau at the end of the story is important because it may shed light on how the final redactor of Genesis imagined the ways in which election might affect relations between the chosen and the nonchosen, or at least one possible model of such a relationship.[167]

---

163. For a similar point, see Fretheim, "Genesis," 574.
164. Spina, *Faith*, 26.
165. Ibid., 27.
166. Levenson, *Death*, 68. Cf. Westermann, *Genesis 12–36*, 530.
167. Kaminsky, *Yet I Loved Jacob*, 54.

When read in the context of the larger framework of the ancestral narratives, Esau can indeed be seen as an exemplary picture of the non-elect. This seems especially poignant in light of Gen 4 and the story of Cain and Abel. Both Cain and Esau are unchosen sons who feel wronged and express anger concerning their situations. But, while Cain is unable to overcome the sin crouching at his door, Esau does overcome his rage by acting as a true brother, an encounter that for Jacob has resonance with the divine. As Kaminsky adroitly observes, "Esau appears to have mastered his envy of his brother's status in a way that Cain could not."[168]

As noted in the introduction to this chapter, the narrative of Gen 32–33 is fraught with ambiguity and complexity. And yet, when given due attention the narrative can be rewarding as well. We have in these chapters a picture of the complex nature of humanity, often driven by fear and self-interest. But we are also shown an image of what humanity can be at its best: a model of divine forgiveness and hospitality in the face of pain and loss. The fact that it is Esau who models this divine character is yet one more unexpected twist in Israel's story.

168.   Ibid., 56.

Chapter 6

GENESIS 36: THE GENEALOGY OF ESAU

1. *Introduction*

Skimming over Gen 36, one would assume, is not an uncommon occurrence. A genealogy can seem uninteresting at the best of times; when it is over forty verses in the genealogy of a supporting character, and thus seemingly inconsequential for the broader storyline, the temptation to pass over the chapter as quickly as possible is understandable. And yet, the question needs to be asked: why does Israel's book of origins contain an entire chapter devoted to the lineage of Esau?

Not surprisingly, because of the nature of the chapter, Gen 36 has been the subject of much historical inquiry. While these studies have been fruitful, historical issues which lie behind the text will not be the focus here.[1] Instead, we will focus on the role that Gen 36 plays in the story of

---

1.   The historical and archaeological studies which have been done in relation to the various facets of Gen 36 are numerous. For historical studies on Gen 36 in general, see Ernst Axel Knauf, "Genesis 36, 1–43," in Macchi and Römer, eds., *Jacob*, 291–300; Knauf, "Supplementa Ismaelitica," *BN* 45 (1988): 62–81; Lars Eric Axelsson, *The Lord Rose Up from Seir: Studies in the History and Traditions of the Negev and Southern Judah* (trans. Frederick H. Cryer; ConBOT 25; Lund: Almqvist & Wiksell, 1987), 66–72; Bartlett, *Edom and the Edomites*, 86–90, 94–102. Older accounts can be found in Eduard Meyer, *Die Israeliten und Ihre Nachbarstämme* (Halle: Niemeyer, 1906), 328–54, and Cannon, "Israel and Edom, I," 129–40.

Detailed studies on the names found in Gen 36, their counterparts in the LXX, and further Arabic connections can be found in Bernhard Moritz, "Edomitische Genealogien. I," *ZAW* 44 (1926): 81–93; and Walter Kornfeld, "Die Edomiterlisten (Gn 36; 1C 1) im lichte des altarabischen namensmateriales," in *Mélanges bibliques et orientaux en l'honneur de M. Mathias Delcor* (ed. André Caquot; Kevelaer: Butzon & Bercker, 1985), 231–36. The similarity and overlap between names in the Edomite genealogy and Judean names has also been well documented. See Gary N. Knoppers, "Intermarriage, Social Complexity, and Ethnic Diversity in the Genealogy of Judah," *JBL* 120 (2001): 15–30, especially 24–27; and Juan Manuel Tebes, "'You Shall Not Abhor an Edomite, for He is Your Brother': The Tradition of Esau and the Edomite Genealogies from an Anthropological Perspective," *JHS* 6

Esau and Jacob and the world of the biblical narrative itself. We will begin by looking at the structure and unity of Gen 36, and what a helpful framework might be for reading the chapter as a whole. Secondly, several elements within Gen 36 will be explored, including various connections of Esau with Edom, as well as the Edomite king list. Finally, the overall purpose of Gen 36 in the context of the Jacob and Esau cycle of stories will be examined. This will be followed by an excursus on Esau's wives and the role they play in the story of Esau.

2. *The Form and Function of Genesis 36*

a. *The Nature of Genealogies*
At the most basic level, a genealogy is a "written or oral expression of the descent of a person or persons from an ancestor or ancestors."[2]

(2006): 1–30 (13–15). This has led some to conclude that there was, at some point, an absorption of Edomite tribes into Judah, or at the very least a strong Edomite presence in the Negeb. This will be discussed below with reference to Obadiah. Cf. A. Zeron, "The Swansong of Edom," *JJS* 31 (1980): 190–98 (190–91).

Work on some of the other people groups found in Gen 36 can be found in Ernst Axel Knauf, "Horites," *ABD* 3:288; Knauf, "Seir," *ABD* 5:1072–73; Roland de Vaux, "Les Hurrites de l'histoire et les Horites de la Bible," *RB* 74 (1974): 482–503; and Gerald L. Mattingly, "Amalek," *ABD* 1:169–71.

Societal and cultural aspects of Edomite history are dealt with in Nelson Glueck, "The Civilization of the Edomites," *BA* 10, no. 4 (1947): 77–84; and Ernst Axel Knauf, "Edom: The Social and Economic History," in Edelman, ed., *You Shall Not Abhor an Edomite*, 93–117.

2.   Robert R. Wilson, *Genealogy and History in the Biblical World* (YNER 7; New Haven: Yale University Press, 1977), 9. Wilson's book offers the fullest account of genealogies, and is supplemented by his other publications: "Genealogy, Genealogies," *ABD* 2:929–32; "The Old Testament Genealogies in Recent Research," *JBL* 94 (1975): 169–89; and "Between 'Azel' and 'Azel': Interpreting the Biblical Genealogies," *BA* 42, no. 1 (1979): 11–22. Another important work in this area, focused on the New Testament genealogies, but touching on those found in the Hebrew Bible, is Marshall D. Johnson, *The Purpose of the Biblical Genealogies, With Special Reference to the Setting of the Genealogies of Jesus* (SNTSMS 8; Cambridge: Cambridge University Press, 1969). In relation to ancient Near Eastern genealogies, see Abraham Malamat, "King Lists of the Old Babylonian Period and Biblical Genealogies," in *Essays in Memory of E. A. Speiser* (ed. William W. Hallo; New Haven: American Oriental Society, 1968), 163–73. Further works on genealogies in Genesis and the Hebrew Bible include Otto Eissfeldt, "Biblos Geneseōs," in *Kleine Schriften*, vol. 3 (ed. Rudolf Sellheim and Fritz Maass; Tübingen: J. C. B. Mohr, 1966), 458–70; David Carr, "Βίβλος γενέσεος Revisited: A Synchronic Analysis of Patterns in Genesis as Part of the Torah (Part One)," *ZAW* 110 (1998): 159–72; Andrew E. Hill, "Genealogy," *DTIB* 242–46.

Because kinship was a major organizing structure for society in the ancient world, genealogies were useful and important in establishing familial relationships. However, genealogies also helped to delineate social, political, and religious connections. "Genealogies, whether from Israel, Egypt, Mesopotamia, Phoenicia, or Greece, are not simply compilations of traditional material, but are assertions about identity, territory, and relationships."[3] Indeed, while Gen 36 is generally referred to as Esau's genealogy, the chapter also exhibits many of these broader characteristics, and it will become apparent that these are vital to our understanding of it.

b. *The Structure of Genesis 36*
Genesis 36 is most often broken down into a series of lists, such as the following:[4]

1. Wives and sons of Esau, vv. 1–5
2. Narrative interlude, vv. 6–8
3. Second genealogy of Esau, vv. 9–14
4. The "chiefs" of Esau, vv. 15–19
5. The sons of Seir, the Horite, vv. 20–28
6. The "chiefs" of the Horites, vv. 29–30
7. A list of Edomite kings, vv. 31–39
8. Second list of the "chiefs" of Edom, vv. 40–43

The breadth and variety of these lists points to this chapter being a collection of various records.[5] Even the traditional ascription of the chapter to P, assigned because of the genealogical nature of the chapter and the use of the term תולדות, has been called into question.[6] This has led some, such as Vawter, to comment that "The editing of the compilation…has been neither thorough nor serious."[7]

---

3. Gary N. Knoppers, *I Chronicles 1–9: A New Translation with Introduction and Commentary* (AB 12; New York: Doubleday, 2003), 18.

4. Wilson, *Genealogy and History*, 167; The NRSV offers a similar breakdown.

5. Coats gives a variety of genres used here, including what he calls organizational lists and king lists (Coats, *Genesis*, 246).

6. This is because of the double use of תולדות in vv. 1 and 9, as well as the various discrepancies with other P material, including the names of Esau's wives as given in Gen 25 and 28. Carr, *Reading the Fractures of Genesis*, 96. Wilson (*Genealogy and History*, 168) has dealt with the complexities of isolating sources in this chapter. Blum has argued for possible divergences within the P school (Blum, *Die Komposition*, 449–51).

7. Vawter, *On Genesis*, 366.

And yet, a case for redactional unity in the chapter can be made.[8] As Wilson comments, "Although Gen 36 gives the immediate impression of disunity, there is nevertheless a definite formal structure to the arrangement of the genealogies in the chapter."[9] This can be seen in the introductions that begin the various units of the chapter, and which provide a rhythm of sorts to the genealogy: ואלה תלדות (v. 1), ואלה תלדות (v. 9), ואלה (v. 29), אלה אלופי (v. 15), אלה בני־שעיר (v. 20), אלה אלופי המלכים (v. 31), ואלה שמות אלופי (v. 40).

Another issue which points to the purposeful shaping of Gen 36 is the fact that equations of "Esau as Edom" and "Esau as the father of the Edomites" bookend the chapter, forming an *inclusio* of sorts for the genealogy. Thus, while it is highly probable that Gen 36 is a compilation of various lists and sources, one could argue that it has been shaped in the end to reflect an extensive account of Esau's lineage, from the patriarch to his people. Whether or not this list is historically accurate by contemporary standards is another question; nonetheless, the narrator wants the list to be *seen* as Esau's extended genealogy.

Taking this into account, a helpful framework for understanding the chapter as a whole may come via a suggestion made by Westermann, who notes that Gen 36 in many ways mirrors the broader history of Israel:

> The importance of ch. 36 is that it attests to those same three stages in society, reduced to genealogies and lists, which also determine the course of history of Israel in the historical books of the Old Testament: from the family…through tribal society…to monarchy… Herein lies the historical importance of ch. 36.[10]

While Westermann says this framework is of historical importance, it might also serve as a heuristic framework hermeneutically: one way to make sense of Gen 36 as a whole is to understand it as the history of Esau and Edom in condensed form, mirroring Israel's story. The same stages in Israel's history will be outlined from the next chapter, Gen 37, down through the books of 1 and 2 Samuel: from ancestor, to family, to tribes, to monarchy.

This is not to eschew the question of historical veracity, which, in relation to genealogies, is a difficult one. However, several issues which are relevant to our study should be noted. To begin with, as Wilson

---

8. Wenham, *Genesis 16–50*, 336.

9. Wilson, *Genealogy and History*, 173; Carr, "Βίβλος γενέσεος," 171.

10. Westermann, *Genesis 12–36*, 568. Fretheim makes a similar statement (Fretheim, "Genesis," 590).

notes, historical questions need to be understood in light of the forms and functions of genealogies.[11] For instance, one of the key characteristics of genealogies is an element of fluidity:

> Where two or more versions of the same genealogy exist, it is usually possible to detect changes in the relationship of names within the genealogy or to note the deletion or addition of names. This sort of fluidity may occur because the names involved are unimportant and thus liable to be forgotten or at least to be poorly remembered. On the other hand, fluidity may be crucial for understanding the genealogies and may indicate significant shifts in social relationships.[12]

For Wilson, this comes back to the question of form and function, and his work in anthropological material shows that "a number of apparently contradictory genealogies may exist at the same time and function in different spheres. The genealogies would not have been considered contradictory by the people who used them, for they would have recognized that each genealogy was accurate when it was functioning in its own particular sphere."[13]

This leads to a related issue, the fact that the genealogies are in some sense "true" in the eyes of those who pass them down:

> [I]n many cases the question of genealogical accuracy may not be a fruitful one because the genealogies involved express a perceived reality which is not open to outside observation. The genealogies express the way in which the writer viewed domestic, political, or religious relationships. Therefore, the genealogies are accurate expressions of the perceptions of the authors but may not correspond with what a Western historian would regard as "objective data."[14]

In sum, Gen 36 may indeed be a collection of various lists which contain historiographical difficulties by contemporary standards. However, there is reason to believe the chapter has been shaped for a specific purpose: to reflect the extended lineage of Esau, Jacob's brother. One way of reading this chapter as a whole, then, is to see it as functioning as the story of Esau/Edom in miniature, a concise portrayal of the history of Esau's

---

11. Wilson, "Between 'Azel'," 11–12.

12. Wilson, *Genealogy and History*, 930–31.

13. Ibid., 181. Wilson gives an extended example of this using the case of Eliphaz. See Wilson, "Between 'Azel'," 20–21.

14. Wilson, "Between 'Azel'," 21. Though note Rendsburg, who argues that the biblical genealogies—particularly in Exodus through Joshua—are more consistent, and perhaps reliable, than often noted. Gary A. Rendsburg, "The Internal Consistency and Historical Reliability of the Biblical Genealogies," *VT* 40 (1990): 185–206.

descendants, mirroring the history of Israel. Several key elements in the text itself may add to this hypothesis.

3. *Key Elements in Genesis 36*

Without offering a verse by verse (or name by name) analysis of Gen 36, there are several elements in the chapter which need to be highlighted.[15] In this section we will focus on the connection of Esau with Edom, the reason for Esau's move to Seir, the use of the term אחזה in 36:43, and the significance of the Edomite king list.

a. *Esau and Edom*

(1) *"Esau is Edom."* One of the more noticeable aspects of Gen 36 is the frequent association of Esau with Edom. In 36:1 we read, ואלה תלדות עשו הוא אדום.[16] This equation (הוא אדום) is repeated in 36:8 and 19, and the designation of Esau as the father of (אבי) the Edomites is found in 36:9 and 43. Thus, five times in this chapter there is an explicit link made between Esau and Edom.[17]

There are several interpretive issues related to this correlation of Esau and Edom. The first is that the term "Edom" can refer to a geographic location, a political entity (nation), a people, and a person.[18] The name "Israel" functions in a similar way in the Hebrew Bible. This might further the claim that this genealogical story of Esau and Edom is, in some way, a mirror of Jacob and Israel's story.

The second issue has to do with the separate notations of Esau "as" Edom and Esau as the "father of" the Edomites. As von Rad, Blenkinsopp, and others have noted, this appears to be two distinct traditions about Esau's direct descendants.[19] However, even if this is the case, it

---

15. The major commentaries offer detailed analyses of the issues, as well as the various text' critical problems. See n. 1, above.

16. Both *Targum Onqelos* and the LXX render this literally, as עשו הוא אדום and 'Hσαû αὐτός ἐστιν 'Εδώμ, respectively.

17. I am dealing here with the literary connection between the two, in the world of the text. On historical dimensions of Esau's relationship to both Seir and Edom, see Bartlett, "Brotherhood of Edom," 2–27; Tebes, "You Shall Not Abhor," 7–16.

18. Diana Vikander Edelman, "Edom: A Historical Geography," in Edelman, ed., *You Shall Not Abhor an Edomite*, 1–11; U. Hübner, "Esau," *ABD* 2:574–75 (575). Cf. Ibn Ezra, who commented on this broad usage in Gen 36. *Ibn Ezra's Commentary, Genesis*, 336.

19. Von Rad, *Genesis*, 344–45; Joseph Blenkinsopp, *The Pentateuch: An Introduction to the First Five Books of the Bible* (ABRL; New York: Doubleday, 1992), 106.

was argued above that Gen 36 is perhaps shaped to reflect Esau's lineage in a condensed fashion. Indeed, it was pointed out that the equations of Esau with Edom and Esau as father of the Edomites bracket the chapter as a whole. One way of reading this, then, is to see it as reinforcing the fact that the entire chapter is to be seen as Esau's lineage, an important part of which is his role as Edom's eponymous ancestor. When the chapter is read as moving from the patriarch to his people, this shift from "Esau is Edom" to Esau as "father of the Edomites" is understandable.

Finally, the language linking Esau to Edom must be mentioned. As noted above, the text reads עשו הוא אדום. The term הוא can have a formulaic use, as it is found appended to names elsewhere in Genesis (14:2, 3; 23:19; 35:19, 27).[20] What are we to make of these literary asides? The use of הוא אדום in Gen 36 is often referred to as a gloss, with little explanation given.[21] Regarding Gen 36 in particular, Fishbane writes, "Patronymic and other personal identifications are…frequently clarified by the ancient Israelite scribes, in the light of their knowledge of other inner-biblical traditions or in their attempt to establish a clear textual meaning."[22] He goes on to say that, "Whether these patronymic annotations…simply reflect the historical penchant of the scribes who copied these historical manuscripts, or reflect a time when even genealogies and boundary lists were 'public' texts for lay audiences who would need such clarifications, cannot be determined."[23] Scholars such as Blank opt for the latter understanding: the mention of "Esau is Edom" so many times is surprising if the connection is as ancient as is often presupposed. Rather, Blank sees this pointing to a later, post-exilic development of this connection, which needed to be explained.[24]

Part of the confusion on this issue is that discussions on this topic tend to conflate the occasion for specific glosses and the antiquity of the identification which is made. The fact that הוא אדום may be a gloss or a late addition does not negate the role that it has in the text as it now stands. Thus, taking on board Blank's assertion that a post-exilic audience would be unfamiliar with this story, I would suggest that equations of Esau with Edom might also be understood on terms which the Bible

20. Michael Fishbane, *Biblical Interpretation in Ancient Israel* (Oxford: Clarendon, 1985), 44–48; cf. H. Ringgren, "הוא," *TDOT* 3:341–52.

21. Wilson, *Genealogy and History*, 169; Gunkel, *Genesis*, 376. Cf. Westermann (*Genesis 12–36*, 562), who refers to this, without explanation, as an "inappropriate gloss."

22. Fishbane, *Biblical Interpretation*, 45–46.

23. Ibid., 46.

24. Sheldon H. Blank, "Studies in Post-exilic Universalism," *HUCA* 11 (1936): 159–91 (176).

itself is familiar with, namely references equating Jacob with Israel.
First, this move from Esau to Edom is important in that it matches a
similar literary move from "Jacob" to "Israel" in Gen 37–50.[25] Second,
the reminder that "Esau is Edom" can be seen as a fulfillment of other
passages that predict nationhood for both Jacob and Esau (e.g. Gen
25:23).[26] Like Jacob, Esau is the eponymous ancestor of a people, fulfill-
ing the promises made to Abraham and Rebekah. Finally, the fact that
this connection is made so many times reinforces the fact, as Koch
highlights, that "Esau is Edom" plays a larger role in Genesis than other
"side stories."[27] While in previous parts of the Jacob Cycle this was
hinted at through various wordplays and more overt references (Gen
25:23; 27:29), it is now stated explicitly, and the reader is allowed to
make the connection. As such, it stands in parallel with and as a pre-
cursor to the transformation of Jacob into Israel.

(2) *Esau's Move to Seir*. A second issue from Gen 36 which needs to be
mentioned is the narrative interlude of vv. 6–8. Here we are given the
description of and reasons for Esau's move from Canaan to Seir.[28] In
vv. 6–8 we read:

> And Esau took his wives and his sons and his daughters and all those
> from his house and all his livestock and cattle, and all that he had
> acquired as property in the land of Canaan, and he went to a land[29] away
> from Jacob his brother. For their possessions were too great to dwell
> together, and the land where they were sojourning was not able to support
> them because of their livestock. So Esau dwelt in the hill country of Seir.
> Esau is Edom.

Not surprisingly, these narrative verses are some of the few in this
chapter that have elicited comment in the history of interpretation.

25. Fretheim, "Genesis," 590.
26. Spina, "The 'Face of God'," 20.
27. Klaus Koch, "Die Toledot-Formeln als Strukturprinzip des Buches Genesis,"
in Beyerle, Mayer, and Strauss, eds., *Recht und Ethos*, 183–91 (189).
28. In Gen 36, Esau and his family move to Seir, named after Seir the Horite
(36:20). Seir is the primary geographic location given in Gen 36, with the exception
of the reference to the kings who reigned in the land of Edom in v. 31. A strong case
can be made that Seir was originally a mountainous area within what would become
known as Edom (e.g. Ezek 35:15). However, as with other aspects in the story, these
lines become blurred, and the two places become virtually synonymous as the
biblical story progresses. If Esau is Edom, then as far as the larger story of the Bible
is concerned, Edom is Seir (see Gen 32:3; Num 24:18; Judg 5:4).
29. The Samaritan Pentateuch and LXX have "from the land of Canaan" here,
while other traditions, including the Peshitta and some targumim, insert Seir.

Genesis Rabbah and Rashi both note that Esau may have left Canaan because of a bond he owed Jacob, or simply because he was ashamed.[30] *Targum Pseudo-Jonathan* adds that Esau left because of a fear of his brother Jacob. *Jubilees* 36:14 has Esau admitting to Isaac that he sold the birthright, and willingly leaving to Edom. In the Christian tradition, commentators have tended to focus on Esau's character flaws. Hence, Calvin has Esau leaving the land because he was "proud and ferocious," and never would have liked to see himself as his brother's inferior, thus leaving the land to Jacob. This, for Calvin, is an example of how "the wicked do good to the elect children of God, contrary to their own intention."[31]

Contemporary scholarship has tended to focus on the fact that, when read in the context of the larger Jacob Cycle, these verses highlight a contradiction regarding the time and reason for Esau's departure from Canaan: Gen 32 seems to infer that Esau is already in the land of Seir, prior to Jacob's return from sojourning with Laban.[32] Genesis 36, meanwhile, narrates the division between the brothers, an event which is based on socio-economic realities (as with Abraham and Lot), rather than any familial strife (as implied in Gen 25; 27; and 32–33).[33] Heard highlights the tension:

> Whereas the narrator had previously depicted Jacob leaving Canaan to avoid a conflict with Esau subsequent to Jacob's theft of Esau's blessing, the narrator now depicts Esau leaving Canaan as a simple matter of resource management. Which version does the narrator want readers to believe? Readers who believe chapter 28 can hardly believe chapter 36, and vice versa, since Esau and Jacob can hardly have separated over resource management issues while Esau was in Canaan and Jacob in Paddan-Aram. Nor can the two accounts be harmonized by supposing that chapter 36 relates to a time period just after the events of chapter 33, for the narrator clearly depicts Esau as already living in Seir at that point (cf. 32:3). Readers determined to read Genesis 12–36 as a coherent, unified narrative might be able to harmonize the accounts by supposing that 36:7 does not reflect any actual conflict or tension between Jacob and Esau, but instead represents Esau's own reasoning in advance of any such problems. Certainly, the description of Seir as a "land away from his brother Jacob" is equally appropriate whether Jacob is in Paddan-Aram at

30. *Gen. Rab.* 82:13; *Rashi's Commentary: Genesis.* 174.

31. Calvin, *Genesis*, 252–53.

32. Sarna, *Genesis*, 249. This issue was noted even in antiquity. Jewish tradition, as Sarna points out, "envisaged Esau as a nomad wandering over an area that covered both Canaan and Seir, until his permanent settlement in Seir after Jacob's return."

33. Fretheim, "Genesis," 590.

the time. Could it be that Esau foresaw the problems that *might* emerge when Jacob returned to Canaan, and voluntarily moved to Seir as a unilateral attempt to forestall any further conflict between himself and his brother? The narrator says nothing that would invalidate such a reconstruction.[34]

Heard himself notes that this is a rather thin and forced reading of the text. However, he goes on to say that

> from a functional perspective they do not need to cohere with one another. Each establishes, in its own way, Esau's voluntary renunciation of Canaan. In Genesis, Esau is neither entitled to nor interested in the territory promised to Abraham and his descendants.[35]

It appears, then, that the conflict tradition is downplayed in this episode, and a more positive construal offered. Indeed, it could be argued that what we see in Gen 36:6–8 is the fulfillment of the blessing in Gen 27:39–40.[36] Esau has done quite well for himself; not only does he have possessions and a family, but he will have his own land on which to become a people. As Spina comments, "There is no editorial attempt to remove this discrepancy by conflating the separate sources. Instead, the chronological problem raised by the textual structure is simply moved to the background, while the larger point that Esau's wealth was equal to Jacob's is highlighted."[37]

(3) *The Use of* אֲחֻזָּה. One final element regarding the connection of Esau and his descendants with Edom and Seir is the use of the term אֲחֻזָּה in 36:43. After the final list of the genealogy we read, "These were the chiefs of Edom, according to their dwellings (לְמֹשְׁבֹתָם) in the land of their possession (בְּאֶרֶץ אֲחֻזָּתָם)."

From the root אחז, the noun אֲחֻזָּה is broadly interpreted as "possession."[38] Because the word is used almost exclusively of land, the term is also understood as "landed property," or "property" in general.[39] Some have argued that the verb and its derivatives are not theological terms.[40]

---

34. Heard, *Dynamics*, 136.
35. Ibid., 178.
36. Alter, *Genesis*, 202; or, for Turner, evidence of the non-fulfillment of Esau's curse (Turner, *Announcements*, 127).
37. Spina, "The 'Face of God'," 19.
38. BDB, 28.
39. *HALOT* 1:31–32.
40. H. H. Schmid, "אחז," *THAT* 1:107–10 (109–10): "Eine eigentlich theologische Bedeutung hat die Wortgruppe nicht." Cf. A. H. Konkel, "אחז," *NIDOTTE* 1:354–58.

In Genesis, for example, the bulk of the occurrences are in reference to burial plots.[41] However, it should be kept in mind that "land of possession" is also linked with the promises to the patriarchs in Genesis. For instance, in Gen 17:8 Abraham is told, "For I will give to you and to your seed after you this land of your sojourning, all the land of Canaan, as an everlasting possession (לאחזת עולם)."[42] Moreover, even the use regarding burial plots has a theological function, as the patriarchs are purchasing plots for burial in the land of promise, and want to be returned there, even from Egypt. It is unclear, then, how someone such as Konkel defines "theological" when he writes: "Though *'ḥz* is used to describe the inheritance of the land as a gift, the term does not have a particularly theological function."[43]

Koopmans offers an alternative:

> Some scholars deny any particular theological importance to the term… However, a number of considerations are worth noting. The references to *'aḥuzzâ* usually imply a gift of property from Yahweh. Josh 22:19 even speaks of *'aḥuzzat yhwh*, "possession of Yahweh," and elsewhere the construction *'aḥuzzat 'ôlām*, "perpetual possession," is employed (Gen 17:8; 48:4; Lev 25:34). These references, along with the use in many other texts, indicate a specific awareness that the possession is a gift from God. Etymologically, the word is related to the concept of "grasping, seizing, holding," but in the context of the OT the predominant connotation is clearly that Israel's possession of land, whether privately and in families or collectively as a nation, is inseparable from the providential gift of Yahweh. The first references to a possession of this sort come in the context of God's covenantal promise of land, described in terms reminiscent of other ancient NE land grants given by a king to his vassals. Subsequent texts repeatedly seek to show how God's provision is being received by his people.[44]

While אחזה appears to be a less legal concept than נחלה,[45] the two can be seen in places functioning as parallels, such as Ps 2:8, where we find, "Ask of me, and I will give the nations as your inheritance (נחלתך), the

---

41. Gen 17:8; 23:4, 9, 20; 49:30; 50:13.

42. See also Gen 48:4.

43. Konkel, *NIDOTTE* 1:357. Cf. Gillis Gerleman, "Nutzrecht und Wohnrecht: Zur Bedeutung von אחזה und נחלה," *ZAW* 98 (1977): 313–24, who argues that both terms in his title should be understood simply as places of settlement.

44. William T. Koopmans, "אחזה," *NIDOTTE* 1:353–60 (359).

45. Friedrich Horst, "Zwei Begriffe für eigentum (besitz): נחלה und אחזה," in *Verbannung und Heimkehr: Festschrift für W. Rudolph* (ed. A. Kuschke; Tübingen: J. C. B. Mohr, 1961), 135–56.

ends of the earth your possession (וַאֲחֻזָּתְךָ)."[46] It would seem, then, that אֲחֻזָּה has a more nuanced range of meaning than is often put forward.

Interestingly, 36:43 is the only use of אֲחֻזָּה outside of references to the patriarchs in Genesis. Hence, it is possible that the use of אֲחֻזָּה here in 36:43 might have theological significance, and it is not unthinkable that "inheritance"-type connotations are in mind.[47] At the very least, stress is being laid on the fact that this land is the property and possession of Esau's descendants, in the same way that the patriarchs have laid claim to (parts of) Canaan. As will be shown in a subsequent chapter, the idea that YHWH has given the descendants of Esau the land of Edom as an inheritance is explicit in Deut 2, where not only is the land given by YHWH as a possession (יְרֻשָּׁה; Deut 2:5), but the previous inhabitants (the Horites) have been driven out before them by YHWH himself (Deut 2:22).[48]

Finally, an interesting comparison can be made between the language used of the Edomite chiefs in 36:43 and that used of Jacob in 37:1. While 36:43 speaks of the Edomite "dwellings (לְמֹשְׁבֹתָם) in the land of their possession (בְּאֶרֶץ אֲחֻזָּתָם)," 37:1 states that "Jacob dwelt (וַיֵּשֶׁב) in the land of his father's sojourning (מְגוּרֵי), in the land of Canaan." Thus, Esau and his descendants have taken possession of the land where they live, while Jacob is still sojourning. In the broader ancestral story, where "the land" is such an elusive and important element, this may be a telling statement.[49]

46. A further example of interchangeable use can be seen in Ezek 44:28. Cf. ibid., 154.

47. In *Targum Onqelos* we find אַחְסָנַתְהוֹן, from אַחְסָנָא, again meaning "property" or "inheritance." See Jastrow, 1:140. The LXX uses κτήσεως; from the root κτῆσις, the word means "acquisition, portion, possession, or property." J. Lust, E. Eynikel, and K. Hauspie, *A Greek–English Lexicon of the Septuagint* (Stuttgart: Deutsche Bibelgesellschaft, 1996), 270. The term אֲחֻזָּה occurs in the Qumran scrolls as well. In 1QS XI 7, for instance, the connotations of "inheritance" are clear: "God has given them to His chosen ones as an everlasting possession (לַאֲחֻזַּת עוֹלָם), and has caused them to inherit the lot of the Holy Ones." Geza Vermes, *The Complete Dead Sea Scrolls in English* (New York: Penguin, 1997), 115. For the Hebrew, see Donald W. Parry and Emanuel Tov, *The Dead Sea Scrolls Reader, Part 1: Texts Concerned with Religious Law* (Leiden: Brill, 2004), 40–41.

48. These same Horites are mentioned in the genealogy of ch. 36 as well, with a personified Seir as their ancestor (36:20–29).

49. Turner, *Announcements*, 138–39. This is another similarity with Deut 1–2, where the Israelites encounter several peoples who are established in their respective God-given lands, while the Israelites continue to wander.

b. *The Edomite King List*

A portion of Gen 36 which has inspired much historical comment is the Edomite king list of vv. 31–39.[50] This section begins with 36:31 stating, "These are the kings (ואלה המלכים) which reigned in the land of Edom before a king reigned before the sons of Israel." Two contextual and hermeneutical issues regarding this list are worth highlighting.

The first issue has to do with the meaning of the word מלך.[51] Some commentators have noted that here the term may be better rendered as "judges," as in the Israelite judges,[52] or as tribal chiefs, as found elsewhere in the Hebrew Bible.[53] This is due to the non-dynastic nature of the king list, and diverging places of origins for the various kings. While there may be some validity in these suggestions, the traditional understanding of these as "kings" of some sort is probably more apt, as the genealogy has already outlined tribes and clans. This may indeed refer to a primitive monarchy; nevertheless, the use of the term מלך seems intentional.

Secondly, the meaning of the final clause of 36:31 is debated. The question is whether the statement refers to any king ruling over Israel, or Israel having a king which ruled over Edom (i.e. David).[54] While a few commentators do opt for the latter understanding,[55] the majority seem to take this as a reference to a time prior to any monarchy in Israel, and the LXX reading of ἐν Ἰσραήλ may corroborate this.[56]

Thus, while a conclusive answer is not possible regarding these issues, it seems reasonable to understand this as a reference to "kings" (of some sort) which ruled over Edom before any monarchy existed in Israel. This, however, leads to a broader hermeneutical issue. The mention of kingship in Israel implies knowledge of an Israelite monarchy, and thus, even within the world of the text, seems to be told from a later historical

---

50. Historical examinations of this list can be found in E. A. Knauf, "Alter und Herkunft der edomitischen Königsliste Gen 36,31–39," *ZAW* 97 (1985): 245–53; Sarna, *Genesis*, 408–10; J. R. Bartlett, "The Edomite King-List of Genesis XXXVI. 31–39 and I Chron. I. 43–50," *JTS* 16 (1965): 301–314.

51. On the semantic range of this word, see K. Seybold, "מלך," *TDOT* 8:346–74, esp. 353–57, 360–62.

52. Levenson, "Genesis," 74.

53. Sarna (*Genesis*, 409) gives examples of Num 31:8 and Josh 13:21. The designation מלך is not the only term in Gen 36 which has been questioned; the term אלוף is also disputed, and has been understood as "chief," "duke," or "clan/group." See Speiser, *Genesis*, 282.

54. Bartlett, "The Edomite King-List," 310.

55. Gunkel, *Genesis*, 379.

56. Sarna, *Genesis*, 252; Alter, *Genesis*, 206.

perspective.[57] The question then becomes, as a narratorial comment, how should this be understood? Why is this statement here at all?

There are several ways this could be explained. On the one hand, the narrator could make mention of this to highlight the fact that the "older will serve the younger" (Gen 25:23), in reference to Israel's eventual subjugation of Edom under David. Some traditional interpretations seem to follow this line of thinking. For instance, *Gen. Rab.* 83:1 quotes Prov 20:21, noting that "an estate may be gotten hastily at the beginning." Luther offers a similar understanding: the people of God should not be jealous of those who obtain worldly prominence before them; God's people will have better things, if only they will wait.[58]

On the other hand, it can be argued that the mention of Edom's kings is indeed a positive statement, and may be seen as a fulfillment of the promise to Abraham that kings would come from his line, even from those outside the line of promise.[59] While the biblical tradition is at times ambivalent regarding kingship, it is also acknowledged that a monarchy is prestigious. As Brett comments,

> the lists of Edomite names and clans includes also a list of *kings* "who reigned in Edom before any king reigned over the children of Israel" (36:31). It would be mistaken to assume that this chapter simply provides some insignificant details about a son of Isaac who is not the bearer of the covenantal promise. On the contrary, genealogical detail is extremely important to the editors of Genesis, and this chapter provides a lengthy illustration of just how the promises to Abraham were already being fulfilled. Nations and kings have descended from Abraham through Esau, even before there were kings descended from Jacob/ Israel. In short, the promises to Abraham have flowed over the borders of any narrow conceptions of covenant and purity. Jacob the trickster is once again, it seems, being taught some patience by an ironic God. Just as the younger sister Rachel had to wait for the blessings of childbirth until Leah had borne all her children, so the elder brother Esau is to enjoy the blessing of kingship first.[60]

Thus, the mention of a monarchy in Edom may be yet another reminder to Jacob and Israel that they are part of a larger story, and that election does not entail a place of privilege in how that story unfolds.

57.   This posed problems for traditional interpretation ascribing authorship of the Torah to Moses, as Ibn Ezra pointed out (*Ibn Ezra's Commentary, Genesis*, 341–42). Cf. Levenson, "Genesis," 74; Speiser, *Genesis*, 281.

58.   Luther, *Lectures on Genesis, Chapters 31–37*, 304–6.

59.   Jon D. Levenson, "The Davidic Covenant and Its Modern Interpreters," *CBQ* 41 (1979): 205–19 (217); Spina, "The 'Face of God'," 20.

60.   Brett, *Genesis*, 106.

c. *The Reference to Amalek*

Two elements in Gen 36 may strike the reader as running counter to the idea that, as a whole, the genealogy should be understood as reflecting positively on Esau and Edom. The first is the inclusion of Amalek in the chapter (36:12, 16), and the second is the reference to Esau's Canaanite wives (36:2). The issue of Esau's wives will be dealt with below; for the time being we will touch briefly on Amalek.

Without doubt, the inclusion of Amalek should cause the reader to sit up and take notice, as the Amalekites were one of the traditional enemies of Israel.[61] That being said, the reference to Amalek is somewhat mitigated by its context in Gen 36. In v. 10 we are told that Eliphaz is Esau's son via Adah, and in v. 11, the sons of Eliphaz are listed. In v. 12, however, the textual flow is interrupted, and we are told that Timnah was a concubine of Eliphaz, and that she bore Amalek. What should we make of this? Sarna offers a possible understanding, one that is rooted in Jewish tradition:

> Behind this parenthetical note lies social and political history. According to verse 22, Timna was "the sister of Lotan," an indigenous Horite. This means that the Edomites who migrated to Seir began to intermarry with the natives but that such alliances were not socially acceptable, which explains Timna's inferior status here as a concubine rather than a wife… The obviously intrusive character of this item, which breaks the connection between the preceding data and the following clause, suggests that its purpose is to draw attention to the Amalekites not being genuine Edomites. This is important because Deuteronomy 23:8–9 forbids an Israelite to "abhor an Edomite," "a kinsman" of Israel.[62]

To be sure, the reference to Amalek may imply that one of Israel's worst enemies came from none other than Esau. Yet, syntactically and grammatically, the text may be mitigating this by drawing a distinction between the descendants of Esau and Amalek.

d. *Key Elements: Preliminary Conclusions*

This section explored several key elements within Gen 36, specifically the connection of Esau and Edom, Esau's move to Seir, the "possession"

---

61. See Deut 25:17–19; for general information, see Mattingly, "Amalek," 1:169–71.

62. Sarna, *Genesis*, 250; cf. Alter, *Genesis*, 204, and Wenham, *Genesis 16–50*, 338. Ramban (*Perusch ha-Torah*) offered a similar reading, distinguishing between the Edomites and the Amalekites. On this reading, see Asaf Turgeman, "Mein bruder ist ein Einzelkind: Die Esau-Darstellung in jüdischen Schriften des Mittelalters," in Langer, ed., *Esau – Bruder und Feind*, 135–53 (151).

of the land, the Edomite king list, and the inclusion of Amalek. Although
not the only possibility for how these elements can be understood, it does
seem that, taken in sum, these elements can be seen as pointing to a positive construal of Esau and his descendants. Even the reference to Amalek,
as we saw, is mitigated. Hence, although not in the chosen line, Esau has
been blessed in his own right, and is the unexpected fulfillment of promises given to his ancestors, including land, a people, and a kingship.

4. *Purpose of Genesis 36*

Thus far I have explored a possible framework for understanding Gen 36,
as well as various literary elements within the text itself. It has been
argued that one way of reading this chapter is as a condensed version of
the story of Esau and Edom, which mirrors that of Jacob and Israel, and
is in general positive in its portrayal. Yet the question remains: What
function does the chapter play in the larger story of Jacob and Israel? It
seems the chapter functions in at least three ways, readings which need
not be mutually exclusive.

First of all, Israel had an obvious historical interest in Edom: "Israel
considered Edom its nearest relative and especially by the fact the [*sic*]
Edom was for Judah the most important of the neighboring nations."[63]
Thus, it is not surprising that a catalogue of Esau's descendants, or
Edom's history, is given. And yet, the size of this list and the amount of
detail given "indicates more than academic interest in nearby foreigners."[64] Indeed, an entire, lengthy chapter in Israel's book of origins is
more space than many "insiders" are given.

Secondly, within the story of Genesis, ch. 36 has a literary function.
Robinson has noted that the genealogies offer a counterbalance to the
narrative sections of Genesis, and yet they play an important role as part
of the narratives, as we instinctively read them to be part of the larger
story.[65] In Genesis in particular, this happens with the term תולדות.[66] Not
only does this term serve as a primary way in which the book of Genesis
is structured, but תולדות is used to introduce both genealogical lists as

---

63. Gunkel, *Genesis*, 376; see also Manfred Weippert, "Edom und Israel," *TRE*
9:291–99 (297).

64. Knauth, "Esau, Edomites," 223.

65. Robert B. Robinson, "Literary Functions of the Genealogies of Genesis,"
CBQ 48 (1986): 595–608.

66. J. Schreiner, "תולדות," *TDOT* 15:582–88; Blum, *Die Komposition*, 432–35;
Childs, *Introduction*, 145–50.

well as narrative portions of the book.[67] Thus, Steinberg's statement that "Genesis is a book whose plot is genealogy"[68] is an important point to keep in mind.

This can be seen when Gen 36 is read in its broader context. For instance, Ishmael also has a genealogy to his name (Gen 25:12–18). While Esau's list precedes the תולדות of Jacob's family, Ishmael's precedes that of Isaac. Hence, the two elder sons are listed before their younger, promise-bearing brothers.[69] In the more immediate context, Gen 36 follows on directly after the death and burial of Isaac in ch. 35. In Gen 27:41, Isaac's death was to be the event which would allow Esau to take vengeance on his brother for the deception regarding the blessing. Here, however, the two brothers bury their father in peace, again like Ishmael and Isaac before them, allowing the story of Abraham's descendants to continue.[70] Thus, if we are attuned to the literary context, we might be expecting Esau's genealogy as the next logical part of the story.

But again, we are given more information in Gen 36 itself than needed for moving the larger story forward. As Wilson remarks, "The genealogies are far more detailed than they need to be in order to link two narrative complexes."[71] For Wilson, this means that the genealogies once had a role outside of their present context. While this may very well be the case, it might also show that these details were considered important in Israelite tradition. After all, it is worth remembering that these are Israel's history and Scriptures, and much of what we know of Edom comes from the biblical record. Why would they include *so much* information?

A reading strategy that accounts for the complex issue of election may add to the discussion. The *toledot* structure of Genesis is meant to narrow down the story "with fewer and fewer participants."[72] After all, the biblical

67. On this varied use, see Koch, "Die Toledot-Formeln," 183–91.

68. Naomi Steinberg, "The Genealogical Framework of the Family Stories in Genesis," *Semeia* 46 (1989): 41–50 (41).

69. The genealogies of these two "unchosen sons" also bracket the entire Jacob Cycle (Walters, "Jacob Narrative," 600).

70. Levenson, *Death*, 67. While not dismissing the fact that this scene may be presenting a different tradition of the fraternal strife between Jacob and Esau (or lack thereof), Alonso Schökel has argued that the death of or concern for the father is a motif which brings brothers together in several Genesis narratives. Thus, Abraham's death brings Ishmael and Isaac back together, and Judah's concern for Jacob opens up the possibility of the reunion with Joseph. See Luis Alonso Schökel, "Gn 35,28–29: Muerte de Isaac y reconcilación fraterna," *EstBib* 55 (1997): 287–95.

71. Wilson, *Genealogy and History*, 182.

72. Schreiner, *TDOT* 15:586.

story is about Israel and where it has come from. And yet, here we have a full chapter on Esau and his lineage. Brueggemann comments,

> The most remarkable feature of this genealogy is that it is here at all. It is stunning that the long conclusion of the Jacob tradition concerns Esau. Every listener to the whole story knows that we are ready to move to Joseph, to forget that older generation and move on to the new. But the tradition itself is not in such a hurry. The tradition finds it difficult to turn loose of Esau. And that raises important issues for a tradition undoubtedly shaped by the pressures and loyalties of the Jacob family.[73]

Fretheim similarly observes,

> it may be thought that because this chapter focuses on those who are "not chosen," whose history seemingly goes nowhere, it need not delay the reader. Yet, the inclusion of the stories of these peoples (known only from Israelite sources) is significant, for it makes the reader pause over the place of nonchosen ones and ponder their relationship to the chosen. Their story is not expunged or reduced to something of no account by the narrators of the story of the chosen people. The testimony of this chapter, with its references to Esau's land, material blessings, and the succession of generations is that God the Creator is indeed at work outside Israel, giving life and blessing to the nonchosen. The blessings given to Esau (27:39–40) continue to be realized down through the centuries.[74]

This, I would suggest, also helps make sense of the extended genealogy of Esau in 1 Chr 1:35–54. The Chronicler begins the history of Israel by placing the story in the broader context of the world in genealogical format.[75] Within the list of 1 Chr 1, the genealogy of Esau reappears, again directly before Israel's lineage.[76] Even here Esau's lineage is given 20 verses, and it seems that the Chronicler draws from and reworks the Genesis material.[77] Why is Esau's line recounted here? Regarding the

---

73. Brueggemann, *Genesis*, 285.

74. Fretheim, "Genesis," 591.

75. Knoppers, *I Chronicles 1–9*, 245; Johnson, *Purpose of the Biblical Genealogies*, 44–76; Joel P. Weinberg, "Das Wesen und die funktionelle Bestimmung der Listen in I Chr 1–9," *ZAW* 93 (1981): 91–114.

76. H. G. M. Williamson, *1 and 2 Chronicles* (NCB; Grand Rapids: Eerdmans, 1982), 40–45; Ralph W. Klein, *1 Chronicles* (Hermeneia; Minneapolis: Fortress, 2006), 74–81.

77. Indeed, it seems that 1 Chr 1 assumes knowledge of the Genesis text, and has several lacunae that the reader is expected to fill. See William Johnstone, "1 Chronicles 1: Israel's Place Within the Human Family," in *1 and 2 Chronicles. Vol. 1, 1 Chronicles 1–2 Chronicles 9, Israel's Place Among the Nations* (JSOTSup 253; Sheffield: Sheffield Academic, 1997), 24–36 (25); Knoppers, *I Chronicles 1–9*, 290–91.

purpose of this first chapter, Knoppers writes, "Like earlier biblical authors, the Chronicler is most interested in stories about Israel, but he also recognizes that Israel did not emerge out of a vacuum. Indeed, one can only appreciate the experience of Israel within its land if one has some understanding of lands and peoples relevant to Israel and how they are related to Israel."[78] Much like in Genesis, the Chronicler places Israel's story in the context of a broader story where the other branches in the genealogical tree are still important, and indeed are vital for Israel's self understanding.

In summary, Gen 36 can be seen to function as a historical reminder of why Israel's close neighbour Edom is important, and it also plays a role in the overall literary structure of Genesis. However, the scope and diversity of this chapter is illuminated when seen from a theological perspective: even as the unchosen brother, Esau's story, and that of his descendants, is an important one. Esau may not be the son of promise, but he has been blessed in his own right. In a sense, Israel's story is incomplete without the story of Esau and Edom.

5. *Genesis 36: Preliminary Conclusions*

This chapter has focused on Gen 36 and three pertinent issues: a framework in which the chapter as a whole might be understood, relevant literary elements, and the overall purpose of Gen 36 in its broader context. It was suggested that one way of reading Gen 36 is as a condensed version of Esau/Edom's history, paralleling the story of Israel from ancestor, to family, to tribes, to monarchy. This is not to downplay the historical difficulties or composite nature of the text. Rather, it is an attempt to find an approach to the chapter that makes sense of its structure and the scope of the material found therein.

With regard to the content of the chapter, several elements were highlighted, including the connection of Esau with Edom, the reason for Esau's departure from Canaan, the "possession" of the land of Seir, and the Edomite king list. It was argued that these various elements all further the thesis that Esau's story is mirroring Jacob's, and taken together, offer a positive portrayal of Esau with which the story of Esau in Genesis comes to a close: wealth and possessions, family and descendants, land and monarchy are all ascribed to Isaac's elder son.

---

78. Knoppers, *I Chronicles 1–9*, 295. Klein (*1 Chronicles*, 80–81) and Johnstone ("1 Chronicles 1," 24) reiterate this idea.

Finally, the purpose of the chapter within the larger storyline was discussed. While the historical and literary aspects of Gen 36 were recognized as legitimate and important, it was pointed out that the scope of the material may also be helpfully understood from a theological perspective. Genesis 36 is a reminder that election is a complex issue, and that stories outside of Israel's own narrative matter.

In summary, Gen 36 concludes the story of Esau in Genesis by presenting a thorough and perhaps unexpectedly positive portrayal of Esau and his progeny. While not the chosen son, Jacob's brother is blessed with land, descendants, and a future. Brueggemann notes,

> Without one disclaimer, the Esau community belongs to Genesis. To be sure, beyond chapter 36 the Esau memory is not developed. But it is there. It is not rejected or closed. The Bible chooses to follow the Jacob line. But that makes the Esau story no less legitimate. We are required by this carefully placed text to recognize the larger vision of Genesis.[79]

EXCURSUS: ESAU'S WIVES

Before concluding the discussion of the portrayal of Esau in Genesis, one final area needs to be touched on, and that is the issue of Esau's wives. This subject raises two questions which need to be addressed: first of all, how do we account for the confusing presentation of the names of Esau's wives in Genesis? And secondly, how are Esau's marriages portrayed in the text itself, and what do they contribute to the story and characterization of Esau?

a. *The Names of Esau's Wives*
We first learn of Esau's marriages in Gen 26:34, where we are told that he married Judith, daughter of Beeri the Hittite, and Basemath, daughter of Elon the Hittite. Then, in 28:9, we learn that Esau marries Mahalath, daughter of Ishmael, sister of Nebaioth. In 36:2–3, Esau is also said to have three wives. However, here the names are different: Adah, daughter of Elon the Hittite; Oholibamah, daughter of Anah, daughter[80] of Zibeon the Hivite; and Basemath, daughter of Ishmael, sister of Nebaioth. The difficulty lies in the fact that not only are there two lists of names, but there is an overlap between the two lists. Thus, Basemath appears in 26:34 and 36:3; in the first she is a Hittite, while in the second she is a daughter of Ishmael.

Several attempts have been made to explain these divergences. One approach is to claim that Esau had either five or six wives, and the lists are simply reporting different wives. However, the fact that both lists portray Esau with two Canaanite wives and one Ishmaelite wife makes this unlikely.

79. Brueggemann, *Genesis*, 286.
80. The Samaritan Pentateuch, LXX, and Peshitta all have "son of Zibeon" here.

A second approach is to posit some form of name variation, whether it is the case that the wives each had two names, or that the wives were renamed. This was a popular interpretive position in both the Jewish and Christian traditions.[81] J. Abraham offers the fullest contemporary account of this approach.[82] Abraham suggests that Esau's third wife was originally named Basemath. However, one of Esau's other wives was already called this; thus, he renamed her Mahalath. Here the original name is given in 36:3, and the new name in 28:9. This name means "to make sweet or pleasant," and it might also imply, as Rashi suggests, Esau's attempt at receiving forgiveness, as Mahalath may be related to מחל, "to forgive." Esau would go on to change his other wives' names as well. Oholibamah has at its root the word אהל, "tent" ("my tent is a shrine"?), and Abraham suggests this may be done by Esau in order to associate himself with the pastoral life of Jacob, a move away from his life as a hunter. The same goes for Adah, whose name first appears in Gen 4:19–20 as Lamech's first wife, mother of Jabal, "the ancestor of those who dwell in tents." For Abraham, all of this points to the fact that Esau is attempting to appease his parents and show a true change of heart.[83]

Abraham's proposal is creative, and I agree with much of what he says regarding Esau's desire to please his parents. However, Abraham's thesis does have some shortcomings. To begin with, it seems forced to think that in the case of the third wife, the original name appears in 36:3, while in the case of the first two wives, ch. 36 presents their changed names. Moreover, Abraham's (and Rashi's) use of מחל to infer "forgiveness" in Mahalath's name may be forcing the issue, not least because מחל is not a biblical term, but first appears in Mishnaic Hebrew, a fact which Abraham himself points out.[84] Abraham's overarching argument, that Esau is trying to make things right, is one with which I agree; however, the case can be made, in my estimation, without forcing the issue of renaming Esau's wives.

A final approach to the variations in Esau's wives names is to postulate that they come from different genealogical lists or traditions, but that there are only three wives. While not the ideal option for a synchronic reading of the text, this option does have several advantages. First of all, as pointed out above, the origins of the wives are broadly consistent: Hittite, Hivite, and Ishmaelite. While 26:34 lists both wives as Hittite, the Samaritan Pentateuch, LXX, and Peshitta all read "Hivite" for the second reference of "Hittite," thus harmonizing the two lists.[85] Even if we follow the MT, the implication of the three wife texts together is clear: Esau has two wives from the Canaanites, and one from the family of Ishmael.[86] Secondly, it should be

---

81. Luther, for instance, wrote that each wife had two names (*Lectures on Genesis, Chapters 31–37*, 286–88). Rashi (*Rashi's Commentary: Genesis*, 173) and Ibn Ezra (*Ibn Ezra's Commentary, Genesis*, 336) both argued for some variation on the idea that Esau renamed his wives.

82. Jed H. Abraham, "A Literary Solution to the Name Variations of Esau's Wives," *TMJ* 7 (1997): 1–14; Abraham, "Esau's Wives," *JBQ* 25 (1997): 251–59.

83. Abraham, "A Literary Solution," 5–6.

84. Ibid., 11 n. 28.

85. Hamilton, *Genesis 18–50*, 392.

86. Heard, *Dynamics*, 134.

kept in mind, as Wilson points out, that fluidity is one of the hallmarks of genealogies.[87] Thus, name variations should not be surprising.

Taken in sum, I would suggest that the best explanation for understanding the variation in names given to Esau's wives in Gen 26, 28, and 36 is that they come from different sources or traditions, and, for reasons unknown, their differences were allowed to stand in the text as it took shape.[88]

b. *How Are Esau's Marriages To Be Understood?*

A further question which can be asked is: What are the hermeneutical implications of the reports of Esau's marriages for understanding his story? This question relates more to the accounts in 26:34–35 and 28:6–9, and we will focus on these texts.

To begin with, it has been noted that the different backgrounds of Esau's wives may hint at the ethnic diversity seen in the later Edomite population.[89] While there is most certainly some truth in this understanding, it does not fully account for the narrative portions of Gen 26 and 28, specifically the dynamics within the family. A second approach sees Esau's marriages as contributing to or reinforcing his role as the unchosen, much like Ishmael before him.[90] It is common to see 26:34 cited as proof of Esau's unworthiness of being the elect. Sarna outlines Esau's threefold offense: he breaks with social convention by not being arranged in marriage; he does not practice endogamy; and he marries native women.[91] Moreover, Sarna notes that the recurring reference to "Canaanite women" in 28:1–9 and 36:2–3 is most likely derogatory.[92] This view has been reinforced in recent decades with the rise of kinship studies, where various schemes relating appropriate endogamous relation-ships have been put forward.[93] In a variety of ways, these scholars all see Esau's marriages as locating him outside of the chosen line.[94]

Other elements of these narratives can be seen to contribute to this understanding. In 26:35, after the report of Esau's first two wives, we are told, "These were bitter-ness of spirit (מרת רוח) to Isaac and Rebekah." This is the only use of the phrase

---

87. See Wilson, *Genealogy and History*, 174–81, where Gen 36 is specifically shown to be an example of genealogical fluidity, including Esau's wives.

88. Wenham, *Genesis 16–50*, 335.

89. Knauth, "Esau, Edomites," 223.

90. Robert L. Cohn, "Negotiating (with) the Natives: Ancestors and Identity in Genesis," *HTR* 96 (2003): 147–66 (153).

91. Sarna, *Genesis*, 189.

92. Ibid., 247.

93. Mara E. Donaldson, "Kinship Theory in the Patriarchal Narratives: The Case of the Barren Wife," *JAAR* 49 (1981): 77–87, argues for a matrilineal cross-cousin scheme; Steinberg (*Kinship and Marriage*) thinks the appropriate line lies with Abraham's descendants taking a wife from the line of Nahor; Kunin argues that the idea was to marry as close to the nuclear family as possible, without committing incest (Kunin, *Logic of Incest*, 56–61). Further kinship issues are discussed in Robert A. Oden Jr., "Jacob as Father, Husband, and Nephew: Kinship Studies and the Patriarchal Narratives," *JBL* 102 (1983): 189–205.

94. See more recently Tammi J. Schneider, *Mothers of Promise: Women in the Book of Genesis* (Grand Rapids: Baker Academic, 2008), 120–25.

מרת רוח in the Hebrew Bible; while there is some disagreement as to how this might be best rendered,[95] the sense is clear in that Esau's parents are not pleased with these marriages.[96]

This leads to the narrative comments given in 28:6–9. Here Esau learns that Jacob has been sent away, and has been instructed not to marry a Canaanite woman. In 28:8 we read, "And Esau saw (וירא) that the daughters of Canaan were displeasing (רעות) in the eyes of Isaac his father." As Wenham remarks, the fact that Esau only realizes his wives displease his parents in 28:6–9 might imply he is slow, a common characterization of Esau.[97] When Esau does try to remedy this by taking a wife from the family of Ishmael, this is often regarded as "too little, too late." As Bakhos comments, Esau's marriage to Ishmael's daughter "may be understood as Esau's attempt to appease his father after having married the Hittite women." However, "Bringing them together creates a relationship between the two ostracized elder brothers and confirms their shared marginalization."[98]

However, there are shortcomings in these various understandings that put Esau on the outside because of his marriages. To begin with, the various kinship theories offered regarding appropriate marriages are inconclusive. There simply is not enough information on these practices in the Hebrew Bible to develop a comprehensive theory of appropriate marriage relationships.[99] This leads to several of the more prominent theories put forward conflicting with one another.[100]

Moreover, where does responsibility lie with regard to the arranging of marriages? It could be argued that the narrative of 26:34 reflects poorly on Isaac, more so than Esau, showing the father's inability to have his own family follow tradition. If so, this would introduce a theme (Isaac's incompetence) which would continue in the events of Gen 27. As Heard notes,

> Nothing in the text indicates that either of his parents ever told him (in forty years of life!) that they preferred he not marry local women. One might suggest that Isaac would have instructed him properly had Esau involved Isaac in the process of selecting his wives, but Esau ignored protocol and bypassed his father, choosing his wives himself. Perhaps,

95. While the majority of commentators understand מרת as coming from מרר, "bitter," Alter translates this word as "provocation," from מרה, "rebel" or "defy." Alter, *Genesis*, 136.

96. See Mignon R. Jacobs, *Gender, Power, and Persuasion: The Genesis Narratives and Contemporary Portraits* (Grand Rapids: Baker Academic, 2007), 118–21.

97. Wenham, *Genesis 16–50*, 214.

98. Bakhos, *Ishmael on the Border*, 28, 59, 64.

99. Fretheim, "Genesis," 539; Heard, *Dynamics*, 108.

100. A thoroughgoing critique of these theories is offered by Heard, *Dynamics*, 119–26. He notes (125), "both Donaldson's and Steinberg's structural-anthropological explanations of marriage patterns in Genesis have limited value in resolving ambiguities related to Esau's, and for that matter Isaac's and Rebekah's, perception of Esau's marriage to Ishmael's daughter Mahalath. Neither an emphasis on matrilineal cross-cousin marriage nor an emphasis on marrying exclusively within the patrilineage of Terah can be definitively shown to concern either the narrator or the characters in the book of Genesis, and several textual clues resist such emphases."

although one should certainly keep in mind that there is no indication that Terah chose Abram's wife; that Abraham did not himself choose Isaac's wife, but only her homeland; and that Isaac did not himself choose Jacob's wife, but only her father. It is thus misguided of (e.g.) Wenham to charge Esau with a "deliberate rejection of family tradition" or with having "flouted family custom." One incident (in chapter 24) does not constitute a tradition or custom. On such logic, Isaac too must be censured for a "deliberate rejection of family tradition" when he sends Jacob himself to get a wife from Nahor's family rather than sending a servant to bring back a wife from Haran. More telling, Gen 28:8 strongly suggests that Esau did not know that his wives displeased his father until after Isaac had sent Jacob to Paddan-Aram with instructions to marry one of Laban's daughters. Perhaps Rebekah and Isaac were perfectly cordial to Judith and Basemath when the whole family was together, airing their dislike of the two only in the privacy of their own tent. The narrator does not reveal whether they ever expressed a preference about marriage partners prior to his unions with Judith and Basemath. Can Esau really be faulted for violating a parental preference he did not know existed?[101]

Furthermore, Esau's marriage to Mahalath after learning of his father's displeasure can be seen as the elder brother's attempt to redeem himself, to make amends, and to honor his parents.[102] Indeed, there is no reason that 28:6–9 should not be understood as a positive construal of Esau and his actions, regardless of his status as the unchosen son. Heard concludes:

> Neither the narrator nor any character (including God, later in chapter 28) postulates any explicit causal connection between Jacob's and Esau's marriages and their status (or lack of same) as parties to God's covenant with Abraham, nor can the structural anthropological models…establish such a connection. What the narrator wishes readers to conclude with regard to any such connection is simply unclear.[103]

In sum, it is difficult to argue conclusively that Esau's marriages are causally connected to his status as the unchosen son. His marriages to Canaanite women may have added to an already tenuous family situation, and they may also reinforce his status as an outsider as the story progresses. To be sure, the description of these women as "Canaanites" in Gen 36 may well be polemical. But in the world of the text, they in no way impinge on the dynamics of election or familial succession. Indeed, if we are looking at the characterization of the family members, it is once again Esau who makes the first move in attempting to ease the tension of family conflict. Whether or not this move was successful in repairing the bitter spirit of his parents, the text remains silent.

101.   Ibid., 109.
102.   *Rashi's Commentary: Genesis*, 173–74; Brueggemann, *Genesis*, 240, 285; Hamilton, *Genesis 18–50*, 235; Westermann, *Genesis 12–36*, 448; Fretheim, "Genesis," 537.
103.   Heard, *Dynamics*, 125–26.

Chapter 7

ESAU IN GENESIS:
SUMMARY AND CONCLUSIONS

The preceding chapters have attempted to show how Genesis is much more nuanced and positive in its portrayal of Esau than it is often given credit for in the history of interpretation, as well as in popular imagination.

To begin with, the oracle to Rebekah in Gen 25:23 is complex and fraught with ambiguous language. While this scene may push the narrative concerning Jacob and Esau in a particular direction, it does not set in stone the relationship between the brothers or their descendants. Meanwhile, the bartering away of Esau's birthright later in the chapter (25:27–34) may not be Esau's finest hour, but neither brother comes across as particularly fit to be the vessel of divine favor. Indeed, interpretations that understand Esau in a strictly negative light in this episode may be ignoring the complexity and subtlety of the pericope. With regard to the pronouncements which Isaac makes over his sons in Gen 27, it was argued that Isaac's statement to Esau is best understood as a blessing, albeit a lesser blessing than that which Jacob received. In this reading, Esau is promised land and fertility, and though subservient to his brother, Jacob's blessing is mitigated by that which is given to Esau.

In Gen 32–33 we see the climax of the tension which has been building between the twin sons of Isaac. As Jacob returns to the land of promise, the reader is left wondering whether Esau will impede this journey. As it turns out, Esau responds in a manner that causes Jacob to liken it to a divine encounter: to see Esau's face is as seeing the face of God. While the brothers separate in what appears to be a less than perfect resolution, there is reconciliation nonetheless, and we are told in Gen 35:29 that they buried their father together. Finally, Gen 36 outlines in extensive fashion the genealogy of Esau. While there are elements of this chapter which may be understood as reflecting poorly on Esau and his descendants, it was argued that on the whole the chapter can be understood as positive: Esau has his own land, becomes his own people, and will even have a monarchy before Israel. Moreover, this chapter can be seen to mirror the same stages of societal development that the Israelites would go through, from eponymous ancestor, to tribes and clans, to monarchy. In a sense, then, Gen 36 is the story of Esau and Edom in miniature.

How might these readings shape our understanding of the theological concept of election? When one looks at Esau's story arc from Gen 25 to Gen 36, it is clear that Esau, in the tradition of Cain, Ishmael, and Reuben, is the firstborn son who is passed over in favor of the younger son. At points it seems that YHWH plays a role in this choice (Gen 25:23), while at other times the actions of his brother and mother seem to work against Esau (Gen 25:27–34; 27). In and through these various means, however, by the end of Gen 27 it is clear to the reader that Esau has been displaced as the firstborn in his family, and he will not be the bearer of promise in the divine economy.

The key development in Esau's character comes off stage, as it were, in the years when Jacob is sojourning with Laban (Gen 28–31). For when Jacob comes to meet Esau following this absence of several decades, Esau welcomes Jacob home in true brotherly fashion. Without reading too much into this scene, one might say that Esau has come to grips with his status as the displaced firstborn. He has accepted his lot in life, and seems content with what his own blessing has afforded him. (It may be that the reality of Esau's blessed life is spelled out for the reader in Gen 36.) Moreover, as Esau defeats the "sin crouching at his door" in a way that Cain never does, Esau becomes the face of God to his brother. Thus, the wronged and unchosen brother becomes in the end an unexpected picture of grace and favor for the elect.

Several preliminary conclusions might be drawn from this assessment. We might first note that the readings offered above substantiate the idea that election is a mystery and a scandal. The elevation of Jacob and displacement of Esau does not appear to be based on the worth (or unworthiness) of either sibling. Indeed, readings which attempt to offer justification of God's elective choice may be forcing the issue on the text. Secondly, the displacement of Esau in Genesis does not necessitate his being cursed. The depiction of Esau and his kin in Gen 32–33 and 36 makes clear that Esau and his people have done well for themselves. A third and related point is that the non-election of Esau does not eliminate him from the divine economy. His line might not be that from which the Israelites will come; however, Esau is compared favorably to Jacob's

God, and his hospitality marks an important development in that it allows the story of Jacob to move forward. Thus, a reading strategy that understands election in terms of scarcity does a disservice to the text.

Deuteronomy offers a (somewhat surprising) expansion on several of these themes, reiterating the notion that Esau and his descendants are Israel's kin, while making explicit the fact that Esau's progeny have their own story with YHWH, one which in many ways mirrors Israel's story. It is to this portrayal that we now turn.

Chapter 8

DEUTERONOMY'S PORTRAYAL
OF THE SONS OF ESAU AND THE EDOMITES

1. *Introduction*

A brief glance at the standard literature on election will quickly reveal
that Deuteronomy offers an important voice on this issue. Indeed, many
studies on the subject take Deuteronomy as their exegetical starting
point.[1] This is understandable for a number of reasons, most notably the
recurring election-related language found in the book, including what
many consider the *locus classicus* of Deut 7:6–8.[2] However, as Kaminsky notes, while Deuteronomy focuses in on Israel's special status, it is
less clear on the question of "what role this people is to play in relation
to the larger terrestrial world."[3] Part of the reason for this is that both the
Priestly and Deuteronomic materials "are attempts to construct an ideal
Israelite society, and they spend little energy on questions surrounding
the implications of Israel's election for the larger world."[4] As such,
scholars must make use of texts that might not have this concern in mind
in order to come to any conclusions regarding Deuteronomy's view of
the non-elect. Thus, Deuteronomy in places seems to exhibit "a kind of
ethnic triumphalism," while in others "there is room left for other nations
to play their legitimate roles in the larger divine drama."[5]

Miller has offered perhaps the most thorough attempt at investigating
this latter point, exploring such "marginal subthemes" found throughout
Deuteronomy:

1. E.g. Vriezen, *Die Erwählung Israels*, 51–63; Dale Patrick, "Election, Old
Testament," *ABD* 2:434–41 (435).
2. So Vriezen, *Die Erwählung Israels*, 51.
3. Kaminsky, *Yet I Loved Jacob*, 101.
4. Ibid., 103.
5. Ibid., 101; cf. Lohr's comments on Deuteronomy in Lohr, *Chosen and
Unchosen*, 148–93.

There are a few texts in the book of Deuteronomy that, somewhat surprisingly, intimate an involvement of the Lord of Israel with other nations
in ways that are highly reminiscent of Israel's own story with this God.
This is a subtheme of Deuteronomic theology that lacks the kind of insistent articulation devoted to other dimensions of that theology. Indeed, there
are ways in which this theme is so out of sorts with the main emphases
that one must regard it as a kind of marginal issue in Deuteronomy. Its
presence, however, is not to be denied, and the very way in which it cuts
against the grain of Deuteronomy's more persistent concerns, such as the
Shema and the demand for full obedience to the First Commandment, the
gift of the land to Israel, and the conviction of Israel's election press for a
more substantial account of this marginal dimension of Deuteronomic
theology than is ordinarily the case.[6]

It is this "subtheme" that most affects the present study, as the only two
references in Deuteronomy to the sons of Esau and Edom are both,
somewhat surprisingly, positive. Why might this be the case?

I will suggest that the gracious response which Israel is to show the
sons of Esau and Edom in Deuteronomy is grounded in two main concepts: the idea that the nations are kin, and the fact that YHWH has been
personally involved with the giving of land to Esau and Edom. It may be
that this positive disposition toward Esau and Edom can give us renewed
appreciation of the complexity of Deuteronomy's election theology, as
well as the role that Esau and Edom play within the larger tableaux of the
Hebrew Bible.[7]

2. *Deuteronomy 2: Brotherhood and Possession of the Land*

The first mention of Esau/Edom terminology in Deuteronomy occurs in
ch. 2, which is situated in the historical prologue to the book, running
from chs. 1–3.[8] Here Moses is reminding the Israelites of their wilderness

6.   Patrick D. Miller, "God's Other Stories: On the Margins of Deuteronomic
Theology," in *Israelite Religion and Biblical Theology: Collected Essays* (JSOTSup
267; Sheffield: Sheffield Academic, 2000), 593–602 (593).

7.   The present work is not as concerned with Deuteronomy's origins as it is with
the book's portrayal of particular non-Israelites in two specific passages, although
admittedly these issue are not always easily separated. On general historical- and
source-critical issues concerning the book, see the major commentaries, including
Jeffrey H. Tigay, *Deuteronomy* (JPSTC; Philadelphia: The Jewish Publication
Society, 1996); Moshe Weinfeld, *Deuteronomy 1–11* (AB 5; New York: Doubleday,
1991); and A. D. H. Mayes, *Deuteronomy* (NCB; Grand Rapids: Eerdmans, 1979).
For issues surrounding the Deuteronomistic history, consult Moshe Weinfeld, *Deuteronomy and the Deuteronomic School* (Oxford: Oxford University Press, 1972).

8.   On the structure and theology of Deut 1–3, see Norbert Lohfink, "Darstellungskunst und Theologie in Dtn 1,6–3,29," in *Studien zum Deuteronomium und*

journey leading up to their present situation on the plains of Moab, and in this section the encounters between the Israelites and the various nations of the Transjordan are recounted, including the sons of Esau. We are told of three positive encounters (sons of Esau, Moab, and Ammon) and two hostile meetings (Sihon and Og). Several interesting issues are raised in this chapter regarding the descendants of Esau, namely the designation of the sons of Esau as Israel's kin, and the notion that their land has been given to them as a possession by Israel's God. However, before exploring these issues, I will briefly lay out how pre-modern and contemporary interpreters have dealt with this passage, particularly the reference to Esau's descendants.

a. *History of Interpretation*
When considering Deut 2, contemporary scholarship has focused its attention on two main areas. The first is the relationship of the traditions in Numbers and Deuteronomy that depict Israel's encounters in the Transjordan, whether this entails harmonizing the two accounts, or positing priority for either Numbers or Deuteronomy.[9] An example of this can be seen in Weinfeld's commentary, where he spends the bulk of the space devoted to Deut 2 exploring similarities and differences between the Numbers and Deuteronomy accounts, as well as in explanation of the geography of Israel's route. The only comment made regarding why the Deuteronomic material may have been shaped the way it has is the off-handed comment that "the presentation in Deuteronomy reflects a more patriotic attitude. Deuteronomy presents a picture of a proud and strong

der deuteronomistischen Literatur I (SBAB 8; Stuttgart: Katholisches Bibelwerk, 1991), 15–25; and Patrick D. Miller, "The Wilderness Journey in Deuteronomy: Style, Structure, and Theology in Deuteronomy 1–3," in *Israelite Religion*, 572–92. A helpful summary of the history of interpretation of Deut 1–3 is found in Horst Dietrich Preuss, *Deuteronomium* (EdF 164; Darmstadt: Wissenschaftliche Buchgesellschaft, 1982), 75–80.

9. Because of space I am not able to deal with the similar accounts found in Numbers. I note the possible relationship between the encounters in Deuteronomy and Numbers in relation to the present thesis in the concluding chapter of this study. Helpful introductions can be found in David A. Glatt-Gilad, "The Re-Interpretation of the Edomite-Israelite Encounter in Deuteronomy II," *VT* 47 (1997): 441–55; W. A. Sumner, "Israel's Encounters with Edom, Moab, Ammon, Sihon, and Og According to the Deuteronomist," *VT* 18 (1968): 216–28; Jerome T. Walsh, "From Egypt to Moab: A Source Critical Analysis of the Wilderness Itinerary," *CBQ* 39 (1977): 20–33; G. I. Davies, "The Wilderness Itineraries and the Composition of the Pentateuch," *VT* 33 (1983): 1–13; George W. Coats, "The Wilderness Itinerary," *CBQ* 34 (1972): 135–52.

nation that is able to defeat its enemies but is not allowed to encroach on the rights of its neighbors."[10]

A second approach of contemporary scholarship has been the exploration of what socio-political realities could have brought about the positive portrayal of these neighboring lands. An example is Bartlett, who writes,

> Deut 2:1–8 is interesting in that it avoids reference to any hostile action on either side, and underlines the brotherly relationship. The Deuteronomistic author is clearly aware that Edom had been a threat to Israel; but Edom is no longer a threat and is to be treated with respect. This is in striking contrast with all other biblical writers and cries for explanation.[11]

This promising elucidation of the issues, however, is abruptly brought to an end with the following: "Possibly the author writes from a late, post-exilic situation when Edomites are no longer any threat."[12]

These contemporary interpretations have fostered much debate, and have led to important discoveries regarding literary relationships and historical development of traditions. They also, however, have tended to encourage a general neglect of Deuteronomy's theology, and particularly its surprisingly positive portrayal of these three non-Israelite nations.[13]

Though pre-modern interpreters did make mention of the relationship of the two traditions,[14] they also tried to make sense of Deuteronomy's positive disposition toward Esau's descendants (as well as toward Moab and Ammon).[15] Somewhat surprisingly, given the more general tendency

---

10. Weinfeld, *Deuteronomy 1–11*, 166. Cf. von Rad, *Deuteronomy*, 41–43; Mayes (*Deuteronomy*, 135), offers a similar reading, but does note that the Deuteronomist is using explicitly theological language to refer to the divine gift of land.

11. John R. Bartlett, "Edom in the Nonprophetical Corpus," in Edelman, ed., *You Shall Not Abhor an Edomite*, 13–22 (19).

12. Bartlett, "Edom in the Non-Prophetical," 19.

13. Glatt-Gilad, "The Re-Interpretation," 446.

14. For example Rashi, Ibn Ezra, and Rashbam all address these issues. These readings tend toward harmonizing the two traditions in various ways, a famous example being the conflation found in the Samaritan Pentateuch. See Johann Maier, "Israel und 'Edom' in den Ausdeutungen zu Dtn 2:1–8," in *Judentum—Ausblicke und Einsichten. Festschrift für Kurt Schubert* (ed. Clemens Thoma; Frankfurt: Lang, 1993), 135–84, for extensive treatment on the LXX, targumic, and rabbinic portrayals of both accounts.

15. Both the LXX and *Targum Onqelos* offer relatively straightforward readings of Deut 2. The LXX refers to "your brothers the sons of Esau" (των ἀδελφῶν ὑμῶν Ησαυ; 2:4) who have been given Mount Seir as a "possession" or "inheritance" (κλήρω; 2:5). The same root occurs in 2:22, which speaks of the sons of Esau "dispossessing" (κατεκληρονόμησαν) the Horites. Meanwhile, *Targum Onqelos* similarly

of interpreters to castigate Esau and Edom, these positive portrayals are not whitewashed, but are explained in light of broader canonical resonances. Rashi, for example, has YHWH telling Israel that Mount Seir is given to Esau as an inheritance from Abraham:

> I gave ten nations to Abraham, seven of them for you [the seven of Canaan], and the Kenites, the Kenizzites, and the Kadmonites (Gen. 16:18–21), who are Ammon, Moab, and Seir. One of them is for Esau, and the other two are for the children of Lot. As a reward [for Lot] for going with him (Abraham) to Egypt and for keeping silent when Abraham said, regarding his wife, 'She is my sister,' He treated him [Lot] as his [Abraham's] son [to inherit part of the land promised to Abraham].[16]

In this instance, Rashi deduces that Israel was not allowed to have these neighboring lands because of the peoples' respective kinship through Abraham, as well as the deference that Lot accorded Abraham. While Rashi's comments here are pointed at Lot, *Deut. Rab.* 1:17 makes a similar claim in relation to Esau. Noting that because Esau honoured his parents by bringing them meals (Gen 25:28), and that he showed respect for Jacob's possessions (Gen 33:8), *Deuteronomy Rabbah* makes the claim that God rewarded Esau and would not allow his descendants to be provoked. Thus, in both Rashi and *Deuteronomy Rabbah*, kinship with and ethical behavior toward the patriarchs are given as explanation for these neighbors retaining their lands during Israel's journey through the Transjordan. These interpretations are insightful, and the issues noted here will recur in the reading offered below.

In fact, I would suggest that there are two issues that need to be expanded upon in order to understand how this text may aid our understanding of the canonical portrayal of Esau and Edom: first, the significance of the language used, specifically the term "brother" and the reference by name to Esau; and secondly, the reasons the text gives regarding why the Israelites are to treat the sons of Esau in a gracious manner. To be sure, as Miller notes, these positive portrayals of Israel's neighbors are "marginal subthemes" in Deuteronomy, and thus one needs to be careful so as to not overstate their importance. And yet, they are present nonetheless, and are worth exploring.

---

speaks of "your brothers the sons of Esau" (אחיכון בני עשו; 2:4) who have been given Mount Seir as a "possession" (ירותא; 2:5). As such, both LXX and *Targum Onqelos* retain the language of the MT.

16.   Rashi's commentary on Deuteronomy, available online: http://www.chabad. org/library/bible_cdo/aid/9966/showrashi/true. Rashi is here drawing on *Gen. Rab.* 44.

b. *Brother Esau*

In Deut 2:4, YHWH instructs Moses to tell the people the next leg of their journey will bring them to the territory of "your brothers (אחיכם), the sons of Esau (בני־עשׂו), who live in Seir (בשׂעיר)." References to the brotherhood of Jacob/Israel and Esau/Edom are found primarily in the Pentateuch (Gen 25; 27; 32–33; Num 20:14; as well as Deut 2 and 23) and the prophetic literature (Amos 1:11; Obad 10, 12; Mal 1:2).[17] Michael Fishbane has argued, in light of Akkadian treaties and their frequent correspondence in form and content with Deuteronomy, that the Hebrew use of אח can in certain contexts be understood as "treaty partner."[18] This seems to be a valid point, and there are without doubt political implications for Israel's interaction with the inhabitants of Seir in Deut 2. However, the reference to Esau by name in the present context should give us pause, as images of the ancestral narratives and the tumultuous relationship between Jacob and Esau are conjured up, laying stress on the familial link. Moreover, the use of the kinship motif implicitly recurs later in the chapter when Moab (2:9) and Ammon (2:19) are referred to as "descendants of Lot." Thus, the reference to brotherhood in 2:4 may in fact refer to a tradition which knew of a relationship between Jacob and Esau, or it might imply a treaty relationship; in either case, what rhetorical function does it play in the text? Numerous commentators mention the importance of the brotherhood language here, but most tend to leave the issue at that.[19] Others offer brief ethical observations, such as "Kinship language implies that ethnic ties preclude warlike behavior."[20] But again, the discussion is frequently brief.

The key to understanding the use of "brother" may lie in the broader context of Deuteronomy. The term אח occurs in various forms over forty times throughout the book.[21] The term is used almost exclusively to refer

---

17. See Bartlett, "Land of Seir," 1–20, for further literary and historical connections between these two people groups.

18. See Michael Fishbane, "The Treaty Background of Amos 1:11 and Related Matters," *JBL* 89 (1970): 313–18 (314–15). Cf. John Priest, "The Covenant of Brothers," *JBL* 84 (1965): 400–406.

19. See, for instance, Tigay, *Deuteronomy*, 23.

20. Richard D. Nelson, *Deuteronomy* (OTL; Louisville: Westminster John Knox, 2002), 35; cf. Thomas W. Mann, *Deuteronomy* (WeBC; Louisville: Westminster John Knox, 1995), 30.

21. Deuteronomy does infrequently use other terminology as well, such as "son of your mother" (13:7). For more on אח in Deuteronomy, see Lothar Perlitt, "'Ein einzig Volk von Brüdern': Zur deuteronomischen Herkunft der biblischen Bezeichnung 'Brüder'," in *Deuteronomium-Studien* (FAT 8; Tübingen: J. C. B. Mohr, 1994), 50–73.

to the Israelites themselves, in the more strict familial sense, as well as to the idea of a neighbor or the broader national community. When speaking of the people of Israel, the term is often used as a boundary and identity marker for the Israelites, which often includes moral and ethical imperatives.[22] As Miller notes, "the identification of the *'āh*, 'brother/ sister' as a moral category properly has its origins in Deuteronomy. It is clear from this book that such kinship, encountering someone as *'āh*, places a moral responsibility upon the one to whom the other is an *'āh*. Thus special care to provide for and to keep from harm is placed upon the relationship."[23]

It is interesting to note, then, that the "sons of Esau" (2:4, 8) and the "Edomites" (23:8) are the only references within Deuteronomy to "brothers" outside of the Israelites themselves.[24] Might we infer from this that the sons of Esau/Edomites demand a particular response from the Israelites, similar to that which is expected toward fellow Israelites?

Meanwhile, commentators frequently express surprise that "Esau" is used by name in 2:4, instead of "Edom." After all, the parallel accounts of this story in Num 20 and Judg 11 refer to Edom, as does Deut 23:8. It is not an incidental usage, however, as the term recurs in the contextual unit in Deut 2:8, 12, and 22. Perlitt and Nielsen offer a possible explanation, stating that the Deuteronomist uses idealistic language, deflecting the possible negative stigma attached to the state of Edom and nationalistic rivalry.[25] This may well be the case, though the usage of "Edomites" in 23:8 would remain problematic. I would suggest another possibility: that the use of the name Esau here in connection with the inheritance of the land has resonance with the traditions found in Genesis and elsewhere (e.g. Josh 24:4) connecting Esau with Edom and Seir, thus legitimizing the Edomite settlement. This will be expanded upon in the following section.

Taken together, we can see that Deut 2:4 uses the distinctive language of "brotherhood" and "Esau." The use of Esau conjures up images of the ancestral traditions, drawing on an assumed familial relationship. The brotherhood language functions in a similar way; however, it may be the

22. See H. Ringgren, "אח," *TDOT* 1:188–93 (192).
23. Miller, "The Wilderness Journey," 581.
24. Somewhat surprisingly, commentators infrequently make note of this. In the literature which I surveyed this fact was highlighted only by Otto Bächli, *Israel und die Völker: Eine Studie zum Deuteronomium* (ATANT 41; Zurich: Zwingli, 1962), 121–22.
25. Eduard Nielsen, *Deuteronomium* (HAT I/6; Tübingen: J. C. B. Mohr, 1995), 34; Lothar Perlitt, *Deuteronomium* (BKAT 5; Neukirchen–Vluyn: Neukirchener, 1990), 153.

case that this term also adds an ethical dimension, as made of Israel concerning kin elsewhere in Deuteronomy. The responsibility in this case seems to land on the Israelites, who are to act in a particular fashion because of the nature of the relationship. Finally, the use of brotherhood terminology should give us pause, as the sons of Esau/Edomites are the only ones referred to as Israel's brother outside of the Israelite people themselves.

c. *Why the Gracious Treatment of the Sons of Esau?*

As the Israelites are about to pass through Seir, three issues are proffered which are to affect Israel's approach towards the sons of Esau. First of all, we are told the inhabitants of Seir will be afraid of the Israelites, so they are to be careful (2:4). Secondly, the Israelites are not to provoke them—presumably to war—because Mount Seir has been given to Esau "as a possession" (2:5). And finally, if the Israelites wonder why they are commanded to buy food and water from the inhabitants of Seir as they progress, YHWH reminds them that he has blessed them, known them, and watched over them during their extended period of wandering in the wilderness (2:6–7). We will focus below on the second issue, the sons and Esau and their relationship to the land of Seir; however, before that, a brief a word on the first and final reasons which are given might be in order.

With regard to the first issue, the fear of the inhabitants of Seir (2:4) presumably has to do with either the size of the Israelite contingent, and the difficulties of travel and resources associated with this, or perhaps the idea that the nations had heard of YHWH's actions on Israel's behalf (so Rahab in Josh 2:8–11). Regardless, it is notable that YHWH warns the people to be careful about this, and presumably not to use it for their own advantage. Indeed, YHWH's next words are a command not to provoke the inhabitants, implying a respectful crossing through their land.

The final reason (2:6–7) is connected to YHWH's command that the people are to purchase food and drink from the people of Seir: "For YHWH your God has blessed you (ברכך) in all that your hand has done; he knew (ידע) your wandering in this great wilderness, these forty years YHWH your God was with you. You did not lack a thing." The idea of "knowing" (ידע) has a strong connection with election in the Hebrew Bible.[26] In Deut 2:7, YHWH's "knowing" Israel seems to be paralleled

26. G. J. Botterweck, "ידע," *TDOT* 6:448–81 (468). See also the standard literature on election, including Vriezen, *Die Erwählung Israels*, 36–37. For the legal and treaty background of this term, see Herbert B. Huffmon, "The Treaty Background of Hebrew YADA'," *BASOR* 181 (1966) 31–37.

with his blessing and his presence, all of which have ensured that the people have not lacked anything.[27] Thus, the final reason the people of Israel are to treat the inhabitants of Seir well is because YHWH has known Israel and continually provided for them, and will continue to do so on their journey. It is worth keeping in mind, then, that in the midst of this section regarding YHWH's involvement with other nations, Israel's special relationship with YHWH is still a prominent idea and never far from the surface.

(1) *The Possession of Seir*. Surely one of the most unexpected elements of the Israelites' encounter with the nations of the Transjordan is Deuteronomy's assertion that these other nations were given their lands by YHWH, as Canaan would be given to the Israelites. As Nelson notes, there is a vast difference between land not being given to Israel and that land being given exclusively to someone else by Israel's God.[28]

Regarding the sons of Esau, we read in 2:5, "Do not provoke them (אל־תתגרו), for I will not give (לא־אתן) to you from their land (מארצם) even a foot; for as a possession for Esau (כי־ירשה לעשו) I gave (נתתי) Mt Seir." The Israelites are enjoined not to provoke the sons of Esau on their trek through the land of Seir. The reason for this is that the Israelites have no right to the land—it has been given to Esau by YHWH and is thus not rightfully attainable for the Israelites. This endowment of land is not limited to the sons of Esau in Deut 2; the lands where the Moabites and the Ammonites reside have also been granted to these nations. Two elements of these gifts of land are notable: first, the land is given by YHWH as ירש, a "possession" or "inheritance." And second, part of the giving of the land was the driving out of its former inhabitants.

Deuteronomy 2:5 notes that the land (ארץ) is given (נתן) by YHWH as a possession (ירש). Plöger has noted that ארץ in this and similar contexts takes on the meaning of a sovereign territory.[29] This seems the obvious understanding in light of the possessive plural ending given to the word in v. 5, as well as the fact that in v. 4 the people are told they will be passing through the "territory" (בגבול) of their brothers the sons of Esau. The use of נתתי in this context, meanwhile, can be understood to possess

---

27. The idea of "blessing" (root ברך) also has a strong connection to election in the Hebrew Bible. See Franz Josef Helfmeyer, "Segen und Erwählung," *BZ* 18 (1974): 208–23.

28. Nelson, *Deuteronomy*, 34–35.

29. Josef G. Plöger, *Literarkritische, formgeschichtliche und stilkritische Unter-suchungen zum Deuteronomium* (BBB 26; Bonn: Hanstein, 1967), 116. Cf. BDB, 75–76.

theological nuance, as נתן is often used in situations where an inheritance is given, including the inheritance of land.[30] Indeed, the word is used this way throughout Deuteronomy in reference to YHWH giving the land of promise to Israel.[31] The theological dimension of the term נתן takes on further significance when we take into account its use in conjunction with ירשה. The verbal form ירש generally means "to take possession of, inherit, or dispossess," while the nominal form used here is understood as "possession" or "inheritance."[32] Lohfink notes that although the noun does not always denote inheritance, the theological usage throughout Deut 2 (vv. 5, 9, 12, and 19) as well as elsewhere in the Hebrew Bible (2 Chr 20:11; Josh 12:6, 7) implies synonymous usage with נחלה.[33] The relationship between the two may be reinforced by the use of נחלה in Deut 32:8, which also speaks of the nations receiving an inheritance. Finally, Deuteronomy has various passages where the two terms are used in conjunction with one another, as in נחלה לרשתה, "as an inheritance to possess" (Deut 15:4; cf. 25:19; 26:1).

Lohfink describes at length the relationship between the terms נתן and ירשה in the Deuteronomic context:

> Theologically, the crucial point in this stratum is the association of Israel's *yrš* with Yahweh's *ntn*... What do these passages mean by saying that Yahweh "gives" something? In JE, the promise to the fathers may have been based on the model of a donation; here, however, we can see another model at work. If Yahweh, the one God, "gives" various neighboring nations their territories, the "gift" must be interpreted after the analogy of royal allotment of land. This may be conceived as reflecting a feudal privilege, much like enfeoffment (cf. 1 S. 8; 14; 22:7; 27:6); or else it presupposes a system in which the entire land is considered the king's property. In this case, a real estate transaction (although in fact representing a purchase agreement, say, between two private parties) must be construed juridically as (appropriation and) a new "gift" on the part of the king... Our texts do not make clear which of the two possible analogies is intended. Possibly the matter was left deliberately vague so

---

30. BDB, 678–82. Cf. Michael A. Grisanti, "נתן," *NIDOTTE* 3:205–11; e.g. Gen 17:8; Lev 14:34; Num 16:14; 26:54. Jer 27:5–6 is a classic example of this idea, where the creator God gives the earth to anyone he pleases, in this case Nebuchadnezzar. For more on נתן, see Norbert Lohfink, "Dtn 12.1 und Gen 15,18: das dem Samen Abrahams geschenkte Land als der Geltungsbereich der deuteronomischen Gesetze," in *Väter Israels* (Stuttgart: Katholisches Bibelwerk, 1989), 183–210.

31. There are too many examples to list, but in the first chapter alone we have occurrences of נתן with reference to YHWH giving the land in 1:8, 20, 21, 25, 35, 36, and 39.

32. BDB, 439–40.

33. N. Lohfink, "ירש," *TDOT* 6:368–96 (376).

as to accommodate both early feudal notions of the relationship between Yahweh and Israel and parallels to notions of ancient Near Eastern property law that had taken hold in Judah… With respect to their earthly territory, Yahweh's relationship to the nations of the world is that of a king to his subjects with respect to productive land. Yahweh, as king, is lord of every territory. Transfer of title becomes legally valid only through his juridical act, termed "giving."[34]

The ramifications, according to Lohfink, are as follows: "The use of *yrš* in this group of texts set Israel's occupation of the land…in a comprehensive scheme of theological and juridical legitimation."[35]

Given the linguistic and thematic similarities, what Lohfink says of Israel should correspond to Seir/Edom as well, not to mention Moab and Ammon: there is a "theological legitimation" to the possession of these lands. This gift of land to other nations is all the more striking when we take into account the subsequent encounters with the kings Sihon and Og in Deut 2:24–3:11. As the Israelites prepare to meet these leaders they are told that YHWH has "given" (נתתי) the kings and their land into the hands of the Israelites, and that they should "begin to take possession (רש)" and engage them in battle (2:24; 3:2, 12). So while some lands are off limits to the Israelites by divine right, others seem to be allotted as part of the land of promise.

What makes this so? The issue, of course, is complicated. There are historical reconstructions, such as those that read these verses as explaining why Israel did not occupy Edom, or possess it at various points in its history.[36] Limiting oneself to the text itself, one could posit that the issue of kinship plays a role, as the sons of Esau and the descendants of Lot are to be left alone. However, one could also make the case that Sihon and Og are simply in the wrong place at the wrong time, as they dwell in what will be part of the land of promise (3:12–16). For now it will have to suffice to say that the text wishes to highlight the fact that the sons of Esau, Ammonites, and Moabites have been chosen by YHWH to possess land in a way similar to Israel.

A second aspect of the acquisition of Seir that is mentioned in Deut 2 is the driving out of previous inhabitants. Just as YHWH promised to dispossess the people whom the Israelites would encounter on their

34. Ibid., 6:384–85.
35. Ibid., 6:385. On the similarities here with Hittite treaties, see Weinfeld, *Deuteronomic School*, 72: "In the Hittite treaties, as in the book of Deuteronomy, the land is given to the vassal as a gift and he is urged to take possession of it… The granting of the land in the Hittite treaties is very often mentioned together with the explicit warning not to trespass beyond the boundaries set by the overlord."
36. Mayes, *Deuteronomy*, 135–36.

journey into the land of promise (as with Sihon in 2:24 and Og in 3:2), so previous inhabitants were dispossessed so that the sons of Esau, the Moabites, and the Ammonites could possess their lands (2:10–12 and 2:20–22). We are told that the Moabites displaced the Emim in Ar, the sons of Esau dispossessed the Horites in Seir, and the Ammonites replaced the Rephaim in their land.[37]

At first glance these appear to be mere "antiquarian notices."[38] However, these historical explanations as to the causation behind the current inhabitants of the lands reinforce some of the theological themes already present in the chapter. Again the language of ירשׁ is present in these verses, this time denoting "dispossession," and yet again YHWH is an active agent. Thus, not only has YHWH given lands as a possession to these peoples, but he has dispossessed those who have gone before them.[39]

Furthermore, there is an explicit link made in these verses between the perception of the Horites, Emim, Rephaim, and the Anakim (Deut 2:10–11, 20–21). The significance of this lies in the fact that the Anakim were the people who instilled the most fear in the Israelite spies during their survey of Canaan, as both Num 13:28, 33 and Deut 1:28 make clear. The Anakim were considered extremely large people, mythic in proportions.[40] It was this lack of faith in YHWH's ability to provide for Israel's conquest of the land which led to the forty years of wilderness wanderings. And yet here in Deut 2 we have several people groups who apparently did not fear the Anakim-like inhabitants of their future lands, but were able to dispossess them with the help of YHWH.

Lest we forget that this is Israel's story, Deut 2:12 makes it clear that a comparison with Israel is indeed in mind: "And the Horites inhabited Seir before the sons of Esau, but they dispossessed them (ירשׁום) and destroyed them from before them. And they inhabited that place, just as

37. On the identification and history of these various groups, see G. Ernest Wright, "Troglodytes and Giants in Palestine," *JBL* 57 (1938): 305–9. On the Horites, see Knauf, "Horites," *ABD* 3:288. On the Rephaim, see Conrad L'Heureux, "The Ugaritic and Biblical Rephaim," *HTR* 67 (1974): 265–74. On the Anakim, see E. C. B. MacLaurin, "Anak/'ANAΞ," *VT* 15 (1965): 468–74; Gerald L. Mattingly, "Anak," *ABD* 1:222.

38. Mayes, *Deuteronomy*, 137–39. Cf. von Rad, *Deuteronomy*, 42.

39. While Deut 2:12 states that the sons of Esau dispossessed the Horites, 2:21–22 clarify that YHWH was the acting agent in the destruction and displacement of the previous inhabitants. The Samaritan Pentateuch adds YHWH in v. 12 to harmonize the two.

40. The Numbers account (13:33) even links the Anakim to the Nephilim of Gen 6:4.

Israel did to the land of its possession (ירשתו) which YHWH gave (נתן) to them." This points to the more subtle issue that YHWH was at work with other peoples and granting them their land while Israel was stuck in a cycle of disobedience and wandering (as depicted in Deut 1). The contrast with Israel's story could not be clearer.[41]

In summary, Deuteronomy's account of the acquisition of Seir by the sons of Esau contains two important strands concerning YHWH's involvement with other nations and peoples. First, YHWH is responsible for the giving (נתן) of the land as a possession (ירשה) to the sons of Esau (as well as Moab and Ammon), disqualifying it from Israel's conquest. Secondly, YHWH was the acting agent in the dispossession of Seir and other lands, driving out imposing previous inhabitants, much like Israel had failed to do in the past.

d. *Deuteronomy 2: Preliminary Conclusions*

Two key issues have been noted with regard to Israel's encounter with the sons of Esau in Deut 2:1–8. First, the descendants of Esau have a privileged place as being the only non-Israelites named as brothers in Deuteronomy, a designation which will recur in Deut 23:8. While obviously a relational term, its use here may also imply ethical considerations. Secondly, Deuteronomy portrays YHWH as being personally involved in the history of the sons of Esau in a manner similar to Israel's story, particularly through the giving of the land.[42]

How do these issues relate to our larger concern, that of election and non-election? Miller's suggestion is helpful:

> There could not be a clearer or more emphatic way of breaking through the potential hubris and misunderstanding of God's gift of the land to Israel. This is an activity typical of this deity, at least for those who belong to the promise to Abraham and his descendants... The provision of place to live is as sure for these other peoples as for Israel. The same book that makes the strongest case for the particular election of Israel...vigorously resists a misreading of that. Within the election texts themselves, the misreading under attack is the assumption that there is something in Israel that merits or evokes the Lord's favor (7.7; 9.4–5). In chs. 2 and 3 the misreading undermined is the assumption of exclusive benefits accruing from that election. Others have benefited in the same fashion from the Lord's power and grace. Israel thus hears that its story is not the only one going on.[43]

---

41. Similar conclusions are drawn by Miller ("The Wilderness Journey," 583–84).

42. As noted above, both Rashi and *Deuteronomy Rabbah* highlight similar themes in these verses. These two factors are also picked up in Patrick D. Miller, *Deuteronomy* (IBC; Louisville: John Knox, 1990), 38–39.

43. Miller, "The Wilderness Journey," 582.

3. *Deuteronomy 23:8–9: Edom and the* קהל יהוה

The second reference in Deuteronomy to Esau's descendants occurs in Deut 23:8–9,[44] in what is considered the book of the law which forms the core of Deuteronomy. This reference is part of a longer list which details several groups who are excluded or eventually allowed into קהל יהוה, the "assembly of YHWH." Deuteronomy 23:8–9 reads: "Do not abhor an Edomite (לא־התעב אדמי) for he is your brother (אחיך). Do not abhor an Egyptian, for an alien you were in his land. Sons who are born to them in the third generation may come into the assembly of YHWH (בקהל יהוה)." We will begin by briefly exploring the meaning of קהל, as well as the nature of inclusion and exclusion in this passage. Following on from this, we will look specifically at the reference to Edom.

a. *What is the* קהל?

Often translated as "assembly" or "congregation," קהל is a complex term.[45] It occurs 13 times in Deuteronomy, with four of these occurrences in 23:2–9. The remaining uses all point toward the collected wilderness community which gathered to hear Moses or receive the law (e.g. 4:10; 5:22; 9:10; 10:4; 31:30). The literary context of Deut 23:2–9 does not give us much help in defining its usage here, as there are several possibilities in the vicinity of our passage, including familial and military regulations. Early translations were quite literal in their renderings, with *Targum Onqelos* using בקהלא, and the LXX opting for ἐκκλησίαν. Premodern Jewish interpretations tended to understand its use in 23:2–9 as either referring to intermarriage (*Targum Pseudo-Jonathan*; Rashi) or to entry into the Temple (see 4QMMT[b] 39–49, where the term refers to both).

Contemporary scholarship, meanwhile, is divided as to whether or not the קהל is simply a term for the worshipping community in the land of Israel, enrolment in the military, or a general citizenship among the people. All of these understandings have a basis in the framework of the Hebrew Bible.[46] Indeed, it should be noted that these varying ideas concerning קהל would have been closely related in ancient Israel, and to

---

44. The MT and ET have different verse markings, with the English one verse behind the Hebrew. In this section we will refer to the Hebrew delineation.

45. BDB, 874. For more on this term see Heinz-Josef Fabry, "קהל," *TDOT* 12:546–61; Eugene Carpenter, "קהל," *NIDOTTE* 3:882–92 (890–91); H. Cazelles, "Qehal YHWH," *DBSup* 9:601–2; Hans Walter Wolff, "Volksgemeinde und Glaubensgemeinde im Alten Bund," *EvT* 9 (1949/50): 65–82.

46. See Carpenter, *NIDOTTE* 3:888–91.

offer clean delineation between sacral activities, military involvement, intermarriage, and citizenship may be anachronistic. For the purposes of this study it may be sufficient to say that joining the קהל entails some sort of privileged access into the life of the people Israel.[47]

b. *The List of 23:2–9*
The first two groups who are denied access to the קהל differ from the last four groups mentioned as they do not appear to be ethnic groups. The first group mentioned shows a concern for physical deformity, and singles out those who have "crushed testicles" (פצוע־דכא) and those "whose penis is cut off" (וכרות).[48] The text does not say whether or not this emasculation is intentional. The second group mentioned, ממזר, is even more obscure. The only other use of this word in the Hebrew Bible is in Zech 9:6. The contexts of these references in Deuteronomy and Zechariah are not overly helpful in determining their meaning, but there is general agreement that term denotes "bastard" or "child of incest."[49] Both of these groups are excluded from the קהל with no reasoning given, though most commentators suppose cultic purity is an underlying issue.

In Deut 23:4–9 the text shifts to dealing with groups by nationality or ethnicity who are specifically non-Israelite. Two of these groups (the Ammonites and Moabites) are excluded from the קהל, and two (the Edomites and Egyptians) are offered eventual inclusion. The consensus among scholars regarding these verses is that this refers not to the nations or people groups in general, but to aliens residing among the Israelites. The language used referring to generational descendants may reinforce this idea.[50]

---

47. To make matters more complicated, it would appear that these laws were reinterpreted and developed in new ways as the need arose (Isa 56; Ruth). This has been extensively dealt with by Fishbane, *Biblical Interpretation*, 116–29, as well as Shaye J. D. Cohen, *The Beginnings of Jewishness: Boundaries, Varieties, Uncertainties* (Berkeley: University of California Press, 2001), 241–62. Thus, this text is another reminder of the complexity of the formation of Israel's identity in relation to the "other" in Deuteronomy and beyond. See Jon D. Levenson, "Is There a Counterpart in the Hebrew Bible to New Testament Antisemitism?," *JES* 22 (1985): 242–60 (251), for possible reasons why these developments were able to take place within Judaism.

48. The terminology here is somewhat ambiguous, but the meaning is reasonably clear. See Tigay, *Deuteronomy*, 386 n. 23.

49. BDB, 561. Cf. Victor P. Hamilton, "ממזר," *NIDOTTE* 2:971.

50. The restriction on the Ammonites and Moabites in v. 4 reads, "An Ammonite and Moabite shall not enter in the קהל יהוה; even (גם) the tenth generation shall not enter into the assembly of YHWH in perpetuity (עד־עולם)." The main issue here concerns the usage of "tenth generation" along with the phrase עד־עולם. The

Attempts have been made to offer reasons for the addition of the emasculated and the ממזר with the people groups that follow in these verses.[51] Reconstructions such as these, however, tend to be conjectural and difficult to substantiate. Thus, recognizing the eclectic nature of these verses, in what follows I will focus on the four people groups and the reasons which the text itself gives for their access into or denial from the assembly.

As has been noted by both pre-modern and contemporary readers, these verses do not point to "a blanket exclusion of foreigners as such, nor any racial objection to them."[52] Rather, what we see here is the fact that "the ethnic and political history of Israel's relationship with other peoples affected the degree to which they were given access to the worshipping community of Israel."[53] Thus, setting aside for the moment

---

Hebrew עולם is generally translated as "forever" or "eternity," though the base meaning is closer to "most remote time" (E. Jenni, "עולם, 'ôlām, eternity," *TLOT* 2:852–62 [852]; H. D. Preuss, "עולם," *TDOT* 10:530–45 [531]). How should this be understood in relation to the "tenth generation?" We do find the number "ten" used elsewhere in the Hebrew Bible in a hyperbolic sense, and in places it signifies completeness or perfection. This might give credence to the fact that the עד־עולם of v. 4 is intended to mean "forever," and this is compounded by the use of the "tenth generation" (See Israel Abraham, "Numbers, Typical and Important," *EncJud* 12:1254–61. Cf. Gen 31:7; Num 14:22; Job 19:3; Josh 22:14.) Further, the Edomites and Egyptians are not explicitly forbidden as with the previous groups. Instead, we are told in v. 9 that the sons who are born to the third generation may enter the קהל. Like the number "ten," "three" can be a specific number in the Hebrew Bible, but can also symbolically represent a short time period (P. F. Jenson, "שלש," *NIDOTTE* 4:144–46; Abraham, "Numbers, Typical and Important," *EncJud* 12:1255; J. B. Segal, "Numerals in the Old Testament," *JSS* 10 [1965]: 2–20. On the conventional use of three, see R. W L. Moberly, "Preaching for a Response? Jonah's Message to the Ninevites Reconsidered," *VT* 53 [2003]: 156–68). Thus, the references to the third and tenth generations can be understood literally or symbolically. Neither understanding dramatically alters the general meaning of the text. Some groups are forbidden—either permanently or for a very long period of time—from the assembly of YHWH. Others can join in after what is tantamount to a few generations, presumably of sojourning.

51.   A historical reconstruction is offered by Mayes (*Deuteronomy*, 315) who, following Galling, notes that "the most likely setting for the laws is border sanctuaries where the acceptance or rejection of these non-Israelites in Israel's cultic life would have been an issue." Cf. Kurt Galling, "Das Gemeindegesetz in Deuteronomium 23," in *Festschrift Alfred Bertholet zum 80. Geburtstag* (ed. Walter Baumgartner et al.; Tübingen: J. C. B. Mohr, 1950), 176–91.

52.   Tigay, *Deuteronomy*, 211. Rashi makes a similar observation in his comments on v. 9.

53.   Miller, *Deuteronomy*, 175.

the question of what later historical circumstances might have triggered these inclusions and exclusions, it is worth pointing out both the relational and ethical dimensions that are the basis for these statutes in the world of the text itself.

The reason for the exclusion of the Ammonites and Moabites seems to contradict the narrative of Deut 2.[54] In Deut 23:3, the Ammonites and Moabites are listed together. The reasons for their exclusion are given in 23:4, which states, "because they did not meet you with bread and with water on your way from Egypt, and because he hired against you Balaam, son of Beor, from Pethor, Aram Naharaim, to curse you." Some commentators take the first half of the verse as referring to the charge against the Ammonites, with the second half of the verse referring to the Moabites.[55] Both of these are technically possible, as Deut 2:29 mentions the hospitality of Edom and Moab, but not Ammon, and Num 22–24 recounts the hiring of Balaam by Balak, the king of Moab. Others claim that these charges apply to both the Ammonites and the Moabites, as the two are dealt with together.[56] Whichever way one understands the relationship of these two reasons, both groups are excluded from the קהל based on their actions toward Israel. The text goes on in 23:7 to forbid seeking their peace or prosperity (שלמם וטבתם), which may imply comeuppance for those who tried to have Israel cursed. This statement can also be seen to stand in parallel with the prohibition against "abhorring" Edomites and Egyptians.

The next group we encounter is the Edomites. Because of the preceding reference to the reception by Ammon and Moab on the journey from Egypt, it seems reasonable to suppose that this reference to the Edomites has in view the same "sons of Esau, inhabitants of Seir" found in Deut 2:4 on that same journey. The statute of Deut 23:8–9 states that the Israelites are not to abhor (תתעב) an Edomite because of their kinship (אח).[57] Finally, we come to the Egyptians, who are also eventually

---

54. See Tigay, *Deuteronomy*, 211.

55. Deut 23:5 uses a third person masculine singular referring to the hiring of Balaam, while the reference to not meeting the Israelites with resources uses a plural verb. This has been used as rationale for differentiating between the two reasons.

56. Frankel argues that v. 5 does not offer separate reasons, but that there was known to be an Ammonite–Moabite coalition that hired Balaam, and that both refused entry to the Israelites on their journey. See David Frankel, "The Deuteronomic Portrayal of Balaam," *VT* 46 (1996): 30–42 (40–41).

57. Because of the hostility between Israel and Edom, there has been considerable debate on the dating of this reference. Some posit that this is a very late reference, others that it would have to be pre-exilic. See the discussion in Nelson, *Deuteronomy*, 278.

included in the קהל and not to be abhorred, "for you were an alien (גר) in his land" (v. 8). The eventual inclusion of the Egyptians in this context continually baffles interpreters, not least because of the harsh treatment Israel received during their time as slaves in Egypt from which, in the world of the text, they have recently fled. Nevertheless, this idea recurs elsewhere in Deuteronomy (e.g. 10:19).[58]

c. *Do Not Abhor an Edomite, For He Is Your Brother*

What do these verses contribute to the portrayal of Edom, both in Deuteronomy and in the broader canon? To begin with, one might first note the terminology used in relation to Edom, specifically "brother" and "abhor." The concept of "brotherhood" in Deuteronomy was discussed earlier in relation to Deut 2:4. It is worth mentioning again, however, that the sons of Esau and the Edomites are the only references to a "brother" outside of the Israelites themselves in the entire book. Here it is their kinship with Israel that ensures eventual acceptance into the קהל. This has resonance with Deut 2, where "brotherhood" was noted as a relational and ethical category. Thus, once again the use of kinship terminology denotes more than a relationship, but also implies obligations associated with this relationship.

This may also illuminate the use of תעבה, "abhor," which is used in reference to both the Edomites and the Egyptians in relation to their inclusion in the קהל. The general meaning of the nominal תעבה is "persons, things, or practices that offend one's ritual or moral order," and the verbal use "delineates the loathing of that offensive person, thing, or practice."[59] While the usage of "abhor" terminology might alert the reader to cultic overtones in this passage, Glueck has argued that in Deut 23:8–9 תעבה can be seen as the opposite of חסד, and he notes how this relates to the use of kinship terminology: "One may say that the denominative verb from *tô'ēbah* used in verse 8 represents the negative side of the covenant-manner of acting, as *hesed* represents the positive side. Paraphrased in positive form, verse 8 would read: 'thou shalt treat an

---

58. Recent scholarship has begun to make the connection of Joseph and his descendants as the point of reference to this inclusion, particularly because of the use of the term גר. See José E. Ramírez Kidd, *Alterity and Identity in Israel: The* גר *in the Old Testament* (BZAW 283; Berlin: de Gruyter, 1999), 86–90. Rashi makes a similar observation. As van Houten points out, this text seems to highlight "the strength of the notion of obligation which existed in ancient Israelite society." Christiana van Houten, *The Alien in Israelite Law* (JSOTSup 107; Sheffield: Sheffield Academic, 1991), 101.

59. Michael A. Grisanti, "תעב," *NIDOTTE* 4:314–18; Cf. William H. Hallo, "Biblical Abominations and Sumerian Taboos," *JQR* 76 (1985): 21–40.

Edomite in accordance with the covenant rules which in Semitic life bind brother to brother.'"[60] In this sense, the command to "not abhor" stands in contrast to the exhortation to not seek the peace or prosperity of the Ammonites and Moabites.

d. *Deuteronomy 23:8–9: Preliminary Conclusions*
In summary, Deut 23:2–9 is a complex collection of statutes regarding those who are excluded from or eventually included in the קהל יהוה. While it is easy (and perhaps natural) to focus on those who are excluded in this passage, one could also note the rather remarkable fact of Edom's (and Egypt's) inclusion. Indeed, when read in light of the harsh prophetic critique of Edom, this inclusion becomes all the more notable. Whatever historical circumstances might lie behind the formation of this statute, it is the recognition of kinship that is the critical factor in Deuteronomy's eventual inclusion of the Edomites into the קהל יהוה. Kinship in this context is more than recognition of relationship, however; it also places moral demands upon the Israelites, who are to treat these kin in a particular fashion.

4. *The Sons of Esau and Edom in Deuteronomy: Summary and Conclusions*

The book of Deuteronomy has two references to Esau's descendants, both of which are surprising in light of their positive disposition. Both Deut 2 and 23:8–9 instruct the people of Israel to treat the descendants of Esau in a gracious manner, whether it is encountering the people in Seir in the journey up the Transjordan, or in how the Edomite resident aliens among them are to be treated. This gracious treatment seems to stem from the fact that Esau's descendants are referred to as Israel's "brother" (אח), a category that is both relational and ethical, and because YHWH has been personally involved in their story in a fashion similar to Israel's, particularly in the giving of the land.

There are, to be sure, various historical reasons which have been proffered in order to explain this positive portrayal. While not eschewing these reconstructions, this positive and indeed inclusive depiction of the sons of Esau and the Edomites in Deuteronomy is also illuminated when read canonically and with an eye to the theological issue of election. For instance, when these Deuteronomic references to Esau's descendants are read in light of the Genesis materials discussed in the previous chapters,

60. Nelson Glueck, "Deuteronomy 23:8,9," in *Mordecai M. Kaplan Jubilee Volume* (New York: Jewish Theological Seminary of America, 1953), 261–62.

the contribution of Deuteronomy to the canonical portrayal of Esau and Edom becomes evident. While the Genesis narratives make reference to Esau's brotherhood (Gen 33) and his move to the land of Seir (Gen 36), Deuteronomy reinforces these ideas, using overtly theological language. Thus, Esau's descendants are referred to as kin, the only non-Israelites to be treated in such a way in Deuteronomy. Moreover, Esau did not move to Seir simply because of family conflict or to make room for his brother's possessions; rather, Seir was given to Esau and his progeny as a divine inheritance, much like Canaan was given to Israel, affirming YHWH's continued involvement with the unchosen.[61]

The Deuteronomic portrayal of Esau's descendants may also be important for making sense of the how the prophetic traditions handle Esau and Edom. It was noted above that Esau/Edom's status as a brother and its reception of the land of Seir as a possession from YHWH have ramifications for the Israelites: they are to treat the Edomites well, and they are to respect their land as apportioned to Esau's descendants by YHWH. The question may then be asked: If these obligations were in effect for Israel, could it be that they were expected of Edom as well? Might Edom also be expected to live up to the moral obligations of brotherhood, and to honor how the lands have been apportioned by YHWH?[62] I hope to show that it is precisely at these points that the prophets offer their sharpest critiques of Edom.

Taken together, I would suggest that the Deuteronomic portrayal of Esau's descendants is an important canonical link between the (generally positive) Esau traditions of Genesis and the (overtly negative) traditions concerning Edom in the prophets. Deuteronomy is a reminder that Esau's descendants have been blessed in their own right, and it sets the stage for

---

61. One could say that Josh 24:4 bridges these two traditions when it notes, "To Isaac I gave (וָאֶתֵּן) Jacob and Esau, and I gave (וָאֶתֵּן) to Esau Mount Seir to possess (לָרֶשֶׁת) it, but Jacob and his sons went down to Egypt." This verse employs the theological language of נתן and ירש familiar in Deuteronomy, and uses them to describe Esau's relationship to the land of Seir in ways reminiscent of the narrative in Genesis.

62. An interesting rabbinic insight that might lend credence to this idea, particularly with regard to the land, is found in *Gen. Rab.* 74:15. Here we have rabbinic tradition stating that when David wanted to attack the Edomites and Moabites, these nations claimed immunity because of these references in Deut 2. David responds by citing evidence of these other peoples first "breaking the fence," or violating the goodwill from Deut 2. Thus, the rabbis suggest that attacks on Edom and the other nations as well as incursions into their lands were justified because, even though these nations were divinely granted their lands, they forfeited that gift by first attacking Israel.

understanding brotherhood and inheritance of the land as theological themes with ethical dimensions.

Finally, to return to the question with which this chapter began, it is worth reflecting on how these conclusions might affect our understanding of Deuteronomy and Israel's relationship to the "other." Miller insightfully draws out the implications:

> There are many features that enable one to read [Deuteronomy] quite chauvinistically and exclusively. Its focus on the taking of the land..., its emphasis on Israel's election, its legal distinctions between dealing with Israelites...and dealing with foreigners, and its heavy insistence of Israel's exclusive allegiance to the Lord all contribute to a hearing of Deuteronomy as intolerant and exclusive, perpetrating a narrow and nationalistic understanding of God's relation to Israel.[63]

He goes on to note that several texts in Deuteronomy, such as the ones looked at above,

> serve to challenge that notion, suggesting in a way equaled only by the prophet Amos and the book of Genesis that all along the way of history, the Lord of Israel has been at work redemptively and providentially with other peoples and nations. In Deuteronomy, it is made clear that Israel's relation with these other peoples and their gods can not be apart from the awareness of the involvement of the Lord in their stories also.[64]

While Deuteronomy unquestionably affirms that Israel is YHWH's chosen people, the disposition toward Esau's descendants attests to the fact that Israel's story involves non-Israelites, and that these outsiders are not excluded from the divine economy. In this sense, Deuteronomy offers us another surprising reminder that the election theology of the Hebrew Bible is a complex set of ideas which needs to be given appropriate attention.

63. Miller, "The Wilderness Journey," 586.
64. Ibid.

Chapter 9

EDOM IN OBADIAH AND THE PROPHETS

1. *Introduction*

The vitriol with which Israel's prophets speak of Edom is unrivaled in the Hebrew Bible. As noted in Chapter 2, this hostility has been understood in a variety of ways: as a result of Edom's historical actions towards Israel and Judah; as a development of Edom's symbolic or typological connotations; or as part of a post-exilic xenophobic ideology. While not eschewing any of these interpretations, I hope to show that, much like the Pentateuchal portrayal of Esau and Edom, the prophetic critique of Edom can helpfully be understood in light of particular theological motifs, namely kinship and the divine apportioning of land(s). In this chapter I will investigate this phenomenon in more detail, using Obadiah as a starting point and then moving on to the wider prophetic corpus. While other prophets do deal with Edom and Esau's descendants, the short book of Obadiah is especially well suited for our purposes, most notably because Obadiah's focus is primarily on Edom, and, because of its length, it gives us a workable text to engage our subject. This is not to say that Obadiah is without difficulties. Obadiah is a book whose historical circumstances and literary integrity have been the subject of much debate. Nevertheless, Obadiah seems particularly suggestive of how the prophets use themes in relation to Edom that have resonance with those found in the Pentateuch.

In order to understand the portrayal of Edom in Obadiah, several issues need to be addressed. First, a history of pre-modern interpretation will be offered, followed by a brief discussion of several contemporary issues related to reading Obadiah. From there we will explore the motifs of kinship and land possession, and how these relate to the larger thesis of this study. Finally, the usage of these themes elsewhere in the prophetic tradition will be highlighted.

2. *Obadiah: The History of Its Interpretation*

a. *Pre-modern Interpretation*

The rabbinic treatment of Obadiah is evidenced in the work of Rashi.[1] Though not overly concerned with the historical setting of Obadiah, Rashi follows the talmudic association of the prophet Obadiah with the servant of Ahab of the same name who was faithful to YHWH (1 Kgs 18:3–4). Rashi notes,

> Why is Obadiah different that he was chosen to prophesy concerning Edom and did not prophesy any other prophecy? Our Sages of blessed memory stated: Obadiah was an Edomite proselyte. Said the Holy One, blessed be He: From them and in them will I bring upon them. Let Obadiah, who dwelt between two wicked people, Ahab and Jezebel, and did not learn from their deeds, come and impose retribution upon Esau, who dwelt between two righteous people, Isaac and Rebecca, and did not learn from their deeds.[2]

As seen in this quote, part of Rashi's greater concern is to read Obadiah in light of the Genesis stories concerning Jacob and Esau.[3] This comes through in a variety of ways in Rashi's comments; a few examples will suffice. To begin with, Rashi notes that in v. 2 Edom is referred to as being made "small" (קטן), even though Esau is referred to as Isaac's "big" son (בנו הגדל, Gen 27:1). In Obad 3, the text refers to those who dwell in the clefts of rocks. Rashi interprets this to mean that the Edomites are taking refuge in their ancestors, Abraham and Isaac. When v. 7 refers to the eating of bread, Rashi ties this in to the meal which Jacob made for Esau when the elder despised his birthright (Gen 25:27–34). Finally, v. 21 speaks of those who will go up to judge Mount Esau, followed by a statement concerning the kingdom being YHWH's. Rashi explains, "This teaches you that his Kingdom will not be complete until He exacts retribution from Amalek." This is most likely a reference to Esau's genealogy, where Amalek is mentioned as a descendant of Esau (Gen 36:12). Thus, Rashi does not appear to be overly concerned with any particular historical circumstances that would implicate Edom;

---

1. In spite of a notoriously difficult MT, the LXX and *Targum Nebi'im* offer relatively straightforward and similar readings. Variants that may be relevant will be dealt with throughout this chapter.

2. The following references to Rashi are taken from his commentary on Obadiah, online: http://www.chabad.org/library/bible_cdo/aid/16182/showrashi/true.

3. Though some rabbis seem to have understood Obadiah's concern with Edom as actually relating to Rome (*Lev. Rab.* 13:5).

rather, he understands Obadiah as a general (and warranted) condemnation of Esau's descendants.

The history of Obadiah's interpretation in the Christian tradition, as House notes, reflects in many ways the changes that the discipline of biblical studies has undergone as a whole over the past two millennia.[4] The church fathers, while not unaware of the textual difficulties and historical issues, tended to read the book figuratively. Indeed, many early Christian interpreters read Obadiah as an allegory for the church and the ultimate victory of God through Jesus.[5] Thus, Jerome understands the book as an allegory concerning the day of judgment for all heretics,[6] while Augustine notes that "Edom" refers to the nations in Obadiah, and thus can be understood as the church of the Gentiles. which is eventually redeemed and incorporated into the kingdom of God.[7]

Taken together, early interpreters (Jewish or Christian) seem to have had little interest in the historical setting of Obadiah, or to what events the prophet might be referring. One could say that while Rashi points back to story of Jacob and Esau, Christian interpreters point forward to the church, redemption through Christ, and God's eschatological rule. Any commentators who do mention an historical context tend to place the book in the pre-exilic period (possibly because of its early placement in the MT ordering of the Book of the Twelve), and none seem to have equated Obadiah with 587 B.C.E. and the fall of Jerusalem. This would change with the Reformation.

The Reformation commentators began to look for a more literal, historical context to the book of Obadiah. Luther, for instance, is convinced that Obadiah prophesies after the Babylonian captivity, and believes Obadiah to be using Jeremiah as a source. Drawing parallels with Ps 137:7, Luther sees the destruction of Jerusalem at the heart of Obadiah's message.[8] He writes: "Against the Edomites he prophesies that the vengeance of God would occur because the Edomites were quite delighted at the time of the Babylonian captivity that the Jews were being grievously afflicted and led into captivity. Yet, because the Edomites were brothers of the Jews, they should have showed compassion."[9]

---

4. Paul R. House, "Obadiah," *DTIB* 542–44 (542).

5. The use of the term מושיעים, "deliverers" or "saviors," in v. 21 was a natural connection for some in seeing this as pointing to Christ.

6. Jerome, *Commentary on Obadiah*, in ACCS 14:123.

7. Augustine, *City of God* 18.31, in ACCS 14:123.

8. Martin Luther, "Lectures on Obadiah," in *Lectures on the Minor Prophets I*, 193.

9. Ibid., 194.

Luther's literal, historical reading ends with v. 16. Like the church fathers, Luther has a hard time understanding how vv. 17–21 can be read as anything but metaphor for the kingdom of God and the gospel being preached to all people.[10]

Calvin takes note of many of the same issues which Luther does; however, Calvin is unwilling to pinpoint the historical setting as assuredly as his contemporary. Instead, he speaks of a general era when the Edomites "rose up against the Israelites and distressed them by many annoyances."[11] Calvin then notes that the children of Jacob must have struggled seeing the Edomites doing so well for themselves; indeed, "the adoption of God might have appeared worthless." The prophecy of Obadiah, then, is about bolstering the faith of the Israelites by stating what would happen to Edom in the future.[12]

The commentators of the eighteenth and nineteenth centuries would further this focus on the historical aspect of the text, narrowing in on issues of authorship, redaction, and dating.[13] In fact, the question of the historical setting of the book became the defining question of the past several centuries.[14] Recent decades have witnessed a further set of questions reflecting the current state of methodological pluralism in biblical studies: form critics began to investigate the possible *Sitz im Leben* of the book;[15] others began to question whether or not the book can be read as a unified whole;[16] those interested in the Book of the Twelve gave further attention to its contribution to that collection;[17] and ideological works

10. Ibid., 202.

11. Like Luther, Calvin also cites Ps 137, and says that it is unlikely that Obadiah was as early as Isaiah. But the most he is willing to concede is that Obadiah may have been a contemporary of Jeremiah. John Calvin, *Commentaries on the Twelve Minor Prophets*. Vol. 2, *Joel, Amos, Obadiah* (trans. John Owen; Edinburgh: Calvin Translation Society, 1846), 418. Cf. Christopher R. Seitz, *Prophecy and Hermeneutics: Toward a New Introduction to the Prophets* (STI; Grand Rapids: Baker Academic, 2007), 135–36.

12. Calvin, *Joel, Amos, Obadiah*, 417–18.

13. On the history of interpretation in the modern period, see Childs, *Introduction*, 412–13; John Merlin Powis Smith, William Hayes Ward, and Julius A. Bewer, *A Critical and Exegetical Commentary on Micah, Zephaniah, Nahum, Habakkuk, Obadiah and Joel* (ICC; Edinburgh: T. & T. Clark, 1911), 5; Douglas Stuart, *Hosea–Jonah* (WBC 31; Waco: Word, 1987), 402–3.

14. Childs, *Introduction*, 412.

15. Hans Walter Wolff, "Obadja - ein Kultprophet als Interpret," *EvT* 37 (1977): 273–84.

16. S. D. Snyman, "Cohesion in the Book of Obadiah," *ZAW* 101 (1989): 59–71.

17. James Nogalski, *Literary Precursors to the Book of the Twelve* (BZAW 217; Berlin: de Gruyter, 1993), 27–35.

dealing with Obadiah's message have in recent years begun to emerge.[18] While it is not possible to deal with all of these contemporary issues, we will deal with several of them in what follows.

b. *Contemporary Issues in Reading Obadiah*

It is often noted that the critical issues in Obadiah seem to be in inverse proportion to its size.[19] In this section we will look at several of these issues, including the structure and unity of the book, its placement in the Book of the Twelve, and the issue of the book's historical context.

(1) *Structure and Unity*. While the unity of Obadiah was assumed in pre-modern exegesis, commentators such as Calvin and Luther noted a tension by interpreting vv. 17–21 as eschatological and referring to the church, as opposed to their more "historical" renderings of vv. 1–16. Not surprisingly, modern scholarship has identified numerous other issues in this vein.

Questions of literary integrity seem to revolve around various styles and subjects that are inherent in different parts of the book. What one makes of the unity of the book is often a matter of what one sees as the connections between these various styles and subjects. However, a growing number of scholars have noted cohesion in the final form of the book, and that the shape of the book as it now stands makes sense both on its own and in the context of the Book of the Twelve: "The canonical shape of the oracles of Obadiah has interpreted the prophetic message as the promise of God's coming rule which will overcome the evil intent of the nations, even Edom, and restore a holy remnant to its inheritance within God's kingship."[20] Following on from the preceding chapters of this study, we will make use of the received form of Obadiah, presenting diachronic issues as appropriate.[21]

---

18. O'Brien, *Challenging Prophetic Metaphor*, 153–73.

19. E.g. Wilhelm Rudolph, *Joel, Amos, Obadja, Jona* (KAT 13/2; Gütersloh: Gerd Mohn, 1971), 295; this sentiment dates as far back as Jerome.

20. Childs, *Introduction*, 415. Among those arguing for the book's unity are: Snyman, "Cohesion," 70; Paul R. Raabe, *Obadiah: A New Translation with Introduction and Commentary* (AB 24D; New York: Doubleday, 1996), 14–18; Dicou, *Edom, Israel's Brother*, 26–27; Philip Peter Jenson, *Obadiah, Jonah, Micah: A Theological Commentary* (London: T&T Clark, 2008), 5–6. Dissenting from this is John Barton (*Joel and Obadiah: A Commentary* [OTL; Louisville: Westminster John Knox, 2001], 119), who reads the various discrete *parts* of the book holistically.

21. The question of Obadiah's unity is also complex because of the similarities with Jer 49. This text will be covered in the section on other prophets, below. For now it is worth noting that most commentaries deal with this issue, and helpful

Regarding the book's structure, there is again a wide divergence in opinion. Jeremias, Barton, and others note that there are two larger sections in Obadiah (Edom's punishment, vv. 1–14, and Israel's restoration in the context of the nations, vv. 15–21), with several possible subsections within these.[22] Raabe highlights four sections: vv. 1–4, 5–7, 8–18, and 19–21, based on formulaic markers in the text.[23] Others have posited five distinguishable sections based on form, and so on.[24] These are all valid approaches to this short text. If following the received form, it seems to me that a tripartite division is a helpful way of understanding the book's progression: vv. 1–9 outline Edom's coming punishment; vv. 10–14 highlight the accusations against Edom; and vv. 15–21 set Israel's restoration in the context of the nations, while retaining a focus on Edom.[25]

(2) *Obadiah and the Book of the Twelve*. Recent interest in the shape of the Book of the Twelve has necessarily affected research on Obadiah.[26] Those who have argued for a redaction of the Twelve based on key words and literary motifs have seen such moves at work in Obadiah,[27] as have those who posit a thematic, narrative-like structure to the Twelve.[28] While some have added to these developments approvingly,[29] others are more hesitant about this endeavor.[30]

discussions can be found in Raabe, *Obadiah*, 22–31; Hans Walter Wolff, *Obadiah and Jonah* (trans. Margaret Kohl; Minneapolis: Augsburg, 1986), 39–40; Theodor Lescow, "Die Komposition des Buches Obadja," *ZAW* 111 (1999): 380–98 (389–92).

22.   Barton, *Joel and Obadiah*, 118–19; Jörg Jeremias, *Die Propheten Joel, Obadja, Jona, Micha* (ATD 24/3; Göttingen: Vandenhoeck & Ruprecht, 2007), 58–59.

23.   Raabe, *Obadiah*, 18–20.

24.   Stuart, *Hosea–Jonah*, 414; Herbert B. Huffmon, "The Covenant Lawsuit in the Prophets," *JBL* 78 (1959): 285–95 (285). Further structural possibilities are outlined by Snyman, "Cohesion," 59–71 and G. Fohrer, "Die Sprüche Obadjas," in *Studia biblica et semitica Theodoro Christiano Vriezen dedicata* (ed. Wilhelm C. van Unnik and Adam Simon van der Woude; Wageningen: Veenman, 1966), 81–93.

25.   As in Rudolph, *Joel, Amos, Obadja, Jona*, 296.

26.   On the state of research on the Book of the Twelve in general, see James D. Nogalski and Marvin A. Sweeney, eds., *Reading and Hearing the Book of the Twelve* (SBLSymS 15; Atlanta: SBL, 2000).

27.   Nogalski, *Literary Precursors*, 27–35.

28.   Paul R. House, *The Unity of the Twelve* (JSOTSup 97; Sheffield: Almond, 1990), 83.

29.   Rolf Rendtorff, "How to Read the Book of the Twelve as a Theological Unity," in Nogalski and Sweeney, eds., *Reading and Hearing*, 75–87.

30.   Ehud Ben Zvi, "A Deuteronomistic Redaction In/Among 'The Twelve'? A Contribution from the Standpoint of the Books of Micah, Zephaniah and Obadiah,"

The objections begin with the fact that there is a different ordering of the Twelve in the LXX, where Obadiah follows Joel.[31] This and other issues have led to some scholars noting that the antiquity and importance of the ordering of the Twelve in the MT may not be as sure footed an argument as is often assumed.[32] This does not mean that those scholars who are hesitant about placing too much emphasis on the shaping of the Twelve have done away with looking at the role the collection might have. Rather, there has been a renewed emphasis on respecting the integrity of the individual books and hearing their individual voices, while allowing that there may be some relationship to the others in the Twelve.[33]

This cautious approach seems to be a sensible one, and has relevance for the present study. Obadiah's placement directly following Amos in the MT and the reference to Edom in Amos 9:12 seems to be an important one because of key terms that are used. Moreover, Obadiah's placement before Jonah might cause the reader to pause when contemplating the harsh words for Edom, showing that issues of judgment and repentance are by no means univocal in the prophets.[34] Nevertheless, as will be shown, Obadiah has a distinctive voice and much to offer on its own, and may have as much in common with the "Major" prophets as it does with the rest of the Book of the Twelve.

(3) *Historical Context and Setting.* As noted above, the historical context of Obadiah was not of great concern to pre-modern interpreters. The question gained relevance during the Reformation period, and became in many respects the main issue of interpretation during the modern period.[35]

---

in *Those Elusive Deuteronomists* (ed. L. S. Schearing and S. L. McKenzie; JSOTSup 268; Sheffield: Sheffield Academic, 1999), 232–61.

31. Peter R. Ackroyd, "Obadiah, Book of," *ABD* 5:2–4 (2). These differences are helpfully expanded upon in Barry Alan Jones, *The Formation of the Book of the Twelve: A Study in Text and Canon* (SBLDS 149; Atlanta: Scholars Press, 1995).

32. Barton, *Joel and Obadiah*, 116–18.

33. Similar language is used in Seitz, *Prophecy and Hermeneutics*, 136–37; Johan Renkema, *Obadiah* (trans. Brian Doyle; HOTC; Leuven: Peeters, 2003), 25; Leslie C. Allen, *The Books of Joel, Obadiah, Jonah and Micah* (NICOT; Grand Rapids: Eerdmans, 1976), 129.

34. House, *Unity*, 139; Rendtorff, "How to Read," 77.

35. General historical studies on Edom which touch on these issues include Frants Buhl, *Geschichte der Edomiter* (Leipzig: Edelmann, 1893); J. R. Bartlett, "Edom," *ABD* 2:287–95; Myers, "Edom and Judah," 377–92; Weippert, "Edom und Israel," 9:291–99.

Although contemporary scholarship has posited pre-exilic,[36] late exilic,[37] and post-exilic[38] settings for Obadiah, the preponderance of interpreters hold to an early exilic date, not far removed from the events of 587 B.C.E.[39] The connection of Obadiah with 587 B.C.E. is based on the assumption that vv. 10–14 describe the Edomites' complicity in Judah's fateful downfall to the Babylonians. The reference to "exiles" in v. 20 may lend credence to this. Some have questioned whether Edom played any role in the events of 587 B.C.E., and have argued that Obadiah portrays a widespread misrepresentation of the Edomites;[40] a greater number, however, would argue that Edom must have done something to deserve this harsh treatment in the prophets, and the most likely setting is the events surrounding 587 B.C.E.[41]

There seems to be a conflation of (at least) three issues in much of this discussion concerning Obadiah's historical context: (1) what the historical referent of Obadiah might be; (2) the book's date of composition; and (3) how historically reliable the record is.[42] Retrieving Obadiah's exact date of composition would appear to be an impossible task, and the

36.   Jeffrey J. Niehaus, "Obadiah," in *The Minor Prophets, an Exegetical and Expository Commentary* (ed. Thomas Edward McComiskey; 3 vols.; Grand Rapids: Baker, 1993), 2:496–502.

37.   Allen, *Joel, Obadiah, Jonah and Micah*, 129–33.

38.   Blank, "Studies in Post-exilic Universalism," 159–91; Smith, Ward, and Bewer, *Micah, Zephaniah*, 7–9; James Limburg, *Hosea–Micah* (IBC; Atlanta: John Knox, 1988), 131.

39.   Early exilic dates are offered by Georg Fohrer, *Die Propheten des frühen 6.Jahrhunderts* (PAT 3; Gütersloh: Gerd Mohn, 1975), 220; John D. W. Watts, *The Books of Joel, Obadiah, Jonah, Nahum, Habakkuk and Zephaniah* (CBC; Cambridge: Cambridge University Press, 1975), 51; William P. Brown, *Obadiah Through Malachi* (WeBC; Louisville: Westminster John Knox, 1996), 7; Daniel J. Simundson, *Hosea, Joel, Amos, Obadiah, Jonah, Micah* (AOTC; Nashville: Abingdon, 2005), 243–44; Rudolph, *Joel, Amos, Obadja, Jona*, 295–98; Jenson, *Obadiah*, 4–5; Renkema, *Obadiah*, 29–31; Rendtorff, *Canonical Hebrew*, 288; Childs, *Introduction*, 412; Raabe, *Obadiah*, 55–56. Some hold this date for parts of the book, but not the whole. See Barton, *Joel and Obadiah*, 120.

40.   Notably J. R. Bartlett, "Edom and the Fall of Jerusalem, 587 B.C.," *PEQ* 114 (1982): 13–24.

41.   Renkema, *Obadiah*, 34–35; Raabe, *Obadiah*, 52–54. This is implied in Ps 137:7 and Lam 4:21. 1 Esd 4:45 states that it was the Edomites who burned the Temple in Jerusalem. However, the usefulness of all of these texts for historical purposes has been questioned on several fronts. See Ackroyd, "Obadiah, Book of," 5:4.

42.   Ehud Ben Zvi makes a not dissimilar claim in "Obadiah," in Berlin and Brettler, eds., *The Jewish Study Bible*, 1193–94.

possibility of it being a collection of several sources makes this even more unlikely. This does not, however, mean that the discerning reader cannot get a sense of the historical circumstances to which the book refers. It does seem, as Seitz points out, that "the associations with the fall of Jerusalem make a kind of obvious sense in the light of the wider canonical witness." And yet, he notes, "Obadiah does not settle in any hard way on only one historical referentiality in respect of Edom."[43] Instead, Obadiah seems to fall in line with other voices in Israel's history that are concerned with *particular aspects* of Edom's relationship to their brother Israel. If read in this way, Obadiah's historical referent becomes a less urgent issue, and instead the book can be seen as a theological witness to Israel's understanding of her neighbor, based in part, no doubt, on longstanding but perhaps unidentified historical circumstances. In this sense, the pre-modern interpretations outlined above might offer some valuable guidance.

Thus, although I am inclined to agree with the majority of scholarship in placing Obadiah in the exilic period and as having something to do with the events of 587 B.C.E., Seitz's (and Calvin's) comments are worth taking on board. Indeed, the issue of historical setting is not of utmost concern for the present study. Instead, I am attempting to focus on the unique way in which Edom and Esau are portrayed in the prophets, which, given the paucity of historical record, may not easily be reduced to particular events. For our purposes, then, the question might be reframed more constructively around what theological presuppositions underlie Israel's prophets' hostility toward their neighbor.

c. *Summary: Obadiah's History of Interpretation*
This section has briefly explored the pre-modern interpretation of Obadiah, as well as current issues which need to be taken into account when reading Obadiah. The pre-modern interpreters showed little interest in the historical particularity of Obadiah. They were concerned, however, with reading Obadiah in light of Genesis (Rashi) and as a forerunner announcing God's coming kingdom (church fathers). Both of these are attempts to read Obadiah holistically, albeit from differing Jewish and Christian perspectives.

43. Seitz, *Prophecy and Hermeneutics*, 138. This has much in common with the observations of Calvin (*Joel, Amos, Obadiah*, 418), who, noting the points of contact with texts such as Ps 137, nevertheless refuses to settle on a particular historical referent for Obadiah.

The critical issues that have preoccupied modern scholarship—particularly the literary integrity and historical context of the book—are by no means few or inconsequential. They need not, however, deter us from examining particular themes and motifs which permeate the book. In fact, the lack of explicit historical reference in Obadiah might encourage us to look instead at particular literary and theological motifs and how these might relate to the broader theological traditions of Israel.

3. *Brotherhood and the Land in Obadiah*

This section will explore Obadiah's use of the two themes which seem to have resonance with the Jacob–Esau narratives of Genesis and the portrayal of Esau's descendants in Deuteronomy, namely, the issues of brotherhood and relation to the land. It is my contention that these two themes also play a substantial role in Obadiah, and should factor into our interpretation of the book. I will begin by investigating the issue of identity in Obadiah, and how this relates to brotherhood. I will then explore the theme of land and the "possession" language which accompanies it.

a. *Identity and Brotherhood in Obadiah*
While the nomenclature that Obadiah employs in relation to its subjects is varied,[44] a key issue for the present study is the use of the term "brother." Indeed, many commentators have noted the importance of the term "brother" for understanding Obadiah.[45] Ben Zvi concludes that the "Edom as brother" motif is the only reasonable explanation for the vitriol in the book.[46] Barton comments that the brotherhood language creates certain particular expectations so that "this is not simply a general principle applicable to all international relations."[47]

The kinship language employed in Obad 10–12 refers to the violence done to brother Jacob (מחמס אחיך יעקב) and gloating over the brother (ואל־תרא ביום־אחיך) on the day of his misfortune. These reprimands

44.   Edom is spoken of in multiple ways: Edom (v. 1, 8), those who live in the clefts of rocks and dwell on high (v. 3), Esau (v. 6), Mount Esau (vv. 8, 9, 19, 21), brother of Jacob (vv. 10, 12), and the house of Esau (v. 18). For more on Obadiah's use of wordplays and allusions, see Bradford A. Anderson, "Poetic Justice in Obadiah," *JSOT* 35 (2010): 247–55.

45.   Jeremias, *Die Propheten Joel, Obadja*, 59; Wolff, *Obadiah and Jonah*, 52; Rudolph, *Joel, Amos, Obadja, Jona*, 309.

46.   Ehud Ben Zvi, *A Historical-Critical Study of the Book of Obadiah* (BZAW 242; Berlin: de Gruyter, 1996), 238–46.

47.   Barton, *Joel and Obadiah*, 128.

seem to be rooted in the accusation of v. 11: "On the day you stood aside, on the day strangers took captive his wealth, and foreigners entered his gates, and cast lots concerning Jerusalem, you also were as one of them (גַּם־אַתָּה אַחַד מֵהֶם)." In other words, it is the issue of kinship that implies Edom should have acted differently from the others, and is the basis for the prophet's disappointment with his neighbor.[48]

It was noted in Chapter 2 that there are various ways of understanding this kinship motif, including O'Brien's contention that this brotherhood language is little more than an ideological tool, and as such is an abuse of power.[49] While we need to take seriously the rhetorical dimensions of the language used here, the abstraction of the brotherhood language from *any sense of kinship* between Israel and Edom seems forced. Indeed, if we are attempting to "read with the grain" of these texts, then we may need to allow for the possibility that Israel did believe that there was a special relationship that was violated, and judge the prophetic texts accordingly. It may well be that the kinship language has a broader frame of reference than simply a shared history; indeed, as Fishbane and others have observed, the idea that brotherhood language may refer to treaties is not out of the question.[50] However, the sense remains clear: Edom violated a special relationship.

EXCURSUS:
EDOM—A "TYPE" FOR ALL NATIONS?

A common refrain that one comes across in studies concerning Edom is that in the prophetic corpus Edom is a representative or type for all nations.[51] Part of the issue here is the fact that Edom would go on to become a codeword for all of Israel's enemies in post-biblical times, particularly for Rome and the Christian church. However, the question needs to be asked: In Obadiah and the other prophetic texts, is Edom itself in view, or is it a stand-in for all the nations?

Interpreters who see Edom as a type for all nations (or those nations which stand against YHWH) tend to focus on the more eschatological section of vv. 15–21. There is a definite shift in tone, as v. 15 states, "For the day of YHWH is near concerning all nations." The sentiment is repeated in v. 16, which states "all nations will drink."[52]

---

48. Brown, *Obadiah Through Malachi*, 12; Rudolph, *Joel, Amos, Obadja, Jona*, 318; Renkema, *Obadiah*, 160.

49. O'Brien, *Challenging Prophetic Metaphor*, 166.

50. Fishbane, "Treaty Background," 313–18.

51. This is one of the main themes of Dicou, *Edom, Israel's Brother*; cf. Cresson, "Condemnation," 125–48.

52. Most likely referring to the "cup of wrath." An extended discussion can be found in Raabe, *Obadiah*, 206–42.

Here, these scholars argue, Edom is a "type" of the outside, hostile world.[53] What might have started with specific hostility concerning Edom became something larger.[54] Similar arguments are offered with regard to other prophetic texts. For example, the close connection between Edom and the nations in Isa 34—as well as in Isa 63:1–6—has led many to note Edom's representative function in relation to the nations in Isaiah.[55]

Other scholars hold that Edom itself is in view in Obadiah. Renkema comments, "Reference to Edom in Obadiah…is reference to a concrete nation and concrete offences."[56] Still others have tried to offer a mediating position by holding Edom and its role in relation to the nations in tension. Ben Zvi points out that there seems to be some oscillation between the two, and that Edom needs to be seen as both brother and representative of the nations.[57]

The issue is obviously a complex one; there are indeed places where Edom may be used in figurative ways. Yet, in Obadiah and other Edom-related texts, this issue needs to be handled with care, for a number of reasons. To begin with, the ways in which interpreters move from Edom being "hated" to being "symbolic" are often vague and unclear.[58] Relatedly, texts where scholars see Edom as a generalized representative of the nations can be seen as speaking of Edom in *juxtaposition to* the nations (Obad 2–3, 11) or as an *example to* the nations (Isa 34).[59] Neither of these issues are sufficiently raised or explained by proponents of the "symbolic" school of thought. And finally, one could argue that the motifs which recur in the prophetic critique of Edom, notably the brotherhood and land themes, point toward its *particularity* in relationship to Israel.

This is not to deny Edom's typological role in later Jewish and Christian tradition; it most certainly has this function. However, it is not clear that this goes back to the biblical traditions themselves in the way that much of scholarship suggests, even if some of the biblical texts are moving in this direction.[60] This is an area that

---

53. Ackroyd, "Obadiah, Book of," *ABD* 5:4; Jeremias, *Die Propheten Joel, Obadja*, 60.

54. Peter R. Ackroyd, *Exile and Restoration* (OTL; Philadelphia: Westminster, 1968), 224; Dicou, *Edom, Israel's Brother*, 104.

55. Claire R. Matthews, *Defending Zion: Edom's Desolation and Jacob's Restoration (Isaiah 34–35) in Context* (BZAW 236; Berlin: de Gruyter, 1995), 159–61; cf. Matthew J. Lynch, "Zion's Warrior and the Nations: Isaiah 59:15b–63:6 in Isaiah's Zion Traditions," *CBQ* 70 (2008): 244–63 (256–57).

56. Renkema, *Obadiah*, 39. Cf. W. W. Cannon, "Israel and Edom: The Oracle of Obadiah—II," *Theology* 15 (1927): 191–200 (198).

57. Ben Zvi, *Historical-Critical Study*, 25, 242–43. Childs makes a similar claim in *Introduction*, 414–15.

58. Cresson ("The Condemnation of Edom," 147–48) seems a good example of this vagueness.

59. This is noted by Willem A. M. Beuken, *Isaiah Part II, Volume 2: Isaiah Chapters 28–39* (trans. Brian Doyle; HCOT; Leuven: Peeters, 2000), 283–88; Brevard S. Childs, *Isaiah* (OTL; Louisville: Westminster John Knox, 2001), 51. The same "exemplary" idea may be at work in Amos 9:12.

60. Similar conclusions are drawn by Assis, "Why Edom?," 7–9.

admittedly needs further exploration, and is related to the inadequate definitions that often accompany "type," "symbol," and "representative" language with reference to Edom. The line between "example" and "representative" seems to be a fine one, but this is infrequently broached. For now it will have to suffice to say that whatever symbolic function Edom comes to have, its particularity is also stressed in the prophetic texts, and thus needs to be kept in mind.

b. *The Land and Possession in Obadiah*

Another theme that plays a substantial role in Obadiah is that of land. Not only is Edom castigated for acting with violence toward their brother, but there is a recurring theme that Judah's land was violated. For example, v. 11 states that while Edom stood aside, strangers took their wealth,[61] foreigners entered his gates (ונכרים באו שערו),[62] and lots were cast for Jerusalem. Verse 13 states even more explicitly, "Do not enter the gate of my people (אל־תבוא בשער־עמי)." Whatever the "gate" may be referring to here—whether Judah in general (Ruth 3:11) or, more probably Jerusalem itself (Mic 1:9)—the use of "my people" implies that any incursion into the land was not only a violation against Edom's brothers, but against Israel's God.[63]

The rhetoric concerning possession of the land intensifies in the last few verses of the book. In v. 17 we read, "But on Mount Zion there will be escape, and it will be holy. And it will possess, the house of Jacob (וירשו בית יעקב), its possession (את מורשיהם)." This theme of "possessing" is picked up again in vv. 19–21:

> And the Negev will possess (וירשו) Mount Esau, and the Shephelah the Philistines; they will possess (וירשו) the land of Ephraim and the land of Samaria, and Benjamin, Gilead. This company of the exiles of the sons of Israel who are in Canaan until Zarephath, and the exiles of Jerusalem which are in Sepharad will possess (יירשו) the cities of the Negev. And deliverers will go up on Mount Zion to judge Mount Esau (את־הר עשו), and the kingdom will be YHWH's.

The relationship of Israel, YHWH, and the land is an important and complex theme in the Hebrew Bible.[64] How and why does Obadiah pick up on this issue here? There are several ways to answer this question.

---

61. The rendering of חילו here is difficult. See the discussion in Raabe, *Obadiah*, 174.

62. Qere שעריו.

63. Renkema, *Obadiah*, 178.

64. See, e.g., Walter Brueggemann, *The Land: Place as Gift, Promise, and Challenge in Biblical Faith* (OBT; London: SPCK, 1977); and Norman Habel, *The Land is Mine: Six Biblical Land Ideologies* (OBT; Minneapolis: Fortress, 1995).

One approach sees the "land" language in Obadiah as primarily related to the fact that in these last few verses of the book we have a salvation oracle concerning Israel. The picture of Israel re-possessing its land in these closing verses is clearly idyllic: it not only employs archaic geographic terminology (Canaan), but also uses the language of territories related to the Israelite tribes that would cover the four corners of Davidic Israel.[65] Here the references to Zion, as well as the focus on the restoration of all Israel, seem to point to the inextricable linkage we find elsewhere in the prophets concerning YHWH, the people and the land. The restoration of the people is necessarily bound up with the repossession of the land (Ezek 37; Joel 3; Jer 29).[66]

Another approach to this issue is an ideological reworking of the previous option. This approach sees Obadiah (and other prophetic texts) as reflecting "the Second Temple community's ideology of claims to the land."[67] As Stiebert explains, "These claims operate within a mindset characterized by hostility to marriage with Canaanite people and Canaanite women in particular, as well as by a more generalized misogyny and xenophobia. In conjunction with this, the land during the time of the Exile is conceived of as having become defiled."[68] Thus, some would argue that "the land" is used in the context of Obadiah as an (unfounded) ideological tool meant to further ostracize "others" while consolidating the post-exilic Judean community.

Both of these interpretive options are worth considering, and each has its own respective strengths. However, something else is at work in these verses, and that is the recurring use of the key term ירש. This, I would like to suggest, might point toward a third way that Obadiah's use of "land" language and motifs can be understood.

If one keeps in mind broader canonical echoes when reading Obadiah, the idea that the land is a "gift" from YHWH to be received as a possession or inheritance might be taken into account. It was noted above in the discussion on Deuteronomy that there is an important connection between YHWH giving (נתן) and Israel possessing (ירש) the land of promise. This same connection was also made in Deuteronomy with other nations, including the descendants of Esau. For instance, Deut 2:5 states that the Israelites are not to try and take the land of Esau's descendants, "for as a

---

65. Raabe, *Obadiah*, 258. The same could be said for the use of "the house of Jacob" and "the house of Joseph" in v. 18.

66. Wolff, *Obadiah and Jonah*, 67–69; Raabe, *Obadiah*, 251–52; Dicou, *Edom, Israel's Brother*, 197.

67. Stiebert, "Maligned Patriarch," 42.

68. Ibid.

possession/inheritance for Esau I gave (כי־ירשה לעשו נתתי) Mount Seir."
This idea is reconfirmed in Deut 2:22, which states that, as with other
nations, YHWH was a part of the "dispossession" (ויירשם) of the Horites,
who lived in the land before the sons of Esau. The same terms are found
in Josh 24:4, which reads: "And I gave (ואתן) to Isaac Jacob and Esau,
and I gave to Esau (ואתן לעשו) Mount Seir to possess it (לרשת אותו), and
Jacob and his sons went down to Egypt."

In light of this, what would seem to be an important issue in a
canonical reading is the use of land-related terminology in Obadiah (and
other prophets) in proximity to Esau and Edom.[69] As noted above,
Obadiah repeatedly uses the term ירש in the closing verses of the book.[70]
Edom's failure to act as a brother, coupled with their disrespect for
Israel's inheritance/possession, will lead to a reversal of fortune: not only
will Israel repossess the land of promise, but Edom will be dispossessed
(v. 19). In a canonical reading, both Israel's and Edom's lands have been
divinely apportioned; thus, incursions into Israel's land are an affront to
both Israel and YHWH.

The theological significance of this idea can be seen in Jer 12:14–17,
where related, though not identical, language is used. Here an oracle is
given to the exiles explaining what will happen to those who have been a
part of Israel's dispossession, particularly their neighbors. Even though
the prophetic traditions are well aware of Israel's guilt and need for
punishment (Jer 12:1–13), this does not mean the land of promise is a
"free for all" for other nations:

> Thus says YHWH concerning all my evil neighbors, the ones touching the
> inheritance (הנגעים בנחלה) which I gave (אשר־הנחלתי) to my people
> Israel: behold, I will pull them up from their lands, and I will pull Judah
> up from among them. And it will be that after I pull them up I will turn,
> and I will have compassion on them and I will return each one to his
> inheritance (לנחלתו) and each to his land. And it will be that if they truly

69. This connection, as far as I can tell, is not explored in any of the commentaries. Wolff (*Obadiah and Jonah*, 67) notes that ירש is a key term here, and Deut 2 is
mentioned in passing by Raabe (*Obadiah*, 258). However, in my research no commentators refer to the broader canonical resonance of ירש with Esau/Edom. Though
the term is not used exclusively in Obadiah in relation to Edom (see vv. 19–20), it is
used specifically of Edom in v. 19a, and indirectly in v. 17b. As v. 21 makes clear,
Edom/Mount Esau is never far from the author/redactor's mind.

70. For more on this, see the discussion in the preceding chapter on Deuteronomy, and Lohfink, *TDOT* 6:368–96. For the uses of ירש in Obadiah, *Targum
Nebi'im* uses חסן, "to take possession of" (Jastrow, 1:488–89). The LXX, meanwhile,
uses κατακληρονομέω, "to receive possession or inherit"; cf. Werner Foerster,
"κλῆρος," *TDNT* 3:758–85, esp. 767–69.

> learn the things of my people and swear by my name, saying, "As YHWH
> lives"—as they taught my people to swear by Baal—then they will be
> built up amongst my people. But if they do not listen, then I will pull this
> nation up completely and destroy it, declares YHWH. (Jer 12:14–17)

There are two pertinent factors in this text. To begin with, Jeremiah
seems to acknowledge that the neighbors have their own inheritance
(נחלה, v. 15), using language which parallels that of Israel's inheritance.
Secondly, the implication is that the "touching" of Israel's inheritance
would have repercussions, as it is YHWH who gave the land to his people
(v. 14). When read in this way, Obadiah may represent a further example
of a neighbor encroaching on Israel's possession, with the result that
their own inheritance is taken from them.

I would suggest that a canonical reading, which takes on board the
theological significance of YHWH's divine apportioning of the lands (as
seen in Deut 2 and Jer 12), might help us better understand Obadiah's
use of "land" and "possession" motifs. It is not simply the case that the
"land" motif occurs here because Israel's restoration and their land go
hand in hand, nor that Israel wishes to ostracize the "others" which
surround them—though elements of both of these understandings may
very well be at work. Instead, when one recognizes the possibility that
the tradition sees both Israel and Edom as having been given their lands
by YHWH as a possession, it becomes apparent that to interfere with the
others' land is to dishonor both YHWH and the inheritances he has
granted.

(1) *Edom as "Dispossessor"?* Because of the association of Obadiah
with the events of 587 B.C.E., and the language of "On the day…" (v. 11),
one can get the impression that Edom's defiling of Israel's land was a
one-time event. However, it is worth exploring the possibility that the
strong prophetic condemnation of Edom is related to the idea that Edom
made incursions into Judahite/Israelite territory in order to settle there,
and was thus considered a "dispossessor" of Israel's inheritance. This
idea is prominent in Ezekiel (see below), where the text speaks of Edom
wanting to "possess" Judah and Israel (Ezek 35:10), as well as Edom
giving to themselves the land (of Judah) as a possession (36:5). Several
issues may substantiate this idea that Edom was seen as a long-term
threat to Israel's land.

The first is a text-critical issue in Obadiah. There are textual variants
regarding v. 17b, where the MT reads וירשו בית יעקב את מורשיהם. The
final word is pointed as מוֹרָשֵׁיהֶם in *BHS*, which is the noun מורש in the
construct state with a third masculine plural suffix, rendered "their
possession." However, several ancient variants understood this to be a

Hiphil participle from ירש, pointed מוֹרִישֵׁיהֶם, and translated as "those who had possessed them," or "their dispossessors." This rendering is followed by the LXX, Vulgate, and Peshitta.[71] With the first option, Israel is repossessing the land of promise. In the variant reading, this reclamation is a dispossessing of those who had presumably taken over the land. Both alternatives make sense of the text. Whether or not one follows the variant offered by the LXX and various other versions, one hypothesis that can be drawn from this is that early traditions saw fit to equate Edom with Israel's dispossessor.

There is further textual evidence that might support this idea. For instance, there are biblical traditions that hint at this being an ongoing issue in Judah/Israel's history. In 2 Chr 20:10–11, for example, we find the following prayer from Jehoshaphat:

> And behold, now, the sons of Ammon and Moab and Mount Seir, whom you did not give to Israel to go into them when they came from the land of Egypt, so they avoided going up to them and did not destroy them. And behold they are repaying us by coming to drive us out from your possession which you gave us as a possession (מִירֻשָּׁתְךָ אֲשֶׁר הוֹרַשְׁתָּנוּ).

Here Ammon, Moab, and Seir—the three "other" lands that Deut 2 says were given as a possession by YHWH—are seen as a threat to Israel's "possession." Texts such as this one, Lindsay argues, offer a picture in the biblical corpus of a long-term Edomite advancement into southern Judah.[72] This appears to complement archaeological discoveries from the ninth to sixth centuries B.C.E., which have led to similar conclusions: that Edom made incursions into Judah, and over time developed a presence in the Negeb.[73] This might also help make sense of why Obad 19 specifically mentions that the Negeb will possess Mount Esau.

Thus, textual and archaeological evidence seem to corroborate the idea that Edom had a presence in Judah/Israel. It would not be surprising if

71. The LXX renders this τοὺς κατακληρονομήσαντας αὐτούς. Recent interpreters who follow this variant reading include Wolff (*Obadiah and Jonah*, 60), Allen (*Joel, Obadiah, Jonah, Micah*, 163), Stuart (*Hosea–Jonah*, 413), and the NRSV. Those that opt for the MT include Renkema (*Obadiah*, 201–2) and Raabe (*Obadiah*, 245–46), who both offer extended treatments, as well as the NIV and NASB.

72. John Lindsay, "Edomite Westward Expansion: The Biblical Evidence," *ANES* 36 (1999): 48–89, who cites 2 Kgs 24:2, 8–17; 1 Chr 4:34–43; 2 Chr 28:16ff., as well as the prophetic texts noted above. Several texts in 1 Esdras (4:45, 49–50; 8:68–69) seem to corroborate this idea.

73. Itzhaq Beit-Arieh, "New Data on the Relationship Between Judah and Edom Toward the End of the Iron Age," in *Recent Excavations in Israel: Studies in Iron Age Archaeology* (ed. Seymour Gitin and William G. Dever; AASOR 49; Winona Lake: Eisenbrauns, 1989), 125–31; Myers, "Edom and Judah," 377–92.

this presence came to affect the portrayal of Edom, especially at a time when Israel's land appeared to be in jeopardy.[74] As Glazier-McDonald comments, the "transformation of Edom from 'an' enemy to 'the' enemy is clearly attributed to Edom's movement from its own land to southern Judah, which is Yahweh's land."[75]

c. *Brotherhood and Possession in Obadiah: Preliminary Conclusions*

Obadiah's harsh condemnation of Edom and Esau's descendants has various components, but two issues seem to be prominent: brotherhood and land. To begin with, Edom fails to live up to the expectations of kinship, and does not act as a brother should. Instead, they are simply just like the other nations. Secondly, there has been a dishonoring of the divinely appointed land that will lead to Israel repossessing its land of promise, and Edom being dispossessed of its inheritance. While these issues do not do away with all of the difficulties in the biblical portrayal of Edom, taken together these themes may help make sense of Obadiah's strong words.[76] More was expected from Edom because there was a special relationship, and because they were recipients of their own inheritance from YHWH. Their actions are seen as a twofold affront against both kin and a divine inheritance. These are, as will be shown below, motifs that recur in the broader prophetic depiction of Edom.

4. *Edom's Brotherhood and Inheritance in the Prophetic Tradition*

The themes of brotherhood and land in relation to Esau and Edom can be found elsewhere in the prophets. This section will briefly examine the more substantial oracles concerning Edom in Isaiah, Jeremiah, Ezekiel, and Amos.[77]

74. Assis, "Why Edom?," 15.

75. Glazier-McDonald, "Edom in the Prophetical," 31; cf. Cresson, "The Condemnation of Edom," 137.

76. I have not dealt explicitly with how Obadiah relates to the broader genre of Oracles Against the Nations. For more on this, see John H. Hayes, "The Usage of Oracles Against Foreign Nations in Ancient Israel," *JBL* 87 (1968): 81–92; and Raabe, who extensively outlines Obadiah's function in this regard. Paul R. Raabe, "Why Prophetic Oracles Against the Nations?," in *Fortunate the Eyes That See: Essays in Honor of David Noel Freedman in Celebration of His Seventieth Birthday* (ed. Astrid B. Beck et al.; Grand Rapids: Eerdmans, 1995), 236–57.

77. Malachi also uses the same imagery of brotherhood and inheritance (1:2–5). This will be dealt with in Chapter 10. There are also several less substantial references to Esau in the prophets that will not be dealt with here: Isa 11:14; 21:11–12;

a. *Isaiah 34*

Isaiah's main oracle concerning Edom (chs. 34–35) is not set amongst the other oracles against the nations, but between the blocks of chs. 28–33 and 36–39.[78] Here the context seems to be YHWH's anger with all nations (34:1–4), with Edom as an example of this anger. In v. 5 we see the transition from the nations to Edom: "For my sword has drunk its fill in the heavens. Behold, upon Edom it will descend, and upon the people I have devoted to the ban for judgment." The following verses expand on this judgment with stark imagery of Edom's slaughter. First, animal imagery is used, evoking a picture of sacrifice (vv. 6–7). This is followed by a depiction of the land, which becomes desolate and uninhabitable (vv. 9–15). It is in these verses that we encounter the familiar language of "possession." In 34:11a it states concerning Edom, "The hawk and the hedgehog will possess it (וירשוה). The owl and the raven will dwell in it." The following verses make it clear that the only inhabitants of Edom will be the wild animals. The chapter closes with a reminder that YHWH ordains these happenings (34:17): "He casts lots for them, and his hand divides them with the line. In perpetuity they will possess it (יירשוה), and from generation to generation they will dwell in it."

While we are given few specifics as to Edom's crimes, we once again encounter the motif of Edom's land becoming desolate and dispossessed—this time by desert animals, as decreed by YHWH.[79] Elsewhere Isaiah uses the term ירש almost exclusively with reference to Israel's relationship to the land of promise; one exception is this reference to Edom's dispossession.[80] Moreover, Edom's dispossession is juxtaposed with Israel's restoration, which is highlighted in Isa 35, and this occurs apart from references to other nations. As will be seen below, this is a

63:1; Jer 9:24–25; 25:21; Ezek 32:29; and Joel 4:19. A helpful summary of Edom in the prophets that includes these texts can be found in Raabe, *Obadiah*, 33–47.

78. On this literary placement, see Beuken, *Isaian 28–39*, 283–84; Christopher R. Seitz, *Isaiah 1–39* (IBC; Louisville: John Knox, 1993), 236–37; Childs, *Isaiah*, 253–56.

79. Scholars are unsure on the reasoning for the animals used. Beuken (*Isaiah 28–39*, 300–301) argues that unclean animals are used here so that by Deuteronomic standards, Edom is an abomination. Seitz (*Isaiah 1–39*, 237) posits that the references to barren landscape and paired animals may be an allusion to the flood narrative of Genesis, and that Edom's fate is that of those who choose to dishonor the vineyard of YHWH, which he himself protects (27:3).

80. See, e.g., Isa 57:13; 60:21; 61:7; 63:18; 65:9. The other exceptions are 14:21, which speaks of evildoers not possessing the earth, and 14:23, which uses the nominal form (מורש), where once again it is the hedgehog that possesses Babylon.

theme which recurs in other prophetic texts, and may potentially signify Edom's unique status in relation to Israel.[81]

b. *Jeremiah 49:7–22*
The oracle concerning Edom in Jer 49:7–22 contains a host of parallels with the text of Obadiah. Yet, this passage is placed in a series of oracles against the nations, and it appears to be a statement of condemnation with no reasoning given, and the oracle is not specifically tied to Israel's restoration. In fact, Jer 49:7–22 is the one prophetic text that lacks specific reference to either the brotherhood or inheritance motifs.[82]

This does not mean, however, that Jeremiah lacks any implicit reference to these themes. As in Obadiah, this passage does mention both Edom and Esau (49:7, 8–10). Moreover, Jeremiah's oracle against Edom makes clear that there are repercussions concerning the land and its inhabitants: 49:18 states that no one will live in Edom, and 49:19 has YHWH declaring that he will chase Edom from its land.[83] Thus, Jeremiah makes the connection between Esau and Edom, and is concerned with matters of the land, even if explicit language regarding brotherhood and possession is missing.[84]

81. Seitz, *Isaiah 1–39*, 238–39.
82. In point of fact, Jer 49:1–2 uses the language of inheritance and possession only with regard to Ammon, and not Edom. "Concerning the Ammonites, thus says YHWH: Has Israel no sons, has he no heirs (יוֹרֵשׁ)? Why has Milcom possessed (יָרַשׁ) Gad, and his people dwelt in its towns? Therefore, behold the days are coming, declares YHWH, when I will sound the battle cry against Rabbah, sons of Ammon. And it will become a desolate mound, and its villages burned with fire. Then Israel shall dispossess those who dispossessed him (וְיָרַשׁ יִשְׂרָאֵל אֶת־יֹרְשָׁיו), declares YHWH." A similar usage occurs in Ezek 25:1–11, where "possession" language is used of both Ammon and Moab. In Deut 2:8–23 we read that the Moabites and Ammonites were also given their land as an inheritance by YHWH because they were the descendants of Lot. One could argue that Jeremiah and Ezekiel are making use of the same theological argument with regard to the Moabites and Ammonites and their land that Obadiah, Ezekiel, and others make with regard to Edom and its land: the land once gifted as an inheritance will be dispossessed because of actions taken toward Israel's land.
83. For more on Jeremiah's oracle on Edom, see Terence E. Fretheim, *Jeremiah* (SHBC 15; Macon: Smyth & Helwys, 2002), 197–98; William McKane, *A Critical and Exegetical Commentary on Jeremiah*. Vol. 2, *Commentary on Jeremiah XXVI–LII* (ICC; Edinburgh: T. & T. Clark, 1996), 1213–30.
84. Haney has recently shown in an extensive structural study that Jeremiah's oracle concerning Edom exhibits many of the traits that accompany divine warnings to Israel. She notes, "the attitude YHWH takes toward Edom in this oracle in Jeremiah is of such a nature and expressed in such language as would be used if

c. *Ezekiel 35–36:12*

The theme of brotherhood does not appear in the Ezek 35 oracle concerning Edom, nor in the salvation message of ch. 36.[85] Ezekiel 35–36 refer to Mount Seir and Edom, but not to Esau. In 35:5, we are told that Mount Seir held an "ancient hostility" (אֵיבַת עוֹלָם) against Israel, which led to them giving the Israelites over to their enemies. One could interpret this as a reference to the events of Gen 25 and 27, though we are given no further indication of this. The next verse, 35:6, makes reference to the fact that Mount Seir will be given over to bloodshed and bloodshed will pursue it: "since you did not hate blood, so blood will pursue you (וּרְדָפְךָ)." There may be an allusion here to the tradition which says that Edom pursued its brother with a sword (Amos 1:11).[86] Nevertheless, there is a conspicuous absence of any explicit kinship terminology.

These chapters are, however, rife with references to land possession and inheritance. In 35:10 the reason for Edom's desolation is given: "Because you have said, 'These two nations and two lands, they will be mine, and we will possess them (וִירַשְׁנוּהָ),' and yet YHWH was there."[87]

YHWH were speaking to Israel. Jeremiah wrote of an Edom that seemed to be in covenant relationship with YHWH, of an Edom that, like Israel, had broken the covenant... YHWH's involvement combined with the use of the language of Deuteronomy in covenant promises and curses indicates that Edom had a much closer relationship to both Israel and YHWH than has been previously recognized." Linda Haney, "YHWH, the God of Israel...and of Edom? The Relationships in the Oracle to Edom in Jeremiah 49:7–22," in *Uprooting and Planting: Essays on Jeremiah for Leslie Allen* (ed. John Goldingay; LHBOTS 459; London: T&T Clark, 2007), 78–115 (114–15). Haney's reading has several points of contact with the present study, most notably that Edom has a special relationship with both YHWH and Israel. If Haney's reading is correct, then Jeremiah highlights this special relationship which Edom has with YHWH and Israel without expressly using the language found elsewhere in the prophets, namely brotherhood and land possession.

85. Though note the phonetically similar הֶאָח in 36:2, which is rendered as "Aha!" The term is also absent in the briefer reference to Edom in Ezek 25:12–14. For more on this text, see W. T. Koopmans, "Poetic Reciprocation: The Oracles Against Edom and Philistia in Ezek. 25:12–17," in *Verse in Ancient Near Eastern Prose* (ed. J. C. de Moor and W. G. E. Watson; AOAT 42; Neukirchen–Vluyn: Neukirchener, 1993), 113–22.

86. Greenberg points out that some Jewish interpreters, including Rashi, took "blood" here to refer to brotherhood: "you were an enemy of blood, so blood will pursue you." See Moshe Greenberg, *Ezekiel 21–37: A New Translation with Introduction and Commentary* (AB 22A; New York: Doubleday, 1997), 713.

87. The two nations here most likely refer to Israel and Judah. As Greenberg notes, "Since the two once were, and are destined to become again, one nation,

This theme continues in 35:12–14, where it is made clear that Edom took advantage of Judah in a time of calamity, and this was taken as an offence against YHWH. Ezekiel 35:15 continues, "As you rejoiced over the inheritance (לנחלת) of the house of Israel when it was desolate, thus I will do to you."

The theme of inheritance and possession continues into the salvation-oriented oracle of Ezek 36. In 36:2–3 we read, "Thus says the Lord YHWH: Because the enemy said concerning you, 'Aha! The ancient high places have become a possession (למורשה) for us.' Therefore prophesy and say, 'Thus says the Lord YHWH: "Because they desolated and crushed you from all sides so that you became a possession (מורשה) for the rest of the nations…"'" This idea is picked up again in v. 5b, with specific reference to the nations, and particularly Edom, who "whole-heartedly gave my land to themselves for a possession (נתנו־את־ארצי להם למורשה)." In 36:12, YHWH speaks to the mountains and the land itself, stating: "I will cause people, my people Israel, to walk upon you; and they will possess you (וירשוך) and you will be for them an inheritance (לנחלה)."

There are various elements at work in these two chapters that should catch our attention. To begin with, the placement of chs. 35–36 within the book of Ezekiel points the reader toward the issue of the land, as it follows the key text outlining the fall of Jerusalem (Ezek 33:21) and precedes the famous "dry bones" oracle of Ezek 37 with its promise of restoration. As with Isa 34, an oracle concerning Edom appears at first to be out of place, as the other oracles against nations appear elsewhere in the book; yet the surrounding chapters of Ezekiel are also concerned with the status of the land of promise.[88] In Ezek 33:23–29, those inhabiting Jerusalem after its fall to the Babylonians are addressed, and the language of "possessing" (ירש) the land again is used. Ezekiel appears to be comforting those in exile by assuring them that these inhabitants will not be the ones to inherit the land simply because they remain in the land. This is followed by a rebuke of Israel's shepherds and how this relates to the loss of the land (Ezek 34), and then the message concerning Edom (Ezek 35–36). One could argue, then, that the main concerns the

Ezekiel regards an encroachment on the southern flank of the land an offense against both temporarily separated constituents. By nevertheless calling them two lands Ezekiel heightens Seir's greed" (ibid., 715). Cf. Walther Zimmerli, *Ezekiel 2* (trans. James D. Martin; Hermeneia; Philadelphia: Fortress, 1983), 235.

88. Walther Eichrodt, *Ezekiel: A Commentary* (trans. Cosslett Quin; OTL; London: SCM, 1970), 485–86; Leslie C. Allen, *Ezekiel 20–48* (WBC 29; Nashville: Thomas Nelson, 1990), 171.

exiles had with regard to the repossession of their land had to do with, first of all, those who were now inhabiting the land (33:23–29), and secondly, the Edomites. Thus, Edom lies at the heart of Ezekiel's message concerning Israel's restoration, perhaps indicating its special relationship with Israel in this regard.

Second, Ezekiel uses two terms, נחל and יָרֵשׁ, concerning Israel's relationship to her land, and how the Edomites view it. Both of these words seem to carry theological significance here for inheritance and possession.[89] Indeed, when 36:5 states that Edom "gave" (נתן) YHWH's land to themselves as a possession (מוֹרָשָׁה), this seems to be a complete reversal of the prescriptions laid out in Deut 2, where it is YHWH who gives the land as a possession. One could say that Edom's attempt to displace Israel in her land shows an implicit dissatisfaction with its own inheritance. Ezekiel 35:11 might confirm this, noting that YHWH will deal with Edom according to the "anger and jealousy" (כְּאַפְּךָ וּכְקִנְאָתְךָ) which they themselves showed. Moreover, Ezekiel refers to Edom's downfall and desolation and her land being made a desolation (35:9–15), again juxtaposing the loss of Edom's land with Israel's restoration.

Therefore, it would appear that Ezekiel sees Edom's greatest transgression as taking advantage of the desolate state of Judah, and not respecting the land which was given by YHWH to his people, a land which, according to 35:10, YHWH was still guarding.[90] Once again, this theme is expressed using the language of possession and inheritance. Moreover, Edom is yet again dealt with in isolation from other oracles concerning nations, and the restoration of Israel is coupled with the downfall of Edom, showing the special function which Edom and her land play in relation to Israel.

d. *Amos 1:6–12; 9:11–15*
The book of Amos has two sections that reference Edom, 1:6–12 and 9:11–15, and each deals separately with the motifs of brotherhood and possession of the land.

The first occurs in Amos 1, in the context of Amos's oracles against the nations.[91] In 1:6 and 9, Gaza and Tyre are castigated for selling com-

---

89. The two are used in parallel in 36:12. For more on נחלה, see E. Lipiński, "נחל," *TDOT* 9:319–35; cf. Zimmerli, *Ezekiel 2*, 236–38.

90. Some of these ideas are touched on in Woudstra, "Edom and Israel," 30–33.

91. On the general context, see John Barton, *Amos's Oracles Against the Nations: A Study of Amos 1.3–2.5* (SOTSMS 6; Cambridge: Cambridge University Press, 1980). Cf. Andrew E. Steinmann, "The Order of Amos's Oracles Against the Nations: 1:3–2:16," *JBL* 111 (1992): 683–89; M. Haran, "Observations on the Historical Background of Amos 1:2–2:6," *IEJ* 18 (1968): 201–12.

munities of captives to Edom. In v. 9 this is said to disregard "a covenant of brotherhood (ברית אחים)." The oracle against Edom commences in 1:11, where we read: "Thus says YHWH: for three sins of Edom, and for four, I will not turn back. Because he pursued his brother with the sword (על־רדפו בחרב אחיו), and cast off all compassion; and he maintained his anger perpetually, and kept his fury forever."

It is unclear what the "covenant of brotherhood" refers to in v. 9, and whether the brother in question is Tyre or Edom.[92] Some have argued that the brotherhood language in Amos 1 may in fact simply be treaty terminology; as in Deuteronomy and Obadiah, one would not want to disregard this possibility.[93] Nevertheless, it is striking that we have two references to brotherhood connected with Edom in close proximity. Moreover, one is hard pressed *not* to make the association of the brotherhood of Jacob and Esau when this terminology is used in Amos regarding Israel and Edom.[94] One can point to Gen 27:40, where, in Esau's blessing, he is told that he will "live by the sword." Indeed, the noun used in parallelism with "brother" in Amos 1:11 is "compassion" (רחם), a term which denotes "natural affection for closest kin."[95] In any reading, what is clear is that a relationship was violated by the actions of those involved, and this lies behind Amos's strong denunciation. There is no reason to think that ancient kinship and political treaties might not both here be in view.[96]

The second reference to Edom is found at the very end of Amos, in 9:11–12. This section deals with the restoration of Israel and the return to the land. These verses read: "On that day I will raise up the fallen booth of David. And I will repair its breaches, and its ruins I will raise up, and build it as in the days of antiquity; in order that they may possess (יירשו)

92. Nowhere else in the Hebrew Bible is Tyre referred to as Israel's brother, while it is a common designation for Edom. It can be understood, then, as Tyre's actions violating a treaty between Israel and Edom.

93. Fishbane, "The Treaty Background," 313–18.

94. Barton, *Amos's Oracles*, 21.

95. See Francis I. Andersen and David Noel Freedman (*Amos: A New Translation with Introduction and Commentary* [AB 24A; New York: Doubleday, 1989], 265), who point out that there may be another pun here as this is also the root for "womb" (רחם). The LXX follows this understanding, as do some rabbinic texts. Cf. Barton, *Amos's Oracles*, 21.

96. The question of historical circumstances giving rise to Amos's critique is, as with Obadiah, difficult. The book as a whole can be understood as relating to pre-exilic, eighth-century B.C.E. Judah. However, some hold that this is an insertion outlining Edom's role in the events of 587 B.C.E. For more on this question, see Andersen and Freedman, *Amos*, 274–77.

the remnant of Edom and all the nations which are called by my name, declares YHWH, the one who does this." The book concludes by noting in v. 15 that YHWH will plant the uprooted people back in their land, the land which he has given to them (נתתי). Once again the *leitwort* ירש is used in relation to Edom, as is the theological language of land as "gift" from YHWH. While "all the nations" seem to be implied in Israel's future dispossession, it is Edom once again that is singled out. Thus, while this passage is short on specific reasons for these events, it is reasonably clear that we have here a reversal of fortune, as also seen in Obadiah, Isaiah, and Ezekiel: while Edom's remnant is dispossessed, Israel reclaims the land of promise.

Taken together, these two references to Edom in Amos highlight the themes outlined above: brotherhood and possession of the land. Edom is chastised for not acting as a true brother should (even if covenant treaties are in mind), and the result is their dispossession.[97]

5. *Edom in Obadiah and the Prophets: Summary and Conclusions*

I have attempted to make the case in this chapter that the motifs of brotherhood and relationship to the land might help make sense of the prophetic vitriol toward Edom, particularly in Obadiah, but also in the broader prophetic tradition. In this reading, Edom fails to live up to the expectations of kinship; even when explicit kinship language is absent, Edom seems to have a unique relationship to Israel, as it often appears apart from other oracles against nations and its downfall is frequently juxtaposed with Israel's restoration. Moreover, Edom also disrespects the divine apportioning of lands, and the familiar terminology of possession and inheritance recurs frequently in this depiction. Taken together, Edom fails in its obligations to both Israel and YHWH, leading to its dispossession.

---

97. These themes are introduced with little exposition in Amos; it is for this reason that some have postulated that Obadiah's placement following Amos in the MT might lead us to see Obadiah as a commentary on Amos's oracles. See, e.g., Jörg Jeremias, *The Book of Amos: A Commentary* (trans. Douglas W. Stott; Louisville: Westminster John Knox, 1998), 169–70; Seitz, *Prophecy and Hermeneutics*, 236–37. It should be noted that the variant reading of Amos 9:12 in the LXX is a substantial difference, as both "Edom" and "possession" are missing in the Greek, which instead speaks of a "remnant of mankind." This may reflect the fact that Obadiah follows Joel and not Amos in the LXX ordering of the Twelve. See Jones, *Formation*, 175–77. Note, however, that *Targum Nebi'im* retains the reference to Edom.

Before concluding our examination of the prophetic depiction of Edom, one further text needs to be explored: Mal 1:2–5. While Malachi employs familiar themes in its portrayal of Esau and Edom, we will see that it is also unique in its representation of these motifs.

Chapter 10

ESAU AND EDOM IN MALACHI 1:2–5

1. *Introduction*

The first oracle of the book of Malachi (1:2–5) provides one of the most succinct yet forceful comments on Esau and Edom in the Hebrew Bible. The importance of this text is reiterated by its placement in the canon (the end of the Book of the Twelve and the conclusion of the Old Testament in the Christian canon), as well as the history of its interpretation, most notably in Rom 9:13. The question remains, however, as to what canonical function Mal 1:2–5 might have when read within the broader context of the Hebrew Bible. Does this text simply sum up what the Hebrew Bible has to say on the matter of the elect status of the twin brothers and their descendants, or are there other elements at work?

In order better to understand this difficult text, we will begin by looking briefly at the history of its reception. This will be followed by a discussion of various contemporary reading strategies and interpretive frameworks that have been used to understand these verses. Finally, a reading of Mal 1:2–5 will be put forward which rethinks the relationship of the clauses within this text. When read in light of these issues, I hope to show that this challenging passage need not be understood simply as an epitomizing statement of the Hebrew Bible's portrayal of Esau and Edom, but may instead be read as a witness to YHWH's continued elective love for Israel as seen throughout the rich and complex traditions regarding Jacob's brother and Israel's neighbor.

2. *Pre-modern Interpretation*

While not without difficulties, the historical and critical issues in Malachi are not as pressing as in other prophetic books. For example, in spite of relatively sparse historical data within the book itself, its placement at the end of the Book of the Twelve, as well as several grammatical markers, led to it being recognized from antiquity as a post-exilic work,[1] a consensus which is maintained in contemporary scholarship (though there is debate as to its precise *Sitz im Leben*). Rather, it is conceptual and existential issues that have plagued interpreters of Malachi throughout the history of its interpretation, particularly the opening oracle. With this in mind, we will focus on how Mal 1:2–5, and the various conceptual difficulties therein, have been read and understood, both in premodern and contemporary contexts.[2]

a. *Jewish Interpretation*
The LXX and *Targum Nebi'im* offer fairly straightforward readings of Mal 1:2–5, with few major interpretive interpolations.[3] Some Jewish traditions did use Mal 1:2–5 as a chance to castigate Esau. For instance, Pseudo-Philo amplifies the text by stating that "God loved Jacob, but he hated Esau because of his deeds."[4] However, the disparagement of Esau

1. For example, Rashi, commenting on Mal 2:11, observes that the sages ascribed the book to Ezra from an early stage. See Rashi's commentary on Malachi, available online: http://www.chabad.org/library/article.asp?print=true&AID=16219 &showrashi=true.
2. Detailed information on the historical background, authorship, and dating of Malachi can be found in Andrew E. Hill, *Malachi: A New Translation with Introduction and Commentary* (AB 25D; New York: Doubleday, 1998), 1–83; Pieter A. Verhoef, *The Books of Haggai and Malachi* (NICOT; Grand Rapids: Eerdmans, 1987), 153–84; Ralph L. Smith, *Micah–Malachi* (WBC 32; Dallas: Word, 1984), 296–301. On the social background, structure, and thematic elements of Malachi, see G. Wallis, "Wesen und Struktur der Botschaft Maleachis," in *Das Ferne und Nahe Wort: Festschrift Leonhard Rost zur Vollendugn seines 70. Lebensjahres* (ed. Fritz Maass; BZAW 105; Berlin: Töpelmann, 1967), 229–37; J. W. Rogerson, "The Social Background of the Book of Malachi," in *New Heaven and New Earth, Prophecy and the Millennium: Essays in Honour of Anthony Gelston* (ed. P. J. Harland and C. T. R. Hayward; VTSup 77; Leiden: Brill, 1999), 171–79; Paul L. Redditt, "The Book of Malachi in Its Social Setting," *CBQ* 56 (1994): 240–48; James A. Fischer, "Notes on the Literary Form and Message of Malachi," *CBQ* 34 (1972): 315–20; Steven L. McKenzie and Howard N. Wallace, "Covenant Themes in Malachi," *CBQ* 45 (1983): 549–63. Mal 1:2–5 is generally taken as a coherent unit, separated from the superscription of 1:1 and the oracle against the priests in 1:6–2:9. It is worth noting that Calvin takes 1:2–6 as the contextual unit in his exegesis, primarily because he wants to stress the fact that God's love is the reason for the chastisement that follows in the verses to come (John Calvin, *Commentaries on the Twelve Minor Prophets*. Vol. 5, *Zechariah and Malachi* [trans. John Owen; London: Banner of Truth, 1986], 463). This idea will be discussed below.
3. The Greek rendering of "abode" (δόματα) for the MT "jackals" (לתבות) in 1:3b will be dealt with below.
4. *L.A.B.* 32:5.

was not the only way in which Jewish interpreters made sense of this text. In fact, later commentators would offer a variety of surprising readings of Mal 1:2–5. As usual, Rashi's comments are insightful. To begin with, Rashi equates YHWH's love of Jacob in 1:2 with the giving of the land, clarifying the verse by adding the following to YHWH's statement of love: "and I gave him (Jer 3:19) 'a desirable land, an inheritance of the desire of hosts of nations'; a land that all the hosts of nations desire."[5] Rashi's comments on Mal 1:3 continue this theme of land. With regard to YHWH's hatred of Esau, he writes, "And I hated him: to push him off to a land because of Jacob, his brother…and I made his mountains desolate: They do not compare to the mountains of Israel."[6] Finally, Rashi's comments on Mal 1:4 tie Edom's continued frustration to its relationship to Jerusalem: "And if Edom says, 'At first we were poor, but from now on we will be rich from the spoils of Jerusalem.' "[7] Edom's continued frustration at the hands of YHWH is perhaps read here as recompense for their complicity in the ransacking of Jerusalem, again playing on the land motif.[8] Taken together, Rashi's comments regarding Mal 1:2–4 and the "loving" and "hating" of Jacob and Esau are framed almost entirely around the issue of land. However, he also differentiates between the giving of the land to the patriarchs and the reasoning for Edom's present punishment (their actions toward Jerusalem).

Subsequent Jewish interpreters would offer yet further nuanced portrayals of Esau and Edom in these verses.[9] For instance, noting the semantic range of the word "hate" (שׂנא), some suggested that the term might mean that YHWH loved Esau less intensely than he did Jacob, as seen in the story of Jacob's wives (Gen 29:31, 33) or in the legislation of Deut 21:15–17.[10] Thus, Mal 1:2–5 is not concerned with YHWH's literal hatred of Esau, but with his preferential love of Jacob.

Taken together, these examples of Jewish interpretation are interesting; although there are examples of early Jewish interpretation reading Esau's evil deeds into Mal 1:2–3 (Pseudo-Philo), this is not always the case. Indeed, later interpreters would read Mal 1:2–5 in light of the issue of land (Rashi) as well as YHWH's preferential love (Radak).

5. Rashi at Mal 1:2.
6. Rashi at Mal 1:3.
7. Rashi at Mal 1:4.
8. Rashi may be commenting here on Obad 11 and 13, which specifically portray Edom as complicit in stealing from Jerusalem in its time of distress.
9. These and other counterintuitive interpretations of Esau and Edom are helpfully summarized in Jonathan Sacks, "The Other Face of Esau," *The Jewish Press*. Online: http://www.jewishpress.com/pageroute.do/41514.
10. See, e.g., Radak's comments in *Mikra'oth Gedoloth*. Cf. Ibid.

b. *Christian Interpretation*

The theme of YHWH's preference of Jacob is one which would dominate Christian interpretation of these verses. This is due in large part to Paul's quotation of Mal 1:2–3 in conjunction with Gen 25:23 in Rom 9:13. Here Paul is arguing that the divine freedom to choose is a key component of the unfolding divine plan (Rom 9:11–12), and that Jacob and Esau are an example of God's inscrutability, as God chose Jacob and rejected Esau before either had done anything. As Dunn notes,

> it needs to be remembered that Paul includes the idea of divine rejection in order to explain what he regards as a temporary phenomenon—viz., God's rejection of Israel in order to achieve a wider election, which will then include Israel (11:25–32). The main thrust of the whole is not in terms of an even-handed, equal-weighted selection and rejection, but of an overall purpose in which rejection has a part only in order to achieve a final outcome of "mercy upon all" (11:32)… In short, Paul's concern is not to expound a doctrine of predestination…whatever corollaries in this connection may legitimately be pressed from his argument, but to explain the situation in which he finds himself where God's word of promise to Israel (9:6) seems to have been called in question both by the Gentiles' acceptance of his own gospel about the Jewish Messiah and particularly by Israel's large-scale rejection of it.[11]

Not surprisingly, Augustine's interaction with Mal 1:2–5 occurs via Paul's argument in Romans. Because of this, Augustine also understands the "love" and "hate" as referring to God's election of Jacob and rejection of Esau. However, Augustine's main concern is to *explain and defend* God's actions (which is what he assumes Paul is doing as well). Thus, Augustine explains Paul's use of Mal 1:2–3 as given in order to help us

> understand plainly by the later utterance what was hidden in the pre-destination of God by grace before they were born. For what did he love but the free gift of his mercy in Jacob, who had done nothing good before his birth? And what did he hate but original sin in Esau, who had done nothing evil before his birth? Surely he would not have loved in the former a goodness which he had not practiced, nor would he have hated in the latter a nature which he himself had created good.[12]

Augustine's apologetic interpretation appears to cut across the thrust of Paul's argument in Romans: while Rom 9 makes the case that God's free choice is the issue, Augustine cannot get away from the subject of future action. Thus, Jacob is shown undeserved grace, and Esau is given

---

11. James D. G. Dunn, *Romans 9–16* (WBC 38B; Dallas: Word, 1988), 546.
12. Augustine, *Letter* 194; cf. *Enchiridion* 25:98, in ACCS 14:285–86.

deserved punishment.[13] Moreover, this juxtaposition of grace and punishment shifts in subtle fashion the discussion of election. Hence, we are no longer dealing with God's choice of one over the other as part of his elective purposes, but are instead moving toward the idea that election is related to salvation and damnation. This understanding of election, as we will see, would dominate later Christian interpretation.

Beginning with Aquinas, and carrying forward into the reformers, Mal 1:2–3 began to play a serious role in more systematically focused theological consideration. For instance, Aquinas argues against those who would try to soften the doctrine of reprobation, and his key text in defending the idea is Mal 1:2–5. After listing several objections, he writes,

> I answer that, God does reprobate some. For…predestination is a part of providence. To providence, however, it belongs to permit certain defects in those things which are subject to providence… Thus, as men are ordained to eternal life through the providence of God, it likewise is part of that providence to permit some to fall away from that end; this is called reprobation… Reprobation includes the will to permit a person to fall into sin, and to impose the punishment of damnation on account of that sin.[14]

Again, the issue of election is dealt with almost exclusively in relation to salvation and reprobation.

The theological works of Calvin and Luther follow Aquinas in focusing on these verses from Malachi, and their respective theological proclivities are on display. In his *Institutes*, Calvin reads Mal 1:2–5 as one of the paradigmatic examples of double predestination.[15] Luther, meanwhile, argues that Mal 1:2–5 is a prime example of the immutable and eternal God choosing whom he may, juxtaposed with the idea of "free will" and any merit-based theology that might attach itself to it.[16] Taken together, the theologically focused works of Aquinas, Calvin, and Luther all tend to read Mal 1:2–5 apart from any consideration of its literary or historical context, shifting the discussion toward distinctively Christian categories of predestination and reprobation.

13. Augustine specifically refers to "penal judgment" in the *Enchidirion* citation.

14. *Summa Theologica* Pt. 1, Q. 23, Art. 3. Quotation from *Summa Theologica of St. Thomas Aquinas* (trans. Fathers of the English Dominican Province; New York: Benziger Brothers, 1947), 1:127.

15. See his *Institutes of the Christian Religion* (ed. John T. McNeill; trans. Ford Lewis Battles; LCC 21; Philadelphia: Westminster, 1960), 2:926–32.

16. See Martin Luther, *Bondage of the Will* (trans. J. I. Packer and O. R. Johnston; Cambridge: James Clarke, 1957), 222–29. Luther's exegetical lectures on this passage are relatively sparse.

Calvin's exegetical commentary on Malachi, however, is another matter. In this instance, Calvin takes time to read the passage in context, both in Malachi and in the broader Hebrew Bible. Here Calvin's theology comes through, though in a more nuanced fashion than in his *Institutes*. His comments are worth considering at length.

To begin with, Calvin explains why he chooses to explicate Mal 1:2–6 as one section:

> I am constrained by the context to read all these verses; for the sense cannot be otherwise completed. God expostulates here with a perverse and an ungrateful people, because they doubly deprived him of his right; for he was neither loved nor feared, though he had a just claim to the name and honor of a master as well as that of a father. As then the Jews paid him no reverence, he complains that he was defrauded of his right as a father; and as they entertained no fear for him, he condemns them for not acknowledging him as their Lord and Master, by submitting to his authority. But before he comes to this, he shows that he was both their Lord and Father; and he declares that he was especially their Father, because he loved them.[17]

God reminds the people of this "gratuitous adoption with which he had favored the seed of Abraham" in order to condemn them regarding their ingratitude toward this love. Calvin goes on to note that this is not a general love, but a special love given to Israel. He then frames the issue in terms of election when he states that Jacob was "chosen" by God and Esau was "rejected." Thus, Calvin understands these verses as primarily concerned with election, and specifically as a reminder of God's elective love for Jacob and Israel. This is stated at the beginning of Malachi because what lies ahead is a rebuke for Israel's rejection of the one who has loved them.

Offering a reading similar to that found in Rashi, Calvin comments that the hatred or rejection of Esau was that he was driven away from the land of promise to a desolate land. This, for Calvin, does not necessarily imply that Canaan was an infinitely better land than Seir; rather, it is the fact that God chose to dwell in Jerusalem, and not anywhere else:

> But were any to object and say, that this was no remarkable token of hatred, as it might on the other hand be said, that the love of God towards Jacob was not much shown, because he dwelt in the land of Canaan, since the Chaldeans inhabited a country more pleasant and more fruitful, and the Egyptians also were very wealthy; to this the answer is—that the land of Canaan was a symbol of God's love, not only on account of its fruitfulness, but because the Lord had consecrated it to himself and to his

---

17. Calvin, *Zechariah and Malachi*, 463.

chosen people. So Jerusalem was not superior to other cities of the land, either to Samaria or Bethlehem, or other towns, on account of its situation, for it stood, as it is well known, in a hilly country, and it had only the spring of Siloam, from which flowed a small stream; and the view was not so beautiful, nor its fertility great; at the same time it excelled in other things. For God had chosen it as his sanctuary; and the same must be said of the whole land. As then the land of Canaan was, as it were, a pledge of an eternal inheritance to the children of Abraham, the scripture on this account greatly extols it, and speaks of it in magnificent terms. If Mount Seir was very wealthy and replenished with everything delightful, it must have been still a sad exile to the Idumeans, because it was a token of their reprobation; for Esau, when he left his father's house, went there; and he became as it were an alien, having deprived himself of the celestial inheritance, as he had sold his birthright to his brother Jacob. This is the reason why God declares here that Esau was dismissed as it were to the mountains, and deprived of the Holy Land which God had destined to his chosen people.[18]

Calvin goes on to give an interesting reading of Mal 1:4, where the hatred or rejection of Esau's posterity is understood in light of Israel's restoration.

For though the Assyrians and Chaldeans had no less cruelly raged against the Jews than against the Edomites, yet the issue was very different; for after seventy years the Jews returned to their own country, as Jeremiah had promised: yet Idumea was not to be restored, but the tokens of God's dreadful wrath had ever appeared there in its sad desolations. Since then there had been no restoration as to Idumea, the Prophet shows that by this fact the love of God towards Jacob and his hatred towards Esau had been proved; for it had not been through the contrivance of men that the Jews had liberty given them, and that they were allowed to build the temple; but because God had chosen them in the person of Jacob, and designed them to be a peculiar and holy people to himself.[19]

According to Calvin, the reverse is true for Edom: "But as to the Edomites, it became then only more evident that they had been rejected in the person of Esau, since being once laid waste they saw that they were doomed to perpetual destruction."[20]

In summary, Calvin focuses on God's gratuitous choice of Jacob, and Israel's inappropriate response to this love (something which Calvin reiterates in closing his comments on Mal 1:6). Like Rashi, he connects Esau's rejection to the land to which Esau and his descendants would go. Furthermore, Calvin sees Edom's perpetual punishment as a continuation

18. Ibid., 466–67.
19. Ibid., 467.
20. Ibid.

of Esau's rejection. Thus, Calvin's commentary comes to similar conclusions as found in his *Institutes*, though rooted more firmly in exegesis
of the text itself: Esau's rejection is irrevocable, and is seen throughout
the history of his descendants.

c. *Summary: Pre-modern Interpretation of Malachi 1:2–5*

It is not surprising that the history of Christian interpretation of Mal 1:2–
5 has been heavily influenced by Paul's quotation of the text in Rom
9:13, often in ways that seem tangential to the argumentation of Romans,
let alone Malachi. More often than not, the statement of God's loving
and hating is extricated from its surrounding context in Malachi and the
wider Hebrew Bible, and distinctly Christian questions of predestination
and reprobation overwhelm the discussion. Esau in these instances often
becomes an abstract example of the hated, rejected, and reprobate.

As one might expect, Jewish interpretation does focus at points on
negative aspects of Esau's character when interpreting Mal 1:2–5. There
are, however, some interesting construals of these verses in later Jewish
tradition, including the focus on land as integral to the oracle (Rashi) as
well as the preferential nature of God's love of Jacob (Radak). As these
issues have obvious resonance with the present study, these insights will
resurface in the discussion that follows.

3. *Contemporary Reading Strategies*

To continue our investigation of Mal 1:2–5, it may be helpful to identify
reading strategies which have been employed by contemporary commentators to make sense of this difficult text. Three possibilities will be
mentioned here: the text can be variously understood as nationalistic
ideology, abusive patriarchy, or under the rubric of covenant and election.

a. *Nationalistic Ideology*

First, when Mal 1:2–3 speaks of loving Jacob and hating Esau, some
understand this as nationalistic ideology. Here the presence of Jacob and
Esau in the text is understood as nothing more than a way to speak of
contemporary national issues. There is no reference to the past; there
is merely the situation post-exilic Israel finds itself in *vis-à-vis* Edom.
This anti-Edom rhetoric fits well with what some call a "damn Edom"
theology that has been attached to the Edomite traditions. What we have
in these verses, then, is a hatred for a neighboring country, and reaffirmation of love for Israel. Those who read the text in this way see Israel
boosting its national self-confidence at the expense of the Edomites, who
are hated, some would say, for no good reason.

While there may be an element of truth with this understanding, there are also shortcomings. The most pressing issue is that reading 1:2–5 as nationalistic ideology ignores the larger context of the book of Malachi, which, as was already noted by Calvin, is more concerned with Israel's faltering ways than in chastising Edom. If anything, the totality of the book offers a substantial critique of Israel that far outweighs the mention of Esau and Edom. Indeed, there seems to be an important correlation between YHWH's love and the chastisement which follows.[21] There are, to be sure, examples of nationalistic ideology in the Hebrew Bible; Mal 1:2–5, however, may not be the best example of such rhetoric.

b. *Abusive Patriarchy*
Another interpretive option for reading this passage is to understand it as an abusive father who is willing to love one son (Jacob) and hate the other (Esau). This is, for some, another example of patriarchal abuse in the Hebrew Bible. In relation to Malachi's use of father–son language, for instance, O'Brien notes that "the relationship is one of sheer power."[22] Commenting on 1:2–3, she writes,

> In this opening disagreement between God and Israel, God contends that he has demonstrated his love for Jacob by hating the twin son Esau. The clear message is that Jacob only survives by the pleasure of a father who is willing to hate his own son. A father, it seems, can choose to hate his own son, while a son is not granted the privilege of hating his father.[23]

This abusiveness is not limited to Esau and Edom, however. In Malachi, God is a scolding father who expects fear from the son whom he does love, Israel. "Priests and people have been disrespectful sons, and they must be shamed back into their proper place."[24] Thus, Malachi is a problematic text on at least two fronts: first of all, God is a father who arbitrarily loves one son and hates the other. Secondly, even toward the son whom he loves, God is a vindictive father who demands fear and reverence.

O'Brien's reading is helpful as it forces us to engage the problematic language in the text. There are elements of Malachi that require careful consideration, particularly by those who are part of traditions which continue to read the book as Scripture. Moreover, readings such as

21. See, e.g., Amos 3:2, which paints a similar picture.
22. Julia M. O'Brien, "Judah as Wife and Husband: Deconstructing Gender in Malachi," *JBL* 115 (1996): 241–50 (242).
23. Ibid.
24. Ibid., 243.

O'Brien's offer a needed corrective in traditions (religious and academic) which too often have been ignorant or turned a blind eye to issues of patriarchy and abuse.

Nevertheless, O'Brien's reading also seems to do a disservice to the text by not taking into account several contextual issues. For instance, O'Brien gives no attention to more nuanced understandings of "love" and "hate" in the Hebrew Bible, such as the "preferential love" understanding offered by Radak. Instead, she appears to focus on modern, emotive understandings of these terms. Carrying on from this, O'Brien's contention with Malachi appears at times to be anachronistic because she reads the text through various modern conceptions, such as that of parent–child relationships. While it is no doubt important to consider contemporary social contexts if one is concerned with present day implications of the text, it does not negate the fact that we need to allow the book to function as an ancient text and the product of a different time and culture. For example, O'Brien does not engage with ancient Near Eastern understandings of covenant, which can be seen to function as a conceptual framework for the book, and which may help us understand the way in which YHWH interacts with Israel in Malachi. Considering these issues will not do away with all of the conceptual difficulties in the book or in this passage in particular. Nonetheless, they do seem to be significant exegetical issues that need to be taken into account if we are to do justice to the text.

c. *Covenant and Election*
A third possible reading strategy for understanding this text can be described as a framework of covenant and election.[25] This framework is substantiated by several issues: (1) the use of covenantal themes and language in Malachi; (2) the placement of 1:2–5 in the broader context of Malachi; and (3) the use of "love" and "hate" in other covenant and election-related contexts.

(1) *Covenantal Framework in Malachi*. It is not uncommon for scholars to note the role of covenant in Malachi, particularly as three covenants are mentioned in the book: the covenants of Levi in 2:8, of the fathers in 2:10, and of marriage in 2:14. However, most works that do mention

---

25. Though these two are sometimes distinguished, for the present study they serve similar purposes, and thus will be dealt with as one theme. For a differentiation of the two, see S. D. Snyman, "Antitheses in Malachi 1, 2–5," *ZAW* 98 (1986): 436–38 (437).

covenant attempt to specify which covenants are being referred to and which traditions may lay behind these references.[26] McKenzie and Wallace, meanwhile, offer the most comprehensive attempt at reading Malachi as a whole in light of covenant. While they look at the three above-mentioned references to covenant, they also investigate covenant-related themes that occur in the book: the messenger of the covenant (3:1), covenantal violations by priests and people (1:6–14 and 2:4–16), and YHWH's covenant love (1:2–5).[27] Their conclusions are as follows:

> Three specific covenants are said to have been violated in the Book of Malachi: the covenants of Levi (2:4–9), the fathers (2:10), and marriage (2:14). The covenant of marriage is contained within the section relating to the violation of the covenant of the fathers (2:10–16). It is thus an example of the greater issue, the profaning of the covenant of the fathers. The redactor of Malachi, then, is concerned with two major covenants: the covenant of Levi which the priests have violated (2:1–9) and the covenant of the fathers which the people have violated (2:10–16), although, as 1:6–14 shows, the sins of priests and people are not isolated. At the beginning of the book there is an oracle (1:2–5) which defends Yahweh's covenant faithfulness. The very placement of it suggests that in the redactor's mind the statement of Yahweh's faithfulness applies to the covenants of Levi and the fathers, in both of which Yahweh is a partner. If…the patriarchal covenant lies behind 1:2–5 and the priests and people are in close association, then the patriarchal covenant is seen as the over-riding covenant applying to the postexilic community. This seems to be the case in 2:17–3:12 where judgment and salvation involve both priests and people. The reference to the fathers (3:7), Jacob (3:6), and the nature of the blessings (3:10–12) indicates that the patriarchal covenant is in view. It binds the entire community.[28]

The conclusions reached regarding covenant and election are enlightening for the present study:

> In the case of the covenant with the patriarchs as well as the covenant with Levi, the purpose of casting the origins of the covenant back to the patriarchal ancestors seems to be bound up with an emphasis on election. Malachi stresses in 1:2–5 and 3:6 that Yahweh chose Jacob over Esau and that Jacob's descendants remain Yahweh's elect… For Malachi, then, covenant and election are bound together, and both apply throughout the generations.[29]

---

26. E.g. Fischer, "Notes on Literary Form," 317.
27. McKenzie and Wallace, "Covenant Themes," 550–59.
28. Ibid., 558–59.
29. Ibid., 559.

Studies on Malachi's placement in the Book of the Twelve may reiterate the importance of covenant and election themes. For instance, in the context of a study on the relationship of Malachi to the Book of the Twelve, Berry has noted the complex canonical function which Malachi exhibits. One of the key areas he notes is that of covenant. "This organizing theme best accounts for the whole of the book. Malachi does not define covenant, but it assumes it. The concept of covenant present in Malachi draws from various segments of the canon of law and prophets."[30] On the relationship of Malachi and the Twelve he writes: "the unity of the basic message of the twelve...presents: (1) Israel as God's elect; (2) the nature of the people as subject to rebellion and punishment in the past and present; and (3) God's ideal community (covenant) as a conception of the future... So Malachi sums up the message of the twelve and prepares for the future."[31]

Thus, elements within Malachi itself, as well as its function in relation to the Book of the Twelve, point toward Israel's election and covenant relationship with YHWH as a plausible framework from which to understand the message of the book as a whole.[32]

(2) *Placement Within Malachi*. As noted above, there is a broad consensus that Mal 1:2–5 stands on its own as a distinct unit within the book. One might then ask, however, why this oracle is placed at the beginning of the book, directly following the superscription of 1:1. How should this placement affect one's reading of the text?

Malachi 1:2–5 is often seen as the first of six separate oracles found in Malachi, the others being 1:6–2:9, 2:10–16, 2:17–3:5, 3:6–12, and

---

30. Donald K. Berry, "Malachi's Dual Design: The Close of the Canon and What Comes Afterward," in *Forming Prophetic Literature: Essays on Isaiah and the Twelve in Honor of John D. W. Watts* (ed. James W. Watts and Paul R. Redditt; JSOTSup 235; Sheffield: Sheffield Academic, 1996), 269–302 (287).

31. Ibid., 300–301.

32. The social and religious milieu that post-exilic Israel found itself in may add further weight to the importance of covenant. Much of the post-exilic literature is concerned with the issue of identity following the exile (Ezra, Nehemiah). As Rogerson notes, the same seems to hold true for Malachi: "The community in which Malachi was produced is to be seen as a community in crisis. It is in crisis about its own identity" ("Social Background," 179). Thus, it should not be surprising that a renewed focus on covenant election would be a priority in a community trying to re-establish its identity as the people of YHWH. Cf. Wilhelm Rudolph, *Haggai–Sacharja 1–8–Sacharja 9–14–Maleachi* (KAT 23/4; Gütersloh: Gütersloher Verlagshaus Gerd Mohn, 1976), 254–55.

3:13–21.[33] Stuart notes that oracles two through six are all concerned with "unfaithfulness to the covenant" on behalf of the priests and the people, a subtitle he gives to each section.[34] But what of covenant in the first oracle? It would seem that a covenantal reading as proposed by McKenzie and Wallace might help make sense of the placement of 1:2–5 in the book as a whole. If the book is read in a covenantal framework, then it is understandable to begin the message with an oracle reminding the people of YHWH's covenantal love. Moreover, this introductory use of love may be all the more important when one takes into account the rather harsh nature of the rest of the book (cf. Calvin). In order to rouse a people to live up to their covenantal status, which they are presently failing to do, the people need to be reminded of their special relationship with YHWH.[35]

Levenson has helpfully noted several literary allusions within Malachi that may corroborate the election-focused nature of the book in light of the opening pericope. He begins by noting,

> It is conceivable that Malachi's ringing endorsement of Jacob's status as the beloved son derives from a tradition that knows nothing of the story of the double deceit by which Jacob became the third patriarch. More likely, however, is the supposition that Malachi did indeed know of that story—and spoke of Jacob as YHWH's beloved nonetheless.[36]

---

33. This breakdown is common; see Fischer, "Notes on Literary Form," 316; and James Nogalski, *Redactional Processes in the Book of the Twelve* (BZAW 218; Berlin: de Gruyter, 1993), 182–83.

34. Douglas Stuart, "Malachi," in McComiskey, ed., *The Minor Prophets*, 3:1245–1396 (1249).

35. The form-critical analysis of the passage offered by Weyde comes to a similar conclusion regarding the text's function. Weyde challenges the received understanding that Mal 1:2–5 is an example of a "disputation oracle," offering instead a form-critical analysis that places this text within the sphere of cultic lament and salvation oracles. He concludes, "since Mal 1:2–5 contains a divine salvation oracle to the addressees, YHWH's election of them is in focus, and not the rejection of Edom; his rejection of Edom 'forever' (v. 4) is elaborated to emphasize a positive message: YHWH's covenantal faithfulness to those addressed. The unmotivated announcement of disaster against Edom stresses that the election of the addressees remains unchanged." Karl William Weyde, *Prophecy and Teaching: Prophetic Authority, Form Problems, and the Use of Traditions in the Book of Malachi* (BZAW 288; Berlin: de Gruyter, 2000), 94. Thus, form-critical studies that have questioned the status quo concerning Malachi's form and function have in the end come to similar conclusions regarding the covenant and election themes which permeate the text.

36. Levenson, *Death*, 64.

Levenson goes on to point out two passages that back up this claim: Mal 2:10 and 3:6–9. He notes that in 2:10 we should take notice of an allusion to brothers from the same father who act deceitfully toward one another: "Is there not one father for us all? Has not one God created us? Why does each deal treacherously with his brother, to profane the covenant of our fathers?"

He then comments on 3:6–9, which reads:

> For I Y<small>HWH</small> have not changed, and you, sons of Jacob (בני יעקב), have not ceased to be.[37] From the days of your fathers (אבתיכם) you have turned away from my statutes and have not kept them. Turn to me and I will turn to you, says Y<small>HWH</small> of hosts. But you say, "How should we turn?" Will a man defraud (היקבע) God? For you are defrauding (קבעים) me. And you say, "How are we defrauding (קבענוך) you?" In tithes and offerings. With a curse you are suffering, but you go on defrauding (קבעים) me, the whole nation of you.

Levenson remarks,

> The use of the rare verb *qāba'* four times in Mal. 3:8–9—it occurs in only one other verse in the entire Bible (Prov. 22:23)—strongly suggests a pun on the name Jacob (*ya'ăqōb*) in v 6. The root of the verb is comprised of the same three consonants as appear in the root of Jacob's name and in the verb translated as "supplant" in Gen. 27:36 and as "take advantage" in Jer. 9:3, of which the verb in Mal. 3:6–8 is probably but a variant. Informed by the tradition about Jacob's defrauding his brother, Malachi calls upon "the children of Jacob" to return to God and his laws, specifically the laws about sacred donations. The opening oracle of the book makes clear, however, that the return for which the prophet calls will not restore the status quo ante: Jacob will still be "loved" and Esau "hated," even after the wrongs deplored in 3:8 have been righted.[38]

If Levenson's readings of these subsequent texts in Malachi are accurate, it furthers the argument that Malachi's harsh message of covenantal infidelity is introduced with a reminder of Y<small>HWH</small>'s covenantal and elective love.[39]

(3) *"Love" and "Hate" in Covenantal and Elective Contexts.* Moran's article on "The Ancient Near Eastern Background of the Love of God in Deuteronomy" decisively shaped the discussion on "love" as a

---

37. This last clause follows Levenson's translation.
38. Levenson, *Death*, 64.
39. This has resonance with Amos 3:2, where it is the specific issue of Israel's election that sets them apart for punishment.

covenantal term, and as such is important for our study.[40] Moran argues that Deuteronomy and its strong emphasis on love is not indebted to Hosea, but to the ancient Near Eastern milieu, where extra-biblical texts exhibit usage of the term "love" "to describe the loyalty and friendship joining independent kings, sovereign and vassal, king and subject."[41] Citing several examples from the ancient Near East, Moran clearly shows how "love" had strong covenantal overtones in the ancient world, with similar usage appearing in Deuteronomy.[42] This idea has had widespread implications, and has been used in relation to prophetic voices such as Hosea.[43]

Beyond covenantal use, it has been observed that the term "love" is used elsewhere in the Hebrew Bible in the context of YHWH's election of Israel. The primary location for such use is again Deuteronomy, where one finds that love and election border on being used as synonyms.[44] For example, though using a different term for "love" (חשׁק), Deut 7:7, often considered the paradigmatic text on Israel's election, explicitly links YHWH's love for and election of Israel. Using the term found in Malachi, אהב, the same idea is found again in Deut 4:37 and 10:15, the former reading: "And so because he loved (אהב) your fathers, he chose (בחר) their descendants after them." There are instances from the prophetic books that seem to corroborate this connection of "loving" and "choosing." Jeremiah 31:3 reads, "And with an everlasting love I have loved you (ואהבת עולם אהבתיך); therefore I have drawn you with loving-kindness." And in Hos 11:1 we find, "When Israel was a child I loved him (ואהבהו) and from Egypt I called my son."

"Love" and "hate" can also be used in secular circumstances to denote the preference for one person or object over another.[45] This idea can be seen in Gen 29:31 and 33, where we find the word "hate" used in reference to Jacob's wife Leah: "And when YHWH saw that Leah was hated (שׂנואה), he opened her womb. But Rachel was barren… And she conceived again and she bore a son and she said, 'Because YHWH heard

40. Moran, "Ancient Near East Background," 77–87. For more on this term, see G. Wallis, "אהב," *TDOT* 1:99–118.

41. Moran, "Ancient Near East Background," 78.

42. Ibid., 79–81. Examples of "love" in Deuteronomy which can be read this way include 5:10; 6:5; 7:9; 10:12; 11:1; 13:4; 15:6; 30:6.

43. Lohfink followed Moran's lead to argue that "love" and "hate" in Hos 9:15 are both used in a covenantal context of loyalty relationship. See his "Hate and Love in Osee 9. 15," *CBQ* 25, no. 4 (1963): 417.

44. G. J. Botterweck, "Jakob habe ich lieb-esau hasse ich," *BibLeb* 1 (1960): 28–38 (34–35).

45. As noted above, this was recognized by Radak, amongst others.

that I am hated (כִּי־שְׂנוּאָה), thus he has given me this son also.'" As Konkel notes, "The use of loved and hated to describe the attitude toward a preferred wife as opposed to the one who was tolerated or even rejected (Gen 29:31, 33) lends to hate the sense of being unloved or not chosen, or even abandoned and rejected."[46]

Taken together, there is precedence throughout the Hebrew Bible for a more nuanced understanding of YHWH's "love" and "hate" beyond the idea of emotive feeling, including love as a covenantal term in the Deuteronomic tradition, as well as the prevalent use of love and hate in relation to election, whether this be a preferential choice or the choosing of one and rejecting of another.

These examples have led many who see Mal 1:2–5 as fitting in a covenantal or elective framework to read this phrase in generally one of two ways. On the one hand, critics such as Elliger feel love and hate should be understood in a relative sense: "I have loved Jacob more, and Esau less."[47] On the other hand, there are those such as Levenson who feel Malachi is using stark language of choice. Levenson translates the phrase as, "I have accepted Jacob, but I have rejected Esau."[48] Meinhold agrees, stating that love in this context is Malachi's "personalsten Erwählungswort."[49] The latter reading seems to be supported by the strong antithetical tone of the passage, an issue which the relative use of these terms may not capture in this instance.[50]

d. *Summary: Contemporary Reading Strategies*
There are various reading strategies that can be employed to understand Mal 1:2–5. Examples include the frameworks of national ideology and abusive patriarchy, readings which helpfully highlight problematic aspects of Malachi's opening statement. However, one should also bear

46. A. H. Konkel, "שׂנא," *NIDOTTE* 3:1256–60 (1257). This same idea seems to be present in the statute regarding the transfer of the birthright in Deut 21:15–16, which also speaks of the "loved" and "hated" wife.

47. K. Elliger, *Das Buch der Zwölf Kleinen Propheten 2: Die Propheten Nahum, Habakuk, Zephanja, Haggai, Sacharja, Maleachi* (ATD 25; Göttingen: Vandenhoeck & Ruprecht, 1982), 190.

48. Levenson, *Death*, 63. While the targumim and LXX do not appear to offer any clues in this regard, *4 Ezra* 3:16 supports this reading: "You set apart Jacob for yourself, but Esau you rejected." See Bruce M. Metzger, "The Fourth Book of Ezra," in *The Old Testament Pseudepigrapha*. Vol. 1, *Apocalyptic Literature and Testaments* (ed. James. H. Charlesworth; New York: Doubleday, 1983), 528.

49. Arndt Meinhold, *Maleachi (1,1–2,9)* (BKAT XIV/8 i; Neukirchen–Vluyn: Neukirchener, 2000), 40.

50. See Snyman, "Antitheses," 436–38.

in mind a covenantal and elective framework for interpreting this passage, based on (1) the covenantal themes which Malachi exhibits; (2) the function that 1:2–5 plays in relation to the remainder of Malachi; and (3) the use of "love" and "hate" terminology in other covenantal and elective contexts. A reading which takes covenant and election as its starting point does not rid the text of its difficulties, nor does it preclude the other interpretive frameworks noted above; nonetheless, it may give the reader a frame of reference from which to understand Mal 1:2–5 both within the book itself and in the broader context of the Hebrew Bible.

4. *Making Sense of Malachi 1:2–5*

Thus far we have explored the pre-modern history of interpretation of Mal 1:2–5, as well as contemporary reading strategies employed when interpreting it. I have suggested that a reading strategy which employs covenant and election as its controlling idea may be helpful when interpreting Mal 1:2–5. However, this does not resolve all interpretive questions regarding these verses. Indeed, even where election is seen to be the controlling factor in the text, scholars differ widely on what exactly Mal 1:2–5 is saying regarding this theological theme. Levenson, for instance, argues that YHWH's disregard for the birth order of the twins in Genesis is commented on in Mal 1:3, where "the preference affects far more than familial relations: it determines the exaltation of Israel, the people descended from Jacob, and the humiliation of Edom, the nation that issued from Esau."[51] Conversely, Hill, citing Gen 25, remarks that Esau and Edom symbolized "all those who in their arrogance and independence rejected the tokens of Yahweh's covenant and despised Israel as Yahweh's elect."[52] This is followed with the statement that, "The story of Esau is one of selfishness and disdain for the tokens of Yahweh's covenant,"[53] therefore validating YHWH's hatred of Esau and his ancestors.

What is one to make of these varied, and indeed contradictory, interpretations? Is this text highlighting YHWH's gratuitous divine choice, or should it be read as an indictment of Esau and Edom? A possible way forward may come via an examination of the clauses within this passage, and how they might be understood in light of one another.

---

51. Levenson, *Death*, 63–64.
52. Hill, *Malachi*, 149.
53. Ibid., 164.

a. *The Relationship of the Clauses in Malachi 1:2–5*

Most pre-modern and contemporary interpreters of Malachi understand the reference to the hatred of Esau and the desolation of his inheritance as causally connected. As seen in the quotations above, Levenson regards the elective preference of YHWH for Jacob over Esau as having an effect on Esau and his descendants down through the ages, while Hill sees Esau's disdain for the things of YHWH as having an effect on his progeny. What if, however, the hatred of Esau and the desolation of his inheritance are not causally connected, but instead are two separate examples of YHWH's covenantal love for Jacob and Israel? Such a reading would require us to rethink the relationship of the clauses in this text. In what follows I offer a possible suggestion along these lines.

(1) *Malachi 1:2–3a: YHWH's Love for Jacob and Hatred of Esau.* To begin with, YHWH declares his love for the addressees (אהבתי אתכם). The verb אהבתי in v. 2a is a *qatal* first person masculine singular. This is generally understood as a stative verb, and as such the primary tense in *qatal* is that of the present: "I love you."[54] However, the *qatal* of stative verbs can also make reference to the past with a definite or imperfect sense: "I have loved you."[55] Hill, for instance, describes the form as durative stative perfect, noting that, "The reported audience response 'How have you loved us?' indicates that the restoration community understood the *durative* sense of *'āhbtî*. The skeptical response…is prompted by the lack of any contemporary evidence justifying the prophet's declaration of God's covenant love for Israel."[56] This initial question from YHWH and rejoinder from the audience set the stage for the remainder of the oracle, as the remaining clauses can all be seen as responding to this issue.

When the people ask, "How have you loved us?," YHWH responds with a question concerning the brotherhood of Jacob and Esau (הלוא־אח עשו ליעקב). As with other texts concerning Esau and Edom, the issue of identity is a complex one, and I have tried to argue for cautiousness in this regard throughout this study. Nevertheless, it seems reasonable, for a number of reasons, to conclude that it is specifically the patriarchs Jacob and Esau, the twin sons of Isaac, that are referred to here.[57]

54. See, e.g., the use of "love" in Gen 22:2, 27:4, 9 and 44:20. Cf. JM §112a.
55. An example being Gen 27:14. JM §112b.
56. Hill, *Malachi*, 147–48; cf. Smith, *Malachi*, 20.
57. Contra Glazier-McDonald, who understands Jacob and Esau here as symbolic of Israel and Edom (Beth Glazier-McDonald, *Malachi: The Divine Messenger* [SBLDS 98; Atlanta: Scholars Press, 1987], 34).

To begin with, the absence of any verb implies that this phrase can be translated as either a past or present reference to the brotherhood of Jacob and Esau, the former perhaps hinting that the continued relationship might be in mind.[58] However, the interrogative ה with the negative particle לוא is often used for "pointing to a fact in such a way as to arouse the interest of the person addressed or to win his assent."[59] Thus, this can be understood as a rhetorical question, pointing toward something which is well known to the audience. If this is the case, then the text is commenting on YHWH's choice of Jacob, as seen in the subsequent clause: ואהב את־יעקב, translated with near unanimity as "yet I loved Jacob."[60] Secondly, the syntactical relationships of the verbs in the statement ואהב את־יעקב ואת־עשו שנאתי seem to imply it is the past to which is being referred. As Niccacci notes, "both qatal forms אהבתי (1:2a) and שנאתי (1:3a), being stative verbs, usually indicate a present situation; here, however, their continuation forms wayyiqtol…[making] it clear that a past situation is intended."[61]

Thus, the specific reference to Jacob and Esau, YHWH's rhetorical question, as well as the syntactical relationship of the verbs, all seem to point toward the fact that Mal 1:2–3 is dealing primarily with the past. To answer the question from the people as to how he has loved them, YHWH responds by noting that from the very beginning of their establishment as a people, his free choice of Jacob, and corresponding rejection of Esau, is a reminder of his love.

(2) *Malachi 1:3b: The Desolation of Edom's Inheritance.* After commenting on the past rejection of Esau, Mal 1:3b reads, "And I set his mountains as a wasteland (ואשים את־הריו שממה), and his inheritance for the jackals of the wilderness (ואת־נחלתו לתבות מדבר)." Several issues are worth commenting on in this clause.

We might first note that Malachi employs the familiar language of "his mountains" (את־הריו), and "his inheritance" (ואת־נחלתו) in 1:3, both references pointing back to the subject Esau earlier in the verse. Mountainous terminology is used right through the Hebrew Bible to refer to Esau and Edom's habitation in the land of Seir/Edom. Moreover, the

---

58. On the issue of verbless (nominal) clauses, see the collection of articles in Cynthia L. Miller, ed., *The Verbless Clause in Biblical Hebrew: Linguistic Approaches* (LSAWS; Winona Lake: Eisenbrauns, 1999).
59. BDB, 520.
60. NRSV, NASB, NIV. See also the title of Kaminsky's work, *Yet I Loved Jacob*.
61. A. Niccacci, "Poetic Syntax and Interpretation of Malachi," *LASBF* 51 (2001): 55–107 (71).

use of the term "inheritance" (נחלה) has resonance with the larger Esau
and Edom traditions which associate Seir/Edom as the possession or
inheritance of Esau and his descendants. As noted in the previous chapter, the majority of prophetic references to Edom's land (or its view of
Israel's land) use the root ירש, "to possess" or "possession" (Ezek 35:10;
Obad 17, 19; Amos 9:12). Malachi, however, uses the more technical
term נחלה, "inheritance." This term is not used elsewhere in the Hebrew
Bible to refer to Edom/Seir in relation to Esau and his descendants.
Nevertheless, it is striking that this particular inheritance-related language is used here of Edom, given its frequent use in connection with
Israel and its land.[62] And, as the term has a certain amount of semantic
overlap with the root ירש, it seems possible to understand Esau's
"inheritance" in Mal 1:3 as the land which was given to Esau and his
descendants, as seen in Deut 2, Josh 24:4, and throughout the prophetic
corpus. Thus, it seems a strong possibility that Mal 1:3 is drawing on the
tradition that Seir/Edom was considered the possession or inheritance of
Esau and his descendants.

Secondly, the language used in Mal 1:3–4 to describe the current
desolate state of Esau's inheritance is reminiscent of the language used
elsewhere in the prophetic books regarding the future plight of Esau and
Edom. While Obad 18, Jer 49:10–12, and Amos 1:11–12 all refer in
general terms to the future destruction of Edom, there are texts that
employ the exact terminology of "jackals" and "wasteland" to describe
Edom's future. There are textual difficulties with the rendering of
"jackals" in Mal 1:3, and several emendations have been proposed.[63]

---

62. I am employing the traditional translation of "inheritance." See, however, the
discussion in Habel, who notes that נחלה "in its primary meaning, is not something
handed down from generation to generation, but the entitlement or rightful property
of a party that is legitimated by a recognized social custom, legal process, or divine
character" (Habel, *The Land is Mine*, 35). Habel thus prefers to translate נחלה as
portion, share, entitlement, allotment, or rightful property. However, bearing in mind
the quote above, translating the term as "inheritance" in a broad sense does not seem
inappropriate. Indeed, given the criteria offered by Habel, this would reiterate the
significance of this term being used with regard to Esau's land: it implies entitlement
that is recognized as legitimate by the reader.

63. The MT reads לתנות, the preposition *lamed* with a feminine plural of תן,
"jackal." This is problematic as the feminine plural of תן is not found elsewhere in
the Hebrew Bible, but only the masculine plural (Isa 13:22; Mic 1:8). The LXX renders this as δόματα, "dwellings," giving the sense of "dwellings of the wilderness"
(a similar idea is found in Syr). Based on this, *BHS* proposes a variant reading of נות,
from נוה, "pasture," "abode," or "habitation." This emendation has been followed
by several commentators (e.g. Elliger, *Das Buch der Zwölf*, 190–91). However, a
number of recent commentators have noted that the MT can rightfully be read as

However, Isa 34:13b describes Edom's future with the following: "It will be a dwelling for jackals (נוה תנים), an abode for the offspring of ostriches." Thus, the use of jackal terminology in Isa 34:13 shows that this concept is not foreign to the prophetic material referencing Edom's fate. Ezekiel 35:3, meanwhile, notes that YHWH's hand is against Mount Seir, stating that "I will set you as a desolation and a waste (ונתתיך שממה ומשׁמה)." The root שׁממה occurs five more times in Ezek 35 in reference to Edom's future, in vv. 4, 7, 9, 14, and 15.[64]

Accordingly, Malachi's depiction of Esau and Edom's land in 1:3b has much in common with the broader biblical traditions. To begin with, Esau's land is a mountainous region, and is depicted as an "inheritance" for Esau and his descendants. Furthermore, the depiction of Edom's demise uses imagery found elsewhere in the prophetic tradition for this event, notably "jackals" and "wasteland." Malachi's description of Edom's desolation differs from the other prophetic accounts, however, in that it pictures the events in the past tense, as already having taken place (the verb ואשׂים is a *wayyiqtol*; see the quote from Niccacci, above). Hence, one way of reading Mal 1:3b is to see it as commenting on the fulfillment of the prophecies elsewhere in the prophetic literature that, in their received form, predicted the downfall of Edom, Esau's inheritance, and used familiar language to do so.

To be sure, other interpreters have pointed out these links. Hill, for instance, notes the following:

> Malachi's wordplay upon the "inheritance"…of Edom is interesting in that Obadiah also envisioned a reversion of territory as "Mount Zion" dispossessed "Mount Esau" (vv 17–21). By framing his prediction of repatriation with Israel's possession of the Negev (vv 19a//20d), Obadiah indicates that the fall of Edom should be viewed as the trigger event setting in motion the fulfillment of Yahweh's covenant promises to Israel. Perhaps this text lies behind Malachi's use of Edom's recent history as an illustration of Yahweh's love for Israel?[65]

"jackals." See Hill, *Malachi*, 155; Glazier-McDonald, *Malachi*, 33. Fuller discussion can be found in Meinhold, *Maleachi*, 22–23, and Hill, *Malachi*, 154–55, who outline several possible variant readings.

64. The reference in Ezek 35:4 also uses the same verb as Mal 1:3, אשׂים, to describe the action of Edom's desolation.

65. Hill, *Malachi*, 168. Hill is not alone in making this link; see Glazier-McDonald, *Malachi*, 34; Rudolph, *Maleachi*, 255–56. From a historical standpoint, it seems probable that Edom did indeed face its demise during this general period, and thus it is reasonable that those who shaped the final form of Malachi were referring to a well-known event. One possible historical referent for Edom's collapse is the campaign of Nabonidus in the region (suggested by, amongst others, Bartlett,

How does this affect our reading of Mal 1:2–5 and the relationship of the clauses therein? As argued in the previous chapter, the prophecies against Edom in Obadiah and elsewhere are not based simply on the fact that Edom is not Israel. Instead, Edom is castigated for not acting as a true brother to Israel, and for not respecting the lands which were apportioned by YHWH. If Malachi is making reference to the prophetic tradition of Edom's demise, then one might conclude that it is specifically Edom's *attitudes and behavior* that are the unspoken reason for the desolation of its inheritance in Mal 1:3b, as in the other prophets. If this is so, then 1:2–3a stands in contrast to 1:3b, the former highlighting the gratuitous choice of YHWH in electing Jacob over Esau.

One way to make sense of this tension is to break away from the general assumption that the statement of YHWH's hatred of Esau in 1:3a is causally connected to the downfall of Edom in 1:3b. Rather, they might be read as two distinct examples of YHWH's love for his people. The former refers to YHWH's choice of Jacob over Esau, an example of YHWH's love from Israel's very inception as a people. If the *waw* in וָאָשִׂים is understood as having an aspect of continuation but not of causality, then 1:3b can be taken as referring to Edom's destruction, a fulfillment of the prophetic traditions that predicted Edom's downfall because of her attitudes and actions toward Israel. Edom's desolation is a further example of YHWH's love for Israel, punishing those who have wronged it, but not necessarily a continued explanation of YHWH's rejection of Esau.[66]

(3) *Malachi 1:4–5: Edom's Future Frustration*. We come, then, to Mal 1:4, the final clause referring to Edom, where it is the future which is envisioned: "If Edom says (כִּי־תֹאמַר אֱדוֹם),[67] 'We are shattered but we will return and rebuild,' thus says YHWH of hosts: 'They may rebuild, but I will tear down, and they will be called the territory of wickedness (גְּבוּל רִשְׁעָה) and the people with whom YHWH is indignant in perpetuity (עַד־עוֹלָם).'" This, too, is to be a reminder of YHWH's love and special

---

"Edom," 2:293; cf. Bartlett, "From Edomites to Nabataeans: A Study in Continuity," *PEQ* 111 [1979]: 53–66). Nevertheless, scholars are divided as to what this calamity entails and how it came about. Cf. Rudolph, *Maleachi*, 254; Glazier-McDonald, *Malachi*, 35–41; Meinhold, *Maleachi*, 35; Cresson, "The Condemnation of Edom," 138; Marvin A. Sweeney, *The Twelve Prophets* (BO; Collegeville: Liturgical, 2000), 723.

66. In theological parlance, Mal 1:2–3 can thus be seen to exhibit elements of both divine initiative and human response as seen throughout the Esau and Edom traditions. We will return to this theme in the concluding chapter.

67. On the conditional aspect of כִּי, see GKC §159aa-bb.

relationship with Israel, as seen in Mal 1:5: "And your eyes will see this (תראינה), and you will say (ואמרתם), 'Great is YHWH beyond the territory of Israel!'" As with the previous clauses in this text, the references to Edom as the "territory of wickedness"[68] as well as "the people with whom YHWH is indignant forever" are given with no explication. What are we to make of these references?

Nogalski argues that there may be a relationship between the description of Edom as the wicked territory in 1:4 and the distinction between righteous and wicked in Mal 3. The feminine form of "wicked" (רשעה) is one which recurs in Mal 3:15 and 3:18, with the masculine form occurring in 3:19 and 3:21 (ET 4:1 and 4:3). These occurrences take place in a section dealing with arrogance against YHWH. Malachi 3:15 reads, "And now we call the arrogant blessed; and not only are the doers of wickedness built up (עשי רשעה גם־נבנו), but they test God and escape." Nogalski notes, "This verse [3:15] appears to contain a deliberate play on words with Mal 1:2–5 in which Esau (עשו) is called a territory of wickedness (רשעה) who threatens to rebuild (בנה) after YHWH destroys their dwelling place."[69] Nogalski's claim that Mal 3:15 may be an allusion to Edom is feasible; in this reading, Edom is used as a reminder in 1:4 that wickedness does not go unpunished, a theme to which the text will return in Mal 3 in relation to Israel. If this is the case, then Edom's "wickedness" might reasonably be linked to its past behavior.[70]

The idea that Edom's "wickedness" is alluding to it past transgressions might be corroborated by further resonances between Obadiah and Mal 1:4. As Nogalski points out,

> Obad 10 states that Edom will be cut off forever (לעולם) which parallels the statement in Mal 1:4 naming them a people against whom YHWH is indignant forever (עד־עולם). Obad 7 predicts Edom will be driven from the territory (literally to the border [עד הגבול]), whereas Mal 1:4f contrasts the wicked territory (גבול) of Edom with the power of YHWH over the territory (גבול) of Israel… Obad 3 portrays Edom as self-deceptive in its delusion over the security of its lofty dwelling place. Mal 1:4 takes this deception one step further by portraying Edom as still suffering under the misapprehension of its strength.[71]

---

68. For more on the term "territory" and its use here, see Magnus Ottosson, "גבול," *TDOT* 2:361–66 (365).

69. Nogalski, *Redactional Processes*, 193.

70. As noted above, Rashi hints at the connection of Edom's action concerning Jerusalem and their continued frustration in his commentary on v. 4: "And if Edom says, 'At first we were poor, but from now on we will be rich from the spoils of Jerusalem.'" Thus, there is a pre-modern precedent for this reading.

71. Nogalski, *Redactional Processes*, 192.

Thus, Malachi's use of language similar to that found in Obadiah might imply that the same issues are of continued concern to Malachi, even though Edom's initial desolation has already taken place.

Bearing this in mind, Assis's argument concerning the post-exilic state of mind in Yehud is helpful.[72] Assis argues that the exilic and post-exilic community saw Edom as a threat to its elect status, and thus the anti-Edomite thread throughout the prophets was in response to this threat. In Malachi, Assis argues, the promise of Edom's continued demise is to assure the post-exilic community that what Edom has done to them in the past will not be done to them again. While I am not convinced by Assis's broader claim that Israel saw Edom as a threat to its elect status, his ancillary argument is more compelling: YHWH's indignation with Edom "in perpetuity"[73] is stated to assuage any lingering fears that Israel may still harbor concerning what has happened to them in the not-too-distant past. Assis's reading not only makes sense of this difficult clause, but it also builds on the line of reasoning made above, namely that YHWH's choice of Israel and continued covenant fidelity is the controlling theme of this passage.

Taken together, it would appear that one way to make sense of the classification of Edom as "the territory of wickedness" as well as its continued frustration by YHWH in Mal 1:4 is to understand it as commenting on Edom's past behavior towards Israel, for the purpose of assuring a concerned post-exilic community of YHWH's continued faithfulness toward them. What has happened in the past will not happen again, another reminder of YHWH's covenantal love.

b. *Summary: Making Sense of Malachi 1:2–5*
In this section I have tried to offer a reading of Mal 1:2–5 that makes sense of the passage within the canonical context of the Hebrew Bible, as well as within the interpretive framework of covenant and election. I argued that this may require the reader to rethink the relationship of the various clauses within these verses, and noted that the text can be seen to deal with the distant past (the patriarchs Jacob and Esau; 1:2–3a), the recent past (Edom's destruction; 1:3b), and the future (Edom's continued frustration; 1:4). All of these are to be reminders of YHWH's love

---

72. Assis, "Why Edom?" 14.

73. The phrase עד־עולם is generally translated as "forever" or "eternity." Jenni notes, however, that "eternity" can be a misleading translation because it may "introduce a preconceived concept of eternity, burdened with all manner of later philosophical or theological content" (E. Jenni, "עולם," *TLOT* 2:852–62 [853]). To allow for the indistinct nature of this term, it may be best rendered as "perpetually," or "in perpetuity." Cf. Preuss, *TDOT* 10:531–36.

for Israel: he chose Jacob, their ancestor. He has punished those who have mistreated them. And he will continue to protect them into the future. In this reading, there is not necessarily a causal connection between YHWH's hatred of Esau and the subsequent desolation of Edom. They are instead distinct examples of YHWH's covenantal love. In diverse ways, the relationship of Jacob and Esau as well as Israel and Edom should be a continued reminder to Israel of YHWH's love for them.

5. *Malachi 1:2–5: Preliminary Conclusions*

In this chapter we have examined various interpretive issues surrounding Mal 1:2–5, including soundings from the pre-modern history of interpretation, an exploration of contemporary reading strategies, and an investigation into how one might read this text in a canonical context. In the end I contended that the passage is best understood when read in the framework of covenant and election. In addition, I suggested that we may need to rethink the relationship between the various clauses in Mal 1:2–5. The result is a reading which highlights YHWH's covenantal love for Israel throughout history: he chose their ancestor Jacob over Esau; he has punished those who mistreated them, including Edom; and he will continue to look after them into the future by frustrating those who would do them harm. All of these are proofs of YHWH's opening statement, "I have loved you" (אהבתי אתכם).

Returning to the issue which was raised at the beginning of this chapter, it is worth reflecting on what Malachi has to say about Esau and Edom in light of the broader context of the Hebrew Bible. Do these verses simply sum up what the Hebrew Bible has to say concerning Esau and Edom? Based on the reading which was offered above, I hope it is clear that the text cannot be reduced so easily. Instead of understanding Mal 1:2–5 as a concluding summary epitomizing what the Hebrew Bible has to say concerning Esau and Edom, the reading offered here suggests an alternative: the text can be understood as commenting on the rich and complex history of Esau and Edom in relation to Israel, and how this relationship has been a constant reminder of YHWH's covenantal love for Israel in the past, and will continue to be in the future.

This reading does not negate the difficulty of these verses, nor does it exempt us from asking questions about a God who chooses some and not others. Nevertheless, when read in the way here suggested, Mal 1:2–5 might be seen to mirror the complexity of the Hebrew Bible's election theology, raising the persistent issues of divine initiative and human response that run throughout the pages of the Hebrew Bible. These are issues to which I will return in the concluding chapter.

Chapter 11

EDOM IN THE PROPHETIC CORPUS:
SUMMARY AND CONCLUSIONS

The previous two chapters have surveyed the more substantial references to Edom in the prophets: following on from Obadiah, we have looked at Isa 34, Jer 49, Ezek 35–36, Amos 1 and 9, and finally Mal 1:2–5. How do these texts relate to the motifs of brotherhood and inheritance?

1. Of these texts, three use explicit kinship language in describing Esau and Edom: Obad 10, 12, Amos 1:9, 11, and Mal 1:2.[1] One further text, Jer 49, makes mention of Esau, and thus draws attention to the patriarchal relationship, without explicitly mentioning "brotherhood." The term "brother" is used almost exclusively in the prophets to refer to fellow Israelites, or as a term denoting a neighbor or "everyman." The only use of this term with regard to non-Israelites is in reference to Esau and Edom, highlighting the special status of this neighbor, whether this is treaty-related terminology or simply recognition of shared history by the nations.[2]

2. Several texts unexpectedly speak of Edom in isolation from other references to nations or peoples (Isa 34–35; Ezek 35–36; Amos 9; Obadiah). Moreover, these texts also tend to juxtapose

1. The only questionable reference here is whether Amos 1:9 refers to Tyre or Edom. One other text that implicitly highlights this relationship without mentioning Esau or Edom is Hos 12:4, which states that Jacob grasped his brother's heel while still in the womb.

2. As noted above, the same limited use of אח can be found in Deuteronomy, where Esau/Edom is the only non-Israelite recipient of the term. Note, however, that other familial language is used in the prophets for other nations. In Jeremiah, for example, God not only refers to Israel as "daughter," but the term is also used of Ammon, Egypt, and Babylon, perhaps implying kinship ties as "God's children." See Fretheim, *Jeremiah*, 609.

Edom's downfall with Israel's restoration. While some have argued that this implies a typological role for Edom in relation to the nations, it may also serve to highlight the particularity of Edom and its unique relationship to Israel, thus reinforcing Edom's special relationship with Israel apart from explicit kinship terminology, as well as the role that land plays in the relationship of the two nations.

3.   Five of these prophetic texts employ "possession" (ירש) and "inheritance" (נחלה) terminology in relation to Israel and Edom (Isa 34; Ezek 35–36; Amos 9; Obadiah; Mal 1). In this "land" motif, stress is often laid on Edom's dispossession and Israel's repossession of its land. Edom is by no means the only nation whose relationship to its land is the subject of prophetic pronouncement. There is, however, a recurring theme of the land in virtually all of the passages concerning Edom, as well as the theological use of possession and inheritance terminology.

In review, all of these prophetic voices concerning Edom explicitly touch on either the issue of kinship or possession/inheritance (with the possible exception of Jer 49), and half of them directly mention both themes (Amos, Obadiah, and Malachi). Moreover, Edom's loss of land is often tied with Israel's restoration, suggesting an important link between the two. Even when language explicit to these motifs is absent, the issues of Edom's special relationship *vis-à-vis* Israel, YHWH, and the land are never far from the surface.

Taken together, these themes may aid our understanding of why Edom receives such harsh treatment in the prophets: not only was Edom considered to have violated a special relationship of brotherhood, but they were considered to have encroached on Israel's inheritance, their land. This encroachment was a dishonoring of YHWH's divine appointment of the land of Judah, as well as a disrespecting of Edom's own inheritance from YHWH. Thus, Edom falls short on two counts: as a brother to Israel/Judah, and as an heir to an appointed land from YHWH.[3]

Two election-related issues might be raised in light of these findings. First of all, Edom's role as a non-elect nation does not exempt it from certain ethical obligations. If Deuteronomy was insistent that Israel respect Edom's kinship and its land, then the prophets seem to expect the same in return from Edom. And that leads to a second, and related, issue:

---

3.   Some interpreters have indeed highlighted the themes of Edom's actions and its encroachment on Israel's land (e.g. Dicou, *Edom, Israel's Brother*, 196–97). However, the theological and canonical dimensions have been left unexplored.

when read in this light, the prophetic critiques of Edom are in many ways similar to the biblical prophecies against Israel, which was also chastised (and punished) for its lack of covenantal fidelity toward both God and "others." It is to these and other issues that we now turn in drawing this study to a conclusion.

Chapter 12

CONCLUSION:
THE RELATIONSHIP OF THE
ESAU AND EDOM TRADITIONS AND THE
IMPLICATIONS FOR ELECTION THEOLOGY

In the preceding chapters I have examined the Esau and Edom traditions found in Genesis, Deuteronomy, and the prophets. By way of conclusion, I wish to address how these traditions might be understood in light of one another, and what the implications might be for election theology.

1. *The Relationship of the Traditions*

As noted in the survey of literature in Chapter 2, there are various ways the issue of the relationship between the Esau and Edom traditions has been approached. Without rehashing the entire conversation, it is worth recalling how pre-modern and modern interpreters have in general understood this relationship.

Pre-modern interpreters generally offered a straightforward and linear reading of the Bible that took the association of Esau and Edom at face value. This seems reasonable, as there is an obvious element of continuity between Esau and Edom drawn explicitly by the biblical texts themselves (Gen 36:1, 8). However, as noted previously, this straightforward reading of the Esau and Edom traditions became problematic in the modern period, due in part to questions of a historical nature concerning the ancestral period as well as the deconstruction of the assumption that the linear presentation of the Bible mirrored a similar linearity in its development.

Modern critical scholarship attempted to answer the question of the relationship of the traditions from the vantage point of dependence and priority, often assuming discontinuity between them: is one tradition dependent on the other and, if so, how? The question, of course, is complex. The more traditional understanding was that the prophets drew from the Genesis material, and the prophetic depiction of Edom was shaped in light of Genesis. However, the trend of placing the composition of the Pentateuch in the post-exilic period might imply the opposite: that the prophets may have come first, or developed these themes independently of Genesis. A mediating position has been offered by some who note that because both Genesis and individual prophetic oracles are so difficult to date precisely, the best we can say is that the prophets were aware of the ancestral traditions, such as the kinship of Jacob and Esau. This does not mean, however, they were familiar with *Genesis*, but with the traditions that would come to make up Israel's foundation story. Adding a further complication is the fact these discussions concerning dependence tend to focus on Genesis and the prophetic material in isolation from the Deuteronomic material, which I have argued touches on similar themes, and thus questions concerning the dating of other textual traditions are not often factored into these hypotheses.

What might we conclude, then, in terms of reading these texts canonically in light of the difficulties inherent in both pre-modern and modern approaches? One possible way of moving the discussion forward is to investigate the relationship of these traditions in terms of *intertextuality*, recognizing that

> as texts are read by individual readers and reading communities who enter into conversation with them, they are rewoven or rewritten out of the threads of innumerable other texts. From this perspective, texts acquire meaning to the extent that they are situated in relation to other texts in a web of mutual interference and illumination.[1]

Consequently, while we may not be able to ascertain definitively which sources or traditions were dependent on others, it remains the case that their placement in a larger canon (in this case the Hebrew Bible) encourages us to read them in light of one another and allows their resonances to reverberate. With this in mind, I would suggest that a more fruitful way of understanding the relationship of the Esau and Edom traditions in a canonical reading might come via a recognition of intertextual resonances in their overarching theological concerns or subject matter.

---

1. George Aichele and Gary A. Phillips, "Introduction: Exegesis, Eisegesis, Intergesis," *Semeia* 69/70 (1995): 7–18 (8), in the volume dealing with intertextuality and the Bible. Elsewhere Aichele has made the case that the biblical canon acts as a controlling rather than meaning-generating force (George Aichele, *The Control of Biblical Meaning: Canon as Semiotic Mechanism* [Harrisburg: Trinity Press International, 2001]). As has been pointed out by others, there is no reason why the canon cannot function as both. See, e.g., Robert M. Fowler's review of Aichele's 2001 study in *RBL* (2004), available online at http://bookreviews.org/pdf/1400_669.pdf.

We might first note that elements in all of these traditions exhibit the kinship motif, entailing a special relationship between Jacob and Esau as well as Israel and Edom. And secondly, the traditions in question appear to understand Esau and Edom as having their own story which includes blessing by YHWH, nationhood, and a special relationship to their land.[2] To use the language I have employed elsewhere in this study, both traditions exhibit the themes of brotherhood and inheritance.

Where these traditions differ, however, is in the depiction of these themes. In Genesis, Esau is the unchosen brother who nevertheless receives his own blessing. Initially Esau is understandably unhappy losing to his younger brother both the rights of primogeniture and his father's blessing. In time, however, Esau responds graciously by welcoming his brother home (Gen 33). And, in the story, he makes peace with the move to Seir, which is described as his descendants' "possession" (אֲחֻזָּה, Gen 36:42).

Deuteronomy seems to echo these themes, and pronounces them in more starkly theological language: when Israel is moving toward Canaan, they are forbidden from taking any land from the descendants of Esau, because they are kin (אָח), and because the land has been gifted from YHWH as an inheritance (יְרֻשָּׁה, Deut 2:5). This recognition of kinship—which can be understood as relational *and* ethical—is extended to those Edomites who may join the Israelites as resident aliens, as they are to be granted eventual access to the קָהָל (Deut 23:8–9).

The prophetic tradition, meanwhile, tells another side to the story. While Esau is depicted as gracious to his brother, the prophetic texts seem to suggest the opposite for Edom. Whether in the events of 587 B.C.E., or, in Calvin's words, a series of "many annoyances" over time, the Edomites are portrayed as acting in a fashion unbecoming of kin. When they should have been different from the other nations because of this relationship, they were not (Obad 10–12). Moreover, Edom is painted as disrespecting Israel's inheritance, its land, by entering its gates (Obad 11, 13) and claiming it as its own possession (Ezek 35). Because of these offences—which, it seems, are offences against both Israel and YHWH (Jer 12:14–17)—it is Edom who the prophets proclaim will be dispossessed. Thus, the actions of Edom are portrayed in the prophetic corpus as, in a sense, a reversal of what is established in Gen 25–36 and Deut 2 and 23.[3] When Obadiah and the other prophetic oracles against

---

2. Other texts outside of these two broad traditions validate this as well: Josh 24:4 speaks of Jacob and Esau as brothers, with Esau given Seir to "possess" it.

3. It was noted above that Deuteronomy and Numbers present wilderness encounters that have much in common, yet also contain substantial differences.

Edom are read in light of Genesis and Deuteronomy, these resonances are illuminating. As kin with an inheritance of their own, Edom chose, in the eyes of Israel, to honor neither of these realities. Instead, both brotherhood and inheritance were disregarded.

2. *Implications for Election Theology*

The theological issue of election has been used as a heuristic frame of reference throughout this study for reading the various texts in question. What, then, can be said about election with reference to the entirety of these traditions? It might first be worth noting that this study has attempted to stay clear of questions concerning the nature of or reasons for YHWH's election of individuals or nations. Instead, I have assumed that, according to the biblical text, some are chosen and some are not. As such, the underlying theological question of this study has been: What does it mean to be unchosen, both in relation to those who are elect, as well as the one who chooses? In this respect, I would posit that a canonical reading of the Esau and Edom traditions can be seen to offer a picture of the dynamics of election, particularly divine initiative and human response.

To begin with, Esau is without doubt the unchosen son, passed over in the end by both his family and YHWH. And yet, Genesis paints a quite favorable picture of Esau, and his displacement does not limit his development as a character, nor his place in the divine economy: he is blessed nonetheless, and he and his descendants have land and nationhood, much like their neighbor Israel. Deuteronomy and other texts (e.g. Josh 24:4) reinforce this positive disposition, laying stress on the special kinship relationship Esau's descendants have with Israel, as well as noting YHWH's personal involvement in the story of Esau and his descendants in the giving of the land. Thus, YHWH's plans might include a specific patriarch and people, but this does not preclude others from

---

While a thorough study of the issues is not possible here, it is interesting that the texts in Numbers that refer to Edom seem to cohere more closely to the negative prophetic picture of Edom than to that of Esau in Genesis: Num 20:14–22 makes mention of Israel as Edom's brother (אח), but Edom will not allow them to pass through their land, in spite of this kinship. In Num 24:18, Balaam pronounces that Edom and Seir will be a "possession" (ירשה). Thus, these two references in Numbers retain the usage of the brotherhood and inheritance themes, but in them Edom does not behave like a brother, and its dispossession is prophesied. Hence, one could say that while Deuteronomy resonates with the positive portrayal of Esau in Genesis, Numbers has resonance with the negative prophetic portrayal of Edom.

having a role in the larger storyline, nor does it entail cursing for those who are unchosen.

Secondly, Esau's response to this divine initiative which left him as the unchosen son is important. In this respect, Gen 33 seems to be a key text within the overarching story of Jacob and Esau, Esau's response to Jacob earns him a comparison with Jacob's God, and displays for the reader what a true brother looks like. In a sense, Esau is the "anti-Cain," responding well to the difficulties with which life has presented him. One could even say, drawing on the Abrahamic blessing (Gen 12:3; 27:29), that it is this right response from Esau that, in the world of the text, opens the door to future blessing for Esau and his descendants.

It would have been tempting, then, to conclude the study at this point, highlighting the Hebrew Bible's rather positive portrayal of the non-elect. However, there is another side to this story which can be seen in relation to the Edomites as depicted in the prophets. These texts also employ the themes of brotherhood and relationship to the land, and imply that Edom's land is indeed their "inheritance." But while Esau responds graciously to his brother, according to the canonical story, the Edomites do not respond in like fashion to their kin. Moreover, Edom disrespects the divine apportioning of the lands. Edom, it would appear, had a special relationship with both Israel and YHWH, yet violated both of these relationships. Edom's inappropriate response to YHWH and Israel leads to their inheritance being taken from them.

When read in this way, the portrayal of Edom has resonance with the broader trajectory of the Hebrew Bible, which depicts YHWH as responsive to those with whom he is involved (Jer 18:6–10). It is, in the end, right response that YHWH desires, regardless. or in spite of, circumstances. This is true of the foreign nations, as well as Israel itself. Indeed, the pattern which occurs in the Edom traditions can also be seen in the story of Jacob's descendants, who, because of their inability to live in covenantal relationship with YHWH and one another, also have an inheritance (the land, Temple) taken away. As Lohr notes, "To be unchosen is to be on one side of the equation in relation to God. To be chosen is to be on the other side, but both sides entail a relationship to God and a responsibility to 'the other'."[4] Thus, it could be said that although one is chosen and one is not, the Hebrew Bible construes YHWH's interaction with Israel and Edom in similar terms: each has obligations to YHWH and the "other," and the ways in which these relationships are nurtured is taken up in YHWH's responsiveness to both nations.

4. Lohr, *Chosen and Unchosen*, 200.

Taken together, the canonical portrayal of Esau and Edom attests to the fact that the one who has planted and built up is also the one who can uproot and tear down. In both blessing and judgment, the Hebrew Bible portrays YHWH as ever responsive to those with whom he is involved—even the unchosen.

BIBLIOGRAPHY

Aberbach, Moses, and Bernard Grossfeld. *Targum Onkelos to Genesis: A Critical Analysis Together With an English Translation of the Text (Based on A. Sperber's Edition)*. New York: Ktav, 1982.

Abraham, Israel. "Numbers, Typical and Important." *EncJud* 12:1254–61.

Abraham, Jed H. "A Literary Solution to the Name Variations of Esau's Wives." *TMJ* 7 (1997): 1–14.

———. "Esau's Wives." *Jewish Bible Quarterly* 25 (1997): 251–59.

Ackroyd, Peter R. *Exile and Restoration*. OTL. Philadelphia: Westminster, 1968.

———. "Obadiah, Book of." *ABD* 5:2–4.

Ahroni, Reuben. "Why Did Esau Spurn the Birthright? A Study in Biblical Interpretation." *Judaism* 29 (1980): 323–31.

Aichele, George. *The Control of Biblical Meaning: Canon as Semiotic Mechanism*. Harrisburg: Trinity Press International, 2001.

Aichele, George, and Gary A. Phillips. "Introduction: Exegesis, Eisegesis, Intergesis." *Semeia* 69/70 (1995): 7–18.

Albertz, Rainer, Hans-Peter Müller, Hans Walter Wolff, and Walther Zimmerli, eds. *Werden und Wirken des Alten Testaments; Festschrift für Claus Westermann zum 70. Geburtstag*. Göttingen: Vandenhoeck & Ruprecht, 1980.

Allen, Leslie C. *The Books of Joel, Obadiah, Jonah and Micah*. NICOT. Grand Rapids: Eerdmans, 1976.

———. *Ezekiel 20–48*. WBC 29. Nashville: Thomas Nelson, 1990.

Alonso Schökel, Luis. "Gn 35,28–29: Muerte de Isaac y reconcilación fraterna." *EstBib* 55 (1997): 287–95.

Alter, Robert. *The Art of Biblical Narrative*. New York: Basic, 1981.

———. *Genesis: Translation and Commentary*. New York: W. W. Norton, 1996.

Andersen, Francis I., and David Noel Freedman. *Amos: A New Translation with Introduction and Commentary*. AB 24A. New York: Doubleday, 1989.

———. *Hosea: A New Translation with Introduction and Commentary*. AB 24. Garden City: Doubleday, 1980.

Anderson, Bradford A. "The Inversion of the Birth Order and the Title of the Firstborn." *VT* 60 (2010): 655–58.

———. "Poetic Justice in Obadiah." *JSOT* 35 (2010): 247–55.

Ap-Thomas, R. "Some Aspects of the Root HNN in the Old Testament." *JSS* 2 (1957): 128–48.

Aquinas, Thomas. *Summa Theologica of St. Thomas Aquinas*. Translated by Fathers of the English Dominican Province. New York: Benziger Brothers, 1947.

Assis, Elie. "Why Edom? On the Hostility Towards Jacob's Brother in Prophetic Sources." *VT* 56 (2006): 1–20.

Attridge, Harold W. *Hebrews*. Hermeneia. Philadelphia: Fortress, 1989.

Axelsson, Lars Eric. *The Lord Rose Up from Seir: Studies in the History and Traditions of the Negev and Southern Judah*. ConBOT 25. Translated by Frederick H. Cryer. Lund: Almqvist &Wiksell, 1987.

Bächli, Otto. *Israel und die Völker: Eine Studie zum Deuteronomium*. ATANT 41. Zurich: Zwingli, 1962.

Bakhos, Carol. *Ishmael on the Border: Rabbinic Portrayals of the First Arab*. Albany: SUNY Press, 2006.

Bar-Efrat, Shimon. *Narrative Art in the Bible*. London: T&T Clark International, 2004.

Barr, James. "Theophany and Anthropomorphism in the Old Testament." Pages 31–38 in *Congress Volume: Oxford, 1959*. Leiden: Brill, 1960.

Barth, Karl. *Church Dogmatics*. Translated by G. W. Bromiley. Edinburgh: T. & T. Clark, 1968.

Bartlett, J. R. "The Brotherhood of Edom." *JSOT* 4 (1977): 2–27.

———. "Edom." *ABD* 2:287–95.

———. *Edom and the Edomites*. JSOTSup 77. Sheffield: JSOT, 1989.

———. "Edom and the Fall of Jerusalem, 587 B.C." *PEQ* 114 (1982): 13–24.

———. "Edom in the Nonprophetical Corpus." Pages 13–22 in Edelman, ed., *You Shall Not Abhor an Edomite*.

———. "The Edomite King-List of Genesis XXXVI. 31–39 and I Chron. I. 43–50." *JTS* 16 (1965): 301–14.

———. "The Election of the Community." §34, page 216 in *Church Dogmatics* 2.2. Translated by G. W. Bromiley. Edinburgh: T. & T. Clark, 1968.

———. "From Edomites to Nabataeans: A Study in Continuity." *PEQ* 111 (1979): 53–66.

———. "The Land of Seir and the Brotherhood of Edom." *JTS* 20 (1969): 1–20.

Barton, John. *Amos's Oracles Against the Nations: A Study of Amos 1.3–2.5*. SOTSMS 6. Cambridge: Cambridge University Press, 1980.

———. *Joel and Obadiah: A Commentary*. OTL. Louisville: Westminster John Knox, 2001.

Beattie, D. R. G., and M. J. McNamara, eds. *The Aramaic Bible: Targums in Their Historical Context*. JSOTSup 166. Sheffield: JSOT, 1994.

Beit-Arieh, Itzhaq. "New Data on the Relationship Between Judah and Edom Toward the End of the Iron Age." Pages 125–31 in *Recent Excavations in Israel: Studies in Iron Age Archaeology*. Edited by Seymour Gitin and William G. Dever. AASOR 49. Winona Lake: Eisenbrauns, 1989.

Bellis, Alice Ogden, and Joel S. Kaminsky, eds. *Jews, Christians, and the Theology of the Hebrew Scriptures*. SBLSymS 8. Atlanta: Society of Biblical Literature, 2000.

Ben Zvi, Ehud. "A Deuteronomistic Redaction In/Among 'The Twelve'? A Contribution From the Standpoint of the Books of Micah, Zephaniah and Obadiah." Pages 232–61 in *Those Elusive Deuteronomists*. Edited by L. S. Schearing and S. L. McKenzie. JSOTSup 268. Sheffield: Sheffield Academic, 1999.

———. *A Historical-Critical Study of the Book of Obadiah*. BZAW 242. Berlin: Walter de Gruyter, 1996.

———. "Obadiah." Pages 1193–97 in Berlin and Brettler, eds., *The Jewish Study Bible*.

Berlin, Adele. *Poetics and Interpretation of Biblical Narrative*. BLS. Sheffield: Almond, 1983.

Berlin, Adele, and Marc Zvi Brettler, eds. *The Jewish Study Bible*. Oxford: Oxford University Press, 2004.

Berry, Donald K. "Malachi's Dual Design: The Close of the Canon and What Comes Afterward." Pages 269–302 in *Forming Prophetic Literature: Essays on Isaiah and the Twelve in Honor of John D. W. Watts*. Edited by James W. Watts and Paul R. Redditt. JSOTSup 235. Sheffield: Sheffield Academic, 1996.

Beuken, Willem A. M. *Isaiah Part II, Volume 2: Isaiah Chapters 28–39*. HCOT. Translated by Brian Doyle. Leuven: Peeters, 2000.

Beyerle, Stefan, Günter Mayer, and Hans Strauss, eds. *Recht und Ethos im Alten Testament - Gestalt und Wirkung: Festschrift für Horst Seebass zum 65. Geburtstag*. Neukirchen–Vluyn: Neukirchener, 1999.

Bienkowski, Piotr, ed. *Early Edom and Moab: The Beginning of the Iron Age in Southern Jordan*. SAM 7. Sheffield: J. R. Collis, 1992.

Blank, Sheldon H. "Studies in Post-exilic Universalism." *HUCA* 11 (1936): 159–91.

Blenkinsopp, Joseph. "Biographical Patterns in Biblical Narrative." *JSOT* 20 (1981): 27–46.

———. *The Pentateuch: An Introduction to the First Five Books of the Bible*. ABRL. New York: Doubleday, 1992.

Blum, Erhard. *Die Komposition der Vätergeschichte*. WMANT 57. Neukirchen–Vluyn: Neukirchener, 1980.

———. "Genesis 33,12–20: Die Wege trennen sich." Pages 227–38 in Macchi and Römer, eds., *Jacob*.

———. "Gibt es die Endgestalt des Pentateuch?" Pages 46–57 in Emerton, ed., *Congress Volume: Leuven, 1989*.

Botterweck, G. J. "Jakob habe ich lieb-esau hasse ich." *BibLeb* 1 (1960): 28–38.

Brenner, Athalya. *Colour Terms in the Old Testament*. JSOTSup 21. Sheffield: JSOT, 1982.

Brett, Mark G. *Genesis: Procreation and the Politics of Identity*. OTR. London: Routledge, 2000.

Briggs, Richard S. "Speech-Act Theory." Pages 75–108 in *Words and the Word: Explorations in Biblical Interpretation and Literary Theory*. Edited by David J. Firth and Jamie A. Grant. Leicester: Apollos, 2008.

Brown, William P. *Obadiah Through Malachi*. WeBC. Louisville: Westminster/John Knox, 1996.

Bruce, F. F. *The Epistle to the Hebrews: The English Text with Introduction, Exposition and Notes*. NICNT. Grand Rapids: Eerdmans, 1990.

Brueggemann, Walter. *Genesis*. IBC. Atlanta: John Knox, 1982.

———. *The Land: Place as Gift, Promise, and Challenge in Biblical Faith*. OBT. London: SPCK, 1977.

Buechner, Frederick. *The Magnificent Defeat*. San Francisco: HarperOne, 1985.

Buhl, Frants. *Geschichte der Edomiter*. Leipzig: Edelmann, 1893.

Butterweck-Bensberg, Annelise. "Die Begegnung zwischen Esau und Jakob (Gen. 33,1–18) im Spiegel rabbinischer Ausdeutungen." *BN* 116 (2003): 15–27.

Calvin, John. *Commentaries on the First Book of Moses Called Genesis*, vol. 2. Translated by John King. Edinburgh: Calvin Translation Society, 1850.

———. *Commentaries on the Twelve Minor Prophets*. Vol. 2, *Joel, Amos, Obadiah*. Translated by John Owen. Edinburgh: Calvin Translation Society, 1846.

———. *Commentaries on the Twelve Minor Prophets*. Vol 5, *Zechariah and Malachi*. Translated by John Owen. London: Banner of Truth, 1986.

————. *Institutes of the Christian Religion.* Vol. 2. LCC 21. Translated by Ford Lewis Battles. Edited by John T. McNeill. Philadelphia: Westminster, 1960.

Cannon, W. W. "Israel and Edom: The Oracle of Obadiah - I." *Theology* 15 (1927): 129–40.

————. "Israel and Edom: The Oracle of Obadiah - II." *Theology* 15 (1927): 191–200.

Carr, David M. "Βίβλος γενέσεος Revisited: A Synchronic Analysis of Patterns in Genesis as Part of the Torah (Part One)." *ZAW* 110 (1998): 159–72.

————. *Reading the Fractures of Genesis: Historical and Literary Approaches.* Louisville: Westminster John Knox, 1996.

Cathcart, K. J., and R. P. Gordon. *The Targum of the Minor Prophets.* ArBib 14. Edinburgh: T. & T. Clark, 1989.

Cazelles, H. "Qehal YHWH." Pages 601–2 in vol. 9 of *DBSup.*

Charles, R. H., ed., *The Book of Jubilees.* London: SCM, 1917.

Childs, Brevard S. *Biblical Theology of the Old and New Testaments: Theological Reflection on the Christian Bible.* Minneapolis: Fortress, 1992.

————. *Introduction to the Old Testament as Scripture.* Philadelphia: Fortress, 1979.

————. *Isaiah.* OTL. Louisville: Westminster John Knox, 2001.

Chung, Il-Seung. "Liberating Esau: A Corrective Reading of the Esau–Jacob Narrative in Genesis 25–36." Ph.D. diss., University of Sheffield, 2008.

Clarke, Ernest G. *Targum Pseudo-Jonathan: Deuteronomy.* ArBib 5b. Edinburgh: T. & T. Clark, 1998.

Clifford, Richard J. "Genesis 25:19–34." *Int* 45 (1991): 397–401.

Clines, David J. A. *What Does Eve Do To Help?, and Other Readerly Questions to the Old Testament.* JSOTSup 94. Sheffield: JSOT, 1990.

Coats, George W. *Genesis, with an Introduction to Narrative Literature.* FOTL 1. Grand Rapids: Eerdmans, 1983.

————. "Strife without Reconciliation: A Narrative Theme in the Jacob Traditions." Pages 82–106 in Albertz et al., eds., *Werden und Wirken.*

————. "The Wilderness Itinerary." *CBQ* 34 (1972): 135–52.

Cohen, Gerson D. "Esau as Symbol in Early Medieval Thought." Pages 19–48 in *Jewish Medieval and Renaissance Studies.* Edited by Alexander Altmann. Cambridge: Harvard University Press, 1967.

Cohen, Jeffrey M. "The Jacob–Esau Reunion." *Jewish Bible Quarterly* 21 (1993): 159–63.

Cohen, Norman J. "Two that are One: Sibling Rivalry in Genesis." *Judaism* 32 (1983): 331–42.

Cohen, Shaye J. D. *The Beginnings of Jewishness: Boundaries, Varieties, Uncertainties.* Berkeley: University of California Press, 2001.

Cohn, Robert L. "Negotiating (with) the Natives: Ancestors and Identity in Genesis." *HTR* 96 (2003): 147–66.

Cotter, David W. *Genesis.* BO. Collegeville: Liturgical, 2003.

Cresson, Bruce C. "The Condemnation of Edom in Post-Exilic Judaism." Pages 125–48 in *The Use of the Old Testament in the New and Other Essays: Studies in Honour of William Franklin Stinespring.* Edited by James M. Efird. Durham, N.C.: Duke University Press, 1972.

Daube, David. "How Esau Sold His Birthright." *CLJ* 8 (1942–44): 70–75.

————. *Studies in Biblical Law.* Cambridge: Cambridge University Press, 1947.

Davies, Eryl W. "The Inheritance of the First-Born in Israel and the Ancient Near East." *JSS* 38 (1993): 175–91.

———. "The Meaning of *pî šenayim* in Deuteronomy XXI 17." *VT* 36 (1986): 341–47.

Davies, G. I. "The Wilderness Itineraries and the Composition of the Pentateuch." *VT* 33 (1983): 1–13.

De Vaux, Roland. "Les Hurrites de l'histoire et les Horites de la Bible." *RB* 74 (1974): 482–503.

Dicou, Bert. *Edom, Israel's Brother and Antagonist: The Role of Edom in Biblical Prophecy and Story.* JSOTSup 169. Sheffield: JSOT, 1994.

———. "Jakob en Esau, Israël en Edom: Israël tegenover de volken in de verhalen over Jakob en Esau in Genesis en in de grote profetieën over Edom." Ph.D. diss., University of Amsterdam, 1990.

Dillmann, August. *Die Genesis.* Leipzig: Hirzel, 1892.

Donaldson, Mara E. "Kinship Theory in the Patriarchal Narratives: The Case of the Barren Wife." *JAAR* 49 (1981): 77–87.

Driver, S. R. *The Book of Genesis.* WC. London: Methuen, 1909.

Dunn, James D. G. *Romans 9–16.* WBC 38B. Dallas: Word, 1988.

Edelman, Diana Vikander. "Edom: A Historical Geography." Pages 1–11 in Edelman, ed., *You Shall Not Abhor an Edomite.*

———, ed. *You Shall Not Abhor an Edomite for He is Your Brother: Edom and Seir in History and Tradition.* ABS 3. Atlanta: Scholars, 1995.

Eichrodt, Walther. *Ezekiel: A Commentary.* OTL. Translated by Cosslett Quin. London: SCM, 1970.

Eissfeldt, Otto. "Biblos Geneseōs." Pages 458–70 in *Kleine Schriften.* Volume 3. Edited by Rudolf Sellheim and Fritz Maass. Tübingen: J. C. B. Mohr, 1966.

Elliger, K. *Das Buch der Zwölf Kleinen Propheten 2: Die Propheten Nahum, Habakuk, Zephanja, Haggai, Sacharja, Maleachi.* Das Alt Testament Deutsch 25. Göttingen: Vandenhoeck & Ruprecht, 1982.

Emerton, J., ed. *Congress Volume: Leuven, 1989.* VTSup 43. Leiden: Brill, 1991.

Eslinger, L. M. "Hosea 12.5a and Genesis 32:29: A Study in Inner Biblical Exegesis." *JSOT* 18 (1980): 91–99.

Ferreiro, Alberto, ed. *The Twelve Prophets.* ACCS 14. Downers Grove: IVP, 2003.

Fischer, James A. "Notes on the Literary Form and Message of Malachi." *CBQ* 34 (1972): 315–20.

Fishbane, Michael. *Biblical Interpretation in Ancient Israel.* Oxford: Clarendon, 1985.

———. *Biblical Text and Texture: A Literary Reading of Selected Texts.* Oxford: Oneworld, 1979.

———. "Composition and Structure in the Jacob Cycle (Gen. 25:19–35:22)." *JJS* 26 (1975):15–38.

———. "The Treaty Background of Amos 1:11 and Related Matters." *JBL* 89 (1970): 313–18.

Fohrer, G. *Die Propheten des frühen 6.Jahrhunderts.* PAT 3. Gütersloh: Gerd Mohn, 1975.

———. "Die Sprüche Obadjas." Pages 81–93 in *Studia biblica et semitica Theodoro Christiano Vriezen dedicata.* Edited by Wilhelm C. van Unnik and Adam Simon van der Woude. Wageningen: Veenman, 1966.

Fokkelman, J. P. *Narrative Art in Genesis: Specimens of Stylistic and Structural Analysis.* SSN 17. Assen: Van Gorcum, 1975.

Fowler, Robert G. Review of George Aichele, *The Control of Biblical Meaning: Canon as Semiotic Mechanism. RBL* (2004). Cited 20 April 2010. Online: http://bookreviews. org/pdf/1400_669.pdf.

Frankel, David. "The Deuteronomic Portrayal of Balaam." *VT* 46 (1996): 30–42.

Freedman, D. N. "The Original Name of Jacob." *IEJ* 13 (1963): 125–26.

Freedman, Harry. "Jacob and Esau: Their Struggle in the Second Century." *JBQ* 32 (1995): 107–15.

Fretheim, Terence E. "The Book of Genesis." Pages 319–674 in *NIB*, vol. 1.

———. "The Jacob Traditions: Theology and Hermeneutic." *Int* 26 (1972): 419–36.

———. *Jeremiah*. SHBC 15. Macon: Smyth & Helwys, 2002.

———. "Which Blessing Does Isaac Give Jacob?" Pages 279–92 in Bellis and Kaminksy, eds., *Jews, Christians*.

Friedman, Richard Elliot. *Commentary on the Torah*. San Francisco: HarperSanFrancisco, 2001.

Galling, Kurt. "Das Gemeindegesetz in Deuteronmium 23." Pages 176–91 in *Festschrift Alfred Bertholet zum 80. Geburtstag*. Edited by Walter Baumgartner, Otto Eissfeldt, Karl Elliger, and Leonhard Rost. Tübingen: J. C. B. Mohr, 1950.

Gammie, John G. "Theological Interpretation By Way of Literary and Tradition Analysis: Genesis 25–36." Pages 117–34 in *Encounter with the Text: Form and History in the Hebrew Bible*. Edited by Martin J. Buss. Philadelphia: Fortress, 1979.

Gerleman, Gillis. "Nutzrecht und Wohnrecht: Zur Bedeutung von אחזה und נחלה." *ZAW* 98 (1977): 313–24.

Gevirtz, Stanley. "Of Patriarchs and Puns: Joseph at the Fountain, Jacob at the Ford." *HUCA* 46 (1975): 33–54.

Ginsburger, M. *Pseudo-Jonathan (Thargum-Jonathan ben Usiël zum Pentateuch)*. Berlin: Calvary, 1903.

Ginzberg, Louis. *The Legends of the Jews*. Vol. 1, *Bible Times and Characters from the Creation to Jacob*. Translated by Henrietta Szold. Philadelphia: Jewish Publication Society, 1954.

Glatt-Gilad, David A. "The Re-Interpretation of the Edomite-Israelite Encounter in Deuteronomy II." *VT* 47 (1997): 441–55.

Glazier-McDonald, Beth. "Edom in the Prophetical Corpus." Pages 23–32 in Edelman, ed., *You Shall Not Abhor an Edomite*.

———. *Malachi: The Divine Messenger*. SBLDS 98. Atlanta: Scholars Press, 1987.

Glueck, Nelson. "The Civilization of the Edomites." *BA* 10, no. 4 (1947): 77–84.

———. "Deuteronomy 23:8,9." Pages 261–62 in *Mordecai M. Kaplan Jubilee Volume*. New York: Jewish Theological Seminary of America, 1953.

Golka, Friedemann W. "BECHORAH und BERACHAH: Erstgeburtsrecht und Segen." Pages 133–44 in Beyerle, Mayer, and Strauss, eds., *Recht und Ethos*.

Gordon, Robert P. *Studies in the Targum to the Twelve Prophets*. VTSup 51. Leiden: Brill, 1994.

Gosse, Bernard. "Détournement de la vengeance du Seigneur contre Edom et les nations en Isa 63,1–6." *ZAW* 102 (1990): 105–10.

———. "Isaïe 34–35: Le chatiment d'Edom et des nations, salut pour Sion." *ZAW* 102 (1990): 396–404.

Greenberg, Moshe. *Ezekiel 21–37: A New Translation with Introduction and Commentary*. AB 22a. New York: Doubleday, 1997.

Greenspahn, Frederick E. *When Brothers Dwell Together: The Preeminence of Younger Siblings in the Hebrew Bible*. Oxford: Oxford University Press, 1994.

Grossfeld, Bernard. *The Targum Onqelos to Deuteronomy*. ArBib 9. Edinburgh: T. & T. Clark, 1988.

———. *The Targum Onqelos to Genesis, Translated with a Critical Introduction, Apparatus, and Notes*. ArBib 6. Edinburgh: T. & T. Clark, 1988.

Gunkel, Hermann. *Genesis*. MLBS. Translated by Mark E. Biddle. Macon: Mercer University Press, 1997.

Habel, Norman. *The Land is Mine: Six Biblical Land Ideologies*. OBT. Minneapolis: Fortress, 1995.

Hadas-Lebel, Mireille. "Jacob et Esau ou Israel et Rome dans le Talmud et le Midrash." *RHR* 201 (1984): 369–92.

Haller, Max. "Edom in Urteil der Propheten." Pages 109–17 in *Vom Alten Testament. Festschrift K. Marti*. Edited by K. Budde. BZAW 41. Giessen: Töpelmann, 1925.

Hallo, William H. "Biblical Abominations and Sumerian Taboos." *JQR* 76, no. 1 (1985): 21–40.

Hamilton, Victor P. *The Book of Genesis, Chapters 18–50*. NICOT. Grand Rapids: Eerdmans, 1995.

Hamori, Esther J. *"When Gods Were Men": The Embodied God in Biblical and Near Eastern Literature*. BZAW 384. Berlin: de Gruyter, 2008.

Haney, Linda. "YHWH, the God of Israel…and of Edom? The Relationships in the Oracle to Edom in Jeremiah 49:7–22." Pages 78–115 in *Uprooting and Planting: Essays on Jeremiah for Leslie Allen*. Edited by John Goldingay. LHBOTS 459. London: T&T Clark, 2007.

Haran, M. "Observations on the Historical Background of Amos 1:2–2:6." *IEJ* 18 (1968): 201–12.

Hayes, John H. "The Usage of Oracles against Foreign Nations in Ancient Israel." *JBL* 87 (1968): 81–92.

Hayward, C. T. R. *Interpretations of the Name Israel in Ancient Judaism and Some Early Christian Writings: From Victorious Athlete to Heavenly Champion*. Oxford: Oxford University Press, 2005.

———. "A Portrait of the Wicked Esau in the Targum of Codex Neofiti 1." Pages 291–309 in Beattie and McNamara, eds., *The Aramaic Bible*.

———. "Targum Pseudo-Jonathan to Genesis 27:31." *JQR* 84 (1993–1994): 177–88.

Heard, R. Christopher. *Dynamics of Diselection: Ambiguity in Genesis 12–36 and Ethnic Boundaries in Post-Exilic Judah*. SBLDS 39. Atlanta: Society of Biblical Literature, 2001.

Helfmeyer, Franz Josef. "Segen und Erwählung." *BZ* 18 (1974): 208–23.

Hendel, Ronald S. *The Epic of the Patriarch: The Jacob Cycle and the Narrative Traditions of Canaan and Israel*. HSM 42. Atlanta: Scholars, 1987.

Hill, Andrew E. "Genealogy." *DTIB* 242–46.

———. *Malachi: A New Translation with Introduction and Commentary*. AB 25D. New York: Doubleday, 1998.

Holladay, W. L. "Chiasmus, the Key to Hosea XII 3–6." *VT* 16 (1966): 53–64.

Holmgren, Fredrick C. "Holding Your Own Against God: Genesis 32:22–32 (In the Context of Genesis 31–33)." *Int* 44 (1990): 5–17.

Horst, Friedrich. "Zwei Begriffe für eigentum (besitz): אחזה und נחלה." Pages 135–56 in *Verbannung und Heimkehr: Festschrift für W. Rudolph*. Edited by A. Kuschke. Tübingen: J. C. B. Mohr, 1961.

House, Paul R. "Obadiah." *DTIB* 542–44.

———. *The Unity of the Twelve*. JSOTSup 97. Sheffield: Almond, 1990.

Houten, Christiana van. *The Alien in Israelite Law*. JSOTSup 107. Sheffield: Sheffield Academic, 1991.

Houtman, C. "Jacob at Mahanaim: Some Remarks on Genesis xxxii 2–3." *VT* 28 (1978): 37–44.

Hübner, U. "Esau." *ABD* 2:574–75.

Huffmon, Herbert B. "The Covenant Lawsuit in the Prophets." *JBL* 78 (1959): 285–95.

———. "The Treaty Background of Hebrew YADA'." *BASOR* 181 (1966): 31–37.

Humphreys, W. Lee. *The Character of God in the Book of Genesis: A Narrative Appraisal*. Louisville: Westminster John Knox, 2001.

Jacob, B. *Das Erste Buch Der Tora: Genesis, Übersetzt und Erklärt*. Berlin: Schocken, 1934.

Jacobs, Mignon R. *Gender, Power, and Persuasion: The Genesis Narratives and Contemporary Portraits*. Grand Rapids: Baker Academic, 2007.

James, M. R., ed., *Liber antiquitatum biblicarum*. The Biblical Antiquities of Philo. New York: Ktav, 1971.

Jenson, P. P. *Obadiah, Jonah, Micah: A Theological Commentary*. London: T&T Clark, 2008.

Jeremias, Jörg. *The Book of Amos: A Commentary*. Translated by Douglas W. Stott. Louisville: Westminster John Knox, 1998.

———. *Die Propheten Joel, Obadja, Jona, Micha*. Das Alt Testament Deutsch 24/3. Göttingen: Vandenhoeck & Ruprecht, 2007.

Johnson, Marshall D. *The Purpose of the Biblical Genealogies, With Special Reference to the Setting of the Genealogies of Jesus*. SNTSMS 8. Cambridge: Cambridge University Press, 1969.

Johnstone, William. "1 Chronicles 1: Israel's Place Within the Human Family." Pages 24–36 in *1 and 2 Chronicles*. Vo. 1, *1 Chronicles 1–2 Chronicles 9, Israel's Place among the Nations*. JSOTSup 253. Sheffield: Sheffield Academic, 1997.

Jones, Barry Alan. *The Formation of the Book of the Twelve: A Study in Text and Canon*. SBLDS 149. Atlanta: Scholars, 1995.

Kaminsky, Joel S. "Did Election Imply the Mistreatment of Non-Israelites?" *HTR* 96 (2003): 397–425.

———. "Humor and the Theology of Hope: Isaac as a Humorous Figure." *Int* 54 (2000): 363–75.

———. *Yet I Loved Jacob: Reclaiming the Biblical Concept of Election*. Nashville: Abingdon, 2007.

Kampling, Rainer. "Wieder kein Segen—Esau im Neuen Testament." Pages 231–41 in Langer, ed., *Esau – Bruder und Feind*.

Kellermann, U. "Israel und Edom. Studien zum Edomhass Israels n 6.–4. Jahrhundert v. Chr." Unpublished Habilitationsschrift, Münster, 1975.

———. "Psalm 137." *ZAW* 90 (1978): 43–58.

Kelley, Page H., Daniel S. Mynatt, and Timothy G. Crawford. *The Masorah of Biblia Hebraica Stuttgartensia: Introduction and Annotated Glossary*. Grand Rapids: Eerdmans, 1998.

Keukens, Karlheinz H. "Der irreguläre Sterbesegen Isaaks Bemerkungen zur Interpretation von Genesis 27,1–45." *BN* 19 (1982): 43–55.

Kidd, José E. Ramírez. *Alterity and Identity in Israel: The גר in the Old Testament.* BZAW 283. Berlin: de Gruyter, 1999.

Kingsbury, Edwin C. "He Set Ephraim Before Manasseh." *HUCA* 38 (1967): 129–36.

Klein, Ralph W. *1 Chronicles.* Hermeneia. Minneapolis: Fortress, 2006.

Knauf, Ernst Axel. "Alter und Herkunft der edomitischen Königsliste Gen 36,31–39." *ZAW* 97 (1985): 245–53.

———. "Edom: The Social and Economic History." Pages 93–117 in Edelman, ed., *You Shall Not Abhor an Edomite.*

———. "Genesis 36, 1–43." Pages 291–300 in Macchi and Römer, eds., *Jacob.*

———. "Horites." *ABD* 3:288.

———. "Seir." *ABD* 5 1072–73.

———. "Supplementa Ismaelitica." *BN* 45 (1988): 62–81

Knauth, R. J. D. "Esau. Edomites." Pages 219–24 in *DOTP.*

Knoppers, Gary N. *1 Chronicles 1–9: A New Translation with Introduction and Commentary.* AB 12. New York: Doubleday, 2003.

———. "Intermarriage, Social Complexity, and Ethnic Diversity in the Genealogy of Judah." *JBL* 120 (2001): 15–30.

Koch, K. "Die Toledot-Formeln als Strukturprinzip des Buches Genesis." Pages 183–91 in Beyerle, Mayer, and Strauss, eds., *Recht und Ethos.*

Koopmans, W. T. "Poetic Reciprocation: The Oracles against Edom and Philistia in Ezek. 25:12–17." Pages 113–22 in *Verse in Ancient Near Eastern Prose.* Edited by J. C. de Moor and W. G. E. Watson. AOAT 42. Neukirchen–Vluyn: Neukirchener Verlag, 1993.

Kornfeld, Walter. "Die Edomiterlisten (Gn 36; 1C 1) im lichte des altarabischen namensmateriales." Pages 231–236 in *Mélanges bibliques et orientaux en l'honneur de M. Mathias Delcor.* Edited by André Caquot. Kevelaer: Verlag Butzon & Bercker, 1985.

Kraft, Robert A. "A Note on the Oracle of Rebecca (Gen. xxv.23)." *JTS* 13 (1962): 318–20.

Kühlewein, Johannes. "Gottesfahrung und Reifungsgeschichte in der Jakob-Esau-Erzählung." Pages 116–30 in Albertz et al., eds., *Werden und Wirken.*

Kunin, Seth D. *The Logic of Incest: A Structuralist Analysis of Hebrew Mythology.* JSOTSup 185. Sheffield: Sheffield Academic, 1995.

LaBianca, Øystein S., and Randall W. Younker. "The Kingdoms of Ammon, Moab and Edom: The Archaeology of Society in Late Bronze/Iron Age Transjordan (ca. 1400–500 BCE)." Pages 399–415 in *Archaeology of Society in the Holy Land.* Edited by Thomas E. Levy. London: Leicester University Press, 1995.

Langer, Gerhard, ed. *Esau – Bruder und Feind.* Edited by Gerhard Langer. Göttingen: Vandenhoeck & Ruprecht, 2009.

———. "Esau im Buch der Jubiläen." Pages 55–62 in Langer, ed., *Esau – Bruder und Feind.*

———. "Esau in der hebräischen Bibel." Pages 17–30 in Langer, ed., *Esau – Bruder und Feind.*

Lescow, Theodor. "Die Komposition des Buches Obadja." *ZAW* 111 (1999): 380–98.

Levenson, Jon D. "The Davidic Covenant and its Modern Interpreters." *CBQ* 41 (1979): 205–19.

————. *The Death and Resurrection of the Beloved Son: The Transformation of Child Sacrifice in Judaism and Christianity*. New Haven: Yale University Press, 1993.

————. "Genesis." In Berlin and Brettler, eds., *The Jewish Study Bible*.

————. "Is There a Counterpart in the Hebrew Bible to New Testament Antisemitism?" *JES* 22 (1985): 242–60.

Levine, Baruch. "Firstborn." *EncJud* 6:1306–8.

L'Heureux, Conrad. "The Ugaritic and Biblical Rephaim." *HTR* 67 (1974): 265–74.

Limburg, James. *Hosea–Micah*. IBC. Atlanta: John Knox, 1988.

Lindsay, John. "Edomite Westward Expansion: The Biblical Evidence." *Ancient Near Eastern Studies* 36 (1999): 48–89.

Loewenstamm, Samuel E. "Prostration from Afar in Ugaritic, Accadian and Hebrew." *BASOR* 188 (1967): 41–43.

Lohfink, Norbert. "Darstellungskunst und Theologie in Dtn 1,6–3,29." Pages 15–25 in *Studien zum Deuteronomium und der deuteronomistischen Literatur I*. SBAB 8. Stuttgart: Katholisches Bibelwerk, 1991.

————. "Dtn 12,1 und Gen 15,18: das dem Samen Abrahams geschenkte Land als der Geltungsbereich der deuteronomischen Gesetze." Pages 183–210 in *Väter Israels*. Stuttgart: Katholisches Bibelwerk, 1989.

————. "Hate and Love in Osee 9. 15." *CBQ* 25 (1963): 417.

Lohr, Joel N. *Chosen and Unchosen: Concepts of Election in the Pentateuch and Jewish-Christian Interpretation*. Siphrut 2. Winona Lake: Eisenbrauns, 2009.

Long, Burke O. *The Problem of Etiological Narrative in the Old Testament*. BZAW 108. Berlin: Töpelmann, 1968.

Lust, J., E. Eynikel, and K. Hauspie. *A Greek–English Lexicon of the Septuagint*. Stuttgart: Deutsche Bibelgesellschaft, 1996.

Luther, Martin. *Bondage of the Will*. Translated by J. I. Packer and O. R. Johnston. Cambridge: James Clarke, 1957.

————. *Lectures on Genesis, Chapter 31–37*. Luther's Works 6. Edited by Jaroslav Pelikan. Saint Louis: Concordia, 1966.

————. *Lectures on the Minor Prophets I: Hosea, Joel, Amos, Obadiah, Micah, Nahum, Zephaniah, Haggai, Malachi*. Edited by Hilton C. Oswald. Translated by Richard J. Dinda. Luther's Works 18. St. Louis: Concordia, 1975.

Lynch, Matthew J. "Zion's Warrior and the Nations: Isaiah 59:15b–63:6 in Isaiah's Zion Traditions." *CBQ* 70 (2008): 244–63.

Maag, Victor. "Jakob-Esau-Edom." *TZ* 13 (1957): 418–29.

Macchi, Jean-Daniel, and Thomas Römer, eds. *Jacob: Commentaire à plusieurs voix de Gen 25–36; Mélanges offerts à Albert de Pury*. MdB 44. Geneva: Labor et Fides, 2001.

MacLaurin, E. C. B. "Anak/'ANAΞ." *VT* 15 (1965): 468–74.

Maher, Michael. *Targum Pseudo-Jonathan: Genesis, Translated, with Introduction and Notes*. ArBib 1B. Edinburgh: T. & T. Clark, 1992.

Maier, Johann. "Israel und 'Edom' in den Ausdeutungen zu Dtn 2:1–8." Pages 135–84 in *Judentum - Ausblicke und Einsichten. Festschrift für Kurt Schubert*. Edited by Clemens Thoma. Frankfurt: P. Lang Verlag, 1993.

Malamat, Abraham. "King lists of the old Babylonian period and biblical genealogies." Pages 163–73 in *Essays in Memory of E. A. Speiser*. Edited by William W. Hallo. New Haven: American Oriental Society, 1968.

Malul, M. " *'āqēb* 'Heel' and *'āqab* 'to Supplant' and the Concept of Succession in the Jacob–Esau Narratives." *VT* 46 (1996): 190–212.

Mann, Thomas W. *Deuteronomy*. WeBC. Louisville: Westminster John Knox, 1995.

Marcus, David. "Traditional Jewish Responses to the Question of Deceit in Genesis 27." Pages 293–306 in Bellis and Kaminksy, eds., *Jews, Christians*.

Matthews, Claire R. *Defending Zion: Edom's Desolation and Jacob's Restoration (Isaiah 34–35) in Context*. BZAW 236. Berlin: de Gruyter, 1995.

Mattingly, Gerald L. "Amalek." *ABD* 1:169–71.

———. "Anak." *ABD* 1:222.

Mauss, Marcel. *The Gift: The Form and Reason for Exchange in Archaic Societies*. Translated by W. D. Halls. New York: W. W. Norton, 1990.

Mayes, A. D. H. *Deuteronomy*. NCB. Grand Rapids: Eerdmans, 1979.

McComiskey, Thomas Edward. *The Minor Prophets: An Exegetical & Expository Commentary*. Grand Rapids: Baker, 1998.

McKane, William. *A Critical and Exegetical Commentary on Jeremiah, Volume II, Commentary on Jeremiah XXVI–LII*. ICC. Edinburgh: T. & T. Clark, 1996.

McKenzie, Steven L. "The Jacob Tradition in Hosea XII 4–5." *VT* 36 (1986): 311–22.

McKenzie, Steven L., and Howard N. Wallace. "Covenant Themes in Malachi." *CBQ* 45 (1983): 549–63.

McNamara, M. *Targum Neofiti 1: Deuteronomy*. ArBib 5a. Edinburgh: T. & T. Clark, 1997.

———. *Targum Neofiti 1: Genesis*. ArBib 1A. Edinburgh: T. & T. Clark, 1992.

Meinhold, Arndt. *Maleachi (1,1–2,9)*. BKAT XIV/8i Neukirchen: Neukirchener Verlag, 2000.

Mendelsohn, I. "On the Preferential Status of the Eldest Son." *BASOR* 156 (1959): 38–40.

Metzger, Bruce M. "The Fourth Book of Ezra." Pages 517–60 in *The Old Testament Pseudepigrapha*. Vol. 1, *Apocalyptic Literature and Testaments*. Edited by James. H. Charlesworth. New York: Doubleday, 1983.

Meyer, Eduard. *Die Israeliten und Ihre Nachbarstämme* Halle: Niemeyer, 1906.

Miller, Cynthia L., ed. *The Verbless Clause in Biblical Hebrew: Linguistic Approaches*. LSAWS. Winona Lake: Eisenbrauns, 1999.

Miller, Patrick D. *Deuteronomy*. IBC. Louisville: John Knox, 1990.

———. "God's Other Stories: On the Margins of Deuteronomic Theology." Pages 593–602 in *Israelite Religion*.

———. *Israelite Religion and Biblical Theology: Collected Essays*. JSOTSup 267. Sheffield: Sheffield Academic, 2000.

———. "The Wilderness Journey in Deuteronomy: Style, Structure, and Theology in Deuteronomy 1–3." Pages 572–92 in *Israelite Religion*.

Miller, William T. *Mysterious Encounters at Mamre and Jabbok*. BJS 50. Chico: Scholars, 1984.

Mitchell, Christopher Wright. *The Meaning of BRK "To Bless" in the Old Testament*. SBLDS 95. Atlanta: Scholars, 1987.

Moberly, R. W. L. *At the Mountain of God: Story and Theology in Exodus 32–34*. JSOTSup 22. Sheffield: JSOT, 1983.

———. *Genesis 12–50*. OTG. Sheffield: Sheffield Academic, 1992.

———. "The Nature of Christian Biblical Theology." Pages 141–57 in *From Eden to Golgotha: Essays in Biblical Theology*. SFSHJ 52. Atlanta: Scholars, 1992.

———. "Preaching for a Response? Jonah's Message to the Ninevites Reconsidered." *VT* 53 (2003): 156–68.

———. *The Theology of the Book of Genesis*. OTT. Cambridge: Cambridge University Press, 2009.

Moran, William L. "The Ancient Near East Background of the Love of God in Deuteronomy." *CBQ* 25 (1963): 77–87.

Moritz, Bernhard. "Edomitische Genealogien. I." *ZAW* 44 (1926): 81–93.

Myers, J. M. "Edom and Judah in the Sixth-Fifth Centuries B.C." Pages 377–92 in *Near Eastern Studies in Honor of William Foxwell Albright*. Edited by Hans Goedicke. Baltimore: The Johns Hopkins University Press, 1971.

Navon, Mois A. "The Kiss of Esau." *JBQ* 35 (2007): 127–31.

Nelson, Richard D. *Deuteronomy*. OTL. Louisville: Westminster John Knox, 2002.

Neusner, Jacob. *Genesis Rabbah: The Judaic Commentary to the Book of Genesis: A New American Translation*. Vol. 2, *Parashiyyot Thirty-Four through Sixty-Seven on Genesis 8:15–28:9*. BJS 105. Atlanta: Scholars, 1985.

———. *Genesis Rabbah: The Judaic Commentary to the Book of Genesis, A New American Translation*. Vol. 3, *Parashiyyot Sixty-Eight through One Hundred, on Genesis 28:10 to 50:26*. BJS 106. Atlanta: Scholars, 1985.

Niccacci, A. "Poetic Syntax and Interpretation of Malachi." *LASBF* 51 (2001): 55–107.

Niditch, Susan. *"My Brother Esau Is a Hairy Man": Hair and Identity in Ancient Israel*. Oxford: Oxford University Press, 2008.

———. *Underdogs and Tricksters: A Prelude to Biblical Folklore*. NVBS. San Francisco: Harper & Row, 1987.

Niehaus, Jeffrey J. "Obadiah." Pages 2:495–542 in McComiskey, ed., *The Minor Prophets*.

Nielsen, Eduard. *Deuteronomium*. HAT I/6. Tübingen: J. C. B. Mohr, 1995.

Nogalski, James D. *Literary Precursors to the Book of the Twelve*. BZAW 217. Berlin: de Gruyter, 1993.

———. *Redactional Processes in the Book of the Twelve*. BZAW 218. Berlin: de Gruyter, 1993.

Nogalski, James D., and Marvin A. Sweeney, eds. *Reading and Hearing the Book of the Twelve*. SBLSymS 15. Atlanta: Society of Biblical Literature, 2000.

O'Brien, Julia M. *Challenging Prophetic Metaphor: Theology and Ideology in the Prophets*. Louisville: Westminster John Knox, 2008.

———. "Judah as Wife and Husband: Deconstructing Gender in Malachi." *JBL* 115 (1996): 241–50.

Oden, Robert A. Jr. "Jacob as Father, Husband, and Nephew: Kinship Studies and the Patriarchal Narratives." *JBL* 102 (1983): 189–205.

Parry, Donald W., and Emanuel Tov. *The Dead Sea Scrolls Reader, Part 1: Texts Concerned with Religious Law*. Leiden: Brill, 2004.

Patrick, Dale. "Election, Old Testament." *ABD* 2:434–41.

Perlitt, Lothar. *Deuteronomium*. KAT 5. Neukirchen–Vluyn: Neukirchener Verlag, 1990.

———. "'Ein einzig Volk von Brüdern': Zur deuteronomischen Herkunft der biblischen Bezeichnung 'Brüder'." Pages 50–73 in *Deuteronomium-Studien*. FAT 8. Tübingen: J. C. B. Mohr, 1994.

Petersen, David L. "Genesis and Family Values." *JBL* 124 (2005): 5–24.

Plaut, W. Gunther, ed. *The Torah: A Modern Commentary*. New York: Union of American Hebrew Congregations, 1981.

Plöger, Josef G. *Literarkritische, formgeschichtliche und stilkritische Untersuchungen zum Deuteronomium*. BBB 26. Bonn: Hanstein, 1967.

Preuss, H. D. *Deuteronomium*. EdF 164. Darmstadt: Wissenschaftliche Buchgesellschaft, 1982.

———. *Old Testament Theology*. Translated by Leo G. Perdue. 2 vols. OTL. Edinburgh: T. & T. Clark, 1995; 1996.

Priest, John. "The Covenant of Brothers." *JBL* 84 (1965): 400–406.

Prouser, Joseph H. "Seeing Red: On Translating Esau's Request for Soup." *CJ* 56, no. 2 (2004): 13–20.

Pury, Albert de. "Le cycle de Jacob comme légende autonome des origines d'Israël." Pages 78–96 in Emerton, ed., *Congress Volume: Leuven, 1989*.

Raabe, Paul R. *Obadiah: A New Translation with Introduction and Commentary*. AB 24D. New York: Doubleday, 1996.

———. "Why Prophetic Oracles Against the Nations?" Pages 236–57 in *Fortunate the Eyes That See: Essays in Honor of David Noel Freedman in Celebration of His Seventieth Birthday*. Edited by Astrid B. Beck et al. Grand Rapids: Eerdmans, 1995.

Rad, Gerhard von. *Deuteronomy*. OTL. Translated by Dorothea Barton. London: SCM, 1966.

———. *Genesis: A Commentary*. Revised edition. Translated by John H. Marks. OTL. London: SCM, 1972.

Rahlfs, A., ed., *Septuaginta*. 2 vols. 4th ed. Stuttgart: Württembergische Bibelanstalt, 1950.

"Rashi's Commentary on Deuteronomy." Cited 20 March 2008. Online: http://www. chabad.org/library/bible_cdo/aid/9966/showrashi/true.

"Rashi's Commentary on Obadiah." Cited 10 July 2009. Online: http://www.chabad. org/library/bible_cdo/aid/16182/showrashi/true.

"Rashi's Commentary on Malachi." Cited 26 January 2006. Online: http://www.chabad. org/library/article.asp?print=true&AID=16219&showrashi=true.

Redditt, Paul L. "The Book of Malachi in Its Social Setting." *CBQ* 56 (1994): 240–55.

Reed, William L. "Some Implications of HEN for Old Testament Religion." *JBL* 73 (1954): 36–41.

Rendsburg, Gary A. "The Internal Consistency and Historical Reliability of the Biblical Genealogies." *VT* 40 (1990): 185–206.

Rendtorff, Rolf. *The Canonical Hebrew Bible: A Theology of the Old Testament*. Translated by David E. Orton. Leiden: Deo, 2004.

———. "How to Read the Book of the Twelve as a Theological Unity." Pages 75–87 in Nogalski and Sweeney, eds., *Reading and Hearing*.

Renkema, Johan. *Obadiah*. HCOT. Translated by Brian Doyle. Leuven: Peeters, 2003.

Richards, Kent Harold. "Bless/Blessing." *ABD* 1:753–55.

Robinson, Robert B. "Literary Functions of the Genealogies of Genesis." *CBQ* 48 (1986): 595–608.

Rogerson, J. W. "The Social Background of the Book of Malachi." Pages 171–79 in *New Heaven and New Earth, Prophecy and the Millennium: Essays in Honour of Anthony Gelston*. Edited by P. J. Harland and C. T. R. Hayward. VTSup 77. Leiden: Brill, 1999.

Rosenbaum, M., and A. M. Silbermann, eds. *Pentateuch with Targum Onkelos, Haphtaroth and Prayers for Sabbath and Rashi's Commentary: Genesis*. London: Shapiro, Vallentine & Co., 1929.

Rosenthal, Franz. *A Grammar of Biblical Aramaic*. PLO 5. Wiesbaden: Harrassowitz, 1995.

Rowley, H. H. *The Biblical Doctrine of Election*. London: Lutterworth, 1950.

Rudolph, Wilhelm. *Haggai – Sacharja 1–8 – Sacharja 9–14 – Maleachi*. KAT 23/4. Gütersloh: Gütersloher Verlagshaus Gerd Mohn, 1976.

———. *Joel, Amos, Obadja, Jona*. KAT 13/2. Gütersloh: Gerd Mohn, 1971.

Sacks, Jonathan. "The Other Face of Esau." Cited 18 November 2009. Online: http://www.jewishpress.com/pageroute.do/41514.

Sarna, Nahum M. *Genesis*. JPSTC. Philadelphia: The Jewish Publication Society, 1989.

———. *Understanding Genesis: The Heritage of Biblical Israel*. New York: Schocken, 1970.

Schmid, Konrad. "Die Versöhnung zwischen Jakob und Esau (Gen. 33,1–11)." Pages 211–26 in Macchi and Römer, eds., *Jacob*.

Schneider, Tammi J. *Mothers of Promise: Women in the Book of Genesis*. Grand Rapids: Baker Academic, 2008.

Schwartz, Regina M. *The Curse of Cain: The Violent Legacy of Monotheism*. Chicago: University of Chicago Press, 1997.

Seeligmann, I. L. "Hebräische Erzählung und biblische Geschichtsschreibung." *TZ* 18 (1962): 305–25.

Segal, J. B. "Numerals in the Old Testament." *JSS* 10 (1965): 2–20.

Seitz, Christopher R. "Canonical Approach." *DITB* 100–103.

———. *Isaiah 1–39*. IBC. Louisville: John Knox, 1993.

———. *Prophecy and Hermeneutics: Toward a New Introduction to the Prophets*. STI. Grand Rapids: Baker Academic, 2007.

Simian, Horacio. *Die theologische Nachgeschichte der Prophetie Ezechiels: Form- und traditionskritische Untersuchung zu Ez 6; 35; 36*. FB. Würzburg: Echter, 1974.

Simundson, Daniel J. *Hosea, Joel, Amos, Obadiah, Jonah, Micah*. AOTC. Nashville: Abingdon, 2005.

Ska, Jean Louis. "Genése 25,19–34: Ouverture du Cycle de Jacob." Pages 11–21 in Macchi and Römer, eds., *Jacob*.

Skinner, John. *A Critical and Exegetical Commentary on Genesis*. ICC. Edinburgh: T. & T. Clark, 1930.

Smith, Craig A. "Reinstating Isaac: The Centrality of Abraham's Son in the 'Jacob–Esau' narrative of Genesis 27." *BTB* 31 (2001): 130–34.

Smith, John Merlin Powis, William Hayes Ward, and Julius A. Bewer. *A Critical and Exegetical Commentary on Micah, Zephaniah, Nahum, Habakkuk, Obadiah and Joel*. ICC. Edinburgh: T. & T. Clark, 1911.

Smith, Ralph L. *Micah–Malachi*. WBC 32. Dallas: Word, 1984.

Smith, S. H. "'Heel' and 'Thigh': The Concept of Sexuality in the Jacob–Esau Narratives." *VT* 40 (1990): 464–73.

Snyman, S. D. "Antitheses in Malachi 1, 2–5." *ZAW* 98 (1986): 436–38.

———. "Cohesion in the Book of Obadiah." *ZAW* 101 (1989): 59–71.

Soggin, J. Alberto. *Das Buch Genesis, Kommentar*. Darmstadt: Wissenschaftliche Buchgesellschaft, 1997.

Sohn, Seock-Tae. *The Divine Election of Israel*. Grand Rapids: Eerdmans, 1991.

Speiser, E. A. *Genesis: A New Translation with Introduction and Commentary*. AB 1. Garden City: Doubleday, 1983.

Sperber, Alexander. *The Bible in Aramaic, Based on Old Manuscripts and Printed Texts.* Vol. 1, *The Pentateuch According to Targum Onkelos*. Leiden: Brill, 1973.

Spero, Shubert. "Jacob and Esau: The Relationship Reconsidered." *JBQ* 32 (2004): 245–50.

Spina, Frank A. "The 'Face of God': Esau in Canonical Context." Pages 3–25 in *The Quest for Context and Meaning: Studies in Biblical Intertextuality in Honor of James A. Sanders*. Edited by Craig A. Evans and Shemaryahu Talmon. Leiden: Brill, 1997.

———. *The Faith of the Outsider: Exclusion and Inclusion in the Biblical Story*. Grand Rapids: Eerdmans, 2005.

Steinberg, Naomi. "The Genealogical Framework of the Family Stories in Genesis." *Semeia* 46 (1989): 41–50.

———. *Kinship and Marriage in Genesis: A Household Economics Perspective*. Minneapolis: Fortress, 1993.

Steinmann, Andrew E. "The Order of Amos's Oracles Against the Nations: 1:3–2:16." *JBL* 111 (1992): 683–89.

Steinmetz, Devora. *From Father to Son: Kinship, Conflict and Continuity in Genesis*. LCBI. Louisville: Westminster John Knox, 1991.

Stiebert, Johanna. "The Maligned Patriarch: Prophetic Ideology and the 'Bad Press' of Esau." Pages 33–48 in *Sense and Sensitivity: Essays on Reading the Bible in Memory of Robert Carroll*. Edited by Alastair G. Hunter and Philip R. Davies. JSOTSup 348. Sheffield: Sheffield Academic, 2002.

Strickman, H. Norman, and Arthur M. Silver, trans. *Ibn Ezra's Commentary on the Pentateuch: Genesis (Bereshit)*. New York: Menorah, 1988.

Stuart, Douglas. *Hosea–Jonah*. WBC 31. Waco: Word, 1987.

———. "Malachi." Pages 3:1245–396 in McComiskey, ed., *The Minor Prophets*.

Sumner, W. A. "Israel's Encounters with Edom, Moab, Ammon, Sihon, and Og According to the Deuteronomist." *VT* 18 (1968): 216–28.

Sweeney, Marvin A. *The Twelve Prophets*. BO. Collegeville: Liturgical, 2000.

Syrén, Roger. *The Forsaken First-Born: A Study of a Recurrent Motif in the Patriarchal Narratives*. JSOTSup 133. Sheffield: JSOT, 1993.

———. "Ishmael and Esau in the Book of Jubilees and Targum Pseudo-Jonathan." Pages 310–15 in Beattie and McNamara, eds., *The Aramaic Bible*.

Tebes, Juan Manuel. "'You Shall Not Abhor an Edomite, for He is Your Brother': The Tradition of Esau and the Edomite Genealogies from an Anthropological Perspective." *JHS* 6 (2006): 1–30.

Thiselton, Anthony. "The Supposed Power of Words in the Biblical Writings." *JTS* 25 (1974): 283–99.

Thompson, Thomas L. *The Historicity of the Patriarchal Narratives*. Berlin: de Gruyter, 1974.

Tigay, Jeffrey H. *Deuteronomy*. JPSTC. Philadelphia: The Jewish Publication Society, 1996.

Turgeman, Asaf. "Mein bruder ist ein Einzelkind: Die Esau-Darstellung in jüdischen Schriften des Mittelalters." Pages 135–53 in Langer, ed , *Esau—Bruder und Feind*.

Turner, Laurence A. *Announcements of Plot in Genesis*. JSOTSup 96. Sheffield: JSOT, 1990.

Urbrock, William J. "Blessings and Curses." *ABD* 1:755–61.

Van Seters, John. *Prologue to History: The Yahwist as Historian in Genesis.* Zurich: Theologischer Verlag, 1992.

Vawter, Bruce. *On Genesis: A New Reading.* London: Chapman, 1977.

Verhoef, Pieter A. *The Books of Haggai and Malachi.* NICOT. Grand Rapids: Eerdmans, 1987.

Vermes, Geza. *The Complete Dead Sea Scrolls in English.* New York: Penguin, 1997.

Vermeylen, Jacques. "Le vol de la bénédiction paternelle: une lecture de Gen 27." Pages 23–40 in *Pentateuchal and Deuteronomistic Studies: Papers Read at the XIIIth IOSOT Congress, Leuven 1989.* Edited by C. Brekelmans and J. Lust. Leuven: Leuven University Press, 1990.

Visotzky, Burton L. *The Genesis of Ethics: How the Tormented Family of Genesis Leads Us to Moral Development.* New York: Crown, 1996.

Vriezen, Th. C. *Die Erwählung Israels nach dem Alten Testament.* ATANT. Zurich: Zwingli, 1953.

Wallis, G. "Wesen und Struktur der Botschaft Maleachis." Pages 229–37 in *Das Ferne und Nahe Wort: Festschrift Leonhard Rost zur Vollendugn seines 70. Lebensjahres.* Edited by Fritz Maass. BZAW 105. Berlin: Töpelmann, 1967.

Walsh, Jerome T. "From Egypt to Moab: A Source Critical Analysis of the Wilderness Itinerary." *CBQ* 39 (1977): 20–33.

Walters, Stanley D. "Jacob Narrative." *ABD* 3:599–608.

Waltke, Bruce K., and Cathi J. Fredricks. *Genesis: A Commentary.* Grand Rapids: Zondervan, 2001.

Walton, Kevin. *Thou Traveller Unknown: The Presence and Absence of God in the Jacob Narrative.* PBM. Milton Keynes: Paternoster, 2003.

Watts, John D. W. *The Books of Joel, Obadiah, Jonah, Nahum, Habakkuk and Zephaniah.* CBC. Cambridge: Cambridge University Press, 1975.

Weinberg, Joel P. "Das Wesen und die funktionelle Bestimmung der Listen in I Chr 1–9." *ZAW* 93 (1981): 91–114.

Weinfeld, Moshe. *Deuteronomy 1–11.* AB 5. New York: Doubleday, 1991.

———. *Deuteronomy and the Deuteronomic School.* Oxford: Oxford University Press, 1972.

Weippert, Manfred. "Edom und Israel." Pages 291–99 in vol. 9 of *TRE.*

Wenham, Gordon J. *Genesis 16–50.* WBC 2. Dallas: Word, 1995.

Wesley, John. "Wesley's Notes on the Bible." Cited 21 February 2010. Online: http://www.ccel.org/ccel/wesley/notes.pdf.

Westermann, Claus. *Blessing in the Bible and the Life of the Church.* Translated by Keith Crim. OBT. Minneapolis: Fortress, 1978.

———. *Genesis 12–36.* Translated by John J. Scullion. A Continental Commentary. Minneapolis: Fortress, 1995.

———. *The Promises to the Fathers: Studies on the Patriarchal Narratives.* Translated by David E. Green. Philadelphia: Fortress, 1980.

Weyde, Karl William. *Prophecy and Teaching: Prophetic Authority, Form Problems, and the Use of Traditions in the Book of Malachi.* BZAW 288. Berlin: de Gruyter, 2000.

Whiston, William, ed. *Antiquities of the Jews.* The Works of Flavius Josephus 2. Grand Rapids: Baker, 1984.

White, Hugh C. *Narration and Discourse in the Book of Genesis.* Cambridge: Cambridge University Press, 1991.

Whitt, William D. "The Jacob Traditions in Hosea and Their Relation to Genesis." *ZAW* 103 (1991): 18–43.

Williamson, H. G. M. *1 and 2 Chronicles*. NCB. Grand Rapids: Eerdmans, 1982.

Willi-Plein, I. "Genesis 27 als Rebekkageschichte. Zu einem historiographischen Kunstgriff der biblischen Vätergeschichten." *TZ* 45 (1988): 315–34.

Wilson, Robert R. "Between 'Azel' and 'Azel': Interpreting the Biblical Genealogies." *BA* 42 (1979): 11–22.

———. *Genealogy and History in the Biblical World*. YNER 7. New Haven: Yale University Press, 1977.

———. "Genealogy, Genealogies." *ABD* 2:929–32.

———. "The Old Testament Genealogies in Recent Research." *JBL* 94 (1975): 169–89.

Wolff, Hans Walter. *Hosea*. Translated by Gary Stansell. Hermeneia. Philadelphia: Fortress, 1974.

———. *Obadiah and Jonah*. Translated by Margaret Kohl. Minneapolis: Augsburg, 1986.

———. "Obadja - ein Kultprophet als Interpret." *EvT* 37 (1977): 273–84.

———. "Volksgemeinde und Glaubensgemeinde im Alten Bund." *EvT* 9 (1949–50): 65–82.

Woudstra, M. H. "Edom and Israel in Ezekiel." *CTJ* 3 (1968): 21–35.

Wright, G. Ernest. "Troglodytes and Giants in Palestine." *JBL* 57 (1938): 305–9.

Zeron, A. "The Swansong of Edom." *JJS* 31 (1980): 190–98.

Zimmerli, Walther. *Ezekiel 2*. Hermeneia. Translated by James D. Martin. Philadelphia: Fortress, 1983.

Zobel, Hans-Jürgen. "Der bildliche Gebrauch von smn im Ugaritischen und Hebräischen." *ZAW* 82 (1970): 209–16.

INDEXES

INDEX OF REFERENCES

INDEX OF AUTHORS